The Greatest Mirror

The Greatest Mirror

Heavenly Counterparts in the Jewish Pseudepigrapha

Andrei A. Orlov

On the cover: *The Baleful Head*, by Edward Burne-Jones. Oil on canvas, dated 1886–1887. Photo credit: Art Resource, NY.

Published by State University of New York Press, Albany

© 2017 State University of New York

All rights reserved

Printed in the United States of America

No part of this book may be used or reproduced in any manner whatsoever without written permission. No part of this book may be stored in a retrieval system or transmitted in any form or by any means including electronic, electrostatic, magnetic tape, mechanical, photocopying, recording, or otherwise without the prior permission in writing of the publisher.

For information, contact State University of New York Press, Albany, NY
www.sunypress.edu

Production, Dana Foote
Marketing, Fran Keneston

Library of Congress Cataloging-in-Publication Data

Names: Orlov, Andrei A., 1960– author.
Title: The greatest mirror : heavenly counterparts in the Jewish Pseudepigrapha / Andrei A. Orlov.
Description: Albany, New York : State University of New York Press, [2017] | Includes bibliographical references and index.
Identifiers: LCCN 2016052228 (print) | LCCN 2016053193 (ebook) | ISBN 9781438466910 (hardcover : alk. paper) | ISBN 9781438466903 (pbk. : alk. paper | ISBN 9781438466927 (ebook)
Subjects: LCSH: Apocryphal books (Old Testament)—Criticism, interpretation, etc.
Classification: LCC BS1700 .O775 2017 (print) | LCC BS1700 (ebook) | DDC 229/.9106—dc23
LC record available at https://lccn.loc.gov/2016052228

10 9 8 7 6 5 4 3 2 1

For April DeConick

... in the season when my body was completed in its maturity, there immediately flew down and appeared before me that most beautiful and greatest mirror-image of myself.

—*Cologne Mani Codex* 17

Contents

Preface · xi

Abbreviations · xiii

Introduction · 1

Chapter One: The Heavenly Counterpart Traditions in the Enochic Pseudepigrapha · 7

Chapter Two: The Heavenly Counterpart Traditions in the Mosaic Pseudepigrapha · 43

Chapter Three: The Heavenly Counterpart Traditions in the Pseudepigrapha about Jacob · 61

Chapter Four: The Heavenly Counterpart Traditions in *Joseph and Aseneth* · 119

Conclusion · 149

Notes · 153

Bibliography · 267

Index · 295

Preface

This study represents the culmination of several years of work. My initial interest in the heavenly counterpart imagery was developed in the late 1990s, when I started working on my doctoral dissertation devoted to the development of the Enoch-Metatron tradition. Part of my dissertation dealt with the exploration of heavenly doubles found in such Jewish works as the *Book of the Similitudes*, *2 Enoch*, the *Exagoge* of Ezekiel the Tragedian, the *Prayer of Joseph*, and the *Ladder of Jacob*.[1] Many of these initial probes into doppelganger lore were subsequently reported in several articles published in various journals and edited volumes.[2] In the last decade, I also extended the scope of my study to Jewish demonological reinterpretations of otherworldly counterparts, which resulted in the publication of several articles and two books devoted to the symmetrical correspondences between heavenly and demonic realities.[3] In 2011, during my sabbatical in Jerusalem, as a fellow of the Institute of Advanced Studies of the Hebrew University of Jerusalem, I began to work systematically on a monograph concerning heavenly counterpart traditions in the Jewish pseudepigrapha, which I was able to finish only now, six years later.

Several people helped me in my work on this project. I would like to express my appreciation to Paul Pasquesi, who helped to improve the manuscript's grammar. I am especially grateful to my research assistant, Caroline Redick, who worked very hard through different versions of the manuscript to help improve the text in both style and substance. I also extend my gratitude to Michael Cover, who read the manuscript at its various stages of evolution and offered numerous constructive ideas.

I owe special thanks to my colleagues at the Department of Theology of Marquette University for their continued human and scholarly support and encouragement.

I am grateful to Art Resource, New York, for permission to use a digital reproduction of Edward Burne-Jones' painting, *The Baleful Head*, as the cover image.

Sincere thanks are also due to Rafael Chaiken, Dana Foote, and the editorial team of SUNY Press for their help, patience, and professionalism during the preparation of the book for publication.

—Andrei Orlov
Milwaukee
The Feast of the Dormition of the Theotokos, 2017

Abbreviations

ÄAT	Ägypten und Altes Testament
AAWG	Abhandlungen der Akademie der Wissenschaften in Göttingen
AB	Anchor Bible
AC	*Anthropology of Consciousness*
ACF	*Annuaire du Collège de France*
AGAJU	Arbeiten zur Geschichte des antiken Judentums und des Urchristentums
AnBib	Analecta Biblica
ANRW	*Aufstieg und Niedergang der römischen Welt*
AOASH	*Acta Orientalia Academiae Scientiarum Hungaricae*
ArBib	Aramaic Bible
ASOR	American Schools of Oriental Research Series
ASTI	*Annual of the Swedish Theological Institute*
BEATAJ	Beiträge zur Erforschung des Alten Testaments und des antiken Judentums
BI	Beiträge zur Iranistik
BIS	Biblical Interpretation Series
BJS	Brown Judaic Studies
BKP	Beiträge zur klassischen Philologie
BSJS	Brill's Series in Jewish Studies
BZAW	Beihefte zur Zeitschrift für die alttestamentliche Wissenschaft
CBQ	*Catholic Biblical Quarterly*
CBQMS	Catholic Biblical Quarterly Monograph Series
CEJL	Commentaries on Early Jewish Literature
CEUSH	Central European University Studies in Humanities
CMC	*Cologne Mani Codex*
COIDR	*Chtenija v Obschestve Istorii i Drevnostej Rossijskih*
Corp. Herm.	*Corpus Hermeticum*
CRINT	Compendia rerum iudaicarum ad Novum Testamentum

CSCO	Corpus scriptorum christianorum orientalium
DSD	*Dead Sea Discoveries*
EB	Eichstätter Beiträge
ECLS	Early Christian Literature Series
EJL	Early Judaism and Its Literature
EPRO	Études préliminaires aux religions orientales dans l'Empire romain
EvQ	*Evangelical Quarterly*
ExpTim	*Expository Times*
Frag. Targ.	*Fragmentary Targum*
FRLANT	Forschungen zur Religion und Literatur des Alten und Neuen Testaments
FSBP	Fontes et Subsidia ad Bibliam Pertinentes
GAP	Guides to Apocrypha and Pseudepigrapha
GCS	Die griechischen christlichen Schriftsteller der ersten drei Jahrhunderte
Gen. Rab.	*Genesis Rabbah*
Gos. Phil.	*Gospel of Philip*
Gos. Thom.	*Gospel of Thomas*
HAR	*Hebrew Annual Review*
HNT	Handbuch zum Neuen Testament
HR	*History of Religions*
HSM	Harvard Semitic Monographs
HTR	*Harvard Theological Review*
HUAS	Hebrew University Armenian Studies
ICS	*Illinois Classical Studies*
Imm	*Immanuel*
IORJS	*Izvestija Otdelenija Russkago Jazyka i Slovesnosti*
JAOS	*Journal of the American Oriental Society*
JBL	*Journal of Biblical Literature*
JCS	*Journal of Cuneiform Studies*
JJS	*Journal of Jewish Studies*
JNES	*Journal of Near Eastern Studies*
Jos. Asen.	*Joseph and Aseneth*
JPsJ	*Journal of Psychology and Judaism*
JQR	*Jewish Quarterly Review*
JR	*Journal of Religion*
JRelS	*Journal of Religious Studies*
JSHRZ	Jüdische Schriften aus hellenistisch-römischer Zeit
JSJ	*Journal for the Study of Judaism in the Persian, Hellenistic and Roman Period*

JSJSS	Journal for the Study of Judaism in the Persian, Hellenistic and Roman Period: Supplement Series
JSNT	*Journal for the Study of the New Testament*
JSNTSS	Journal for the Study of the New Testament. Supplement Series
JSOR	*Journal of the Society of Oriental Research*
JSOTSS	Journal for the Study of the Old Testament. Supplement Series
JSP	*Journal for the Study of the Pseudepigrapha*
JSPSS	Journal for the Study of the Pseudepigrapha. Supplement Series
JSQ	*Jewish Studies Quarterly*
JTS	*Journal of Theological Studies*
KEK	Kritisch-exegetischer Kommentar über das Neue Testament
Keph.	*Kephalaia*
LCJP	Library of Contemporary Jewish Philosophers
LCL	Loeb Classical Library
LIS	Literatura Intertestamentària Supplementa
LSAAR	Lund Studies in African and Asian Religions
MAS	Mitteilungen aus der Ägyptischen Sammlung
MH	*Museum Helveticum*
NedTT	*Nederlands Theologisch Tijdschrift*
NHC	Nag Hammadi Codex
NHMS	Nag Hammadi and Manichaean Studies
NHS	Nag Hammadi Studies
NovT	*Novum Testamentum*
NovTSup	Supplements to Novum Testamentum
NPAJ	New Perspectives on Ancient Judaism
NSBT	New Studies in Biblical Theology
NTOA	Novum Testamentum et Orbis Antiquus
NTS	*New Testament Studies*
OBO	Orbis biblicus et orientalis
PPS	Popular Patristic Series
PRE	*Pirke de Rabbi Eliezer*
PTS	Patristische Texte und Studien
PVTG	Pseudepigrapha Veteris Testamenti Graece
QM	Qumranica Mogilanensia
REJ	*Revue des études juives*
RevQ	*Revue de Qumrân*
RHR	*Revue de l'Histoire des Religions*
SAALT	State Archives of Assyria Literary Texts
SANE	Sources from the Ancient Near East
SBLSCS	Society of Biblical Literature Septuagint and Cognate Studies
SBLSP	*Society of Biblical Literature Seminar Papers*

SBLSS	Society of Biblical Literature Symposium Series
SBLTT	Society of Biblical Literature Texts and Translations
SC	Sources chrétiennes
SCL	Sather Classical Lectures
ScrTh	*Scripta theologica*
SHR	Studies in the History of Religions
SII	Studien zur Indologie und Iranistic
SJ	Studia Judaica
SJJTP	Supplements to the Journal of Jewish Thought and Philosophy
SJLA	Studies in Judaism in Late Antiquity
SJS	Studia Judaeoslavica
SNTSMS	Society for New Testament Studies Monograph Series
SOR	Studies in Oriental Religions
SORJS	Sbornik Otdelenija Russkogo Jazyka i Slovesnosti
SPB	Studia Post-Biblica
SR	*Studies in Religion*
SSEJC	Studies in Scripture in Early Judaism and Christianity
SSS	Sagners slavistische Sammlung
STAC	Studien und Texte zu Antike und Christentum
STDJ	Studies on the Texts of the Desert of Judah
STJHC	Studies and Texts in Jewish History and Culture
StSem	Studi Semitici
SVC	Supplements to Vigiliae Christianae
SVTP	Studia in Veteris Testamenti Pseudepigrapha
SVTQ	*St. Vladimir's Theological Quarterly*
Targ. Neof.	*Targum Neofiti*
Targ. Onq.	*Targum Onqelos*
Targ. Ps.-J.	*Targum Pseudo-Jonathan*
TBN	Themes in Biblical Narrative
TLZ	*Theologische Literaturzeitung*
TODRL	*Trudy Otdela Drevnerusskoj Literatury*
TSAJ	Texte und Studien zum antiken Judentum
UNT	Untersuchungen zum Neuen Testament
UUA	Uppsala Universitets Årsskrift
VC	*Vigiliae Christianae*
VTSup	Supplements to Vetus Testamentum
VT	*Vetus Testamentum*
VUI	*Varshavskie Universitetskie Izvestija*
WBC	Word Biblical Commentary
WMANT	Wissenschaftliche Monographien zum Alten und Neuen Testament

WUNT	Wissenschaftliche Untersuchungen zum Neuen Testament
WZKM	*Wiener Zeitschrift fur die Kunde des Morgenlandes*
ZNW	*Zeitschrift für die Neutestamentliche Wissenschaft und die Kunde der älteren Kirche*
ZPE	*Zeitschrift für Papyrologie und Epigraphik*
ZTK	*Zeitschrift für Theologie und Kirche*

Introduction

From one of the Manichaean psalms, we learn that in the final moments of his life Mani was beholding his heavenly double with "eyes of light."[1] This was not the only encounter this Syrian visionary had with his upper celestial identity. The *Cologne Mani Codex* tells us that the heavenly counterpart first manifested himself to Mani at the age of twelve, and he continued his visits, to assist with revelations, until Mani's death. In several texts, Mani's celestial alter ego is designated as a spirit and even called the Paraclete,[2] the same title the Holy Spirit bears in the fourth gospel. The conception of the adept's heavenly correlative also appears in several early Christian accounts, including the *Shepherd of Hermas*, Clement of Alexandria's *Excerpta ex Theodoto*, and Aphrahat's *Demonstrations*. Similar traditions can further be found in early heterodox Christian accounts, including the *Gospel of Thomas*, *Pistis Sophia*, and various apocryphal Acts of the Apostles.

Modern biblical scholars have long puzzled over the conceptual roots of this heavenly counterpart imagery, wondering which religious milieus could have introduced it to mainstream and heterodox Christian literature. In the second half of the twentieth century, the traditions of the heavenly double received some scholarly attention due to the discoveries of the Nag Hammadi library and the Dead Sea Scrolls as well as renewed interest in Jewish and Muslim mystical trends. The rise of Jungian psychology also played a part in invigorating fascination with the concept of a heavenly twin.[3] Around that time, the most original and advanced studies of the subject were by members of the Eranos Seminar, a para-scholarly gathering[4] inspired by the ideas of Carl Gustav Jung. Three distinguished participants of the Eranos Seminar, Henry Corbin,[5] Gilles Quispel,[6] and Gershom Scholem,[7] each made important contributions to the topic in their respective fields of study. While Scholem and Corbin mostly concentrated on the uses of the heavenly twin imagery in later Kabbalistic and Sufi materials, their younger colleague, Quispel, focused on early Christian and Manichaean texts that are rife with vivid accounts of the heavenly alter egos of their traditions' luminaries. These multidisciplinary investigations still serve as salient landmarks in the field with lasting methodological value. The Eranos Seminar research, however, had its limits. While some Christian, Manichaean, Islamic, and later Kabbalistic materials were scrutinized meticulously for the presence of the heavenly counterpart imagery, early Jewish, especially pseudepigraphical, accounts received considerably less or almost no attention.

Why were the early Jewish accounts neglected by these distinguished scholars? In part this was due to their peculiar take on the conceptual roots of the imagery. They focused their interpretive lens on the Iranian or the Greco-Roman origins of Christian, Manichaean, and Islamic traditions and consistently ignored early Jewish Second Temple sources. One of the main proponents of the Greco-Roman roots was Gilles Quispel. April DeConick observes that for Quispel the idea of the heavenly double was linked with "the Greco-Roman concept of the *daimon* or *genius*: each person was believed to have a *daimon* or *genius* which was a guardian spirit or angel who could be described as the exact counterpart to the person to whom he belonged."[8] She notes that Quispel believed "that the Jews picked up [the idea of the heavenly counterpart] from the Greeks and combined it with their own lore about God's image and lore about the angels."[9] Despite these convictions, Quispel never explored early Jewish pseudepigraphical texts where the angelic lore arguably comes to its fore. Henry Corbin also ignored Jewish pseudepigrapha and instead argued for the formative value of the Iranian imagery of *fravaši* and *daēnā*.[10] Even Gershom Scholem, who took great pains to recover various concepts of the heavenly correlative in the *Zohar* and other Kabbalistic testimonies, was not able, in my opinion, to give proper attention to early Jewish accounts in his interpretations. In his thorough analysis of the heavenly counterpart traditions in the *Zohar*, references to the Jewish pseudepigrapha are markedly absent.

Only in the last several decades have scholars begun to take note of the formative value of the heavenly counterpart traditions found in early Jewish accounts. This new scholarship suggests that Christian, Manichaean, and even Kabbalistic specimens of the doppelganger lore might stem, not from the Greco-Roman or Iranian traditions, but from the early Second Temple developments reflected in the Jewish pseudepigrapha. As our study will show, many Christian, Manichaean, Mandaean, Muslim, and Kabbalistic developments are greatly indebted to the early concepts and imagery in the Jewish pseudepigraphical lore, which often depict the seers' heavenly identities in the form of a spirit, an image, a face, a child, a mirror, or an angel of the Presence. This study aims to explore more closely the rich and multifaceted symbolism of heavenly identities in these Jewish materials.

Examining these early Jewish testimonies may not only elucidate the origins of the heavenly counterpart imagery in early Christian or Manichaean literature but also illuminate complex anthropological symbols in the Jewish pseudepigrapha. These materials often describe the seers' radical transformations on their celestial journeys as they acquire new luminous bodies reminiscent of the protoplast's original form, which the first human lost after the fall in the Garden of Eden. In our judgment, the apocalyptic dynamics of acquiring a new celestial shape cannot be fully understood without taking into account the heavenly counterpart traditions since the upper luminous form of the human seers is often envisioned as their celestial alter ego. This apocalyptic imagery suggests that the notion of the heavenly counterpart can be viewed as a crucial conceptual nexus in the anthropology of the Jewish pseudepigrapha.

Further, the heavenly counterpart lore can offer insight into the nature of pseudepigraphical attribution where novel apocalyptic revelations are channeled and adopted in the name of a prominent biblical authority of the past, often represented by primordial patriarchs and prophets. Participation in established authoritative discourse was crucial in the formation of literary streams transmitted in the name of Enoch, Noah, Baruch, and other biblical figures—streams that lasted for millennia and crossed religious, geographical, social, and political boundaries.

Jewish pseudepigrapha often identify their protagonists with exemplars of established literary traditions, such as biblical patriarchs and prophets. This emulation of biblical luminaries, which allows the texts' authors to convey new revelations in the name of some prominent authority of the past, cannot be fully grasped without understanding the heavenly counterpart traditions in which the adept became identified with his or her heavenly alter ego, often in the form of an exalted exemplar. Acquisition of the heavenly identity can thus be seen as a fundamental dynamic in the adept's unification with the exemplar of the literary and mystical tradition and his or her further participation in the exemplar's story through angelic initiation as well as acceptance of the celestial offices of the tradition's founder.

The study will show that the heavenly counterpart traditions in the Jewish pseudepigrapha often unfold amid complex angelology where a special group of angels, the so-called princes of the Presence, help the seer unite with his or her heavenly identity. The intermediate position of these angelic servants who stand between the earthly seer and his heavenly alter ego, often in the form of the divine Face or Glory, serves an important role in mystical and literary emulation. As will be seen, the figure of the angel of the Presence is a transformative and textual device allowing the adept to enter the assembly of immortal beings consisting of both celestial and literary heroes.

Considering that biblical exemplars in the form of exalted patriarchs and prophets play an important role in the Jewish pseudepigrapha, our study will be organized around several biblical figures—Enoch, Moses, Jacob, Joseph, and Aseneth, who, as will be shown later, become crucial vehicles for the development of the heavenly counterpart traditions in early Jewish accounts.

The first chapter of our study will deal with Enochic pseudepigrapha, including early booklets of the so-called *1 (Ethiopic) Enoch*: the *Book of the Watchers*, the *Animal Apocalypse*, and the *Book of the Similitudes*. An examination of the heavenly counterpart traditions in the *Book of the Similitudes* will be especially important in view of the paradoxal identification between Enoch and his upper identity in the form of the Son of Man. We will also closely examine the heavenly counterpart traditions in *2 Enoch* and in *Sefer Hekhalot*, or *3 Enoch*, a text in which the supreme angel Metatron was fashioned as Enoch's doppelganger. In this section, we will also look at how the imagery of the "youth" becomes envisioned as the human protagonist's heavenly alter ego. Although the main focus of our study will be on early Jewish pseudepigraphical materials, relevant Christian, "Gnostic," Mandaean, Manichaean, and rabbinic accounts will be also taken into consideration.

The second chapter will deal with the Mosaic pseudepigrapha—the *Exagoge* of Ezekiel the Tragedian and the *Book of Jubilees*. The *Exagoge*, where the traditional biblical imagery acquires a distinctive apocalyptic mold, leads the heavenly counterpart lore into a new conceptual dimension by assigning several distinctive exalted attributes to Moses' heavenly identity. *Jubilees*, in its turn, also advances the doppelganger lore by fashioning a celestial scribe in the form of an angel of the divine Presence as Moses' alter ego.

The third chapter of our study will deal with the pseudepigraphical accounts connected with Jacob's story—the *Prayer of Joseph* and the *Ladder of Jacob*. Among other things, we will explore the concepts of the image and the spirit as heavenly identities of the patriarch Jacob. To better understand these conceptual currents, the study will offer extensive excursuses into the afterlives of these traditions in talmudic, targumic, and midrashic literature.

In the fourth chapter of our study, we will explore the heavenly counterpart traditions found in *Joseph and Aseneth*, a pseudepigraphon where both male and female protagonists of the story are endowed with celestial identities. In this text, where the female seer interacts with her celestial guide in the form of the patriarch Joseph, several novel symbolic dimensions are added to the doppelganger lore, including bridal chamber imagery, a concept that plays an important role in the Christian accounts of the heavenly counterpart.

Our study will show a remarkable variety of the heavenly counterpart concepts in the Jewish pseudepigrapha, in which the heavenly identity of a human being is rendered by several traditional and novel symbols, being portrayed as an image, a spirit, a mirror, a shadow, a face, a "youth," and an angel of the Presence. Further, we will see that various streams of the heavenly counterpart lore not only contain strikingly different imagery but also offer contrasting conceptions of how the protagonists acquire their celestial identity.

Chapter One

The Heavenly Counterpart Traditions in the Enochic Pseudepigrapha

As has been already mentioned, our study of the heavenly counterpart traditions found in the Jewish pseudepigrapha will be organized around the major mediatorial trends prominent in the Second Temple period and associated with protological characters found in the Hebrew Bible—patriarchical, prophetic, and priestly figures, like Enoch, Noah, Melchizedek, Jacob, Joseph, and Moses, whose stories become greatly expanded in Jewish extrabiblical accounts. We will begin our exploration of the doppelganger symbolism with an analysis of some currents found in the early Enochic lore.

The choice of the Enochic legends as the first step in our analysis of heavenly counterpart imagery is dictated by the fact that nowhere in early Second Temple literature can one find such ardent attention to the realities of the heavenly world and opportunities for a human being to breach the boundaries between earthly and celestial realms.

Scholars have previously noted that the interest of the Enochic tradition in the heavenly realities and the possibilities for breaching the boundaries between realms manifests a striking contrast with conceptual currents reflected in the body of the early Jewish literature gathered in the Hebrew Bible, a collection, which according to some studies, was profoundly shaped by the Zadokite priestly ideology.[1] In contrast to the corpus of early Enochic writings, the student of the Hebrew Bible finds very limited information about the possibility for human beings to traverse the heavens. Few heroes of the biblical accounts are said to be translated into the heavenly abode. Among these unique figures, Enoch and Elijah are notably singled out; yet the biblical references about their translations are quite abbreviated, and they do not provide any details about the content of their heavenly journeys and celestial initiations. Such marked disinterest in the realities of the heavenly world, manifested in the Hebrew Bible, appears to represent a distinctive ideological tendency. Traversing the upper realms is clearly discouraged in such a theological framework, and an attentive reader of the biblical accounts soon learns that all portentous formative encounters between human beings and otherworldly characters take place not in heaven or hell but instead in the terrestrial world—in the wilderness or on a mountain. Thus, Ezekiel receives his vision of the Merkavah not in the heavenly throne room, like Enoch, but instead on the river Chebar, and the son of Amram obtains his revelations from the deity on the mountain. Scholars previously reflected on the topological peculiarities of biblical accounts that attempt to discourage any depiction of humans ascending to upper realms in order to receive the divine revelation. Gabriele Boccaccini rightly observes that in "the primeval history, as edited in the Zadokite Torah (Gen 1–11) . . . any attempt to cross the boundary between humanity and the divine always results in disaster."[2]

Yet, despite these topological proclivities, the possibility of the existence of heavenly counterparts was not entirely abandoned in the Hebrew Bible. In view of the pronounced sacerdotal tendencies of the Zadokite ideology, its application of the counterparts' imagery became permeated by cultic concerns manifesting itself in the idea of a heavenly correlative to the earthly sanctuary.[3] Such traditions of the heavenly counterparts first unfold in the paradigmatic revelation given to Moses on Mount Sinai. Several biblical passages from Exodus and Numbers[4] insist that "the earlier pattern of the tabernacle and the pattern of all its furniture was made after the [heavenly] pattern . . . which was shown . . . on the mountain."[5] A passage from 1 Chronicles 28:19 further affirms the possibility that the plan of the earthly sanctuary came from above.[6] All these passages postulate the idea that earthly cultic settings ought to be faithful imitations of heavenly ones.[7] As one scholar rightly observes, "the goal of history . . . is that the *cultus* will be 'on earth as in heaven.'"[8] This notion that the earthly sanctuary is a replica of the heavenly one makes its first appearance not in the texts of the Hebrew Bible but in early Mesopotamian traditions.[9] There, earthly temples are repeatedly portrayed as counterparts of heavenly realities.[10]

Yet, despite these specimens of sacerdotal counterparts' traditions in biblical accounts, it appears that the conceptual developments pertaining to heavenly identities of human seers play a more prominent role in early Enochic lore, with its marked interest in the realities of the celestial world. We therefore must direct our attention to some of these developments.

The *Book of the Watchers*

Already in one of the earliest Enochic booklets, the *Book of the Watchers*,[11] the reader notices the fascination of the Enochic writers with the heavenly counterparts of the earthly realities, especially the cultic ones. Thus, in *1 Enoch* 14, which portrays the patriarch's travel to the heavenly sanctuary located in the heavenly abode, the structure and the attributes of the celestial shrine are markedly reminiscent of the features of the Jerusalem temple. *1 Enoch* 14:9–18 details the following intriguing portrayal of the heavenly structures:

> And I proceeded until I came near to a wall which was built of hailstones, and a tongue of fire surrounded it, and it began to make me afraid. And I went into the tongue of fire and came near to a large house which was built of hailstones, and the wall of that house (was) like a mosaic (made) of hailstones, and its floor (was) snow. Its roof (was) like the path of the stars and flashes of lightning, and among them (were) fiery Cherubim, and their heaven (was like) water. And (there was) a fire burning around its wall, and its door was ablaze with fire. And I went into that house, and (it was) hot as fire and cold as snow, and there was neither pleasure nor life in it. Fear covered me and trembling, I fell on my face. And I saw in the vision, and behold, another house, which was larger than the former, and all its doors (were) open before me, and (it was) built of a tongue of fire. And in everything it so excelled in glory and splendor and size that I am unable to describe to you its glory and its size. And its floor (was) fire, and above (were) lightning and the path of the stars, and its roof also (was) a burning fire. And I looked and I saw in it a high throne, and its appearance (was) like ice and its surrounds like the shining sun and the sound of Cherubim.[12]

Commenting on this passage, Martha Himmelfarb draws attention to the description of the celestial edifices that Enoch encounters in his progress to the divine Throne. She notes that in the Ethiopic text, in order to reach God's heavenly Seat, the patriarch passes through three celestial constructions: a wall, an outer house, and an inner house. The Greek version of this narrative mentions a house instead of a wall. Himmelfarb observes that more clearly in the Greek, but also in the Ethiopic, this arrangement echoes the structure of the earthly temple with its vestibule, sanctuary, and the Holy of Holies.[13]

God's throne is located in the innermost chamber of this heavenly construction and is represented by a throne of cherubim (*1 Enoch* 14:18). These are the heavenly counterparts to the cherubim found in the Holy of Holies in the Jerusalem temple. In drawing parallels between the descriptions of the heavenly temple in the *Book of the Watchers* and the features of the earthly sanctuary, Himmelfarb observes that the fiery cherubim that Enoch sees on the ceiling of the first house (Ethiopic) or middle house (Greek) of the heavenly structure do not represent the cherubim of the divine throne but are images that recall the figures on the hangings on the wall of the tabernacle mentioned in Exodus 26:1, 26:31, 36:8, and 36:35 or possibly the figures that, according to 1 Kings 6:29, 2 Chronicles 3:7, and Ezekiel 41:15–26, were engraved on the walls of the earthly temple.[14] As one can see, the structure of the heavenly sanctuary and its features are reminiscent of the earthly temple and thus can be viewed as corresponding counterparts, one celestial and another terrestrial.

Moreover, in the course of this encounter, Enoch himself becomes a heavenly counterpart of the earthly sacerdotal servant, the high priest, who once a year on Yom Kippur was allowed to enter the divine Presence. Scholars previously noted these correspondences. For example, George Nickelsburg suggests that Enoch's progressions through the chambers of the celestial sanctuary might indicate that the author(s) of the *Book of the Watchers* perceived him as a servant associated with the activities in these chambers.[15] Similarly, Nickelsburg argues that Enoch's vision of the Throne in the *Book of the Watchers* is "qualitatively different from that described in the biblical throne visions" because of the new active role of its visionary.[16]

Himmelfarb also points to the possibility that in the *Book of the Watchers* the patriarch himself becomes a priest in the course of his ascent,[17] similar to the angels.[18] In this conceptual development, the angelic status of the patriarch and his priestly role[19] are viewed as mutually interconnected. Himmelfarb stresses that "the author of the *Book of the Watchers* claims angelic status for Enoch through his service in the heavenly temple" since "the ascent shows him passing through the outer court of the temple and the sanctuary to the door of the Holy of Holies, where God addresses him with his own mouth."[20]

Helge Kvanvig highlights another aspect of Enoch's dream-vision in *1 Enoch* 14 that is very important for our study of the heavenly counterpart traditions. Kvanvig argues that the dream about the celestial temple "is told by Enoch from two perspectives. The first tells the whole series of events, emphasizing that Enoch stays on the earth during the entire dream. . . . The second perspective focuses on Enoch as the protagonist of the dream itself, and he is carried away to the heavenly temple."[21] If Kvanvig is correct in his assessment of the peculiarities of Enoch's dream, the seer appears to be simultaneously in both realms: dreaming in his sleep on the earth and at the same time installed as the sacerdotal servant in the heavenly temple. As will be shown below, such depiction of the double identity of a human adept is widespread in various accounts of the heavenly counterparts. It especially evokes the later rabbinic accounts about Jacob's heavenly identity where angels behold this patriarch as sleeping on the earth and at the same time installed in heaven.

Kvanvig sees these early Enochic developments found in the *Book of the Watchers* as a crucial conceptual step in the shaping of the subsequent tradition of Enoch's doppelganger in the *Book of the Similitudes* where the patriarch will be openly identified with his heavenly persona in the form of the Son of Man. He notes that "in *1 Enoch* 13–14 Enoch sees himself as a visionary counterpart in heaven. In [the *Similitudes*] 70–71 Enoch is actually taken to heaven to be identified as the Son of Man."[22]

As will be shown below, the *Similitudes* also employs a double perspective in its dream report: Enoch first describes the Son of Man's mighty deeds and then later becomes identified with this celestial figure.[23] Kvanvig notices that "the two perspectives . . . constitute two ways of reporting a dream experience where the dreamer sees himself. In the first the dreamer reports what happened in retrospect, depicting how he sees himself acting in the dream; in the second he remains in the dream experience itself, where only one of the figures is involved, the figure seen in the dream."[24]

Other early Enochic booklets also imply the existence of human beings' heavenly identities. Thus, for example, in the *Animal Apocalypse*,[25] Noah's and Moses' metamorphoses from animal forms to the form of the human being signify, in the zoomorphic code of this book, the transition from human to celestial condition.[26]

The parallelism between heavenly and earthly identities of the various characters of the Enochic lore is further reaffirmed inversely in the destiny of the antagonists of the story. The fallen angels, called the Watchers, during their rebellious descent into the lower realm, encounter their lower "earthly" selves by assuming human roles of husbands and fathers.

All these features demonstrate that already in the earliest Enochic booklets the protagonists and the antagonists of the story are depicted as making transitions between their upper and lower personalities. Yet, in the *Book of the Similitudes*, such imagery comes to a new conceptual level when the seer becomes openly identified with his celestial Self. We should now draw our close attention to the portentous conceptual developments associated with this shift.

The *Book of the Similitudes*

Scholars have previously suggested[27] that the *Book of the Similitudes* entertains the idea of a visionary's heavenly counterpart when it identifies Enoch with the Son of Man in chapter 71. Although this Enochic text is not found among the Qumran fragments of the Enochic books, the current scholarly consensus holds that the book is likely to have been composed before the second century CE.[28] An account of Enoch's celestial metamorphosis found in *Similitudes* 71 offers the following perplexing depiction:

And it came to pass after this that my spirit was carried off, and it went up into the heavens. I saw the sons of the holy angels treading upon flames of fire, and their garments (were) white, and their clothing, and the light of their face (was) like snow. And I saw two rivers of fire, and the light of that fire shone like hyacinth, and I fell upon my face before the Lord of Spirits. And the angel Michael, one of the archangels, took hold of me by my right hand, and raised me, and led me out to all the secrets of mercy and the secrets of righteousness. And he showed me all the secrets of the ends of heaven and all the Storehouses of all the stars and the lights, from where they come out before the holy ones. And the spirit carried Enoch off to the highest heaven, and I saw there in the middle of that light something built of crystal stones, and in the middle of those stones tongues of living fire. And my spirit saw a circle of fire which surrounded that house; from its four sides (came) rivers full of living fire, and they surrounded that house. And round about (were) the Seraphim, and the Cherubim, and the Ophannim; these are they who do not sleep, but keep watch over the throne of his glory. And I saw angels who could not be counted, a thousand thousands and ten thousand times ten thousand, surrounding that house; and Michael and Raphael and Gabriel and Phanuel, and the holy angels who (are) in the heavens above, went in and out of that house. And Michael and Raphael and Gabriel and Phanuel, and many holy angels without number, came out from that house; and with them the Head of Days, his head white and pure like wool, and his garments indescribable. And I fell upon my face, and my whole body melted, and my spirit was transformed; and I cried out in a loud voice in the spirit of power, and I blessed and praised and exalted. And these blessings which came out from my mouth were pleasing before that Head of Days. And that Head of Days came with Michael and Gabriel, Raphael and Phanuel, and thousands and tens of thousands of angels without number. And that angel came to me, and greeted me with his voice, and said to me: "You are the Son of Man who was born to righteousness, and righteousness remains over you, and the righteousness of the Head of Days will not leave you." And he said to me: "He proclaims peace to you in the name of the world which is to come, for from there peace has come out from the creation of the world; and so you will have it forever and for ever and ever. And all . . . will walk according to your way, inasmuch as righteousness will never leave you; with you will be their dwelling, and with you their lot, and they will not be separated from you, forever and for ever and ever. And so there will be length of days with that Son of Man, and the righteous will have peace, and the righteous will have an upright way, in the name of the Lord of Spirits for ever and ever."[29]

For a long time, students of the Enochic traditions were puzzled by the fact that the Son of Man, who in the previous chapters of the *Similitudes* has been distinguished from Enoch, becomes suddenly identified in this chapter with the seventh antediluvian patriarch. James VanderKam, among others,[30] suggests that this puzzle can be explained by the Jewish notion, attested in several ancient Jewish texts, that a creature of flesh and blood could have a heavenly double or counterpart.[31] To provide an example, VanderKam points to Jacob's pseudepigraphical and targumic accounts in which the patriarch's "features are engraved on high."[32] He stresses that this theme of the visionary's ignorance of his higher angelic identity is observable, for example, in the early Jewish pseudepigraphon known to us as the *Prayer of Joseph*.[33] In view of these traditions, VanderKam suggests that "Enoch would be viewing his supernatural double[34] who had existed before being embodied in the person of Enoch."[35]

If indeed in the *Book of the Parables* the Son of Man is understood as the heavenly identity of the seer, in the *Similitudes*, like in some Jacob currents,[36] the adept's heavenly archetype seems to be related to imagery of God's *Kavod*. *1 Enoch* 71:5 reports that Enoch was brought by the archangel Michael to the fiery structure, surrounded by rivers of living fire, which he describes as "something built of crystal stones, and in the middle of those stones tongues of living fire."[37]

There is no doubt that the fiery "structure" in the *Similitudes* represents the Throne of Glory, which in the *Book of the Watchers* is also described as the crystal structure issuing streams of fire.[38] An explicit reference to the deity's Seat in *1 Enoch* 71:8,[39] immediately after the description of the fiery "crystal" structure, makes this clear. The appearance of the four angels of the Presence is also noteworthy, since they will constitute a constant feature in other accounts of the heavenly counterparts overshadowed by the *Kavod* imagery. We will see later in our study that the *Kavod* imagery featured in the *Book of the Similitudes* will continue to exercise its crucial role in other accounts of the heavenly counterparts found in various mediatorial trends.

Several words should be said about the Son of Man figure as the heavenly alter ego of the seventh antediluvian hero in the *Book of the Similitudes*. How novel is this association? It is intriguing that already in its first appearance in Daniel 7, the Son of Man's figure might be envisioned as a doppelganger.[40] Thus, John Collins previously suggested that already in Daniel 7 the Son of Man is understood as a heavenly counterpart. Yet, in Collins' opinion, in Daniel, the

Son of Man is not a celestial alter ego of a single human being but instead an entire human community.[41] Reflecting on the imagery found in chapter 7, Collins offers the following explanation:

> [Son of Man] . . . is not a man, at least in the usual sense of the word, but is rather a heavenly being. A closer analogy is found with the patron deities of nations in Near Eastern mythology. These deities have a representative unity with their peoples, although they are definitely distinguished from them. While "the gods of Hamath and Arpad" (Isa 36:19) cannot be conceived apart from the nations they represent, there is no doubt that any divinity was assumed to have greater power than his people and to be able to act independently over against them. The heavenly counterparts of nations played an important part in apocalyptic literature, most notably in Daniel 10 where the angelic "princes" of Persia and Greece do battle with Michael, "the prince of your people." I have argued elsewhere that the "one like a son of man" in Daniel 7 should be understood in this sense, as the heavenly counterpart of the faithful Jews.[42]

It is also noteworthy that this tendency to depict otherworldly figures as the representatives of human social bodies also appears to be reaffirmed[43] in the functions and attributes of the antagonistic figures found in the Book of Daniel—namely, the four infamous beasts who are understood as the otherworldly representatives of the hostile nations.[44]

If we return again to the Son of Man imagery, one should note that this prominent mediatorial trend was closely intertwined with the imagery of the heavenly counterparts not only in Jewish materials but also in early Christian accounts. According to some scholarly hypotheses, we can find such a conceptual link already in the canonical Gospels where the Son of Man title becomes Jesus' self-definition. Dale Allison raises an intriguing question, asking if it is possible that "some of Jesus' words about the Son of Man were about his heavenly twin or counterpart, with whom he was one or would come one?"[45] He further notes that "already David Catchpole[46] had suggested, with reference to Matt 18:10, that in Luke 12:8–9, the Son of Man is Jesus' guardian angel."[47] Allison concludes that "if Jesus and the heavenly Son of Man were two yet one, this would neatly explain why in some sayings the Son of Man is Jesus on earth, while in others he is a heavenly figure who for now remains in heaven."[48]

Indeed, Luke 12:8–9 represents a distinguished conceptual nexus where the Son of Man seems to be envisioned as the heavenly counterpart of the earthly Jesus. As one may recall, Luke 12:8–9 presents the following words of Jesus: "And I tell you, everyone who acknowledges me before others, the Son of Man also will acknowledge before the angels of God; but whoever denies me before others will be denied before the angels of God."[49]

In his attempt to clarify a possible concept of earthly Jesus' heavenly double in the form of the Son of Man found in this Lukan fragment, David Catchpole brings attention to Matthew 18:10, a portentous passage for future Christian elaborations of the heavenly counterpart imagery, where the μικροί on earth are depicted as *Sarim ha-Panim* who are situated in God's immediate presence.[50] Comparing Lukan and Matthean traditions, Catchpole suggests that

> the point here is that the angel in God's presence is presumed to act either favorably or unfavorably in relation to the person addressed by the saying, depending on whether that person treats the μικρός favorably or unfavorably. For the angel is the guarantor of the μικρός. In the light of such a scheme Lk. 12:8 makes perfect sense. It suggests that the Son of man will act either favorably or unfavorably in respect of the person addressed who either confesses or denies Jesus, precisely because the Son of Man is the heavenly guarantor of the earthly Jesus.[51]

Catchpole further notes that this idea of the heavenly angelic sponsor or guarantor is not unique to Luke's passage and can be found in other Jewish writings, such as Tobit 12:15 and *1 Enoch* 104:1, and therefore "represents an individualizing of the old idea of an angelic ruler for each nation (cf. Dan. 10:12; 12:1; Sir. 17:17)."[52]

Fletcher-Louis then offers some additional illustrations from the Enochic lore that, in his opinion, reinforce[53] the plausibility of Catchpole's hypothesis. He notes that

> the *Similitudes* offer a very close comparison to this human being/heavenly counterpart structure, particularly as they have been read by J.C. VanderKam. Enoch is the human being who was in pre-existence, who is, and then fully realizes his identity as the heavenly Son of Man. VanderKam's own analysis can now be supported by comparison with this gospel tradition. In the gospel Jesus, not Enoch, is the earthly manifestation of the heavenly Son of Man. This pattern is itself parallel to that in the *Prayer of Joseph*, where Jacob and Israel are names for the earthly and heavenly identities of the same individual.[54]

We should note here that the concept of the Son of Man as Jesus' heavenly identity is not limited only to the Gospel of Luke. Thus, in a number of passages from the Gospel of John—namely, John 1:18, 1:51 and 3:13[55]—the speculation about Jesus' heavenly identity appears to be again conflated with the Son of Man tradition.[56] We will explore these important Christian developments later in our study.

2 Enoch

Further development of Enoch's heavenly counterpart imagery continues in another early Jewish pseudepigraphon—*2 Enoch*, where the correspondences between earthly and otherworldly realities reach a new conceptual threshold. This text, which was probably written in the first century CE, before the destruction of the Second Jerusalem Temple,[57] depicts Enoch's heavenly journey to the throne of God where the hero of faith undergoes a luminous transformation into a celestial creature. Akin to the developments found in the *Book of the Similitudes*, the scene of the seer's metamorphosis takes place near the deity's *Kavod*, described in *2 Enoch*'s account as the divine Face.[58] According to the story, after his dramatic transformation in the upper heaven, the patriarch must then return back to the human realm in order to convey the revelations received in the upper realm. Here the heavenly counterpart traditions enter their new conceptual dimension by depicting their protagonist as temporarily abandoning his celestial identity and a luminous heavenly garment associated with it, in order to return to his earthly community.

2 Enoch 39:3–6 depicts the patriarch arriving on earth and describing to his children his earlier dramatic encounter with the divine Face. In the shorter recension of the Slavonic text, the following account can be found:

> You, my children, you see my face, a human being created just like yourselves; I am one who has seen the face of the Lord, like iron made burning hot by a fire, emitting sparks. For you gaze into my eyes, a human being created just like yourselves; but I have gazed into the eyes of the Lord, like the rays of the shining sun and terrifying the eyes of a human being. You, my children, you see my right hand beckoning you, a human being created identical to yourselves; but I have seen the right hand of the Lord, beckoning me, who fills heaven. You see the extent of my body, the same as your own; but I have seen the extent of the Lord, without measure and without analogy, who has no end.[59]

It appears that Enoch's description reveals a contrast between the two identities of the visionary: the earthly Enoch ("a human being created just like yourselves") and his heavenly counterpart ("the one who has seen the Face of God"). Enoch describes himself in two different modes of existence: as a human being who now stands before his children with a human face and body *and* as a celestial creature who has seen God's Face in the heavenly realm.[60] These descriptions of two conditions (earthly and celestial) occur repeatedly in tandem. It is possible that the purpose of Enoch's instruction to his children is not to stress the difference between his human body and the deity's body but to emphasize the distinction between *this* Enoch, a human being "created just like yourselves," and the *other* angelic Enoch, who has been standing before the deity's Face. Enoch's previous transformation into a glorified form and his initiation into the service of the divine Presence in *2 Enoch* 22:7 supports this suggestion. It is unlikely that Enoch has somehow completely abandoned his supra-angelic status and his unique place before the Face of God granted to him in the previous chapters. An account of Enoch's permanent installation can be found in chapter 36 where the deity tells Enoch, before his short visit to the earth, that a place has been prepared for him and that he will be in front of God's face "from now and *forever*."[61] What is significant here for our research is that the identification of the visionary with his heavenly double involves the installation of the seer into the office of the angel (or the prince) of the Presence (*Sar ha-Panim*). The importance of this account for the idea of the heavenly counterpart in *2 Enoch* is apparent because it points to the simultaneous existence of Enoch's angelic double, who is installed in heaven, and its human counterpart, whom God sends periodically on missionary errands.

A similar state of affairs is observable in the *Testament of Isaac* where the archangel Michael serves as angelic double of Abraham. Thus, *Testament of Isaac* 2:1–9 reads:

> It came to pass, when the time drew near for our father Isaac, the father of fathers, to depart from this world and to go out from his body, that the Compassionate, the Merciful One sent to him the chief of the angels, Michael, the one whom he had sent to his father Abraham, on the morning of the twenty-eighth day of the month Misri. The angel said to him, "Peace be upon you, O chosen son, our father Isaac!" Now it was customary every day for the holy angels to speak to him. So he prostrated himself and saw that the angel resembled his father Abraham. Then he opened his mouth, cried with a loud voice, and said with joy and exultation, "Behold, I have seen your face as if I had seen the face of the merciful Creator." Then the angel said to him, "O my beloved Isaac, I have been sent to you from the presence of the living God to take you up to heaven to be with your father Abraham and all the saints. For your father Abraham

is awaiting you; he himself is about to come for you, but now he is resting. There has been prepared for you the throne beside your father Abraham; likewise for your beloved son Jacob. And all of you shall be above everyone else in the kingdom of heaven in the glory of the Father and the Son and the Holy Spirit."[62]

In this pseudepigraphical account, one can see a striking distance between the angelic messenger in the form of Abraham sent here on a missionary journey to the lower realm to instruct Isaac and the "other" Abraham's identity that is awaiting Isaac in heaven.

As will be demonstrated later in our study, some targumic and rabbinic accounts about Jacob also attest to a similar concept of the heavenly counterpart when they depict angels beholding Jacob as one who is simultaneously installed in heaven and sleeping on earth.[63] In relation to this paradoxal situation where the seer not only is unified with his heavenly correlative in the form of the angel of the Presence but also retains the ability to travel back to the earthly realm, Jonathan Smith observes that "the complete pattern is most apparent in the various texts that witness to the complex Enoch tradition, particularly *2 Enoch*. Here Enoch was originally a man (ch. 1) who ascended to heaven and became an angel (22:9, cf. *3 Enoch* 10:3f. and 48C), returned to earth as a man (33:11), and finally returned again to heaven to resume his angelic station (67:18)."[64]

What is also important in *2 Enoch*'s account for our ongoing investigation of the heavenly counterpart traditions is that while the "heavenly version" of Enoch is installed permanently in heaven in the form of an angelic servant of the divine Presence, his "earthly version" is dispatched by God to a lower realm with the mission to deliver the handwritings made by the translated hero in heaven. Thus, in *2 Enoch* 33:3–10, God endows Enoch with the task of distributing those heavenly writings on earth:

> And now, Enoch, whatever I have explained to you, and whatever you have seen in heavens, and whatever you have seen on earth, and whatever I have written in the books—by my supreme wisdom I have contrived it all. . . . Apply your mind, Enoch, and acknowledge the One who is speaking to you. And you take the books which I have written. . . . And you go down onto the earth and tell your sons all that I have told you. . . . And deliver to them the books in your handwritings, and they will read them and know their Creator. . . . And distribute the books in your handwritings to your children and (your) children to (their) children; and the parents will read (them) from generation to generation.[65]

This account is striking in that while commanding the adept to travel to the lower realm with the heavenly books, God himself seems to assume the seer's upper scribal identity. The deity tells Enoch, who is previously depicted as the scribe of the books,[66] that it is He who wrote these books. As we will witness later in our study, this situation is reminiscent of some heavenly counterpart developments found in the Mosaic tradition—namely, in *Jubilees*, where the angel of the Presence also seems to take on the celestial scribal identity of Moses. It is also noteworthy that in *Jubilees*, like in *2 Enoch*, the boundaries between the upper scribal identity of the visionary who claims to be the writer of "the first law" and the deity appear blurred.[67] In *2 Enoch* 33, where the divine scribal figure commands the seventh antediluvian hero to deliver the book in his (Enoch's) handwritings, one possibly witnesses the unique paradoxal communication between the upper and the lower scribal identities.

The fact that in *2 Enoch* 33 the patriarch is dispatched to earth to deliver the books in "his handwritings"—the authorship of which the text assigns to the deity—is also worthy of attention given that in the traditions attested in *Jubilees*, one also encounters the idea of Moses' doppelganger in the form of the angel of the Presence. This angelic servant claims authorship of the materials that the Jewish tradition explicitly assigns to Moses. Here, just like in *2 Enoch*, the production of these authoritative writings can be seen as a process executed simultaneously by both earthly and heavenly authors, although it is the function of the earthly counterpart to deliver them to humans.

3 Enoch or Sefer Hekhalot

Before we proceed to the in-depth investigation of some conceptual developments common to several texts of the Enochic lore, it is worth pausing for a moment to reflect on another crucial, this time rabbinic, document that also entertains the idea of the heavenly alter ego of the seventh antediluvian hero. This text, known to us as *3 Enoch*, or *Sefer Hekhalot* (the *Book of [the Heavenly] Palaces*), unambiguously identifies Enoch with his upper identity in the form of the supreme angel Metatron. Separated by many centuries from the early Second Temple Enochic booklets,[68] this enigmatic rabbinic text attempts to shepherd early apocalyptic imagery into a novel mystical dimension. Thus, an attentive reader of *3 Enoch* soon learns that the apocalyptic résumé of the seventh antediluvian hero has not been forgotten by the Hekhalot authors.

Indeed, some of Metatron's roles and titles elaborated in *Sefer Hekhalot* appear to be connected with those already known from the previous analysis of early Enochic traditions. These offices, in fact, represent the continuation and, in many ways, consummation of the roles of the seventh antediluvian hero. As one remembers, the hero was endowed with these multiple duties upon his dramatic metamorphosis in heaven. In reference to these conceptual developments, Crispin Fletcher-Louis observes that "3 *Enoch's* account of the transformation of Enoch into the principal angel Metatron represents something of the climax of earlier Enoch traditions."[69]

It should be noted that the Metatron tradition found in *Sefer Hekhalot* does not stem solely from the Enochic conceptual currents, but without a doubt is informed by other mediatorial streams. In this respect, Hugo Odeberg's early hypothesis that the identification of Metatron with Enoch represented a decisive formative pattern in the Metatron tradition was criticized by a number of distinguished students of Jewish mystical traditions, including Moses Gaster, Gershom Scholem, Saul Lieberman, and Jonas Greenfield. These experts noted that the concept of Metatron cannot be explained solely by reference to early Enochic lore because Metatron has taken many of the titles and functions that are reminiscent of those that the archangel Michael, Yahoel, and other elevated personalities possess in early Jewish traditions. But as we remember even in early Enochic booklets, including the *Book of the Similitudes*, the seventh antediluvian patriarch already was endowed with the titles and roles of other mediatorial trends' heroes, including the Son of Man. Some scholars even suggested that the Son of Man traditions might play a crucial role in Enoch's acquisition of his celestial alter ego in the form of Metatron. Thus, in relation to these conceptual currents, Alan Segal observes that

> in the Third or Hebrew Book of Enoch, Metatron is set on a throne alongside God and appointed above angels and powers to function as God's *vizier* and plenipotentiary. These traditions are related to the earlier Enoch cycle in apocalyptic literature because Enoch is described by the mystics as having been caught up to the highest heaven (based on Gen 5:24), where he is transformed into the fiery angel, Metatron. This is clearly dependent on the ancient "son of man" traditions which appear in Ethiopian Enoch 70 and 71, but they have been expanded in Jewish mysticism so that Enoch and Metatron are now *alter egos*, while neither the titles "son of man" nor "son of God" appear at all.[70]

Besides the Son of Man traditions, the influence of other apocalyptic mediatorial figures like Yahoel or the archangel Michael should not be forgotten. Gershom Scholem's classic study differentiates between two basic aspects of Metatron's legends that, in Scholem's opinion, were combined and fused together in the rabbinic and Hekhalot literature. These aspects include the Enochic tradition and the lore connected with the exalted figures of Yahoel and Michael. Scholem writes that

> one aspect identifies Metatron with Yahoel or Michael and knows nothing of his transfiguration from a human being into an angel. The talmudic passages concerned with Metatron are of this type. The other aspect identifies Metatron with the figure of Enoch as he is depicted in apocalyptic literature, and permeated that aggadic and targumic literature which, although not necessarily of a later date than Talmud, was outside of it. When the *Book of Hekhaloth*, or *3 Enoch*, was composed, the two aspects had already become intertwined.[71]

Despite the aforementioned critique of Hugo Odeberg's position, the possible influence of the Enochic tradition on the Metatron imagery has never been abandoned by the new approaches, mainly in view of the evidence preserved in *Sefer Hekhalot*. For example, Gershom Scholem repeatedly referred to several conceptual streams of the Metatron tradition, one of which, in his opinion, was clearly connected with early Enochic developments. Scholars, however, often construe this Enochic stream as a later development that joined the Metatron tradition after its initial formative stage.

Indeed, in *Sefer Hekhalot* Metatron appears in several new roles previously unknown in the early booklets included in *1 (Ethiopic) Enoch*, such as the "Youth," the "Prince of the World," the "Measurer/Measure of the Lord," the "Prince of the divine Presence," the "Prince of the Torah," and the "Lesser YHWH."[72] It is possible that some of these designations might have already originated in pre-mishnaic Judaism under the influence of the various mediatorial traditions in which Michael, Yahoel, Adam, Moses, Noah, Melchizedek, and other characters were depicted as elevated figures.

Also in comparison to the early Enochic booklets, *Sefer Hekhalot* provides more elaborate descriptions of how Enoch's earthly identity was dramatically changed into his transcendental Self. One of the most striking portrayals in this respect is situated in *3 Enoch* 15 (*Synopse* §19), which describes the metamorphosis of the patriarch's earthly body into the fiery celestial form of the supreme angel. *3 Enoch* 15 reads:

> R. Ishmael said: The angel Metatron, Prince of the divine Presence, the glory of highest heaven, said to me: When the Holy One, blessed be he, took me to serve the throne of glory, the wheels of the chariot and all the needs of the Shekinah, at once my flesh turned to flame, my sinews to blazing fire, my bones to juniper coals, my eyelashes to lightning flashes, my eyeballs to fiery torches, the hairs of my

head to hot flames, all my limbs to wings of burning fire, and the substance of my body (וְגוּף קוֹמָתִי) to blazing fire.[73]

Moreover, unlike in the early Enochic writings, the heavenly identity of the seer is presented in *Sefer Hekhalot* not simply as angelic but as divine, since he is designated there as the lesser representation of the divine Name.

This concept of Enoch's heavenly archetype as a preexistent divine being who transcends creation and history is very important for understanding the relationship between the patriarch and his doppelganger. It appears, however, that Enoch might not be the only earthly identity of the great angel.

Although Metatron's title "Youth" in *Sefer Hekhalot* suggests that the great angel joined the angelic company quite late,[74] another salient passage in chapter 48 of the same work reveals that Metatron's upper identity precedes Enoch's earthly existence. Thus, *3 Enoch* 48C:1 (*Synopse* §72) details the following tradition: "The Holy One, blessed be he, said: I made him strong, I took him, I appointed him, namely Metatron my servant (עַבְדִּי), who is unique among all denizens of the heights. 'I made him strong' in the generation of the first man. . . . 'I took him'—Enoch the son of Jared, from their midst, and brought him up. . . . 'I appointed him'—over all the storehouses and treasures which I have in every heaven."[75]

Here, Metatron is envisioned as a divine being who was first incarnated during the generation of Adam and then a second time during the generation before the Flood in the form of the seventh antediluvian hero. Thus, analyzing an excerpt from *3 Enoch* 48, Moshe Idel observes that "two stages in the history of Metatron are described in this passage: the first in the generation of Adam, the second in the generation of the Flood, when he was 'taken' and later 'appointed.' Metatron's status in respect of the generation of Adam is not made clear; possibly he is regarded as an entity different from Adam, as we learn from another source as well. This understanding too, however, cannot blur the connection, from the historical aspect, between two conditions of Metatron: an earlier condition in the generation of Adam and a later condition during the Flood generation."[76]

This development is similar to the tradition of Jacob's heavenly counterpart found in the *Prayer of Joseph*, where Jacob is also understood as an incarnation of the primordial angel who "tabernacled" on earth in the body of the patriarch.

Face of God

It is time to discern common conceptual tenets of the Enochic trajectory related to the idea of the heavenly counterpart. We will start our exploration with the theophanic imagery found in the Enochic accounts.

It has already been noticed in our study that the imagery of the divine Glory, *Kavod*, appears to be playing a crucial role in several scenes where human adepts become united with their heavenly identities. Often such *Kavod* imagery is rendered through the symbolism of the divine Face, a portentous terminological interchange, which was first manifested in the biblical Mosaic stories. The imagery of the divine *Kavod* also plays a significant role in early Enochic accounts. Both *2 Enoch* and the *Similitudes* demonstrate striking similarities in their rendering of the *Kavod* imagery and the angelic retinue that surrounds this glorious extent of the deity. Also the seer's approach to the divine Form and his striking metamorphosis are very similar in both narrations. Several details are particularly worth noting:

a. In both accounts (*1 Enoch* 71:3–5 and *2 Enoch* 22:6), Enoch is brought to the Throne by the archangel Michael.

b. The angelology of the Throne in *1 Enoch* 71, similarly to *2 Enoch*,[77] includes three classes of angelic beings: ophanim, cherubim, and seraphim.

c. Both Enochic accounts speak about the transformation of the visionary. Enoch's metamorphosis in *1 Enoch* 71 recalls the description of the luminous transformation of Enoch into a glorious heavenly being in *2 Enoch* 22:8–9.

d. The transformation takes place in front of a fiery "structure," a possible source of both transformations.

e. Studies in the past have noted that in both accounts, the transformation of the visionary takes place in the context of the angelic liturgy (*1 Enoch* 71:11–12; *2 Enoch* 21:1–22:10).[78]

f. In both accounts, Enoch falls on his face before the Throne.[79]

g. The manner in which Enoch is greeted near the Throne of Glory in *1 Enoch* 71:14–17 resembles the scene from *2 Enoch* 22:5–6 where the deity personally greets Enoch. In both accounts, we have an address in which the visionary is informed about his "eternal" status.[80]

These features of both accounts point to the importance of the encounter with the *Kavod* in the process of acquiring knowledge about, and attaining the condition of, the seer's heavenly identity. Similarly in Jacob's doppelganger lore, the vision of God's glory also becomes an important theophanic motif. As we will see later, these motifs are clearly recognizable in the targumic Jacob accounts and in the *Ladder of Jacob*, where reports about Jacob's angelic counterpart are creatively conflated with theophanic traditions about the vision of God's *Kavod*.

Angels of the Presence as Custodians of Heavenly Identities

Notably, both the *Book of the Similitudes* and *2 Enoch* depict angelic guides who acquaint the seers with their upper celestial identities and their corresponding offices as angels of the Presence. It is well known that the earliest Enochic materials already portray numerous appearances of the angel of the Presence under the name Uriel, who is also known in various traditions under the names of Phanuel and Sariel. In one of the earliest Enochic booklets, the *Astronomical Book*, this angel is responsible for initiating the seventh antediluvian hero into the utmost mysteries of the universe, including astronomical, calendrical, and meteorological secrets.

In *2 Enoch* 22–23, the angel Uriel (whose name is rendered in that apocalypse as Vereveil) also plays a primary role during Enoch's initiations near the Throne of Glory.[81] He instructs Enoch about various subjects of esoteric knowledge in order to prepare him for his celestial offices, including the office of the heavenly scribe. During these initiations, Vereveil transfers to the adept celestial writing instruments and heavenly books. Here the transference of books, scribal tools, and the office of the celestial scribe further reaffirms the process of the gradual unification of the seer with his heavenly alter ego.[82] As will be shown later, such constellations will also play a prominent role in Mosaic traditions of the heavenly double.

1 Enoch 71 also refers to the same angel of the Presence who appears to initiate Enoch into the Son of Man, but names him Phanuel.[83] In the *Similitudes*, he occupies an important place among the four principal angels—namely, the place usually assigned to Uriel. In fact, the angelic name Phanuel might be a title, which stresses the celestial status of Uriel-Sariel[84] as one of the servants of the divine *Panim*.[85] As we will see later in our study, the importance of the angels of the divine Presence in the process of the seer's unification with his heavenly counterpart will be reaffirmed in the accounts of Moses' and Jacob's transformations. Thus, the aforementioned title "Phanuel" will play a prominent role in various Jacob accounts of the heavenly correlative. In view of these connections, it is possible that the title itself might have originated from Jacob's lore. In Genesis 32:31, Jacob names the place of his wrestling with God as Peniel—the Face of God. Scholars believe that the angelic name Phanuel and the place Peniel are etymologically connected.[86]

This reference to Uriel-Sariel-Phanuel as the angel who instructs/wrestles with Jacob and announces to him his new angelic status and name is widely documented in Jacob lore dealing with the idea of the heavenly counterparts, including *Targum Neofiti* and the *Prayer of Joseph*. In the *Prayer of Joseph*, Jacob-Israel reveals that "Uriel, the angel of God, came forth and said that 'I [Jacob-Israel] had descended to earth and I had tabernacled among men and that I had been called by the name of Jacob.' He envied me and fought with me and wrestled with me."[87]

In the *Ladder of Jacob*, another portentous pseudepigraphical text dealing with the idea of the heavenly counterpart, Jacob's identification with his doppelganger, the angel Israel, again involves the initiatory encounter with the angel Sariel: the angel of the divine Presence or the Face. The same state of events is observable in Enochic materials where Uriel serves as the principal heavenly guide to another prominent visionary who has also acquired knowledge about his own heavenly counterpart—namely, Enoch-Metatron.

Moreover in some Enochic accounts, including *2 Enoch*, the patriarch not only is initiated by the angel of the Presence but himself becomes the servant of the divine Presence. Enoch's new designation is unfolded primarily in chapters 21–22 of *2 Enoch* in the midst of the *Kavod* imagery. In these chapters, one can find several promises from the mouth of the archangel Gabriel and the deity himself that the translated patriarch will now stand in front of God's Face forever.[88] The adept's role as the servant of the divine Presence and its connection with the traditions of the heavenly counterpart will be explored in detail later in this study.

Enoch as the "Youth"

As we have already learned in this study, the concept of the heavenly alter ego of Enoch was not forgotten in the later Enochic lore, wherein the heavenly persona of the seventh patriarch was often identified with the supreme angel Metatron, a character designated in Hekhalot and rabbinic texts as the celestial "Youth," the title rendered in the Merkavah lore with the Hebrew term נער.[89] This designation is intriguing since in many accounts of the heavenly counterparts in early Jewish and Christian texts, a celestial double of a human protagonist is often portrayed as a child or a youth. For example, in early heterodox Christian developments Jesus' heavenly identity is often rendered through the imagery of a child.[90] Such imagery is widely dissipated in various apocryphal Acts, including, the *Acts of John* 87[91] and 88–89,[92] the *Acts of Andrew and Matthias* 18[93] and 33,[94] the *Acts of Peter* 21,[95] and the *Acts of Thomas* 27.[96] Other early Christian apocryphal materials are also cognizant about Jesus' heavenly identity in the form of the "youth." Thus, such imagery can be found in the *Gospel of Judas* 33:15–20,[97] the *Apocryphon of John*,[98] the *Concept of Our Great Power* 44:32–33,[99] the *Apocalypse of Paul* 18:6,[100] and other early Christian accounts.[101]

The identity of Jesus as a "youth" often has been understood by scholars as a reference to his "immaterial" heavenly Self. Thus, for example, reflecting on Jesus' identity as a child in the *Gospel of Judas*, Paul Foster argues that

> it is against this broader theological outlook of the text that the ability of Jesus to change into the form of a child needs to be understood. Here polymorphic power is not used to illustrate transcendence over death, as in the post-resurrection examples of this phenomenon; rather it declares the possessor's transcendence over the material world. Physical form is not a constraint on such a being, for in essence he does not belong to the material world. Therefore, a fundamental difference needs to be emphasized. The property of polymorphy was particularly attractive in gnostic theology since it allowed for reflection on a divine being able to defy the limitations of the transitory and material world. Here, unlike previous examples, the author of the Gospel of Judas wishes to show that Jesus not only defeats the power of death through his ability to metamorphose, but in fact he is beyond the control of what is viewed as being the inherently corrupted mortal realm.[102]

The symbolism of a child as Jesus' heavenly identity was received into the Manichaean lore, which often speaks of a divine figure under the name "Jesus-Child."[103] Moreover, in some *Kephalaia*'s passages, "Youth" appears to be representing only one of Jesus' multiple identities that is clearly distinguished from his other selves.[104]

The idea of Jesus' heavenly identity as the "Youth" might have its roots already in the New Testament materials. Thus, it is possible that a mysterious "youth" (νεανίσκος) who appears in Mark 14:51–52[105] and 16:5[106] might represent Jesus' doppelganger. In Mark 14:51–52, this "youth" is depicted as initially wearing linen clothes (περιβεβλημένος σινδόνα) from which he was then stripped naked in the course of struggle with his persecutors. In Mark 16:5, the "youth" appears before women in the empty tomb dressed in a white robe (στολὴν λευκήν). The women's amazement and terror might hint to the fact that the youth's attire signifies an angelic garment. The "youth's" knowledge about Jesus' resurrection also points to the fact that he was not an ordinary earthly being. Since there are only two instances of this term in the Gospel of Mark, and in both of these instances, the mysterious "youth" is defined through the clothes he wears, scholars often argue that it refers to the same person.

Scholars previously noticed that details of the young man's passages appear to be mirroring some events of Jesus' story. Harry Fleddermann summarizes these scholarly suggestions by noting that

> Mark associates the young man closely with Jesus. He does not use his usual *akolouthein* but the rare *synakolouthein*. Mark also uses the word *kratein* to link the young man with Jesus. Jesus is arrested (14:46); and the young man is arrested (14:51). The word *sindōn* "linen cloth" links this passage with the pericope of the burial of Jesus. The word is used twice in each pericope and nowhere else in Mark. The young man follows with only a linen cloth about his naked body (14:51). He is arrested, and he flees leaving the linen cloth (14:52). Joseph of Arimathea buys a linen cloth and, taking the corpse down from the cross, he wraps it in the linen cloth (15:46). Finally, Mark links the passage with the account of the empty tomb. The word *neaniskos* "young man" is used only twice in Mark, in the present passage and in the account of the empty tomb (16:5). In both cases the young man's clothing is described using the perfect participle middle of *periballō*. These are the only two uses of the verb in Mark.[107]

In view of these connections, some scholars see this character as a "symbolic representation" of Jesus. Raymond Brown notes that "in chap. 16 the risen Jesus is represented symbolically once more as this young man, only now clothed in heavenly garments, even as the transfigured Jesus appears in garments that have been made white in Mark 9:3."[108] Brown further suggests that the youth here, like in some "Gnostic" materials, might represent the heavenly identity of Jesus. He notes that "a gnostic variation of this symbolism would involve a distinction between the Christ (the heavenly principle) and Jesus (the earthly shell or human appearance)."[109]

If the youth is indeed envisioned in the Gospel of Mark as Jesus' doppelganger, his disrobing in Mark 14:52 is especially noteworthy.[110] The protagonist's unclothing in some heavenly counterpart accounts often signifies an entrapment by negative forces, like in the *Hymn of the Pearl*, where the loss of garment is associated with the transition to the lower demonic realm, symbolically represented by Egypt. The conceptual roots of such an understanding of unclothing is connected with the protoplast's story where the loss of original garments is interpreted as an ominous event coinciding with the exile to a lower realm.

It might be not coincidental that in Mark 14:51–52 the νεανίσκος becomes "unclothed" in the very episode that inaugurates Jesus' passion. Endowment with the luminous garment, on the other hand, signifies rebirth and acquisition of a new, heavenly, identity. In this respect, it is not by happenstance that the "youth" who is present at the scene of the empty tomb, which signifies Jesus' resurrection, is donning the "white robe," the raiment that might suggest the protagonist's new heavenly status. While in Mark the actual status of the mysterious "youth" remained concealed, in Matthew, Luke, and John, his heavenly identity will be "revealed" when he will be openly turned into an angel.[111]

The "youth," as the heavenly identity of Jesus, also has a long tradition of representation in later Christian iconography where the child Jesus is depicted as sitting on the angelic throne represented by the Theotokos.

Moreover, in early Christian traditions, not only is the heavenly identity of Jesus rendered through the imagery of the "youth," but the upper selves of other historical and mythological figures are also depicted through similar symbolism. For example, in various materials, which were circulated in early Christian milieus under the name of the apostle Thomas, the heavenly identity of a protagonist is often described as a child.[112] Similarly, in the *Hymn of the Pearl* found in the *Acts of Thomas*, where the heavenly twin's imagery comes to the fore, the main hero is depicted as an anonymous child. It is noteworthy that this symbolism is evoked in a scene of the adept's reunification with his upper identity.[113]

Some scholars trace this symbolism of children as the heavenly counterparts of humans to the passage in Matthew 18:10,[114] where the imagery of the μικροί is tied to the symbolism of the angels of the Presence who perpetually behold the Face of the heavenly Father in heaven. Here we find a familiar cluster of the peculiar motifs usually associated with the concept of the heavenly correlatives in apocalyptic accounts where one also often encounters the themes of the divine Face and angelic servants of the Presence.

The concept of the heavenly identities of human beings in the form of children might not make its first appearance in early Christian lore but may instead have its ancient roots in Second Temple Jewish materials. Thus, the Jewish pseudepigrapha portray some biblical patriarchs and prophets as miraculous children, whose features and attributes are reminiscent of the celestial beings. This distinguished cohort of the "wonder children"—which includes the figures of Seth,[115] Noah, Melchizedek, and Moses, among others—appears to be understood in some cases as related to the heavenly identities of the protagonists. In view of these developments, the imagery of the "youth" in Enochic literature, and especially in *2 Enoch*, should be explored more closely.

The Jewish esoteric lore derives Metatron's title "Youth" from an exegesis of Proverbs 22:6 (חנוך לנער), which is interpreted as "Enoch was made into the

נער, i.e. Metatron."¹¹⁶ The title "Youth" has several possible theological meanings in the Jewish legends. According to one of them, the name may be explained by the fact that Metatron is constantly rejuvenated upon reaching old age.¹¹⁷ The information about Metatron's title "Youth" is widely disseminated in the rabbinic and Hekhalot materials.¹¹⁸ Despite the abundant information about the title provided by other Hekhalot evidence, 3 Enoch appears to contain a substantial bulk of the unique knowledge pertaining to this sobriquet of Metatron. The appellation occurs several times in the text and becomes a locus of extensive theological deliberation. It is significant for our study that the authors of *Sefer Hekhalot* construe the context and even the origin of the title on the basis of the motifs associated with the Enochic traditions.

The title is first introduced in 3 Enoch 2:2 (*Synopse* §3) in the context of the angelic opposition to the ascension of R. Ishmael. There the designation "Youth" in relation to Enoch-Metatron first comes from the mouth of the angelic hosts who challenge the exalted angel on the subject of the legitimacy of his protégé, Rabbi Ishmael, "the one born of woman," to enter God's presence and behold the Chariot:

> Then the eagles of the chariot, the flaming ophanim and the cherubim of devouring fire, asked Metatron, "Youth (נער), why have you allowed one born of woman to come in and behold the chariot? From what nation is he? From what tribe? What is his character?" Metatron replied, "He is of the nation of Israel, whom the Holy One, blessed be he, chose from the seventy nations to be his people. He is of the tribe of Levi, which presents the offering to his name. He is of the family of Aaron, whom the Holy One, blessed be he, chose to minister in his presence and on whose head he himself placed the priestly crown on Sinai." At once they began to say, "This one is certainly worthy to behold the chariot, as it is written, Happy is the nation of whom this is true, happy is the nation whose God is the Lord."¹¹⁹

The story from 3 Enoch 2:2, which revolves around the theme of the humanity of the visionary, alludes to Enoch's situation, underscored in *Sefer Hekhalot* by the parallel story of the angelic opposition to the seventh antediluvian patriarch.¹²⁰ As mentioned above, in 3 Enoch 4:5–10 (*Synopse* §6), Enoch encountered a similar challenge from the three ministering angels ʿUzzah, ʿAzzah, and ʿAzaʾel at the time of his ascension in the generation of the Flood.

In that passage, as in the account found in 3 Enoch 2, the angelic opposition is provoked by the human status of the visionary who attempts to enter into the celestial realm, violating the boundaries separating human and angelic regions. Both stories also have an identical structure, since in both of them the angels who initially opposed the visionary eventually become persuaded and pacified by the argumentation of the seer's patrons (God and Metatron) and are finally obliged to deliver a similar address praising the social or physical (nation/parents) pedigree of the invader.

It is significant that *3 Enoch* 4 refers to the Adamic tradition by recalling the protoplast's situation. This motif might reflect the Adamic provenance of the stories from *3 Enoch* 2 and 4 and their possible connection with the tradition about the veneration of Adam by some angels and the rejection of such obeisance by others, a tradition that was widespread in early Adamic literature. This motif and its connection with the concept of the heavenly double will be explored in detail later in our study.

In light of our previous investigation, it is noteworthy that the title "youth" also plays an important role in *2 Enoch*, where it possibly designates the patriarch's heavenly persona. Some Slavonic manuscripts of the shorter recension, including *A, B*, and *V*, apply this title several times solely to the patriarch Enoch.

The reader encounters the title already in the first few chapters of the Slavonic apocalypse, which describe the patriarch's celestial voyage through the heavens. In fact, manuscripts *B* and *V* use the title "youth" at the outset in the first chapter of the text. The very first address Enoch's celestial guides utter in these manuscripts is: "Be brave, Youth!" (*derzai junoshe*).[121] This designation is then occasionally repeated by the celestial guides as they lead the seer through the heavens, providing him with detailed explanations of the heavenly surroundings. Thus, in chapter 9 of the shorter recension, an angelic being accompanying the seer on his way through the heavenly realm addresses Enoch as "youth": "This place has been prepared, Youth (*junoshe*),[122] for the righteous. . . ."[123] Shortly after this in chapter 10, the angel captures the visionary's attention with the same title: "This place, Youth (*junoshe*), has been prepared for those who practice godless uncleanness on the earth."[124]

It should be noted that, in contrast to *3 Enoch*, where the information about the origin and usage of the title is unfolded through the narrative framework of the conversation between R. Ishmael and Metatron, in *2 Enoch* the title appears in the direct speech of the angels and the deity. Thus, in the shorter recension of *2 Enoch* 24, God directly addresses the patriarch with the title "Youth": "And the Lord called me [Enoch] and he placed me to himself closer than Gabriel. And I did obeisance to the Lord. And the Lord spoke to me: 'Whatever you see, Youth (*junoshe*), things standing still and moving about were brought to perfection by me and not even to angels have I explained my secrets . . . as I am making them known to you today.'"[125] Some manuscripts of *2 Enoch* 22 also attest to the same direct address of the deity: "And the Lord with his own mouth called me [Enoch] and said: Be brave, Youth! (*junoshe*).[126] Do not be frightened! Stand up in front of my face forever. And Michael, the Lord's archistrategos, brought me in front of the Lord's face. And the Lord tempted his servants and said to them: 'Let Enoch come up and stand in the front of my face forever.' And the glorious ones bowed down and said: 'Let him come up!' "[127]

The differences between the uses of the title in *2 Enoch* and in *Sefer Hekhalot* might indicate that, in its handling of the adept's sobriquets, the Slavonic apocalypse stays very close to the early Enochic booklets in which the titles are often introduced in the same fashion—that is, as direct addresses of main characters. Therefore, in the early Enochic materials, the patriarch's scribal honorifics often come from the mouth of other characters, including God[128] and angels.[129] This feature indicates that the tradition about the title "Youth" in the Slavonic apocalypse does not represent an interpolation from the later Merkavah accounts since this new title is used similarly to other early Enochic titles as an address of other characters.

The tradition of the visionary's doppelganger in the form of the "youth" appears to be found also in another pseudepigraphical account that will be explored later in our study. This account is *Joseph and Aseneth*, where the female seer, in the course of her transformation and unification with a heavenly counterpart, acquires the form of a "young man." Thus, in *Jos. Asen.* 15:1–2, the heavenly visitor tells Aseneth that she can now remove the veil from her head because *her head is as a young man* (ἡ κεφαλή σού ἐστιν ὡς ἀνδρὸς νεανίσκου): "And she went to the man into her first chamber and stood before him. And the man said to her, 'Remove the veil from your head, and for what purpose did you do this? For you are a chaste virgin today, and your head is like that of a young man.' And Aseneth removed the veil from her head."[130] It is significant that this acquisition of the seer's "youth" identity goes simultaneously with the attainment of her new heavenly persona.

Furthermore, the authors of *Jos. Asen.* also appear to be cognizant about the identity as "youth" of another portentous exemplar of the heavenly counterpart lore—the patriarch Jacob. In *Jos. Asen.* 22:7,[131] when Aseneth encounters the angelomorphic father-in-law, he appears to her as the young man (ὥσπερ νεότης ἀνδρός).[132] We will explore these traditions later in our study.

The Priestly "Youth" as the Heavenly Counterpart of the Exemplar

It has been established already in our study that in early Jewish and Christian accounts the protagonist's heavenly alter ego sometimes is envisioned in the identity of a "youth." In view of this important conceptual development, we should now direct our close attention to the imagery of angelomorphic children that often appear in the Second Temple Jewish materials, since these traditions might also pertain to the concept of the doppelganger.

One of the earliest specimens of the lore about an angelomorphic "youth" can be found in the Noachic materials.[133] The early Jewish materials strive to portray Noah as a wonder child: *1 Enoch* 106,[134] the *Genesis Apocryphon*,[135] and possibly *1Q19*[136] depict him with a glorious face and eyes "like the rays of the sun." *1 Enoch* 106:2 relates that when the newborn Noah opened his eyes, the whole house lit up.[137] The child then opened his mouth and blessed the Lord of heaven. Scholars have previously noted[138] that the scene of the glorious visage of the young hero of the Flood delivering blessings upon rising up from the hands of the midwife has a sacerdotal significance and parallels the glorious appearance and actions of the high priest.[139]

It is not coincidental that the angelomorphic child who might be envisioned here as the heavenly identity of the Flood's hero is endowed with priestly credentials. It already has been noted in our study that the writers of early Enochic materials, where Noah first appears in his "youth" identity, were cognizant of the peculiar sacerdotal counterparts that exist simultaneously in heaven and on earth and include sanctuaries and their cultic servants. Here, like in many doppelganger accounts already explored in this study, the sacerdotal settings serve as fertile ground for unfolding the lore about the celestial identities. For example, the story of Enoch's heavenly identity plays a very important role in *2 Enoch*'s sacerdotal debates where the earthly sanctuary is specifically built on the site of Enoch's second ascension to heaven. The Slavonic apocalypse also appears to unveil the heavenly identity of another important priestly character—Melchizedek, who becomes, not coincidently, envisioned in the Slavonic apocalypse, like Noah, as an angelomorphic child. Scholars noted that Melchizedek's birth in *Slavonic Enoch* recalls some parallels with the birth of Noah in *1 Enoch* and in the *Genesis Apocryphon*.[140] The Melchizedek narrative occupies the last chapters of *2 Enoch*.[141] A host of interesting overlaps between the birth of Noah in the early Enochic accounts and the birth of Melchizedek in *2 Enoch* have been previously noticed by scholars.[142] It has been also suggested that the author of *2 Enoch* wants to diminish the extraordinary qualities of Noah's person and transfer these qualities to Melchizedek.[143] The text therefore can be seen as an account drawing on original Noachic themes. Yet the Melchizedek story of *2 Enoch* brings the concept of the "youth" as the heavenly identity of an exemplar to a new level in comparison with the Noachic developments. Thus, while in the aforementioned Noachic accounts the miraculous child is not translated to heaven, *2 Enoch*'s authors depict the voyage of the angelomorphic "youth" to the paradise Eden on the wings of Michael. In this respect, the wunderkind tradition found in *2 Enoch* is more transparent about the heavenly identity of its youngster.

But how valuable are these miraculous child traditions for our explorations of the seventh patriarch's celestial alter ego, and what are their possible connections with Enoch's role as "youth"? Notably, in *2 Enoch* the story of the miraculous child Melchizedek parallels in some details the story of the main protagonist—the patriarch Enoch. Thus, Enoch and Melchizedek are the only two characters of the apocalypse who undergo translation to heaven. Like Enoch, Melchizedek then returns to the earth after his visitation to heaven in order to become a priest after the Flood. In view of these similarities and also the Noachic parallels mentioned before, it is evident that the miraculous child Melchizedek fulfills here the same functions as the child Noah in early Enochic accounts.

In this respect, it is intriguing that there are no stories of the miraculous child Enoch in early Enochic booklets or in *2 Enoch*, although his chief ideological contender, Moses, is often endowed with such a story.[144] Why then is an account of Enoch's miraculous birth so markedly absent from early Enochic lore? It appears that such a miraculous birth account is rendered in early Enochic materials through the imagery of the child Noah (in *1 Enoch* and possibly in the *Genesis Apocryphon*)[145] and the child Melchizedek (in *2 Enoch*). Scholars previously noted that, in the early Enochic booklets, Enoch and Noah often appear in the same roles when Noah serves as the conceptual double of the seventh antediluvian hero.[146] In *2 Enoch*, Melchizedek fulfills similar functions, implicitly elucidating the heavenly identity of Enoch as the "youth." The choice of Melchizedek for illustrating the heavenly "youth" identity of the story's main protagonist in this respect is not coincidental since in some early Jewish and Christian materials this enigmatic priest is often understood as a human being who has his own doppelganger.

Scholars previously noticed that Melchizedek appears to be envisioned in some Qumran materials as a double of the archangel Michael. For example, Florentino García Martínez suggests the following:

> If in *11QMelch* Melchizedek is neither God nor a divine hypostasis, he is definitely a heavenly and exalted being.[147] The text attributes to him dominion over the heavenly armies: he is the chief of all the angels and of all the sons of God. In addition, he is one who leads the battle against Belial and the spirits of his lot, and carries out divine vengeance against them. Melchizedek is described with the same features used in the Rule of the Community and the Damascus Document to describe the "Prince of light" and as a double of the archangel Michael, exactly as described in the War[148] Scroll.[149]

Similarly David Frankfurter argues that "a figure of extensive lore in early Judaism, by the early Christian period Melchizedek had already become a heavenly double for the archangel Michael at Qumran (*11QMelch*), for Christ among the audience of Hebrews (5:5–6; 7), and for the spirit of God among others."[150] Another scholar, James Dunn, arguing along similar lines, pointed out that "the name Melchizedek (king of righteousness) could have been formed as a titular description of the archangel Michael, just as Melchiresha (king of wickedness) seems to have been formed as a titular description of Belial."[151]

Further, some scholars suggested that the peculiar bond between Melchizedek and the archangel Michael appears to be reminiscent of the relationships between Enoch and the Son of Man—the prominent pair of the doppelganger lore, which has already been explored in this study. Thus, Michael Knibb draws attention to the parallels between the tradition of Melchizedek's heavenly alter ego and Enoch's identification with the Son of Man in the *Book of the Similitudes*.[152] James Dunn makes another significant comparison by bringing into the discussion the prominent pair of a seer and his heavenly identity in the form of Enoch-Metatron. He notes that Melchizedek's apotheosis in *11QMelch* "is only paralleled in the (later) equation of Enoch with the Son of Man in *1 Enoch* 71:14 and with Metatron in *3 Enoch* 3–16."[153] It is also noteworthy that various early Jewish and Christian Melchizedek materials feature prominent lists of antediluvian figures that might suggest that these figures are understood in these traditions as the earthly reincarnations of the king of Salem.[154]

In light of these conceptual developments, it is intriguing that in the longer recension of *2 Enoch* the child Melchizedek is transported to heaven on the wings of Michael.[155] Here the earthly priest and his angelic double are paradoxically unified in the course of the human protagonist's transition to the heavenly realm.

The Acquisition of Luminous Garments as Unification with the Heavenly Counterpart

To conclude our investigation into Enochic traditions of the heavenly correlatives, we should now draw our attention to another important feature of *2 Enoch*—namely, the motif of the seer's endowment with the glorious garment during his acquisition of his upper identity.

The symbolism of garments plays a paramount role in many apocalyptic accounts, signaling ontological transitions endured by the human beings who attempt to cross the threshold between their earthly and celestial states, conditions that often become rendered through respective sets of clothing metaphors. In this regard, scholars noticed that "clothing . . . helps to bridge the gap between the worlds above and below. At the very outset one should note that both the heavenly creatures and God appear in the Bible clothed, even if their garments are frequently metaphorical."[156]

It is not coincidental that in the Slavonic apocalypse the clothing metaphors loom large, especially in the scene of the adept's celestial transformation in the upper heaven. Thus, *2 Enoch* 22:9 portrays the archangel Michael extracting Enoch from his earthly "clothes" and anointing him with delightful oil. The text says that the oil's appearance is "greater than the greatest light and its ointment is like sweet dew, and the fragrance [like] myrrh; and it is like rays of the glittering sun."[157] Anointing with oil appears to be understood here as the patriarch's transition from his garments of skin to the luminous garment of an immortal angelic being, one of the glorious ones. This exchange of attire has been previously noted by scholars who suggested that Enoch's covering with the shining oil might represent priestly investiture.[158]

The endowment of the seventh antediluvian hero with the glorious raiment is reiterated in later Enoch tradition. There too the acquisition of the celestial garments coincides with the human seer's transition to his upper identity. Thus, for example, *Sefer Hekhalot* recounts how during Enoch's transition to the state of the supreme angel, Metatron, his earthly attire of skin was altered in a dramatic fiery metamorphosis,[159] and as a result, the patriarch acquired the celestial luminous robe and crown: "R. Ishmael said: Metatron, Prince of the divine Presence, said to me: Out of the love which he had for me, more than for all the denizens of the heights, the Holy One, blessed be he, fashioned for me a majestic robe, in which all kinds of luminaries were set, and he clothed me in it. He fashioned for me a glorious cloak in which brightness, brilliance, splendor, and luster of every kind were fixed, and he wrapped me in it." (*3 Enoch* 12:1–2).[160]

Jarl Fossum observes that in *3 Enoch* "as part of his installation as God's vice-regent in heaven, Enoch is given new clothes . . . a robe of honor on which were fixed all kinds of beauty, splendor, brilliance, and majesty."[161] As one can see in various Enochic accounts, the clothing metaphors help to highlight the process of the subject's transition from his earthly identity to the celestial alter ego, thus accentuating the portentous link between two identities represented by the respective set of "ontological" clothes. In such perspective, the various identities are understood as the "garments" of the adept suitable for different realms of his or her habitation.

Another pseudepigraphical doppelganger account that will be explored in detail later in our study also attests to the motif of change of the seers' garments: in *Jos. Asen.*, the female initiate changes her garments in the process of identifying with her upper counterpart. *Jos. Asen.* 14:12–15 offers the following description of the seer's reclothing:

> And Aseneth rose and stood on her feet. And the man said to her, "Proceed unhindered into your second chamber and put off your black tunic of mourning, and the sackcloth put off your waist, and shake

off those ashes from your head, and wash your face and your hands with living water, 'and dress in a new linen robe (as yet) untouched' and distinguished and gird your waist (with) the new twin girdle of your virginity. And come (back) to me, and I will tell you what I have to say." And Aseneth hurried and went into her second chamber where the chests (containing) her ornaments were, and opened her coffer, and took a new linen robe, distinguished (and as yet) untouched, and undressed the black tunic of mourning and put off the sackcloth from her waist, and dressed in her distinguished (and as yet) untouched linen robe, and girded herself with the twin girdle of her virginity, one girdle around her waist, and another girdle upon her breast. And she shook off the ashes from her head, and washed her hands and her face with living water. And she took an (as yet) untouched and distinguished linen veil and covered her head.[162]

Here, like in *2 Enoch*, the angelic guide directs the seer's reclothing into the new garment. Reflecting on the adept's transformation in *Jos. Asen.*, Ross Kraemer draws attention to the actions of Aseneth's angelic instructor by noting that "as a result of her encounter with the angelic double of Joseph, Aseneth changes her clothing twice. In the first instance, at the angel's command, she removes the filthy garments of mourning she has worn during her week of penance and replaces them with a 'στολὴν καινὴν ἄθικτον'—a new, immaculate robe (14.13). The remainder of her encounter with the angel takes place while she wears this garment. But in 15.10, the angel instructs her to change into a wedding garment, which she only does after the angel departs back up to the heavens."[163]

In the Mosaic traditions of the heavenly counterpart, attested in the *Exagoge* of Ezekiel the Tragedian, the son of Amram might also receive the luminous garment of the doppelganger. Although a garment of the seer is not explicitly mentioned in that account, some implicit details in the description of Moses' heavenly correlative and Raguel's reaction to Moses' changed identity might suggest such a possibility. In its description of Moses' heavenly identity sitting on the lofty throne, the *Exagoge* uses the Greek word φώς/φῶς. Scholars previously reflected on the ambiguity of this Greek term that can signify not only man (φώς) but also light (φῶς)—possibly pointing to the luminous nature of the seer's heavenly identity. Raguel's reaction at the end of the account when he calls Moses a "stranger" also might point to the possibility of the seer's luminous transformation. Moreover, the transference of the celestial man's regalia (a scepter and a crown) to Moses might also suggest the conveyance of the celestial accoutrement to a new "owner."

It appears that the symbolism of the seers' luminous garments is deeply rooted in the Adamic traditions where the acquisition of a celestial raiment is often understood as the return to the prelapsarian heavenly nature of the protoplasts.[164] The Adamic conceptual developments are very important for our investigation of the heavenly counterpart traditions since in these protological currents the transition of the human being from their heavenly identities in the Garden of Eden to their earthly identities on earth became rendered through a set of distinctive clothing metaphors. We, therefore, must explore these Adamic legends more closely.

Biblical developments found in Genesis 1:26–27 and Genesis 3:21 represent pivotal starting points for subsequent Jewish and Christian interpretations about the glorious garments of humanity. Genesis 1:26 describes the creation of humanity after the likeness (דמות) of the image (צלם) of God. Notably Genesis 1:26–27 refers to the צלם *(tselem)* of Adam, the luminous image of God's glory according to which Adam was created.[165] It is often understood that Adam's *tselem* was created after God's own *tselem* (בצלמנו, literally "in our *tselem*")— a kind of luminous "imitation" of the glorious *tselem* of God. Later rabbinic interpretations often argue that the likeness that Adam and God shared was not physicality, in the usual sense of having a body, but rather luminescence.[166] In this context, the first humans' clothing in garments of glory was often taken by later interpreters as a replication of the state of the deity, who, according to some biblical passages, was also clothed in glory and majesty.[167] It is noteworthy that in rabbinic tradition the imagery of *tselem* became very closely intertwined with the terminology of the face (*panim*).

It is therefore especially noteworthy that, amid such major conceptual developments, Genesis 3 contains a cluster of motifs pertaining to the first humans' attire. According to Genesis 3:21, the deity fashioned for his beloved creatures a set of enigmatic clothes—"garments of skin." This passage is usually understood to refer to God's clothing of Adam and Eve's nakedness *after* the Fall. Some scholars, however, argue that sufficient evidence exists to suggest another interpretation of the time reference in Genesis 3:21. According to this alternative reading, the verbs in Genesis 3:21 are to be taken as having pluperfect sense referring to the status of Adam and Eve at their creation *before* the Fall.[168]

Several extrabiblical materials also show familiarity with the traditions of the glorious garments of the first humans.[169] The motif is apparent, for example, in the elaborations of the protoplasts' story found in some versions of the *Primary Adam Books* that allude to the story of the original garments of light once possessed by the first humans. In the Armenian version of the *Primary Adam Books* (at 20:1), a testimony about the tragic loss of the garments comes directly from the mouth of one of the protoplasts, when Eve recollects the dramatic moment of the garments' disappearance: "At that hour I learned with my eyes that I was naked of the glory with which I had been clothed."[170] This passage hints not only at the protoplasts' original possession of the glorious clothes[171] but also at their ominous stripping after the Fall.[172]

Despite this unhappy memory, humanity's return to the glorious garments of the protoplast seems also to be foreshadowed in the *Primary Adam Books*.[173] A suggestive hint appears at the scene of Adam's burial (which is found in the section dealing with Adamic funerary rites). His body is covered with linen vestments brought from Paradise, imagery that serves as a sign of the eschatological reclothing of humanity and its return to the protoplasts' original attire: "After this, God spoke to Michael and said, 'Go to the Garden of the [third] heaven and bring [me] three linen cloths.' When he had brought them, God said to Michael and to Ozel and to Gabriel, 'Bring these linen cloths and cover Adam's body, and bring sweet oil.' They brought them and set them around him and wound him in that garment."[174] The rabbinic materials reaffirm the tradition that the first humans possessed glorious garments. The targumic traditions, both Palestinian[175] and Babylonian,[176] while rendering Genesis 3:21 "the Lord God made for Adam and his wife garments of skin and clothed them," read "garments of glory" instead of "garments of skin." This targumic interpretation is supported by a wide array of midrashic sources. Thus, for example, *Genesis Rabbah* 20:12 says that the scroll of Rabbi Meir read "garments of light" (כתנות אור) instead of "garments of skin" (כתנות עור): "In R. Meir's Torah it was found written, 'Garments of light: this refers to Adam's garments, which were like a torch [shedding radiance], broad at the bottom and narrow at the top.'"[177] Another midrashic compilation, *Pirke de Rabbi Eliezer* 14, also knows the motif of the protoplast's glorious garment: "What was the dress of the first man? A skin of nail and a cloud of glory covered him. When he ate of the fruits of the tree, the nail-skin was stripped off him and the cloud of glory departed from him, and he saw himself naked."[178]

Indeed, this motif continued to be developed in the rabbinic context for millennia. In one of the later Jewish mystical compendiums, the *Book of Zohar* I.36b, one finds an echo of the same tradition about the luminous garments. As was the case at *Gen. Rab.* 20, this Zoharic passage also uses the same word play, אור / עור: "At first they had had coats of light (אור), which procured them the service of the highest of the high, for the celestial angels used to come to enjoy that light; so it is written, 'For thou hast made him but little lower than the angels, and crowned him with glory and honor' (Ps. viii, 6). Now after their sins they had only coats of skin (עור), good for the body but not for the soul."[179]

In Christian materials, the notion of various garments corresponding to various identities (earthly or heavenly) of the seer receives further development. Moreover, in some texts, the garment itself becomes envisioned as the heavenly counterpart of the visionary. Thus, in the *Hymn of the Pearl* 76–80, as we saw above, the following tradition can be found: "On a sudden, when I received it, the garment seemed to me to become like a mirror of myself. I saw it all in all, and I too received all in it, for we were two in distinction and yet again one in one likeness. And the treasurers too, who brought it to me, I saw in like manner to be two (and yet) one likeness."[180]

Analyzing this arcane passage, Gerard Luttikhuizen suggests that here "the poetic story is interlaced with references to the religious meaning of self-knowledge which the prince attains when he is reunited with his precious garment,[181] apparently a metaphor for his better half or heavenly twin."[182]

In Mandaean texts, the adept's heavenly twin (*dmuta*) is also understood as the celestial "garment." Thus, *Left Ginza* II.5 unveils the following imagery: "I shall take you out of the world and cause you to ascend. I shall take you out of it and cause you to ascend and shall leave all behind. I shall leave all, they shall all die and disappear. You are my counterpart (*dmuta*), I shall cause you to ascend and keep you safe in my garment. In my garment, which the Great (Life) gave to me, and in the pure fragrance which is entrusted to me."[183]

The aforementioned Christian and Mandaean traditions of the garment as the heavenly counterpart of a human being can be compared with the tradition of "clothing into the image" found in later Jewish mystical accounts where the *tselem* itself is understood as the attire. Gershom Scholem's research demonstrates that in Jewish mysticism *tselem* became envisioned as a sort of "garment" of the soul that "floats" over it. He observes that "this garment also becomes the soul's heavenly attire when it returns to Paradise after death."[184] These conceptual currents that try to connect *tselem* with the garment will be very important for our study when we turn to Jacob materials where the heavenly counterpart of Jacob will be envisioned as his *tselem*. The concept of the image as the hero's doppelganger will be explored in detail later in our study.

Removal of the Luminous Garment as Parting with the Heavenly Identity

As we already witnessed in our study, in some Adamic accounts the stripping of garments of light from the protagonists and the antagonists of the protological story coincide with their exile into the lower regions where they assume a different set of roles. It is possible that in these legends about stripped garments of light, one can encounter a tradition of parting with respective heavenly identities.

Thus, in the *Primary Adam Books*, Satan's exclusion from the heavenly realm coincides with the stripping of his garments of glory. In this text, the demoted antagonist repeatedly describes his original celestial condition through metaphors of glory and light. These are precisely the formulae often used in the *Primary Adam Books* to describe the first humans' celestial attire. Thus, in the Latin version of the aforementioned text (12.1–16:2), the Adversary describes his lost condition through the symbolism of "glory":

O Adam, all my enmity, jealousy, and resentment is towards you, since on account of you I was expelled and alienated from my glory (*gloria mea*), which I had in heaven in the midst of the angels. Then the Lord God grew angry with me and sent me forth with my angels from our glory (*gloria nostra*). On account of you we were expelled from our dwelling into this world and cast out upon the earth. Immediately we were in grief, since we had been despoiled of so much glory (*gloria*), and we grieved to see you in such a great happiness of delights.[185]

Here the motif of stripping off glorious garments coincides with the transition to a lower realm. Moreover, the demoted Antagonist's alienation from his former glorious state is set several times in parallel to the exaltation and gifts given to the protoplast: "since we had been despoiled of so much glory (*gloria*), and we grieved to see you in such a great happiness of delights."[186]

The same transitional situation, as we already witnessed in this study, can be seen in the story of the protoplasts reflected in various Adamic materials including the *Primary Adam Books*.

Moreover, it appears that not only fallen creatures but even characters in a good standing, like the patriarch Enoch, are also required to "strip" their luminous garments off before their departure into the lower regions. *2 Enoch* 37 recounts the unusual procedure performed on Enoch's "face" at the final stage of his encounter with the deity in the seventh heaven. After the patriarch's glorious transformation and after the utmost mysteries of the universe are revealed to him, God orders Enoch to go back to the realm of humans in order to convey these revelations to the people of the earth. His recently acquired radiant celestial attire, however, appears to pose some problems for his return to earth. In order to remedy this obstacle, God calls one of his senior angels to chill the "face" of Enoch. From the longer recension of *2 Enoch* 37:1-2, we learn the following:

And the Lord called one of the senior angels, *terrifying and frightful* (*strashna i grozna*), and he made him stand with me. And the appearance of that angel was as white as snow, and his hands like ice, having the appearance of great frigidity. And he chilled my face, because I could not endure the terror of the Lord, just as it is not possible to endure the fire of a stove and the heat of the sun and the frost of death. And the Lord said to me, "Enoch, if your face had not been chilled here, no human being would be able to look at your face."[187]

The text says that the angel was "terrifying and frightful," and appeared frozen; he was as white as snow, and his hands were as cold as ice. With these cold hands, he then chilled the patriarch's "face." Right after this chilling procedure, the Lord informs Enoch that if his "face" had not been chilled, no human being would have been able to look at him. In view of terminological peculiarities of the text, the "face" here, similar to *panim* in some Mosaic accounts, signifies the whole luminous extent of the protagonist.

The conceptual currents found in *2 Enoch* 37 are important for our study since they again affirm the connection between the heavenly identity of the seer and his glorious garment. In this respect, it does not appear coincidental that Enoch's transition to the earthly identity during his short visit to the earth requires temporary parting with his luminous attire.

Conclusion

Our study of the Enochic heavenly counterpart traditions demonstrated that they do not stem from Greco-Roman concepts of otherworldly doubles, like Gilles Quispel and other scholars previously suggested, but instead are based on "internal" Jewish developments. In the majority of cases, they represent reinterpretations of the biblical theophanic traditions, in which Jewish prophets, like Moses or Ezekiel, received revelations of otherworldly realities. Early Enochic pseudepigrapha lead these familiar theophanic encounters of Moses and Ezekiel into a new conceptual dimension, in which the heavenly doubles of the human seers become identified with the divine Glory, which son of Buzi once saw on the river Chebar, or with the divine Face, which the son of Amram once encountered on Mount Sinai.

However, the possibility of a "foreign" influence, which may play a part in the Enochic reshaping of classical biblical theophanies, cannot be completely excluded. In this respect, our investigation of the Enochic traditions provide possible hints for another important non-Jewish conceptual pool, so often neglected by students of the heavenly counterpart accounts—that is, Mesopotamian lore. We know that early Enochic authors were cognizant of the Mesopotamian legends concerning the seventh antediluvian king, Enmeduranki, a Mesopotamian prototype of the patriarch Enoch, who was portrayed as a translated figure, once installed in the "council of gods."[188] Similar to the protagonist of *2 Enoch*, Enmeduranki travels back to earth in order to initiate his son and other humans into divine knowledge. A crucial correspondence between the heavenly self of the protagonist and his "earthly" identity appears to be already established in these early Mesopotamian sources, with their keen attention to celestial counterparts that paradoxically mirror earthly realities.

Chapter Two

The Heavenly Counterpart Traditions in the Mosaic Pseudepigrapha

The *Exagoge* of Ezekiel the Tragedian

After our exploration of the heavenly counterpart traditions found in the Enochic materials, we now proceed to some Mosaic accounts that also attest to the idea of the celestial identity of its hero, the son of Amram. One such early Mosaic testimony has survived as a part of the drama *Exagoge*,[1] a writing attributed to Ezekiel the Tragedian, which depicts the prophet's experience at Sinai at his celestial enthronement. Preserved in fragmentary form by several ancient sources,[2] the *Exagoge* 67–90 reads:

> MOSES: I had a vision of a great throne on the top of Mount Sinai and it reached till the folds of heaven. A noble man was sitting on it, with a crown and a large scepter in his left hand. He beckoned to me with his right hand, so I approached and stood before the throne. He gave me the scepter and instructed me to sit on the great throne. Then he gave me a royal crown and got up from the throne. I beheld the whole earth all around and saw beneath the earth and above the heavens. A multitude of stars fell before my knees and I counted them all. They paraded past me like a battalion of men. Then I awoke from my sleep in fear.
>
> RAGUEL: My friend (ὦ ξένε), this is a good sign from God. May I live to see the day when these things are fulfilled. You will establish a great throne, become a judge and leader of men. As for your vision of the whole earth, the world below and that above the heavens—this signifies that you will see what is, what has been and what shall be.[3]

Scholars argue that, given its quotation by Alexander Polyhistor (ca. 80–40 BCE), this Mosaic account can be taken as a witness to traditions of the second century BCE.[4] It is noteworthy that the text also exhibits a tendency to adapt some Enochic motifs and themes into the framework of the Mosaic tradition.[5]

The *Exagoge* 67–90 depicts Moses' dream in which he sees an enthroned celestial figure who vacates his heavenly Seat and hands to the son of Amram his royal attributes. The placement of Moses on the great throne in the *Exagoge* account and his donning of the royal regalia often have been interpreted by scholars as the prophet's occupation of the Seat of the deity. Pieter van der Horst remarks that in the *Exagoge* Moses becomes "an anthropomorphic hypostasis of God himself."[6] The unique motif of God's vacating the throne and transferring occupancy to someone else has long puzzled students of this Mosaic account.[7] An attempt to deal with this enigma by bringing in the imagery of the vice-regent does not, in my judgment, completely solve the problem; the vice-regent in Jewish traditions (e.g., Metatron) does not normally occupy God's throne but instead has his own glorious chair that sometimes serves as a replica of the divine Seat. It seems that the enigmatic identification of the prophet with the divine Form can best be explained, not through the concept of a vice-regent, but through the notion of the heavenly twin or counterpart.

In view of our previous study of the heavenly identity of Enoch, it is possible that the *Exagoge* of Ezekiel the Tragedian also attests to the idea of a heavenly counterpart of the seer when it identifies Moses with the glorious anthropomorphic extent enthroned on the top of Mount Sinai.[8] As we recall, the text depicts Moses' vision of "a noble man" with a crown and a large scepter in the left hand installed on the great throne. In the course of the seer's initiation, the attributes of this "noble man," including the royal crown and the scepter, are transferred to Moses, who is instructed to sit on the throne formerly occupied by the noble man. The narrative thus clearly identifies the visionary with his heavenly counterpart, in the course of which the seer literally takes the place and the attributes of his upper identity. The transference of regalia is noteworthy, since as we remember in Enochic accounts, the protagonist also receives some items from heavenly beings, items that signify his newly acquired celestial office of the heavenly scribe. Here in the Mosaic account, the transference of the regalia also might point to the peculiar roles and functions with which Moses' heavenly persona is endowed.[9]

Moses' enthronement is also reminiscent of some Jacobite accounts of the heavenly counterparts that will be explored later in our study. In these accounts, Jacob's heavenly identity is depicted as being "engraved" or "enthroned" on the divine Seat.[10] The account also underlines that Moses acquired his vision in a dream by reporting that he awoke from his sleep in fear. Here, just as in the Jacob targumic accounts, while the seer is sleeping on earth, his counterpart in the upper realm is identified with the *Kavod*.

Some scholars also make a connection between Moses' enthronement in the *Exagoge* and the Son of Man traditions. Thus, Howard Jacobson points out some similarities with Daniel 7. He notes that "at Daniel 7.9ff the divine being sits on his throne in great splendour and then 'one like a man comes with the clouds of heaven.' Like Moses in Ezekiel, the man approaches the throne and is given sovereignty, glory and kingly power."[11] Christopher Rowland and Christopher Morray-Jones draw attention to these parallels with another cluster of Son of Man traditions found in the *Book of the Similitudes* by noting that, in that Enochic booklet, "the Son of Man or Elect One sits on the throne of glory (e.g. *1 Enoch* 69:29). Elsewhere in the text the throne is occupied by God."[12] These connections are decisive for our study since they likewise attest to the heavenly counterpart traditions as has been already demonstrated.

Transformation of the Adept's Face

In some Jewish accounts, the transformation of a seer into his or her doppelganger often involves the change of his or her bodily appearance. It may happen even in a dream as, for example, in the *Similitudes*' account of the heavenly counterpart where, although Enoch's journey was "in spirit," his "body was melted," and as a result, he acquired the identity of the Son of Man.[13] A similar change in the visionary's identity might be also discernible in the *Exagoge* where Moses is designated by his interpreter Raguel as ξένος. Besides the meanings of "friend" and "guest," this Greek word also can be translated as "stranger."[14] If the *Exagoge* authors indeed had in mind this meaning of ξένος, it might well be related to the fact that Moses' body underwent some sort of transformation that altered his previous physical appearance and made him appear as a stranger to Raguel. The motif of Moses' altered identity, after his encounter with the *Kavod*, is reflected not only in Exodus 34 but also in extrabiblical Mosaic accounts, including the tradition found in Pseudo-Philo's *Biblical Antiquities* 12:1. This passage explains that the Israelites failed to recognize Moses after his glorious metamorphosis on Mount Sinai: "Moses came down. (Having been bathed with light that could not be gazed upon, he had gone down to the place where the light of the sun and the moon are. The light of his face surpassed the splendor of the sun and the moon, but he was unaware of this). When he came down to the children of Israel, upon seeing him they did not recognize him. But when he had spoken, then they recognized him."[15]

The motif of the shining body or, more important, the countenance of Moses is significant for our ongoing discussion of the heavenly counterpart traditions found in Enochic and Mosaic lore. This distinctive mark of the Israelite prophet's identity, his glorious face, which served in biblical accounts as the undeniable proof of his encounter with God, later became appropriated in the framework of Enochic[16] and Metatron[17] traditions as the chief distinguishing feature of the Enochic hero. In this new development, Moses' shining face became nothing more than the later imitation of the glorious countenance of Enoch-Metatron. Thus in *Sefer Hekhalot* 15B, Enoch-Metatron tells Moses about his shining visage: "Son of Amram, fear not! For already God favors you. Ask what you will with confidence and boldness, for light shines from the skin of your face from one end of the world to the other."[18]

Here, as in the case of the rarified visionaries who encountered their heavenly counterparts and beheld the divine Face like their own reflection in a mirror, Moses too finds out that his radiant face is a reflection of the glorious Face of the deity. Yet, there is one decisive difference: this divine Face is now represented by his long-lasting contender, Enoch-Metatron.[19]

The Motif of Standing and the Angel of the Presence

Despite the draw of seeing the developments found in the *Exagoge* as merely the adaptation of Enochic and Jacobite traditions about the heavenly double, it appears that the influence may point in the other direction, and these accounts, in turn, were shaped by the imagery found already in the biblical Mosaic accounts. It is possible that the conceptual roots of the identification of Moses with the celestial figure could be found already in the biblical materials where the son of Amram appears standing before the divine Presence. To clarify the Mosaic background of the traditions about the heavenly counterpart, we must now turn to the biblical Mosaic accounts dealing with the symbolism of the divine Presence or the Face.

As has been already mentioned in our study, one of the earliest identifications of the hero with the peculiar duties of an angel of the Presence, important in the traditions about the heavenly double, can be found in *2 Enoch* where, in the course of his celestial metamorphosis, the seventh antediluvian patriarch Enoch was called by God to *stand* before his Face forever. Pivotal in this portrayal of the installation of a human being into a prominent angelic rank is the emphasis on *standing* before the Face of God. Enoch's role as the angel of the Presence is introduced through the formulae "stand before my face forever." *2 Enoch*'s definition of the office of servant of the divine Presence as standing before the Face of the Lord appears to be linked to the biblical Mosaic accounts in which Moses is described as the one who was standing before the Lord's Face on Mount Sinai. It is significant that, as in the Slavonic apocalypse, where the Lord himself orders the patriarch to stand before his Presence,[20] the biblical Mosaic accounts contain a similar command. In the theophanic account from

Exodus 33, the Lord commands Moses to stand near Him: "There is a place by me where you shall stand (ונצבת) on the rock."

In Deuteronomy, this language of standing continues to play a prominent role. In Deuteronomy 5:31, God again orders Moses to stand with him: "But you, stand (עמד) here by me, and I will tell you all the commandments, the statutes and the ordinances, that you shall teach them." In Deuteronomy 5:4–5, the motif of standing, as in Exodus 33, is juxtaposed with the imagery of the divine *Panim*: "The Lord spoke with you face to face (פנים בפנים) at the mountain, out of the fire. At that time I was standing (עמד) between the Lord and you to declare to you the words of the Lord; for you were afraid because of the fire and did not go up the mountain." Here, Moses is depicted as standing before the Face of the deity and mediating the divine Presence to the people.

These developments of the motif of standing are intriguing and might constitute the conceptual background for the traditions of Moses' heavenly counterpart in the *Exagoge* and, more important, in the *Book of Jubilees*, the account that will be explored later in this chapter.

In this respect, it is noteworthy that the idiom of standing plays a significant part in the *Exagoge* account that has Moses approach and stand (ἐστάθην)[21] before the throne.[22]

In the extrabiblical Mosaic accounts, one can also see a growing tendency to depict Moses' standing position as the posture of a celestial being. Crispin Fletcher-Louis observes that in various Mosaic traditions, the motif of Moses' standing was often interpreted through the prism of God's own standing, indicating the prophet's participation in the divine or angelic nature. He notes that in Samaritan and rabbinic literature, a standing posture was generally indicative of the celestial being.[23] Jarl Fossum points to the tradition preserved in *Memar Marqah* 4:12, where Moses is described as "the (immutable) Standing One."[24]

In 4Q377 2 vii–xii, the standing posture of Moses appears to be creatively conflated with his status as a celestial being: "And like a man sees li[gh]t, he has appeared to us in a burning fire, from above, from heaven, and on earth he stood (עמד) on the mountain to teach us that there is no God apart from him, and no Rock like him. . . . But Moses, the man of God, was with God in the cloud, and the cloud covered him, because [. . .] when he sanctified him, and he spoke as an angel through his mouth, for who was a messen[ger] like him, a man of the pious ones?"[25]

Scholars have previously observed that Moses here "plays the role of an angel, having received revelation from the mouth of God."[26]

In light of the aforementioned Mosaic developments, it is possible that the idiom of standing, so prominent in the depiction of the servants of the Presence in the Enochic tradition of the heavenly double, has Mosaic provenance.[27] Already in Exodus and Deuteronomy, the prophet is portrayed as the one who is able to stand before the deity to mediate the divine Presence to human beings.[28] The extrabiblical Mosaic accounts try to further secure the prophet's place in front of the deity by depicting him as a celestial creature. The testimony found in the *Exagoge*, where Moses is described as standing before the Throne, seems to represent a vital step toward the rudimentary definitions of the office of the angelic servant of the Face.

The Symbolism of the Hand and the Heavenly Counterpart Imagery

One of the constant features of the aforementioned transformational accounts in which a seer becomes identified with his or her heavenly identity is the motif of the divine or angelic hand that embraces the visionary and invites him or her into a new celestial dimension of his existence. This motif is found in Mosaic as well as Enochic traditions, where the hand of God embraces and protects the seer during his or her encounter with the deity in the upper realm.

Thus, in *2 Enoch* 39, the patriarch relates to his children that during his vision of the divine *Kavod*, the deity helped him with his right hand. The hand here is described as having a gigantic size and filling heaven: "But you, my children, see the right hand of one who helps you, a human being created identical to yourself, but I have seen the right hand of the Lord, helping me and filling heaven."[29] The theme of the hand of God assisting the seer during his vision of the Face is not an entirely new development, since it recalls the Mosaic account from Exodus 33:22–23. Here, the deity promises the prophet to protect him with his hand during the encounter with the divine *Panim*: "And while my glory passes by I will put you in a cleft of the rock, and I will cover you with my hand until I have passed by; then I will take away my hand, and you shall see my back; but my face shall not be seen."

The divine hand assisting the visionary is also mentioned in the *Exagoge* of Ezekiel the Tragedian. The account relates that during the prophet's vision of the *Kavod*, a noble man sitting on the throne beckoned him with his right hand (δεξιᾷ δέ μοι ἔνευσε).[30]

It is conceivable that *2 Enoch*'s description is closer to the form of the tradition preserved in Ezekiel the Tragedian than to the account found in Exodus since the *Exagoge* mentions the right hand of the deity beckoning the seer. What is important here is that both Mosaic accounts seem to represent the formative conceptual roots for the later Enochic developments where the motif of the Lord's hand is used in the depiction of the unification of the seventh patriarch with his celestial counterpart in the form of the angel Metatron. Thus, from the Merkavah materials, one can learn that "the hand of God rests on the head of the Youth, named Metatron."[31] The motif of the divine hand assisting Enoch-Metatron during his celestial transformation is prominent in *Sefer Hekhalot*, where it appears in the form of a tradition very similar to the evidence found in the *Exagoge* and *2 Enoch*. In *Synopse* §12, Metatron tells R. Ishmael that during the transformation of his body into the gigantic cosmic extent, matching the world in length and breadth, God "laid his hand" on the translated hero.[32] Here, just as in the Mosaic accounts, the hand of the deity signifies the bond between the seer's body and the divine corporeality, leading to the creation of a new celestial entity in the form of the angelic servant of the Presence.

In some other apocalyptic accounts of the heavenly counterparts, an angelic right hand appears to fulfill a similar function. Accordingly, in *Joseph and Aseneth*, during the initiation of the Egyptian maiden into the mystery of her heavenly identity, the celestial Anthropos embraces the female seer with his right hand. *Jos. Asen.* 16:12–13 reads: "And the man smiled at Aseneth's understanding, and called her to himself, and stretched out his right hand, and grasped her head and shook her head with his right hand. And Aseneth was afraid of the man's hand, because sparks shot forth from his hand as from bubbling (melted) iron. And Aseneth looked, gazing with her eyes at the man's hand."[33]

Chapter 71 of the *Similitudes* depicts the archangel Michael holding the patriarch by his (Enoch's) right hand. It is intriguing that here in the account of the seer's identification with his celestial double, the text specifically invokes the imagery of the right hand. Some later Jewish mystical accounts attest to the tradition of the deity's embrace of the heavenly image of Jacob.[34]

Similar conceptual developments where divine or angelic beings embrace the seers during their unification with their heavenly counterpart can be found also in some heterodox Christian accounts.[35] For example, in *Pistis Sophia* 61:11, Jesus' heavenly twin embraces him:

> When thou wast small, before the Spirit came upon thee, while thou wast in a vineyard with Joseph, the Spirit came forth from the height, he came to me into my house, he resembled thee. And I did not recognize him and I thought that he was thou. And the Spirit said to me: "Where is Jesus, my brother, that I meet him?" And when he said these things to me, I was confused and I thought that he was a phantom to tempt me. But I took him, I bound him to the leg of the bed in my house, until I came out to you in the field, thou and Joseph, and I found you in the vineyard, as Joseph was hedging the vineyard with reeds. Now it happened, when thou didst hear me speaking the word to Joseph, thou didst understand the word and thou didst rejoice. And thou didst say: "Where is he that I may see him? Or else I await him in this place." But it happened

when Joseph heard thee saying these words, he was agitated and we came up at the same time, we went into the house. We found the Spirit bound to the bed. And we looked at thee with him, we found thee like him. And he that was bound to the bed was released, he embraced thee, he kissed thee. And thou also, thou didst kiss him and you became one.³⁶

Gilles Quispel argues that in this passage the Spirit is considered to be the "image (*iqonin*) of Jesus, who forms a whole with him."³⁷ As we will learn later in our study, the heavenly identity of Jacob also will be often envisioned as the *iqonin* in targumic and rabbinic accounts.

The *Book of Jubilees*

The concept of Moses' heavenly counterpart appears also in another early Jewish pseudepigraphical text—the *Book of Jubilees*.³⁸ In this pseudepigraphon, as in some aforementioned accounts, the seer's heavenly identity takes the form of a servant of the divine Presence. Before we proceed to a close analysis of the doppelganger imagery, several words must be said about the conceptual proclivities of the book as the whole. Scholars have previously noted that in *Jubilees* one can find peculiar symmetrical patterns that involve both temporal and spatial dimensions. Thus, reflecting on *Jubilees*' temporal aspect of such imagery James Scott observes that

> *Jubilees* affirms a rigorous temporal symmetry. All human history from creation to new creation is foreordained by God and inscribed in the heavenly tablets, which in turn, are revealed through angelic mediation to Moses on Mt. Sinai, just as they were revealed to Enoch before him. In this presentation, historical patterns are adduced to confirm divine providence over earthly events. A striking example of this is found in the correspondence between *Endzeit* and *Urzeit*. In *Jubilees*, as in other apocalyptic literature, God intends the world ultimately to conform to his original intention for the creation. But *Jubilees* goes even further by implying a nearly complete recapitulation, that is that the *Endzeit* or restoration would almost exactly mirror the *Urzeit* or patriarchal period.³⁹

Scott's research demonstrates that the striking symmetrical patterns discernable in *Jubilees* encompass not only the horizontal, temporal aspect but also the vertical, spatial dimension, with its peculiar imagery of the heavenly and earthly realms that mirror each other. Reflecting on these distinctive correspondences, Scott observes that *Jubilees* affirms "not only a temporal symmetry between *Urzeit* and *Endzeit*, but also, secondly, a spatial symmetry between heaven and earth."[40] These distinctive correspondences between the earthly and heavenly realities are important for our study of the heavenly counterpart traditions. As we already learned in our analysis of the Enochic lore, such spatial correlations are especially evident in the parallelism between heavenly and earthly cultic settings that are often depicted as mirroring each other.[41] We know that such sacerdotal parallelism often constitutes the background of the heavenly counterpart imagery, and it is not coincidental that such a worldview is manifested in *Jubilees* where the chief protagonist became endowed with the upper angelic identity.

One of the enigmatic characters in the *Book of Jubilees* is the angel of the Presence who dictates heavenly revelation to Moses. The book provides neither the angel's name nor a clear picture of his celestial roles and offices. Complicating the picture is the angel's arrogation to himself "what in the Bible are words or deeds of God."[42] In *Jubilees* 6:22, for example, the angel utters the following: "For I have written (this) in the book of the first law in which I wrote for you that you should celebrate it at each of its times one day in a year. I have told you about its sacrifice so that the Israelites may continue to remember and celebrate it throughout their generations during this month—one day each year."[43]

James VanderKam observes that according to these sentences "the angel of the Presence wrote the first law, that is, the Pentateuch, including the section about the Festival of Weeks in the cultic calendars (Lev 23:15–21 and Num 28:26–31, where the sacrifices are specified)."[44] VanderKam further notes that "these passages are represented as direct revelations by God to Moses in Leviticus and Numbers, not as statements from an angel."[45]

In *Jubilees* 30:12, which retells and modifies Genesis 34, the angel's authorial claim is repeated again: "For this reason I have written for you in the words of the law everything that the Shechemites did to Dinah and how Jacob's sons said: 'We will not give our daughter to a man who has a foreskin because for us that would be a disgraceful thing.' "[46]

Even more puzzling is that in these passages the angel insists on personally *writing* the divine words, thus claiming the role of the celestial scribe in a fashion similar to Moses.[47] Also striking is that this nameless angelic scribe posits himself as the writer of the Pentateuch ("For I have written [this] in the book of the first law"), the authorship of which the tradition ascribes to the son of Amram. What are we to make of these authorial claims by the angel of the Presence?

Is it possible that in this puzzling account concerning two protagonists, one human and the other angelic—both of whom are scribes and authors of the same "law"—we have an allusion to the idea of the heavenly counterpart of a seer in the form of the angel of the Presence?[48] As we learn in Jewish apocalyptic and early mystical literature, such heavenly doubles in the form of angels of the Presence are often presented as celestial scribes.

In this Mosaic narrative, like in the previously explored Enochic accounts, the imagery of the angel of the Presence has several conceptual dimensions. In *2 Enoch*, the angel of the Presence initiates the adept into the office of the celestial scribe. Then Enoch himself becomes the angel of the Presence, ordained to stay before the Presence of the deity forever.

A similar conceptual constellation might be present in the *Book of Jubilees* where the angel of Presence initiates the seer by revealing heavenly secrets to him.[49] It parallels the dictation by the archangel Vereveil in *2 Enoch* and also the instruction of Uriel in the early Enochic booklets.

Other parts of the text also indicate that *Jubilees*' author was cognizant of heavenly counterpart traditions. Thus, for example, in rendering Jacob's story, *Jubilees* 36:16–17 relates the following: "If he [Esau] wishes to kill his brother Jacob, he will be handed over to Jacob and will not escape from his control but will fall into his control. Now you are not to be afraid for Jacob because Jacob's guardian is greater and more powerful, glorious, and praiseworthy than Esau's guardian."[50] It is intriguing that the tradition of the powerful and glorious "guardian" of a human being unfolds in the midst of Jacob's story—the character who was so formative and iconic in the development of the doppelganger lore.

Another weighty detail is *Jubilees*' peculiar understanding of the angels of the Presence, a portentous celestial group, prominent in so many accounts of the heavenly counterpart. *Jubilees* 2:18 unveils the following about this angelic cohort: "He [God] told us—all the angels of the Presence and all the angels of holiness (these two great kinds)—to keep sabbath with him in heaven and on earth."[51] Here, it is fascinating that the angels of the presence seem able to coexist in two spatial planes (heavenly and earthly) simultaneously. Moreover, because of their peculiar attributes in *Jubilees*, they are understood as the heavenly counterparts of the Israelites.[52] In relation to such an understanding of the angels of the Presence in *Jubilees*, George Brooke observes that "the Angels of the Presence and the Angels of Holiness have a pre-eminent place in serving God, a pre-eminence which is also marked out by their circumcision (*Jub.* 15.27–28).[53] According to *Jubilees*, by implication, it is these two classes of angels which correspond with the earthly Israel."[54]

Heavenly Counterpart as the Guardian of the Scribal Tradition

One of the key characteristics of the aforementioned visionary accounts, in which the adepts become identified with their heavenly correlatives, is the transference of prominent celestial offices to the new servants of the Presence. Thus, for example, transference is discernable in the *Exagoge* where the "heavenly man" hands to the seer his celestial regalia, scepter, and crown[55] and then surrenders his heavenly seat, which in the Enoch-Metatron tradition is often identified with the duty of the celestial scribe.[56]

The scribal role may indeed represent one of the essential offices that angels of the Presence surrender to the new servants of the Face. As one remembers, *2 Enoch* describes the initiation of the seer by Vereveil (Uriel) in the course of which this angel of the Presence, portrayed in *2 Enoch* as a "heavenly recorder," conveys knowledge and skills pertaining to the scribal duties to the translated patriarch. Important to this account is its emphasis on the act of transference of the scribal duties from Vereveil to Enoch, when the angel of the Presence surrenders to the hero the celestial library and even the pen from his hand.[57]

Jubilees, as the Enochic account, has two scribal figures: the angel of the Presence and a human being. Yet, the exact relationship between these two figures is difficult to establish in view of the scarcity and ambiguity of the relevant depictions. Does the angel of the Presence in *Jubilees* serve, after the fashion of Uriel, as a celestial scribe who is responsible for the initiation of the adept into the scribal duties? Or does he represent the heavenly counterpart of Moses who is clearly distinguished at this point from the seer? This clear distance between the seer and his celestial identity is not unlikely in the context of the traditions about the heavenly counterpart. In fact, this distance between the two identities—one in the form of the celestial person and the other in the form of a human hero—represents a standard feature of such accounts. For example, in the already mentioned account from the *Book of the Similitudes*, Enoch is clearly distinguished from his heavenly counterpart in the form of the celestial Son of Man throughout the whole narrative until the final unification occurring in the last chapter of the book. The gap between the celestial and earthly identities of the seer is also discernable in the targumic accounts about Jacob's heavenly double where the distinction between the two identities is highlighted by a description of the angels who behold Jacob sleeping on earth while at the same time installed in heaven. This distance between the identity of the seer and his heavenly twin is also observable in the *Exagoge* where the heavenly man transfers to Moses his regalia and vacates for him his heavenly seat.

There is, however, another vital point in the stories about the heavenly counterparts that could provide important insight into the nature of pseudepigraphical accounts where these stories are found. This aspect pertains to the issue of the so-called emulation of the biblical exemplars that allows the pseudepigraphical authors to unveil new revelations in the name of some prominent authority of the past. The identity of the celestial scribe in the form of the angel of the Presence might further our understanding of the enigmatic process of mystical and literary emulation of the exemplary figure, the cryptic mechanics of which often remain beyond the grasp of our postmodern sensibilities.

Can the tradition of the unification of the biblical hero with his angelic counterpart be part of this process of emulating the exemplar by an adept? Can the mediating position[58] of the angel of the Presence, ordained to stand "from now and forever" between the deity himself and the biblical hero, serve as a stand-in for the author's identity, representing the fundamental locus of mystical and literary emulation? Is it possible that in *Jubilees*, like in some other pseudepigraphical accounts, the figure of the angel of the Presence serves as a transformative and literary device that allows an adept to enter the assembly of immortal beings consisting of the heroes of both the celestial and the literary world?

Could it be possible that in the traditions of heavenly counterparts we are able to draw nearer to the very heart of the pseudepigraphical enterprise? In this respect, it does not appear to be coincidental that these transformational accounts dealing with the heavenly doubles of their adepts are permeated with the aesthetics of penmanship and the imagery of the literary enterprise.[59] In the course of these mystical and literary metamorphoses, the heavenly figure surrenders his scribal seat, the library of the celestial books, and even personal writing tools to the other earthly identity, who now becomes the new guardian of the authoritative tradition.

Heavenly Counterparts as "Embodied" Mirrors

We now return to the motif of the divine Face so prominent in the Mosaic lore. It has already been noted in our study that the imagery of the divine Countenance plays a crucial role in so many doppelganger accounts where the human adepts are transformed before the divine Face and even acquire the qualities of the divine Visage, becoming in some ways the reflections or the mirrors of that Face.[60] Some of these heavenly counterparts—like the celestial Self of the patriarch Enoch, the supreme angel Metatron[61]—then become openly labelled in the mystical lore as the "Face of God."[62] These correspondences between the deity represented by his Face and the heavenly counterparts who are becoming God's "faces" must now be explored more closely.

I have previously proposed that in the course of the seer's identification with his or her heavenly counterpart, a process that in many visionary accounts occurs in front of the divine Countenance and with the help of the angelic servants of the Face, the adept becomes a "reflection" or a "mirror" of the divine Face.[63] This role is often conveyed in various apocalyptic accounts through the process of either becoming the Prince of the Face (*Sar ha-Panim*)[64]—or the entity engraved on the Face[65]—or just becoming the Face itself. In view of these conceptual developments, in some of which the seer's heavenly identity becomes "reflected" or "inscribed" on the divine Face in the form of the "image," it is possible that the divine Face itself can be understood as a mirror. Such an understanding of the deity's glorious Visage might be already present in some early Jewish and Christian materials, including the Pauline interpretation of the Mosaic imagery found in 2 Corinthians 3. We should now turn our attention to these conceptual developments.

It has already been demonstrated in our study that the vision of the divine Face represents the pinnacle of the seer's visionary experience in so many apocalyptic accounts where various adepts become identified with their upper identities. This role of the divine Face as the goal of visionary experience became prominent in pseudepigraphical accounts as well as later Jewish mystical lore. Thus, in various Hekhalot materials, the imagery of the divine Face continues to play a paramount role, being understood as the "center of the divine event" and the teleological objective for the ascension of the *yorde merkavah*. This motif's importance is illustrated in *Hekhalot Rabbati*, which considers the Countenance of God "the goal of *yored merkavah* and simultaneously revokes this statement in a paradoxical way by stressing at conclusion that one cannot 'perceive' this Face."[66] Analyzing this account, Peter Schäfer observes that for the visionary in the Hekhalot tradition, the Countenance of God is an example "not only of overwhelming beauty, and therefore of a destructive nature,[67] but at the same time the center of the divine event."[68] God's Face thereby becomes the consummation of the heavenly journey since, according to Schäfer, "everything God wishes to transmit to the *yored merkavah* . . . is concentrated in God's Countenance."[69] Is it possible then that the divine Face itself could be understood in these traditions as a medium of revelation, a sort of looking glass that reflects divine disclosures?

In this respect, it is intriguing that some Jewish interpretations of Moses' encounter with the divine Face on Mount Sinai suggest that the prophet received his revelation on the great mountain through a mirror. Thus, in *Leviticus Rabbah* 1:14 the following tradition can be found:[70]

> What difference is there between Moses and all other prophets? R. Judah b. Il'ai and the Rabbis [gave different explanations]. R. Judah said: Through nine mirrors did the prophets behold [prophetic visions]. This is indicated by what is said, And the appearance of the vision which I saw, was like the vision that I saw when I came to destroy the city; and the visions were like the vision that I saw by the River Chebar; and I fell upon my face (Ezek 43:3); but Moses beheld [prophetic visions] through one mirror, as it is said, With him do I speak . . . in a vision, and not in dark speeches (Num 12:8). The

> Rabbis said: All the other prophets beheld [prophetic visions] through a blurred mirror,[71] as it is said, And I have multiplied visions; and by the ministry of the angels have I used similitudes (Hos 12:11). But Moses beheld [prophetic visions] through a polished mirror, as it is said, The similitude of the Lord doth he behold. R. Phinehas said in the name of R. Hosha'iah: This may be compared to a king who allowed himself to be seen by his intimate friend [only] by means of his image. In this world the *Shekhinah* manifests itself only to chosen individuals; in the Time to Come, however, The glory of the Lord shall be revealed, and all the flesh shall see it together; for the mouth of the Lord hath spoken it (Isa 40:5).[72]

This passage postulates that not only Moses' vision of the divine *Kavod* (labeled in biblical Mosaic accounts as the "Face" or *Panim*) has occurred in a mirror but other paradigmatic Jewish seers, including Ezekiel, similarly received their visions of the divine *Kavod* in a looking glass too. For our study, it is important that such speculations do not represent later rabbinic inventions but have ancient roots in Second Temple Jewish lore. Thus, already Philo demonstrates the familiarity with such tradition in his *Leg.* 3.100–103:

> There is a mind more perfect and more thoroughly cleansed, which has undergone initiation into the great mysteries, a mind which gains its knowledge of the First Cause not from created things, as one may learn the substance from the shadow, but lifting its eyes above and beyond creation obtains a clear vision of the uncreated One, so as from Him to apprehend both Himself and His shadow. To apprehend that was, we saw, to apprehend both the Word and this world. The mind of which I speak is Moses who says, "Manifest Thyself to me, let me see Thee that I may know Thee" (Exod 33:13); for I would not that Thou shouldst be manifested to me by means of heaven or earth or water or air or any created thing at all, nor would I find the reflection of Thy being in aught else than in Thee Who art God,[73] for the reflections in created things are dissolved, but those in the Uncreated will continue abiding and sure and eternal.[74] This is why God hath expressly called Moses and why He spake to Him. Bezalel also He hath expressly called, but not in like manner. One receives the clear vision of God directly from the First Cause Himself. The other discerns the Artificer, as it were from a shadow, from created things by virtue of a process of reasoning. Hence you will find the Tabernacle and all its furniture made in the first instance by Moses but afterwards by Bezalel, for Moses is the artificer of the archetypes,

and Bezalel of the copies of these. For Moses has God for Instructor, as He says "thou shalt make all things according to the pattern that was shown to thee in the mount" (Exod 25:40), but Bezalel is instructed by Moses. And all this is just as we should expect. For on the occasion likewise of the rebellion of Aaron, Speech, and Miriam, Perception, they are expressly told "If a prophet be raised up unto the Lord, God shall be known unto him in a vision" and in a shadow, not manifestly; but with Moses, the man who is "faithful in all His house, He will speak mouth to mouth in manifest form and not through dark speeches" (Num 12:6–8).[75]

These traditions in which the son of Amram is depicted receiving his revelations in a mirror are intriguing since they provide additional support to the idea that the divine *Panim* (or the divine *Kavod*) might be envisioned in some early Jewish accounts as the celestial looking glass.

The concept of the divine Face as the mirror of revelation might also be present in some early Christian materials. Thus, in 2 Corinthians 3:18, the Apostle Paul assures his readers that "all of us, with unveiled faces, seeing the glory of the Lord as though reflected in a mirror, are being transformed into the same image from one degree of glory to another." This biblical text has generated enormous attention from the scholarly community. Some scholars have suggested that the Pauline passage draws on the aforementioned Mosaic motifs[76] in which the great prophet saw revelations on Mount Sinai through the divine mirror.[77]

If it is indeed true, it would appear that the Pauline speculation affirms even more forcefully the transformational proclivities[78] of the aforementioned Mosaic "mirror" imagery, by indicating that the seer not only receives a revelation in the mirror of the divine Face, rendered in the Pauline passage with the standard formulae of *Kavod*, but himself becomes the image of the *Kavod*. As we will see later in Jacob's lore, the image[79] will become a standard theological devise for rendering the seer's doppelganger.[80] Such conceptual developments lead some scholars to argue that Paul's vision of the *Kavod* in the mirror should be read in the framework of the heavenly counterpart traditions. Thus, Alan Segal previously proposed that in 2 Corinthians 3:18 "Paul gives us a totally different and at once conceivable notion of a bodily transformation"[81] that comes "with its own experience of the self—not a soul but *an angelic alter ego*."[82]

Segal then compares this Pauline understanding of the "angelic *alter ego*" with the doppelganger complex found in the *Book of the Similitudes*, arguing that "as long as the date of *1 Enoch* 70–71 cannot be fixed exactly . . . Paul himself remains the earliest author explicitly expressing this kind of angelic transformation in Judaism."[83]

Another scholar, April DeConick, also discerns the presence of the heavenly counterpart imagery in 2 Corinthians 3:18 by arguing that "Paul speaks here of *the face-to-face encounter with one's self* by implementing the middle form of the verb κατοπτρίζω which means 'to produce one's own image in a mirror' or 'to behold oneself in a mirror.'"[84] In DeConick's opinion, such "rendering suggests that the vision is *a vision of one's divine Self*. When one sees oneself in a mirror, one is viewing the Lord's Glory. This vision creates change, transforming the person, degree by degree, into the divine Glory which is seen in the mirror. It is obvious that this text belongs to one of the oldest strata of vision mysticism of early Christianity."[85] As one can see, she underlines the transformational tendencies of the Pauline passage that belong in her opinion to so-called vision mysticism. DeConick concludes that "a vision of the *Kavod*, the Image of God, literally resulted in the 're-stamping' of God's image on the soul, restoring it to the original Form and Glory."[86]

It is also important for our study that in 2 Corinthians 3:18, the "mirror" is represented by a divine mediator who is also envisioned as the exemplar of the religious tradition, in this case—Christ. Jan Lambrecht observes that in 2 Corinthians 3:18, "Paul wants to suggest that Christ is the 'mirror' of God. In that mirror we see the glory of the Lord; in Christ we see God reflected in all his glory! According to this explanation Christ is both mirror and image.[87] *He is mirror and also a mirrored reflection, an image of God.*"[88] Lambrecht's nuanced observation is helpful for our investigation. Such understanding of the mediatorial "mirror" that occupies an intermediate position in the course of the human adept's transformation and unification with his or her heavenly identity represents a familiar motif.[89] It brings to memory the notions of celestial "mirrors" found in various Jewish apocalyptic and mystical accounts where some mediatorial figures are depicted as the mirrors of the divine Face,[90] at the same time serving as the reflections of the celestial identities of human seers. This understanding of the mediator as an intermediate mirror, which is instrumental for the seer's transformation, might be found already in Philo. Thus, David Litwa argues that in Philo "the Logos[91] serves as a layer of mediation—the metaphorical mirror—between Moses and the primal God."[92] Often such divine mediators are themselves understood as vice-regents or embodiments of the deity. Litwa suggests that "for Philo, the mirror through which Moses sees God is God himself in the person of the Logos."[93]

The conceptual developments found in the Philonic and Pauline understanding of the mediatorial "mirrors" will continue to exercise formative influence on later Jewish mystical testimonies, including *Sefer Hekhalot*, where another mediator, this time Metatron, is posited as the divine mirror in which Moses sees his revelations. In *3 Enoch*, like in the Bible, the son of Amram finds out that his luminous face is a mere reflection of the glorious Visage of the deity. Yet, in comparison with the biblical accounts, there is one decisive difference: this divine Face is now represented by his long-lasting contender, Enoch-Metatron.[94] One can discern in this text a possible reference to the paradoxical hierarchy[95] of the "mediatorial mirrors"[96] in which the former seers, who already became the reflections of the divine Face, now serve as the embodied mirrors for subsequent human adepts.

Early Jewish and Christian traditions often illustrate this enigmatic succession of the "mirrors" when they depict Enoch, Jacob,[97] Moses, or Christ[98] becoming the personified reflections or the "mirrors"[99] of the divine Face when their own glorious "presences" are able to transform the next generations of human adepts. We already witnessed one specimen of this tradition in the scene of Enoch's metamorphosis in *2 Enoch* to whose transformed face the elders of the earth later approach in order to be redeemed and glorified.[100] Moses' face is also predestined to serve as the embodied mirror of God's Countenance.[101] Scholars previously noted the peculiar parallelism between the deity's Face and the face of the prophet. Thus, Brian Britt observes that "the frightening and miraculous transformation of Moses' face, and its subsequent concealment by a veil, constitute a kind of theophany. Just as the face of God is usually off-limits to Moses (with the exception of Exod 33:11 and Deut 34:10), so the face of Moses is sometimes off-limits to the people. . . . While these parallels may not bear directly on Moses' transformed face, they offer suggestive evidence that theophany and divine enlightenment can appear on the human face."[102]

Conclusion

Our analysis of the Mosaic pseudepigraphic traditions, like the preceding study of Enochic developments, again reaffirms the importance of biblical theophanic traditions for the fashioning of Moses' heavenly counterpart imagery. The memory of these biblical motifs appears to be especially dominant in the *Book of Jubilees*, with its use of biblical angelological traditions in shaping the profile of Moses' otherworldly identity. These formative influences again challenge scholarly hypotheses that postulate that some Greco-Roman concepts, including the notion of *daimon*, were crucial for understanding the origins of the early Jewish notion of the heavenly self. Surprisingly, even in the *Exagoge* of Ezekiel the Tragedian, an account that formally adheres to a genre widespread in the Greco-Roman literary environment, we again were not able to detect any formative influences of *daimon* imagery, or of any other distinctively "Greco-Roman" concept responsible for constructing Moses' heavenly self. Instead, the features of biblical theophanies and the polemical appropriations of extrabiblical Enochic motifs appear to play a decisive role in fashioning the concept of Moses' heavenly counterpart.

Chapter Three

The Heavenly Counterpart Traditions in the Pseudepigrapha about Jacob

Jacob's Heavenly Counterpart in Rabbinic Accounts

It has already been mentioned in our study that some scholars, including James VanderKam and others, have relied on a set of motifs that can be traced to Jacob's story in their analysis of the heavenly counterpart traditions in Jewish pseudepigraphical literature, including chapter 71 of the *Book of the Similitudes*. Indeed, the biblical story of Jacob's vision of the ladder at Bethel, narrated in Genesis 28, without doubt constituted the conceptual background for accounts of the heavenly double in various religious milieus. Although in the pseudepigraphic accounts, Jacob's vision of the ladder is only implicitly tied to the idea of his heavenly double, in later targumic, midrashic, and talmudic elaborations, this connection becomes the locus of intense and explicit speculation. In view of the clarity of these later Jewish testimonies and their unambiguous connection with the notion of the heavenly doppelganger, we will begin our exploration of the Jacobite lore with these rabbinic testimonies that will enable us to discern more clearly similar traditions in Jewish pseudepigraphical accounts.

It is noteworthy that in rabbinic renderings of Jacob's vision of the ladder, the seer's heavenly identity is often portrayed as his image engraved on the throne of glory. These traditions about the heavenly image of Jacob are present in several Palestinian targumic accounts. *Targum Pseudo-Jonathan* offers the following description of the patriarch's celestial identity: "He [Jacob] had a dream, and behold, a ladder was fixed in the earth with its top reaching toward the heavens . . . and on that day they (angels) ascended to the heavens on high, and said, 'Come and see Jacob the pious, whose image is fixed (engraved) in the Throne of Glory, and whom you have desired to see.'"[1]

Another Palestinian text, *Targum Neofiti*, offers a very similar portrayal: "And he dreamed, and behold, a ladder was fixed on the earth and its head reached to the height of the heavens; and behold, the angels that had accompanied him from the house of his father ascended to bear good tidings to the angels on high, saying: 'Come and see the pious man whose image is engraved in the throne of Glory, whom you desired to see.' And behold, the angels from before the Lord ascended and descended and observed him."[2]

Finally, the authors of a third Palestinian text, the so-called *Fragmentary Targum*, are also cognizant of Jacob's heavenly alter ego fixed upon the Throne of Glory: "And he dreamt that there was a ladder set on the ground, whose top reached towards the heavens; and behold the angels that had accompanied him from his father's house ascended to announce to the angels of the heights: 'Come and see the pious man, whose image is fixed to the throne of glory.' "[3]

A distinctive feature of these targumic passages is that Jacob's heavenly counterpart, envisioned as his image, is engraved on a very special celestial entity—namely, on the Throne of Glory. Engraving on the throne indicates an association with the *Kavod*, since the throne is the central part of the *Kavod* imagery—the seat of the anthropomorphic glory of the deity. Here again, like in the previously explored Enochic and Mosaic accounts, the revelation of the heavenly alter ego of the protagonist is unfolded in the midst of the *Kavod* symbolism. Besides the tradition of engraving on the Throne, some rabbinic materials point to an even more radical identification of Jacob's image with the *Kavod*. It has been previously noted[4] that in some rabbinic accounts about Jacob's doppelganger, his image is depicted not simply as engraved on the heavenly throne, but as seated upon the throne of glory.[5] Jarl Fossum argues that this second tradition is original and that it is possibly connected with the Second Temple mediatorial currents. Christopher Rowland also argues that Jacob's image is "identical with the form of God on the Throne of Glory (Ezek 1:26f.)."[6] Such an understanding of Jacob's image as an anthropomorphic Glory is found already in some targumic accounts. Thus, David Halperin's research draws attention to a targumic reading of Ezekiel 1:26 that interprets "the appearance of a human being" as Jacob's image.[7] Fossum offers additional support for the originality of the idea of Jacob's enthronement by pointing out that the Hebrew forms of the Greek loan word εἰκών, used in the Targums, are synonymous with צלם and דמות.[8] He further suggests that "איקונין or דיוקנא can thus be seen to denote a bodily form, even that of God, that is the divine Glory."[9]

Such symbolism of Jacob's heavenly image associated with the deity's Throne is widely diffused in rabbinic literature.[10] What is important for our study is that some of these materials appear to underline a distance between two identities of the patriarch: one heavenly and the other earthly. Thus, Rachel Neis argues that "the rabbinic texts set up a visual symmetry, between an earthly Jacob and a divine iconic Jacob."[11] A possibility that Jacob's celestial identity might be envisioned in these materials as an "icon" deserves our closer attention. In this respect, two rabbinic passages are especially noteworthy. The first passage, found in *Genesis Rabbah* 82:2, details the following tradition:

> R. Isaac commenced: An altar of earth shalt thou make unto me . . . In every place where I cause My name to be mentioned I will come unto thee and bless thee (Exod 20:24). If I bless him who builds an altar in My name, how much the more should I appear to Jacob, whose features are engraved on My Throne, and bless him. Thus it says, And God appeared unto Jacob . . . and blessed him. R. Levi commenced: And an ox and a ram for peace offerings . . . for to-day the Lord appeared unto you (Lev 9:4). If I appear to him who offered a ram in My name and bless him, how much more should I appear to Jacob whose features are engraved on My throne, and bless him. Thus it says, And God appeared unto Jacob . . . and blessed him.[12]

Another passage from *Lamentation Rabbah* 2:2 also depicts Jacob's heavenly identity as a celestial image: "Similarly the Holy One, blessed be He, said to Israel: Do you not provoke Me because you take advantage of the likeness of Jacob which is engraved upon My throne? Here, have it, it is thrown in your face! Hence, He has cast down from heaven unto the earth the beauty of Israel."[13]

It appears that in these rabbinic passages Jacob's image engraved on the Throne has a sacerdotal significance and might be envisioned as an "icon" of the deity in a manner similar to how the prelapsarian Adam, installed in heaven, is understood in the *Primary Adam Books*. In relation to this concept, Neis suggests that in *Lamentations Rabbah* 2:2 "God accuses Israel of taking advantage of the presence of this icon and provoking him with their behavior. He threatens to cast down the icon of Jacob from his throne."[14]

In another rabbinic passage found in *Numbers Rabbah* 4:1, not only Jacob's image but also his name appear to be understood as sort of corresponding visual and auditory representations of the deity through which angels are able to worship God: "There is a scriptural text bearing on this: Since thou art precious in My sight, and honorable, etc. (Isa 43:4). The Holy One, blessed be He, said to Jacob: Jacob, thou art exceedingly precious in my sight. For I have, as it were, set thine image on My throne, and by thy name the angels praise Me and say: Blessed be the Lord, the God of Israel, from everlasting and to everlasting (Ps 41:14)."[15]

As will be shown later in our study, similar conceptual constellations play a prominent role in the Adamic lore about the protoplast's *tselem*.

It appears that Jacob's exalted profile and his association with the *Kavod* posed a formidable challenge to rabbinic monotheistic sensibilities since some midrashic passages about the heavenly image of the patriarch are overlaid with distinctive polemical overtones. For example, *Gen. Rab.* 68:12 presents the following debate between two rabbis:

> R. Hiyya the Elder and R. Jannai disagreed. One maintained: They were ascending and descending the ladder; while the other said: They were ascending and descending on Jacob. The statement that they were ascending and descending the ladder presents no difficulty. The statement that they were ascending and descending on Jacob we must take to mean that some were exalting him and others degrading him, dancing, leaping, and maligning him. Thus it says, Israel in whom I will be glorified (Isa 49:3); it is you, whose features are engraved on high; they ascended on high and saw his features and they descended below and found him sleeping. It may be compared to a king who sat and judged in a [basilica]; people ascend to the basilica and find him [judging], they go out to the chamber and find him [sleeping].[16]

The contestation of the rabbinic authorities involves an interesting point—namely, a suggestion that Jacob himself might represent an anthropomorphic "ladder" that connects earthly and celestial realms. This motif will be explored more closely below.

Further, it appears that the polemical thrust of this passage is not confined merely to a contestation between the rabbis but also involves a rivalry between the otherworldly creatures. Thus, the salient feature of the text is a postulation that some angelic servants seem to oppose Jacob's doppelganger by "degrading . . . and maligning him," thus revealing a familiar motif of the angelic rivalry that has been already explored in our study. This theme of angelic opposition is reflected already in some talmudic materials that constitute the background of these midrashic passages. Thus, *b. Hul.* 91b contains the following tradition: "A Tanna taught: They ascended to look at the image above and descended to look at the image below. They wished to hurt him, when behold, the Lord stood beside him (Gen 28:13). R. Simeon b. Lakish said: Were it not expressly stated in the Scripture, we would not dare to say it. [God is made to appear] like a man who is fanning his son."[17]

Elliot Wolfson notes that in these rabbinic sources the motif of the patriarch's doppelganger "is placed in the context of another well-known motif regarding the enmity or envy of the angels toward human beings. That is, according to the statements in *Gen. Rab.* and *Bavli Hullin* the angels, who beheld Jacob's image above, were jealous and sought to harm Jacob below."[18] He notes that "the influence of the talmudic reworking of this motif is apparent in several later midrashic sources as well."[19]

The theme of Jacob's transcendental Self engraved on the divine Throne has also been transmitted in later Jewish mysticism. These mystical currents often add some novel symbolic dimensions to already familiar imagery. Thus, in *Hekhalot Rabbati* (*Synopse* §164), the tradition of Jacob's alter ego on the throne is overlaid with striking erotic symbolism: "And testify to them. What testimony? You see Me—what I do to the visage of the face of Jacob your father which is engraved for Me upon the throne of My glory (לקלסתר פניו יעקב אביהם שהיא חקוקה לי על כסא כבודי). For in the hour that you say before Men 'Holy,' I kneel on it and embrace it and kiss it and hug it and My hands are on its arms three times, corresponding to the three times that you say before Me, 'Holy,' according to the word that is said, Holy, holy, holy (Isa 6:3)."[20]

Here the deity embraces and kisses Jacob's heavenly identity engraved on his Throne. Yet, the striking difference here, in comparison with the previously explored accounts, is that now not the image but instead Jacob's face (לקלסתר פניו יעקב)—or more precisely a cast (קלסתר)[21] of the patriarch's face—is said to be engraved on the throne. It appears that this conceptual shift is not merely a slip of a Hekhalot writer's pen but a deliberate conceptual shift, since it is also attested to in some other materials.[22] Thus, in some *piyyutim*, which are conceptually very close to the developments found in *Hekhalot Rabbati*, Jacob's heavenly identity again appears to be understood as the "face" on the Throne. In a liturgical poem of R. Yannai, one can find the following depiction:

> Your trust is in Jacob and the proof is Israel. One who sees the image of Jacob will sanctify the holy one of Israel. And those who make mention of the name Jacob will venerate you God of Israel. You are called the God of Jacob and also the God of Israel. And the exemplar of the camps of your angels, this one will call out the name Jacob. And this one will call out the name Israel. This one will say he is holy and this one will say he is blessed. And they will call out to one another. . . . And they will encircle the chariot, and rub with their wings. [. . .] And they will prostrate their entire length to it. And they will cover *the face of the throne*. And a sound will emerge from its wheels. [. . .] Their singing is to Jacob. They sanctify you, Holy One of Jacob.
>
> And they will respond and say: "Holy, holy, holy. The Lord of hosts fills the entire earth with his glory." From his place he [God] descended and brought down his hosts to see the image of Jacob. In his place he [Jacob] was asleep; behold I [God] am with you because

your image is with me. In his place he slept; while you sleep your guardian will not sleep.[23]

One of the curious expressions that occurs in this poem devoted to Jacob's heavenly identity is the phrase "the face of the throne." Rachel Neis notices that "this expression invokes Job 26:9, 'He covers the face of his throne,' but in this setting must also work with the references to Jacob's image and facial features."[24]

Another rabbinic testimony found in *Pirke de Rabbi Eliezer* 35 also attempts to replace the *tselem* imagery with the symbolism of Jacob's *panim* by arguing that the angels went to see the face of the patriarch and that his heavenly countenance is reminiscent of a visage of one of the Living Creatures of the divine Throne:[25]

> Rabbi Levi said: In that night the Holy One, blessed be He, showed him all the signs. He showed him a ladder standing from the earth to the heaven, as it is said, "And he dreamed, and behold a ladder set up on the earth, and the top of it reached to heaven" (Gen 28:12). And the ministering angels were ascending and descending thereon, and they beheld the face of Jacob, and they said: This is the face—like the face of the *Chayyah*, which is on the Throne of Glory. Such (angels) who were (on earth) below were ascending to see the face of Jacob among the faces of the *Chayyah*, (for it was) like the face of the *Chayyah*, which is on the Throne of Glory.[26]

Such peculiar terminological exchanges between *tselem* and *panim* are significant for our study since they evoke the memory of various heavenly counterpart traditions in which the symbolism of the seer's celestial alter ego is closely connected with the *panim* imagery. Thus, in *2 Enoch*, the seventh patriarch's doppelganger is understood as the luminous "face" that mirrors the divine *Panim*.[27] It points to a possibility that the notion of Jacob's celestial identity in the form of "face" is not a later rabbinic invention. As we will see further on in our study, the notion of Jacob's heavenly counterpart in the form of the celestial "face" already plays a prominent conceptual role in an early Jewish pseudepigraphon, known to us as the *Ladder of Jacob*.[28]

In even later Jewish mystical testimonies, we find yet another critical development, already mentioned in our study, in which Jacob's heavenly identity is not simply engraved on the throne but instead seated on the Merkavah. Thus, *Zohar* I.71b–72a offers the following striking interpretation of Ezekiel's vision of the Chariot:

"And above the firmament that was over their heads was the likeness of a throne, as the appearance of a sapphire stone" (Ezek 1:26). This alludes to the "foundation stone," which is the central point of the universe and on which stands the Holy of Holies. "The likeness of a throne," i.e. the supernal holy throne, possessing four supports, and which is symbolic of the Oral Law. "And upon the likeness of the throne was the likeness as the appearance of a man upon it above;" this symbolizes the Written Law. From here we learn that copies of the Written Law should rest on copies of the Oral Law (and not vice versa), because the latter is the throne to the former. "As the appearance of a man" refers to the image of Jacob, who sits on it.[29]

Here the formative Ezekelian account is refashioned as the vision of Jacob's image enthroned on the celestial Seat. Another passage from *Zohar* II.241a offers a very similar reading in relation to Isaiah's theophanic vision: "R. Simeon prefaced his reply with the verse: 'Thus saith the Lord: The heaven is my throne, etc.' (Isa 66:1). 'Observe,' he said, 'that the Holy One, blessed be He, found delight in Israel as His inheritance and portion, brought them near to Himself, and divided them into certain grades after the celestial model, so as to bring into one complete whole all the worlds, both the upper and the lower. Thus "the heaven is my throne" indicates the firmament wherein Jacob dwells, an exalted image, as it were, of the most high divine Throne.'"[30] In this passage, once again, the exalted image of Jacob is depicted as dwelling on the divine Throne.

Another passage from *Zohar* I.168a, which has already been mentioned in our study, connects the tradition of Jacob's image with the symbolism of a mirror, a portentous metaphor that we have already learned became crucial in so many heavenly counterpart accounts: "Hence it is that when the children of Jacob are oppressed, God looks at the image of Jacob and is filled with pity for the world. This is hinted in the passage: 'Then will I remember my covenant with Jacob' (Lev 26:42), where the name Jacob is spelt *plene*, with a *vau*, which is itself the image of Jacob. To look at Jacob was like looking at the 'clear mirror.'"[31]

Moreover, some Jewish accounts appear to extend the symbolism of image as a heavenly identity to other well-known exemplars, already associated with the heavenly counterpart lore in our study. Thus, for example, *Targ. Ps.-J.*, while rendering the account of Moses' shining visage, adds to it the אִיקוֹנִין terminology. *Targ. Ps.-J.* to Exodus 34:29 reads: "At the time that Moses came down from Mount Sinai, with the two tables of the testimony in Moses' hand as he came down from the mountain, Moses did not know that the splendor of the *iqonin* of his face shone because of the splendor of the Glory of the Shekinah of the

Lord at the time that he spoke with him."[32] The next verse (34:30) also uses the
אִיקוּנִין formulae: "Aaron and all the children of Israel saw Moses, and behold,
the *iqonin* of his face shone; and they were afraid to go near him."[33] Finally
verses 33–35 again demonstrate the intense appropriation of the image symbolism: "When Moses ceased speaking with them, he put a veil on the *iqonin* of
his face. Whenever Moses went in before the Lord to speak with him, he would
remove the veil that was on the *iqonin* of his face until he came out. And he
would come out and tell the children of Israel what he had been commanded.
The children of Israel would see Moses' *iqonin* that the splendor of the *iqonin*
of Moses' face shone. Then Moses would put the veil back on his face until he
went in to speak with him."[34]

In these targumic interpretations of the biblical passages about Moses'
shining face, like in the aforementioned Jacob's traditions, one can see the creative interchange between the *panim* and *tselem* symbolism.[35]

Like in the targumim, in later Jewish mysticism, and especially in the
Zohar, the notion of the image as the heavenly Self is eventually bound to transcend the confines of Jacob's story. The *tselem* now becomes the heavenly identity
of every human being, understood as the person's celestial "body." Gershom
Scholem underlines the persistence of this idea in later Jewish mystical lore. He
notes that "already among the twelfth-century Ashkenazic Hasidim, the ancient
motifs of man's personal angel or *daemon* were linked to the image in which
man was created. . . . This angel is now understood as the person's double, about
which nothing is said in the older Jewish sources of Merkavah mysticism. The
sending of this angel to the earthly world even involves manifestations of this
doppelganger to the person."[36]

Scholem further notes that in these later Jewish expansions, the *tselem
Elohim* was understood as the image of a human being's angel that is imprinted
upon the creature at the moment of his or her birth, or even earlier, at
conception.[37]

The notion of *tselem* as the heavenly archetype comes to its clearest expression in several Zoharic passages where the divine image of the righteous man
is understood as an angel. Thus, from *Zohar* I.191a, one learns the following:

> R. Judah said in reply: "The divine image of the righteous man is
> itself the very angel that shuts the mouths of the beasts and puts
> them in shackles so that they do not hurt him; hence Daniel's words:
> 'My God hath sent his angel,' to wit, the one who bears the imprint
> of all the images of the world, and he firmly fixed my image on me,
> thereby shutting the lions' mouths, and making them powerless over
> me. Hence man has to look well to his ways and paths, so as not to
> sin before his Master, and to preserve the image of Adam."[38]

Here the celestial Self of a human being is understood not merely as an angelic being but as a guardian angel,[39] whose functions include protection of a human creature from evil supernatural forces.[40]

Scholem emphasizes the complex multidimensional nature of the *tselem* imagery in the Zoharic materials where the concept of image as a purely personal angel was sometimes replaced by notions of a primordial shape and a preexistent heavenly garment worn by the soul in its paradisiacal existence prior to entering the body.[41] Pure souls thus also require their own clothing, even in their celestial state, and only under extraordinary circumstances would they abandon this attire and appear uncovered before God.[42] Scholem notes that the *Zohar* speculates at length about these celestial garments[43] by unfolding these clothing metaphors in the midst of the *tselem* symbolism.[44] One such speculation can be found in *Zohar* I.226b, which narrates a dream of a famous rabbinic authority: "R. Judah the Elder one day saw in a dream his own image illumined and radiating brightly in all directions. 'What is that?' he said; and the answer came: 'It is thy garment for thy habitation here'; whereupon he was in great joy. R. Judah said: 'Every day the spirits of the righteous sit in rows in the Garden of Eden arrayed in their robes and praise God gloriously, as it is written: "Verily the righteous shall praise thy name; the upright shall sit before thee." ' "[45]

In this passage, Rabbi Judah the Elder receives a vision of his luminous image identified in the text as a celestial garment. It is reminiscent of some early traditions of the heavenly counterpart, especially attested to in the *Hymn of the Pearl*, where the heavenly raiment of the protagonist is envisioned as his celestial doppelganger. Another pivotal allusion found in this passage is a reference to the Garden of Eden that evokes the memory of underlying Adamic currents in which the first humans are said to be endowed with garments of light—the protological attire, which is predestined to be restored to the righteous in the eschaton. Such an allusion points to a formative reception of the protological traditions in shaping the concept of *tselem* in the Zoharic materials. Although the *Zohar*[46] very rarely explicitly states that this concept is identical with the *tselem* of Genesis 1, there is no doubt, in Scholem's opinion, that this was the intention of many Zoharic passages.[47]

Another essential conceptual development that also pertains to the clothing metaphors associated with the *tselem* imagery is the peculiar understanding of this mysterious entity as a raiment of the soul—an ethereal body that determines and interacts with the physical body of the human being.[48] Analyzing the Zoharic developments, Scholem argues that "the ethereal body, which belongs to every human earthly body, is now designated by the *Zohar* as *tselem*. At the same time, it is also a biological principle operating within the human organism and changing its shape along with it. It is formed and impressed within the soul at the moment of conception."[49]

Daniel Matt also proposes that in the *Zohar* the *tselem* is understood as "an ethereal body in which each soul is clothed before entering a human body. This bodily garment resembles the physical body that she will inhabit on earth. A person is created 'in that image,' and as he proceeds through life, the image surrounds him as an aura, departing from him shortly before he dies."[50]

In line with these conceptual currents, *Zohar* III.13b avers that when a human being goes out into the world he or she will grow with the same *tselem*. From *Zohar* II.217b and *Zohar* III.13b,[51] one also learns that the *tselem* leaves a human being immediately before his or her death.[52]

Scholem reflects on this weighty development that envisions the *tselem* as a sort of inner pattern according to which the physical body grows. In this perspective, the human body itself becomes a "shadow" of the inner *tselem*. He considers, "on the one hand, the *tselem* as a principle determined before birth; on the other hand, as the biological principle of the individual life, containing and determining the growth of the organism and its life span."[53] *Zohar* III.104a–b further elaborates this formative influence of the *tselem*:

> At the hour of wedded union on earth, God sends a certain form with the figure of a human being which hovers over the union, and if a man's eye were capable of such a thing it would see such a form over his head. The child is created in that form, and before that form stands over a man's head the child is not created, that form being prepared for it before it issues into the world. In that form it grows up, in that form it goes about, as it is written, "Surely every man walketh in a form" (*tselem*, Ps 39:9). This form is from on high. When the spirits go forth from their places, each one stands before the Holy King with its adornments, with the countenance which it is to wear in this world; and from that adornment comes forth this form (*tselem*). Thus it is the third from the spirit, and it comes down first to this world at the time of wedded union, from which it is never absent. In the case of Israel, who are holy, this *tselem* is holy and from a holy place. But for the heathens it comes from the "evil species," from the side of uncleanness. Therefore a man should not mix his form with that of a heathen, because the one is holy and the other unclean.[54]

Analyzing this passage, Scholem notes that the *tselem* here is envisioned as a third element—a mediating entity between the life soul—*nefesh*, which is the lowest sphere of the human *psychē*, and the body itself. In Scholem's opinion, the *Zohar* thus regards the *tselem* as the astral body that the Israelites receive from the holy realms, while the pagan nations from the unclean and demonic realms.[55]

It is also vital for our study that, according to the Zoharic materials, the *tselem* can in some instances become visible to a human being. Scholem notes that in this case the adept "would experience a kind of *Doppelgänger* phenomenon . . . in which a person encounters the 'shape of himself.'"[56] According to the *Zohar*, the adept in some situations is able to adjure his or her *tselem*. Yet, in contrast with the previously explored apocalyptic accounts where such encounter with the upper identity is a desirable transforming event, this praxis of encountering one's heavenly identity is clearly discouraged in the *Zohar*. According to this mystical compendium, such an event is laden with negative consequences for the adept since in order to behold the *tselem* he or she must make a pact with the forces of the Left Side. *Zohar* III.43a describes a practice of the *tselem*'s adjuration and its grave dangers:

> One who knows how to perform sorcery on the left side and to cling there should stand by the light of a lamp, or in a place where his own images may be seen, and utter certain words and invite his images to those whom he has summoned, and say that they are willingly prepared for their commands. Such a person has left the domain of his Lord and has yielded his pledge to the impure side. By those incantations that he utters, inviting his images, two spirits manifest, and array themselves in his images in human form, and inform him how to harm and benefit at particular times. These are two spirits who were not comprised within a body, and now they are comprised within these images, arrayed in them, and they convey information to this person-one who has left the domain of his Lord and yielded his pledge to the impure side.[57]

As one can see, the praxis of interaction with the adept's heavenly identity is strictly forbidden here. Scholem notes that by doing this, the adept is making a pact with the powers of the Left Side by surrendering to them his or her *tselem*, which is manifested as shadow images.[58] As a consequence of such a ritual, instead of the two forces of holiness that normally accompany the human being, two demonic spirits clothe themselves in his two shadows, serving him as guides and advisors.[59]

Another salient aspect of the *tselem* imagery in the *Zohar*, relevant for our study, is a peculiar understanding of the doppelganger in the form of the image as a reflection, which in the *Zohar* is rendered through the formulae of "shadow." Scholem notes that "in the *Zohar*, exactly as in the famous passage in Dante's *Purgatorio* (canto 25), the astral body is linked to man's shadow, a connection facilitated by the obvious wordplay in Hebrew on *tselem* and *tsel* (shadow)."[60] Scholem argues that this shadow is interpreted by the *Zohar* as none other than an external projection of the inner *tselem*.⁶¹ Such an understanding of the *tselem* as the shadow is important for our study, especially in light of the previously explored Mosaic currents where the symbolism of reflections and mirrors as the heavenly identities of seers and mediators looms large.

Image as the Otherworldly Counterpart in Ancient Greek Literature and Philosophy

There is a certain temptation to view the aforementioned Zoharic speculations about the celestial alter ego in the form of *tselem* as later Kabbalistic inventions completely divorced from the early heavenly counterpart lore. Yet, a similar concept already circulated in ancient Greek literature and philosophy several millennia before the *Book of Zohar* first appeared in Spain in the thirteenth century CE. Thus, already in Homer's writings, a double of a human being was envisioned as an *eidōlon*, a term that in some contexts can be translated as an "image," or "likeness,"⁶² but in the Homeric materials became understood as a "phantom" or a "double."⁶³ One finds this idea in Homer's *Odyssey* where the *eidōlon* of Iphthime, prepared by Athene, appears in Penelope's dream. *Odyssey* 4.795–800 reads: "Then the goddess, flashing-eyed Athene, took other counsel. She made a phantom (εἴδωλον), and likened it in form to a woman, Iphthime, daughter of great-hearted Icarius, whom Eumelus wedded, whose home was in Pherae. And she sent it to the house of divine Odysseus, to Penelope in the midst of her wailing and lamenting, to bid her cease from weeping and tearful lamentation."⁶⁴

Another passage from *Odyssey* (11.601–602) depicts Heracles' *eidōlon* in Hades,⁶⁵ while the hero himself is dwelling upon Olympus with the gods: "And after him I marked the mighty Heracles—his phantom (εἴδωλον); for he himself among the immortal gods takes his joy in the feast, and has to wife Hebe, of the fair ankles, daughter of great Zeus and of Hera, of the golden sandals."⁶⁶

In the aforementioned passages, *eidōlon* is clearly distinguishable from the "earthly" persona it represents, being understood as a sort of "shadow" or "phantom" of that person.⁶⁷ It is also noteworthy that it is sometimes fashioned literally as the person's "twin," who looks exactly like the individual it represents. Reflecting on this feature, Jan Bremmer observes that

> the meaning of *eidōlon* becomes clear from two passages. After Apollo had taken Aeneas away to a temple to be healed after a fight against Diomedes, "he made an *eidōlon* like Aeneas himself" (5.450).⁶⁸ Athena sent Penelope an *eidōlon* which she made like Iphthime (4.796). From these passages it appears that an *eidōlon* is a being

that looks exactly like a person. This becomes especially clear in the case of Achilles when he is visited by the *psychē* of Patroclus in a dream. When Patroclus departs, Achilles tries to embrace him, but Patroclus' *psychē* vanishes without Achilles succeeding. He then realizes that it was "a *psychē* and *eidōlon*," although "it was wondrous like him" (23.104–107).[69] The word *eidōlon*, thus, originally stressed the fact that for the ancient Greeks the dead looked exactly like the living.[70]

Although in Homeric writings, the term *eidōlon* is never used for the souls of the living,[71] in the Orphic and Pythagorean traditions, it became envisioned as a double of a person who was still alive. In respect to these developments, Jean-Pierre Vernant observes that a very different concept of the soul, opposite to the Homeric understanding, was elaborated in the milieu of the philosophical-religious sects like the Pythagoreans[72] and Orphics.[73] Vernant notes that this new conception appeared to be linked to spiritual practices of these esoteric groups, whose intentions were to escape from time, from successive reincarnations, and from death through acts of purifying and liberating the little particle of the divine everyone carries within himself or herself.[74] Vernant notes that in this novel understanding the *psychē* is still defined in the Homeric way like *eidōlon*, yet it is no longer the simulacrum of the dead person after death. Now that it is present within the living person, it can no longer take the form of a ghostly double of a vanished body.[75] Vernant further observes that in its continuous duration, this new entity became the double of a living being: *aiōnos eidōlon*. This double, which is of divine origin and escapes the destruction that is the fate of mortal bodies, slumbers when its limbs are active. It awakens when the body is asleep and shows itself in the form of dreams, thus revealing to us the lot that awaits us in the other world after our death.[76]

In Platonic thought, the concept of *eidōlon* undergoes a further striking evolution. Analyzing these portentous transitions, Vernant points out that in Plato one can see an inversion of the values attributed to the body and the soul. Instead of binding the individual intimately to a physical body and his or her soul (*psychē*), presented like the *eidōlon* of the body that is no longer here, as its phantom or double, for Plato it becomes the immortal *psychē* that constitutes one's real being.[77] In this perspective, the physical body changes its status: it now becomes a "shadow," an illusory image of what we are truly are. In the ghostly world of appearances, the body becomes a semblance of the soul. In Vernant's opinion, it leads to a different understanding of the *eidōlon*. No longer are there *psychai* that possess *eidōla*, phantoms of those whose bodies have been reduced to ashes on the funerary pyre; rather, it is the bodies of the deceased (their corpses) that are the *eidōla* of those who are dead.[78] As Vernant notes, here we have a major transition from the soul as the ghostly double of the body to the body as a ghostly reflection of the soul.⁷⁹

Important terminological changes are also taking place. Thus, in the Platonic philosophy, unlike in Homer, *eidōlon* is understood not as a "phantom" but rather as an "image." Reflecting on these changes, Vernant observes that a reversal of the relation between body and soul explains why Plato, the first theoretician of the image as an imitative artifice and a fiction, uses a term to designate mimetic activity in general that is the most charged with archaic values, the least "modern" of those available at this time in the vocabulary of the image.⁸⁰

The notion of *eidōla* as the chain of successive images/reflections representing "copies of a copy," received its further elaboration in Plotinus in the third century CE.⁸¹

A good illustration of such a usage of *eidōlon* can be found in chapter 6 of the first *Ennead* where this concept is placed in the context of Narcissus' story who once saw his reflection in the water:

> When he sees the beauty in bodies he must not run after them: we must know that they are images, traces, shadows, and hurry away to that which they image. For if a man runs to the image and wants to seize it as if it was the reality (like a beautiful reflection [εἰδώλου καλοῦ] playing on the water, which some story somewhere, I think, said riddlingly a man wanted to catch and sank down into the stream and disappeared) then this man who clings to beautiful bodies and will not let them go, will, like the man in the story, but in soul, not in body, sink down into dark depths where intellect has no delight, and stay blind in Hades, consorting with shadows there and here.⁸²

It has been previously suggested that these philosophical currents⁸³ might influence some heterodox Christian developments with their symbolism of the upper *eidōla* paradoxically reflected in the watery mirrors of the lower realms.⁸⁴ These traditions will be explored in detail later in our study.

Image as the Heavenly Identity in Mandaeism, Manichaeism, and Early Christianity

Some conceptual developments found in Mandaean, Manichaean, and early Christian materials also reaffirm, in their own peculiar way, the antiquity of the understanding of the image as the human being's doppelganger.

Let us first direct our attention to some Mandaean materials, based on oral traditions that can be dated to the first and second centuries CE, where the idea of the *dmuta* or the Lightworld image or likeness[85] can be found.[86] In relation to the concept of *dmuta* as the heavenly counterpart of a human being in the Mandaean texts, Ethel Stefana Drower notes that according to these materials "each individual on earth has his double (*dmuta*) or likeness in [the world of the upper counterparts, called] *Mšunia Kušta* and at the time of death the earthly individual leaves his earthly body and assumes the ethereal body of his double."[87]

Another distinguished student of the Mandaean traditions, Jorunn Jacobsen Buckley, in her analysis of *dmuta* symbolism, emphasizes several features of this arcane entity essential for our study. Buckley notes that

> the term *dmuta* conveys a dynamic relationship between the earthly image and its Lightworld counterpart. More precisely, the Lightworld image dwells in *Mšunia Kušta*, the world of ideal counterparts, which is a specific section of the Lightworld. The earthly image can only function insofar as it is energized by its *dmuta* in the upper world. Everything, every human being and all ʿ*utras*, seem to have such an image. What one might expect of a given mythological figure characterized by great mobility depends on where that figure happens to be at any moment. Due to the *dmuta*, the figure's identity is constant, but the figure may show itself as positive or negative depending on location and on the company it keeps. There is an underlying Mandaean psychological idea at work here, for personality traits may vary, but the fundamental, *dmuta*-given identity remains constant.[88]

Buckley's reflections underline the complex nature of the *dmuta* symbolism found in the Mandaean materials that often operate with notions of both earthly and heavenly identities that are mutually interconnected. Here, like in the aforementioned Jewish mystical testimonies, the heavenly alter ego is envisioned as the formative entity that controls its lower earthly counterpart.

Some scholars also draw attention to the pronounced salvific significance of reunification with the heavenly twin in the form of the *dmuta* in Mandaeism, which is reminiscent of the heavenly counterpart traditions found in Jewish apocalyptic accounts. Thus, Richard Foltz argues that "as in Manichaeism and a number of other belief systems, Mandaeism posits that each human has a heavenly twin (*dmuta*). Thus, the aim of Mandaeans is to ascend to the World of Light and attain reunion with their idealized, spiritual counterparts."[89]

It is also important that in Mandaeism the protagonist's heavenly doppelganger in the form of *dmuta* is often envisioned as a celestial "garment,"[90] which serves as an upper correlative to his or her earthly "garment."[91] As we already learned in our study, such an understanding of the celestial alter ego as an attire can be found also in other heavenly counterpart traditions.

Some Manichaean doppelganger traditions also show familiarity with the notion of the heavenly double as an *eikōn*. Thus, in *Kephalaia* 14:27–15:3, Mani's heavenly counterpart appears to be understood as an "image": "At that same season he [. . .]/my image, I assuming it in the years of Arta[b]anus/the [ki]ng of Parthia. Then, in the years of Ard[ashir], the kin[g] of Persia, I was tended and grew tall and attained the ful[lne]ss of the sea /[so]n. In that same year, when Ard[ashi]r the ki/[ng was c]rowned, the living Paraclete came down t[o me. He sp]oke with me. He unveiled to me the hidden mystery,/the one that is hidden from the worlds and the generations, the myster[y] of the dep[ths]/and the heights."[92]

Reflecting on this Manichaean excerpt, Charles Stang notes that its most tantalizing feature

> is the mention of "my image" (*tab-ikōn*). The verb is no longer legible in this line, and this passage follows on ten lines of which only fragments are legible. Nevertheless, it seems clear that the Paraclete is meant to be in some sense "my image" (Gr. *eikōn*) and that Mani is saying that he "assumed" that image when he had grown to maturity. This is, of course, quite a departure from the Gospel of John. Nowhere does Jesus say that the Paraclete will be an image or *eikōn*. But as we will see in the next section, this tantalizing detail in the *Kephalaia* finds confirmation in the *Cologne Mani Codex*, where Mani proclaims, "Then, at the time when my body reached its full growth, immediately there flew down and appeared before me that most beautiful and greatest mirror image (*katoptron*) of [my self]" (*CMC* 17,1). We will also consider the ways that this "image" and "mirror image" may allude to Paul (and his concept of *eikōn*), Plato (lovers serving as each other's mirror), and the *Gospel of Thomas* (the "image" as opposed to "likeness" in §84).[93]

Stang further argues that the notion of image as the heavenly counterpart becomes an important feature of the Manichaean anthropology of the divine double. He draws attention to the passage found in *Keph.* 36:9–15, where we find the following description of the "Light Form": "The third is the Light Form; the one whom the elect and the catechumens shall receive, should they renounce the world. And also the fifth father is this Light Form; the one who shall appear to everyone who will g[o] out from his body, corresponding to the pattern of the image (*ikōn*) to the apostle; and the thr[ee] great glorious angels who are come with her."[94] Commenting on this passage, Stang notes that

> it is this Light Form on which we need now to focus in order to understand whether there is a universal Manichaean anthropology

of the divine double. Here we learn that the Light Form will appear to both tiers of the Manichaean community—catechumens or "hearers" and the elect. This Light Form "corresponds to the pattern of the image (*ikōn*) to the apostle." We have already seen how Mani's companion or counterpart is understood as his image: "my image (*ikōn*)" (*Kephalaia* 14, 28); "that most beautiful and greatest mirror-image of [myself] (*katoptron ton prosōpou mou*)" (CMC 17, 1–16). Here we learn that the relationship of the apostle to his companion is repeated at the level of the Manichaean faithful: the Light Form appears to the faithful just as his image appears to the apostle.[95]

Another important piece of evidence is found in the *Cologne Mani Codex* 94–96, where "an image of man" in the waters appears several times to the leader of the baptismal sect, Alchasai: "For Elkhasai, the founder of your law, indicates (this): for when he was going to wash in the waters, an image of a man (εἰκὼν ἀνδρὸς) appeared to him from the spring of water. . . . again for a second time, an image of a man (εἰκὼν ἀνδρὸς) appeared to him out of that spring."[96] Some scholars previously argued that this human image is envisioned in this Manichaean text as Mani's heavenly counterpart.[97]

It is possible that the aforementioned Manichaean traditions are drawing on some heterodox Christian developments where the heavenly doppelganger was understood as an image.[98] Gilles Quispel and April DeConick argue that such a notion of the adept's heavenly double can be encountered in several Christian heterodox passages including Logion 84 of the *Gospel of Thomas*[99] (NHC II,7, 47:25–29), where the following tradition can be found: "Jesus said, 'When you see your likeness, you rejoice. But when you see your images which came into being before you, and which neither die nor become manifest, how much you will have to bear!' "[100]

DeConick suggests that the notion of "likeness" in this passage is related to the adept's earthly identity, while the notion of "image" corresponds to the heavenly one.[101] The gist of the passage, according to DeConick, is that one's earthly "likeness" must encounter one's heavenly double or "image."[102] Other scholars also see such correlations. Thus, while analyzing Logion 84, Henri-Charles Puech also connects the notion of the heavenly image in this passage with the concept of the divine Self or the guardian angel that needs to be encountered and rejoined.[103]

Quispel draws his attention to the preceding Logion 83 of the same heterodox gospel that also deals with the notion of image, considering Logion 83 and Logion 84 as doublets: two different versions of the same utterance of Jesus.[104]

Logion 83 (*Nag Hammadi Codex* II, 7, 47:20–24) reads: "Jesus said, 'The images are manifest to man, but the light in them remains concealed in the image of the light of the father. He will become manifest, but his image will remain concealed by his light.'"[105] Here the symbolism of the adept's image is connected to the "image of the light of the deity." The first intriguing detail is that both "images" are associated with the light—this feature, as one remembers, is also prominent in Enochic and Mosaic heavenly counterpart accounts where both the deity's Form and the anthropomorphic extent of the seer are portrayed as luminous. The second valid detail is that the adept's image appears to be concealed in the image of the deity—a motif that often can be found in several doppelganger speculations where the adept's heavenly identity is revealed only upon the adept's encounter with the divine Form.

Quispel also finds a similar understanding of the image in other early Christian texts coming from the Syrian environment, including chapter 112 of the *Acts of Thomas*, which contains the *Hymn of the Pearl*, already familiar to us. In this text, the transcendental Self of the protagonist, envisioned as his celestial garment, is identified as the image of God. The *Acts of Thomas* 112:82–86 reads: "My decorated robe, which was adorned with glorious colors, with gold and beryls and rubies and agates, and sardonyxes, varied in color. And was skillfully worked in its home on high, and with diamond clasps were all its seams fastened; and *the image of the king of kings* was embroidered and depicted in full all over it."[106]

One encounters the same concept of the image as the doppelganger in another cluster of materials associated with the Syrian ideological milieu—namely, in the so-called *Macarian Homilies*, written in Greek at the end of the fourth century CE by a Christian mystic from Mesopotamia. In one of the homilies, the image appears to be understood as the heavenly Self and became identified with the mediatorial figure of the Holy Spirit.[107] Homily II.12.6 reads:

> Since Adam lost his own image and also that heavenly image, therefore, if he shared in the heavenly image, did he have the Holy Spirit (πνεῦμα ἅγιον)? Answer: As long as the Word of God was with him, he possessed everything. For the Word himself was his inheritance, his covering, and a glory that was his defense (Isa 4:5). He was his teaching. For he taught him how to give names to all things: "Give this the name of heaven, that the sun; this the moon; that earth; this a bird; that a beast; that a tree." As he was instructed, so he named them.[108]

Reflecting on the appropriation of the image as the heavenly identity in the *Macarian Homilies*, Quispel observes that "the mystic Macarius, who wrote in Greek but reflects the views of the Syrian church, implies in several passages that Spirit and Icon are identical. . . . The same view is found in the *Hymn of the Pearl* in *Acts of Thomas* 112. There the Self, which comes to encounter the prince, is, on the one hand, the garment left in heaven, the Holy Spirit; and, on the other, the Image (*eikōn*) of the King of Kings, God, was woven into it. The Self is simultaneously Spirit and guardian angel."[109]

Quispel further suggests that one can find a similar concept in very different quarters—namely, in Rome in the second century CE in the *Shepherd of Hermas*.[110] *Vision* 5 of this early Christian text relates the following tradition:

> As I prayed at home sitting on the dining couch, some man came in, splendid to see, dressed like a shepherd, covered with a white goatskin, with a sack on his shoulder and a staff in hand. He greeted me and I greeted him back. He sat down beside me right away and said to me: "I have been sent by the most distinguished angel to live with you for the rest of the days of your life." I thought he was there to test me, and I said: "So who are you?" For I know; I said, "to whom I have been given over." He said to me: "You do not recognize me?" "No," I said. "I am the Shepherd to whom you have been given over." While he was still speaking, his appearance changed, and I recognized the one to whom I had been given over, so that I was suddenly thrown into confusion; fear seized me and I was completely broken up with regret that I had answered him so badly and stupidly. But he answered me: "Do not be overwhelmed with confusion, but take strength in my mandates which I am going to command you. For I have been sent;" he said, "to show you again everything you saw before, the important points that are helpful for you. First of all, write my commandments and parables. Beyond that, you will write as I show you. This is why," he said, "I am telling you to write the mandates and the parables first, so that you can read them right away and keep them." So I wrote the mandates and the parables as he commanded me. Therefore, if you hear them, keep them, go forth in them, and do them with a pure heart, you will receive from the Lord everything he promised you. But if you hear and are not converted, but continue in your sins, you will receive just the opposite from the Lord. All these things the Shepherd commanded me to write, for he is the angel of conversion.[111]

Quispel argues that the guardian angel of Hermas in this description is his heavenly counterpart. Moreover, according to Quispel, this angelic being is presented in the text in the form of the seer's image or *iqonin*. Quispel suggests that "when the angel changes his appearance, then Hermas recognizes him, evidently because he is his image and counterpart. The Jewish concept of the guardian angel as *iqonin* is implied."¹¹² Such an interpretation of the mysterious "shepherd" has enjoyed long-lasting support already from such luminaries as Wilhelm Bousset and Martin Dibelius who held similar opinions by arguing that in this text the protagonist recognizes the heavenly visitor as an image of himself.¹¹³

It is noteworthy that the communication between Hermas and his celestial guardian is reminiscent of peculiar interactions between the angels of the Presence and human seers in the previously explored Jewish pseudepigraphical accounts where the apocalyptic adepts become identified with their celestial alter egos.

Quispel also draws attention to another Christian specimen of such conceptual constellation found in the *Testamentum Domini* where the image of a human being is portrayed as standing on high like an angel of the Presence:¹¹⁴ "Before the foundation of the world there stands the image (*salma*) or type of every soul."¹¹⁵ Quispel notes that the Syriac word *salma* used in this passage "is related to the Hebrew *tselem*, used in Gen 1:27 to indicate the image of God in man."¹¹⁶ He also observes that in this passage "it is not the outward appearance of man, or his reason, or his free will, but his eternal unconscious transcendental Self which is the real image of God."¹¹⁷

Summarizing the lessons of the aforementioned Christian developments, Quispel postulates their Jewish roots by arguing that "the concept of a genius or *daimon* was well known to the Jews in Palestine of Hellenistic times, who called the guardian angel *iqonin* (icon, image) and considered him to be the exact image and counterpart of the man to whom he belonged."¹¹⁸

Adamic and Enochic Roots of Jacob's Heavenly Image

We already noticed that in some of the aforementioned Jewish and Christian materials, in which the image is envisioned as the heavenly identity of a human being, one can see an attempt to evoke implicitly and explicitly the memory of the protoplast—the first human creature endowed with the divine image. Scholars previously have suggested that the traditions about Jacob's image as his heavenly archetype appear to be profoundly shaped by early Adamic lore. Thus, James Kugel argues that "the biblical account of Adam, who was fashioned according to God's 'image' (Gen 1:27) and who himself fathered Seth 'in his [Adam's] likeness and in keeping with his image'—certainly this account and these particular phrases might have been used to suggest that the preexisting image mentioned [in Jacob's accounts] was in fact an image of the first man, one that God consulted in creating him and that was subsequently kept in Heaven."¹¹⁹ Elliot Wolfson effectively sums up the gist of such scholarly intuitions when he notes that "some scholars have suggested that Jacob represents primordial Adam and hence the icon engraved on the throne is to be construed as the universal image of humanity."[120]

These insights from distinguished experts of Jewish lore force us to explore more closely the formative value of some early Adamic accounts and their possible impact in shaping the concept of Jacob's heavenly identity as the image.

Thus, various versions of the *Primary Adam Books*, whose narrative elaborations of the protoplast's story are deeply rooted in Second Temple Jewish conceptual currents,[121] describe the primordial act of the protoplast's endowment with the divine image. After this portentous event, the prelapsarian Adam becomes envisioned as the deity's "icon"—a role very similar to the one that Jacob's image will play in the later rabbinic accounts. In both cases, these anthropomorphic "icons" provoke very similar reactions from the angelic host: on the one hand, the actions of veneration and loyalty, and on the other, feelings of resentment and rejection. As we already know, such complex and multidimensional dialogue between the embodied celestial image and the heavenly servants constitutes the conceptual center of the later targumic, talmudic, and midrashic accounts of Jacob in which the angels will be depicted as constantly interacting with the patriarch's upper Self in the form of *tselem* and his lower "sleeping" identity, connecting them with their ladder-like processions. This motif of the peculiar angelic interactions, however, does not originate in the Jacob lore but instead stems from the formative Adamic accounts of the angelic reaction to the image of God, similar to the ones reflected in the *Primary Adam Books*.[122]

A story found in the Armenian, Georgian, and Latin versions of the *Primary Adam Books* depicts the archangel Michael bringing the newly created Adam into the divine Presence and forcing him to bow down before God.[123] The deity then commands all the angels to bow down to the protoplast.[124] The results of this order are mixed. Some angels agreed to venerate Adam, while others, including Satan, refuse to do obeisance, on the basis that Adam is "younger" or "posterior" to them.[125]

These accounts of the angelic veneration and the denial of such obeisance to the bearer of the deity's image are pertinent to our study. They bring to memory not only the theme of the mixed angelic reaction to Jacob's heavenly identity found in *b. Hul.* 91b and *Gen. Rab.* 68:12 but also the development of such motifs in other doppelganger accounts, including the heavenly counterpart traditions found in *2 Enoch*, where Enoch's transformation into a glorious heavenly creature also coincides with the motif of angelic veneration.

As one remembers, *2 Enoch* 21–22 narrates the final stage of the patriarch's celestial journey during which the seventh antediluvian hero is brought by his angelic guides to the edge of the seventh heaven. At the deity's command, the archangel Gabriel invites the patriarch to stand before the deity's Face. Enoch agrees, and the archangel carries him to the glorious Countenance of God where the patriarch does obeisance to the deity. God then personally repeats the invitation to Enoch to stand before him forever. After this invitation, another archangel, Michael, brings the patriarch to the front of the deity's *Panim*. God then tells his angels, sounding them out: "Let Enoch join in and stand in front of my face forever!" In response to the deity's command, the angels do obeisance to Enoch.[126]

Scholars have noted that *2 Enoch* 21–22 is reminiscent of the account of Adam's elevation and his veneration by angels. Michael Stone notes that, along with the motifs of Adam's elevation and his veneration by angels, the author of *2 Enoch* also appears to be aware of the motif of angelic disobedience and refusal to venerate the first human. Stone draws attention to the phrase "sounding them out,"[127] found in *2 Enoch* 22:6, which another translator of the Slavonic text rendered as "making a trial of them."[128] Stone suggests that the expressions "sounding them out" or "making a trial of them" imply that the angels' obedience is being tested.[129]

In view of these developments, Stone argues that *2 Enoch* 21–22 is reminiscent of the traditions found in the Armenian, Georgian, and Latin versions of the *Primary Adam Books*. The similarities include three chief events:

a. Installation on high. In the *Primary Adam Books*, Adam is created and situated in heaven; in *2 Enoch*, the seventh antediluvian patriarch is brought to heaven.

b. Veneration of the deity. In the *Primary Adam Books*, Adam does obeisance to God; in *2 Enoch*, the seventh antediluvian hero does obeisance to the deity.

c. Initiation into the celestial community: angelic veneration of the protagonist and Satan's refusal to bow down. In the *Primary Adam Books*, God commands the angels to bow down. All the angels do obeisance. Satan and his angels disobey. In *2 Enoch*, the angelic rebellion is assumed. God tests whether this time the angels will obey.[130]

It is also significant that the tradition of the angelic veneration in the Slavonic apocalypse appears to be related to the concept of the heavenly counterpart. In this respect, it is intriguing that in some manuscripts of *2 Enoch* the patriarch's title "youth," the designation so important in various doppelganger accounts, suddenly appears in the context of the angelic veneration.[131]

Angelic veneration in the midst of the seer's identification with his heavenly double occurs also in the *Exagoge* of Ezekiel the Tragedian. As one remembers, this account narrates the "multitude of stars" who fell before Moses' knees.[132] Considering Enochic influences on the *Exagoge*, where the stars often designate angelic beings,[133] the multitude of stars kneeling before the seer might be a reference to the angelic veneration.

The tradition of the angelic veneration of humanity was not forgotten in later Enochic lore where it reappeared in *Sefer Hekhalot*. There, too, such a motif was closely tied to the concept of the heavenly identity of Enoch, designated as "Youth."

Sefer Hekhalot 4:1–10 depicts Rabbi Ishmael questioning his celestial guide Metatron about his name "Youth":

> R. Ishmael said: I said to Metatron: ". . . you are greater than all the princes, more exalted than all the angels, more beloved than all the ministers . . . why, then, do they call you 'Youth' in the heavenly heights?" He answered: "Because I am Enoch, the son of Jared . . . the Holy One, blessed be he, appointed me in the height as a prince and a ruler among the ministering angels. Then three of ministering angels, ᶜUzzah, ᶜAzzah, and ᶜAzaʾel, came and laid charges against me in the heavenly height. They said before the Holy One, blessed be He, 'Lord of the Universe, did not the primeval ones give you good advice when they said, Do not create man!' . . . And once they all arose and went to meet me and prostrated themselves before me, saying Happy are you, and happy your parents, because your Creator has favored you. Because I am young in their company and mere youth among them in days and months and years—therefore they call me 'Youth.'"[134]

Commenting on this passage, Gary Anderson suggests that if "we remove those layers of the tradition that are clearly secondary . . . we are left with a story that is almost identical to the analog we have traced in the Adam and Eve literature and in *2 Enoch*."[135]

Anderson further notes that the acclamation of Enoch as "Youth," in *Sefer Hekhalot*, is intriguing because the reason *3 Enoch* supplies for this title is deceptively simple and straightforward: "Because I am young in their company and a mere youth among them in days and months and years—therefore they call me 'Youth.'" Anderson proposes that the title might point to its Adamic provenance since the explanation for the epithet "youth" recalls the reason for the angelic refusal to worship Adam in the *Primary Adam Books* on the basis of his inferiority to them by way of his age.[136]

Similarities between the angelic veneration of Adam as the divine image and the veneration of Enoch in front of the divine Face brings us to a key question: Can divine image traditions, which play such an important role in some accounts of the heavenly counterparts, also be found in *2 Enoch*? Although the Slavonic apocalypse does not mention explicitly the divine image as the heavenly identity of the seventh patriarch, it constantly refers to another pivotal celestial entity—the divine Face. This entity plays a paramount role in the process of the seer's unification with his celestial alter ego and the angelic veneration of the hero takes place in the immediate proximity to this entity.

It is possible that in *2 Enoch*, like in some rabbinic and Hekhalot accounts, the divine *Panim* might take on the role of the divine *Tselem*. As has been already shown in our study, the divine Countenance in *2 Enoch* 22 represented the cause and the prototype after which Enoch's new celestial identity was formed. The new creation after the Visage signifies the return to the prelapsarian condition of Adam, who was also modeled, according to some testimonies found in the Slavonic apocalypse, after the Face of God. Support for this view can be found in *2 Enoch* 44:1, where one learns that the protoplast was also created after the *Panim* of God. The text says that "the Lord with his own two hands created humankind; in a facsimile of his own face, both small and great, the Lord created [them]."[137] It is intriguing that *2 Enoch* departs here from the canonical reading attested in Genesis 1:26–27 where Adam was created not after the face of God but after his image (*tselem*).[138] Francis Andersen observes that *2 Enoch*'s "idea is remarkable from any point of view. . . . This is not the original meaning of *tselem*. . . . The text uses *podobie lica* [in the likeness of the face], not *obrazu* or *videnije*, the usual terms for 'image.'"[139] It is clear, however, that this reading did not arise in the Slavonic environment but belonged to the original argument of *2 Enoch*, where the creation of the luminous protoplast after the deity's Face corresponded to a similar angelic creation of the seventh antediluvian patriarch.

In light of these terminological parallels, it is possible that the notion of the heavenly counterpart attested to in *2 Enoch* might be also connected with the *tselem* conceptual currents, similar to the ones found in Jacob's lore. As we already learned above, this rendering of *tselem* imagery through formulae of the divine Countenance, or *Panim*, will continue to exercise its formative influence in later rabbinic accounts about Jacob's heavenly identity.[140]

Prayer of Joseph

Our in-depth examination of various Jacob doppelganger traditions in the later rabbinic lore has provided us with important spectacles that enable us more clearly to see initial traces of these conceptual developments in early Jewish lore. With this knowledge, we should now proceed to the assessment of early pseudepigraphical accounts.

For our explorations of the heavenly counterpart traditions in early Jacob legends, one early account holds a very special value. It is a Jewish pseudepigraphon known to us as the *Prayer of Joseph*. Only three fragments of the *Prayer* are currently extant.[141] According to some scholars, the original composition represented "a midrash on the Jacob narrative in Genesis."[142] The pseudepigraphon is usually dated to the first century CE. Thus, Jonathan Smith argues that "the *Prayer* is most likely to be situated within . . . [the] first-century Jewish groups, both in Palestine and in the Diaspora, both before and after the destruction of the Temple."[143] The surviving fragments reveal the following striking content:

Fragment A

I, Jacob, who is speaking to you, am also Israel, an angel of God[144] and a ruling spirit.[145] Abraham and Isaac were created before any work. But, I, Jacob, who men call Jacob but whose name is Israel am he who God called Israel which means, a man seeing God because I am the firstborn of every living thing to whom God gives life.[146] And when I was coming up from Syrian Mesopotamia, Uriel, the angel of God, came forth and said that "I [Jacob-Israel] had descended to earth and I had tabernacled among men and that I had been called by the name of Jacob." He envied me and fought with me and wrestled with me saying that his name and the name that is before every angel was to be above mine. I told him his name and what rank he held among the sons of God. "Are you not Uriel, the eighth after me? And I, Israel, the archangel of the power of the Lord and the chief captain among the sons of God? Am I not Israel, the first minister before the face of God? And I called upon my God by the inextinguishable name."

Fragment B

For I have read in the tablets of heaven all that shall befall you and your sons.

Fragment C

[Origen writes] Jacob was greater than man, he who supplanted his brother and who declared in the same book from which we quoted "I read in the tablets of heaven" that he was a chief captain of the power of the Lord and had, from of old, the name of Israel; something which he recognizes while doing service in the body, being reminded of it by the archangel Uriel.¹⁴⁷

It has been noted that the leading idea of these fragments appears to be that "angels can become incarnate in human bodies, live on earth in the likeness of men, and be unconscious of their original state."¹⁴⁸ Several scholars have previously suggested that the *Prayer of Joseph* might contain heavenly counterpart traditions. Thus, for example, Dale Allison argues that "although this obscure fragment probably equates Jacob with the angel Israel, who has come to earth and somehow forgotten his true identity, it must be related to the well-known tradition that the features of the patriarch Jacob/Israel have a heavenly correlative on or near God's throne. It seems likely enough, reading between the lines, and as James Kugel has suggested, that some Jews held the earthly Jacob to have a heavenly counterpart."¹⁴⁹

Allison further suggests that "such a belief could have arisen from the Hebrew of Gen 32:29 (שרית עם־אלהים), taken to mean, 'you [Jacob] have been exalted with God,' and/or from the popular etymology of Israel's name, 'the man who sees God' (ישראל being supposed to derive from איש ראה אל)."¹⁵⁰

A close look at the surviving fragments reveals a cluster of familiar motifs that have been previously encountered in our analysis of the heavenly counterpart traditions. The first important detail that catches the eye is the presence of Uriel, a distinctive angelic servant who often appears in other accounts where the seers become unified with their heavenly Selves. Here in the *Prayer*, like in the previously explored Enochic accounts, this angelic servant appears to be assisting a human adept in the acquisition of his heavenly identity.¹⁵¹ Thus, from the *Prayer*, we learn that it was indeed Uriel who conveyed to Jacob the mystery of his transcendental Self.¹⁵² The interaction between Jacob and Uriel might also point to a possible initiatory endeavor that plays a pivotal role in various heavenly counterpart accounts when the angels of the Presence transfer their former offices to the new favorites of the deity who become the new guardians of celestial books and secrets.

Another aspect of the account is an accentuated conceptual gap between the heavenly Self and the earthly "incarnation" of the protagonist. Here one can observe the already familiar ascent-descent pattern,¹⁵³ prominent also in *2 Enoch* where the seventh patriarch has a capacity to travel back and forth between upper and lower realms¹⁵⁴ and as a consequence is able to reside or "tabernacle" temporarily on earth,¹⁵⁵ while his heavenly persona was permanently installed as the angel of the Presence on high. This is especially reminiscent of Enoch's descent in the second part of *2 Enoch* where he is sent by the deity to the lower realm in order to transmit final instructions to his sons and to the people of the earth while his heavenly identity remained installed "forever" before the Face of God.

The Spirit as the Heavenly Counterpart

Another of Jacob's pivotal functions reflected in the *Prayer* that pertains to the heavenly counterpart traditions is his pneumatological task. Fragment A of the *Prayer* opens with a line where Jacob-Israel reveals his role as the sovereign or ruling spirit (Gk. πνεῦμα ἀρχικόν).[156] The reference to the patriarch's identity as a "spirit" is intriguing since various heavenly counterpart currents attempt to portray upper identities of human protagonists as "spirits" or even as the Holy Spirit. Although this designation has not previously drawn much scholarly attention,[157] the peculiar confluence of this title with the motif of Jacob's self-acclamation that he is "the firstborn of every living thing" brings to memory some pneumatological developments prominent in other heavenly counterpart accounts.

Although the motif of the heavenly Self as a spirit played a certain role in early Jewish and Christian developments, it received its most articulated expression in the Manichaean lore where the heavenly twin of the founder of this religious tradition, Mani (216 CE–276 CE), was envisioned as a spirit.[158] Several Manichaean documents, including the *Kephalaia of the Teacher* and *CMC*, extensively speculate about Mani's heavenly *Zwilling*.[159] According to these documents, the Twin-Spirit was sent to Mani already at the age of twelve and then again at age twenty-four[160] revealing to the adept his unique mission in this world.[161] During the first encounter, Mani was told to break with his religious past and step on the path of the ascetic lifestyle.[162] The Twin-Spirit[163] then accompanied Mani during his lifetime, helping him with continuous revelations[164] and even transmitting writings to him.[165] From the Manichaean psalms, one learns that the mission of the Twin-Spirit continued even in the final hours of Mani's life.[166] According to one Manichaean psalm, at the end of his earthly journey, Mani was gazing at his Twin-Spirit "with the eyes of light."[167]

For our study, it is important that Mani's heavenly twin is often depicted not simply as a "spirit" but as the Holy Spirit—Paraclete. Iain Gardner observes that Mani "believed himself to be the recipient of direct revelation from his divine Twin Spirit, which being is understood to be the Paraclete foretold by Jesus, and with whom Mani became 'one body and one Spirit.'"[168] Thus, *Keph.* 14:4–7 relates the following pneumatological tradition in which Mani's twin is portrayed as the Paraclete: "[Wh]e[n] the church of the saviour was raised to the heights, my apo/stolate began, which you asked me about! From that time on was sent the Paraclete, the Spirit of truth; the one who has / co[me] to you in this last generation. Just like the saviour sa/id: When I go, I will send to you the Paraclete."[169] In *Keph.* 14:27–15:3, the tradition about the Paraclete is repeated again: "At that same season he [. . .]/my image, I assuming it in the years of Arta[b]anus/the [ki]ng of Parthia. Then, in the years of Ard[ashir], the kin[g] of Persia, I was tended and grew tall and attained the ful[lne]ss of the sea/[so]n. In that same year, when Ard[ashi]r the ki/[ng was c]rowned, the living Paraclete came down t[o me. He sp]oke with me. He unveiled to me the hidden mystery,/ the one that is hidden from the worlds and the generations, the myster[y] of the dep[ths]/and the heights."[170]

Reflecting on these passages, Johannes van Oort observes that "in the *Kephalaia*, the Paraclete has precisely the same function as the Twin or *Syzygos* as described in the *CMC*. In short: the Paraclete and the Twin are identical in Manichaean theology."[171] It is noteworthy that although in *Keph.* 14–16 Mani's heavenly twin is called the Paraclete, in some other Manichaean passages Mani himself is expressly named as the "Paraclete."[172] It again affirms another tenet of the heavenly counterpart lore when a human adept assumes the offices of his heavenly Self. Thus, van Oort notes that "in a fragment from his Gospel, which was transmitted by the tenth century Muslim historian al-Biruni, it is explicitly stated 'that he [Mani] is the Paraclete who had been announced by the Messiah.'"[173] The same designation is repeated in *CMC* 46,[174] *CMC* 63,[175] and in *CMC* 70.[176] Van Oort notes that "from these quotations from Baraies' testimonies incorporated into the *CMC* (which in turn go back to autobiographical statements of Mani), it is completely clear that Mani considered himself to be the Paraclete."[177] Analyzing the Manichaean pneumatological developments van Oort asks an essential question—namely: "Was Mani, then, the Paraclete (which in orthodox Christian circles was—and is—identified with the Holy Spirit)? Or was the Paraclete (or Holy Spirit) in Mani? And, in what manner may the evidence that both the *Nous* and the *Syzygos* are named as Paraclete match to each other?"[178] In van Oort's opinion, such queries can be resolved through the notion of the heavenly counterpart. He proposes that

> the dilemma of . . . the seeming contradiction that both the *Nous* and the *Syzygos* are called "Paraclete" may be solved by a further examination of the Manichaean (and typical Gnostic) concept of the *Syzygos*. When Mani, i.e., the *Nous* of Mani, was sent into the world, a mirror image of this *Nous*, i.e., his *alter ego*, remained behind in heaven. One ego, Mani's Light-*Nous*, was imprisoned in his body and thus forgot his mission. Then the *Syzygos*, the *alter ego*, was sent to him from heaven: as it is told throughout the *CMC*, this Twin brought Mani the revelation by reminding him of his divine nature and mission; and, like his guardian angel, he protected him. The *Nous* of Mani and his *Syzygos* should therefore be treated as two complementary aspects of Mani's identity. Because Mani's *Nous* (or real Self) and his *Syzygos* were considered to be one and the same

identity, this implies that, if one of them is the Paraclete, the other must be the Paraclete.[179]

Gardner also notes that united with his divine twin Mani thus "becomes the Paraclete foretold, as according to John 14:16 where Jesus promises the disciples that he will ask the Father who will send them another helper, the Spirit of truth, who will remain with them forever."[180]

The aforementioned Manichaean speculations that attempt to portray Mani's heavenly twin as the Holy Spirit appear to be stem from early Jewish and Christian developments in which the celestial Self of a human being is also sometimes envisioned as a spirit. It is intriguing that some of these developments reveal a set of already familiar themes found in the Enoch and Jacob traditions of the heavenly counterparts, including the symbolism of the servants of the divine Face and the motif of the heavenly Self as an image. We will now try to explore these conceptual developments more closely.

One of the crucial biblical references that often appears in the deliberations about the heavenly counterparts as "spirits" in various Christian materials is Matthew 18:10 in which Jesus warns his disciples to not despise little children because their angels continually behold the deity's face in heaven. In some Christian passages, the angelic alter egos of the "little children" became envisioned as the Holy Spirit. Such pneumatological development constitutes an interesting parallel to the Manichaean traditions where Mani's celestial alter ego is envisioned as the Paraclete. One such refashioning is found in Aphrahat's *Demonstrations* where the guardian angels of the little ones, who eternally behold the Face of God, are understood as the Holy Spirit. Thus, *Demonstrations* 6:15 reads:

> This Spirit which the prophets received is likewise the one we (received), my beloved. She is not all the time to be found with those who receive her, rather, at times she goes off to Him who sent her, and at times she comes back to the person who received her. Listen to what our Lord said "Do not despise a single one of these small ones who believe in me, for their angels in heaven continually behold the face of my Father" (Mt 18:10). *This same Spirit all the time goes and stands before God and beholds His face*, and against the person who harms the temple in which she resides she will lay complaint before God.[181]

Scholars previously suggested that Aphrahat is speaking here not simply about the Holy Spirit but also about his (or her) role as the heavenly counterpart of a human being.[182] Thus, Gilles Quispel notes that "Aphrahat has given a very curious interpretation of [the] guardian angel. With an allusion to Matthew 18:10, he speaks about the guardian angels of the little ones, who eternally behold the Face of God and goes on to say that this is the Holy Spirit who permanently goes and stands before God, contemplates his face, and accuses everybody who does harm to the man in which he dwells."[183]

It is also significant for our study that in Aphrahat the Holy Spirit assumes the role of the servant(s) of the divine Face—the office so decisive for the acquisition of the seer's heavenly identity in many pseudepigraphical accounts. Yet, Aphrahat's angelological deliberations are not entirely novel. Thus, the motif of the spirits as the servants of the divine Face in connection with the famous Matthean passage is found already in the writings of Clement of Alexandria,[184] who identifies the Holy Spirit with the seven "first-created" servants of the Face[185] called the *Protoktists* or the *Protoktistoi*. In *Excerpta ex Theodoto* 10, 6–11, 2, Clement discusses the following tradition:

> They (the First-Created) "always behold the face of the Father"[186] and the face of the Father is the Son, through whom the Father is known. Yet that which sees and is seen cannot be formless or incorporeal. But they see not with an eye of sense, but with the eye of mind, such as the Father provided. When, therefore, the Lord said, "Despise not one of these little ones. Verily, I say unto you, their angels do always behold the face of the Father,"[187] as is the pattern, so will be the elect, when they have received the perfect advance. But "blessed are the pure in heart, for they shall see God." And how could there be a face of a shapeless being?[188]

In this account, the Matthean motifs of the "angels" and the "face" are reshaped into the tradition about the heptad of the Holy Spirit represented by the seven highest-ranking members of the celestial hierarchy who are perpetually gazing upon Christ, the Face of God.[189] Scholars discerned that the *Protoktistoi* are often envisioned as heavenly identities or guardian angels of the faithful Christians. Thus, Quispel observes that in Clement's passage "the guardian angels of the faithful are identified with the *Protoktistoi*, who are the Spirit. Guardian angel and Holy Spirit are one and the same."[190]

In the light of these angelological developments, it is important that the *Prayer of Joseph* also defines Jacob as the servant of the divine Face when he himself acknowledges his role as "the first minister before the Face of God."[191] This title is reminiscent of some Enochic developments and, especially, the motif of Enoch's access to the divine Presence and his installation as one of the *Sar ha-Panim* in *2 Enoch* and *Sefer Hekhalot*. This peculiar connection between the pneumatological role and the role of the servant of the divine

Face demonstrates that the concept of the heavenly counterpart as a spirit is surrounded in the *Prayer of Joseph* by other crucial developments prominent in the doppelganger lore.

Jacob's Image

Another development pertinent to our exploration of the doppelganger currents in the *Prayer of Joseph* is the presence of the concept of the image or *tselem* of God—a prominent trend of later Jacob legends. In this respect, it is essential that immediately after the introduction of his title "ruling spirit" Jacob mentions his unique place in God's creation by uttering the following striking statement: "I, Jacob, who is speaking to you, am also Israel, an angel of God and a ruling spirit. Abraham and Isaac[192] were created before any work (προεκτίσθησαν).[193] But . . . I am the firstborn (πρωτόγονος) of every living thing to whom God gives life."[194]

The designation of Jacob as πρωτόγονος[195] might point to his role as the image of God, which is similar to the office that Adam occupies in some Jewish accounts. The connection of this designation with the protoplast's figure has often been noticed by scholars. Thus, for example, Howard Schwartz argues that such expression "suggests that Jacob was a kind of proto-human, an Adam-like figure."[196] Jarl Fossum reflects on another key parallel, previously noticed by other scholars as well,[197] a possible connection with Colossians 1:15 where Christ's role as "the image of the invisible God" (εἰκὼν τοῦ Θεοῦ τοῦ ἀοράτου) is juxtaposed with his designation as πρωτότοκος πάσης κτίσεως (the firstborn of all creation). Fossum argues that "the closest parallel to the phrase in Col 1:15b is found in a fragment of the *Prayer of Joseph* preserved by Origen."[198]

Another important detail that might point to the presence of the *tselem* concept in the *Prayer of Joseph* is the motif of angelic opposition that, as we already learned, often accompanies the *tselem* traditions in Adam's and Jacob's lore. Thus, in the *Prayer*, Jacob mentions that the angel Uriel envied him, wrestled with him, and argued that his name was above Jacob's.[199] Although obviously the *Prayer of Joseph* is drawing on the biblical story of Jacob's wrestling with a supernatural contender at the river Jabbok—the motifs of angelic jealousy and the angel's arguments about his superior status are entirely new developments here in comparison with the biblical account. In relation to these novel interpretations, Richard Hayward notes that "the Bible gives no motive for the supernatural attack on Jacob [at Jabbok]. . . . The *Prayer*, however, attributes the attack to jealousy, and adds something entirely foreign to both the Bible and Philo: what is at issue between the two combatants is their relative status as angels, and their exact positions within the celestial hierarchy."[200] Uriel's jealousy and peculiar arguments about his superiority to the patriarch bring to memory the motif of the angelic opposition to Adam as the image of God in the *Primary Adam Books*. There his chief antagonist, Satan, also expresses similar feelings of jealousy,[201] and he explains his refusal to do obeisance to Adam on the basis of the protoplast's inferior celestial status in comparison with his own, more exalted, standing.[202] The theme of the angelic jealousy and resistance thus implicitly affirms here the existence of the *tselem* tradition.

In view of these connections, it is possible that in the *Prayer of Joseph*, Jacob's heavenly identity is envisioned as both the spirit and the image. If it is indeed so, it is noteworthy that in some doppelganger's accounts the symbolism of the image and the spirit as designations for the adept's heavenly counterpart are often conflated. Quispel draws attention to some texts where such parallels between the concept of the spirit and the concept of the image are present. Thus, he notices that in the *Hymn of the Pearl* "the Self, which comes to encounter the prince, is, on the one hand, the garment left in heaven, the Holy Spirit; and, on the other, the Image (*eikōn*) of the King of Kings, God, was woven into it."[203] The seer's upper identity thus is understood here simultaneously as the spirit and the image.

Quispel also draws attention to a passage from the *Shepherd of Hermas* that details a female figure shrouded in peculiar pneumatological symbolism. According to Quispel, "the Woman that manifests herself to Hermas is in reality the Holy Spirit (*Sim.* 9:1). This then presupposes the well-known Jewish Christian concept according to which the Holy Spirit is a mother. Secondly, the name of the writing refers to the guardian angel of Hermas to whom the latter has been committed (at baptism). When the angel changes his appearance, then Hermas recognizes him, evidently because he is his image and counterpart."[204]

In Quispel's opinion, the same constellation of the concepts of image and spirit can be found in the already mentioned passage from *Pistis Sophia* 61.[205] He notes that "in the *Pistis Sophia*, Mary, the mother of the Lord, tells that, before the Spirit has descended upon Jesus at his baptism, this same Spirit came to her into her house, resembling (*epheine*) Jesus. Mary did not recognize him and thought he was Jesus. The Spirit said to her: where is Jesus, my brother, that I may encounter him? Mary binds him to a leg of the bed and goes to fetch Jesus, who returns home. 'And we looked at you and him and found you resembling him.'"[206] Quispel suggests that "the Holy Spirit here is considered to be the guardian angel and image (*iqonin*) of Jesus, who forms a whole with him."[207]

Concluding this section of our study, we should note that the identification of the protagonist's heavenly identity with the spirit in the Jewish pseudepigrapha is not confined solely to the *Prayer of Joseph* but can be found also in other early pseudepigraphical accounts. In this respect, it is intriguing that in the doppelganger account found in *Similitudes* 71, where Enoch is identified with his heavenly Self in the form of the Son of Man,[208] the title "spirit" also looms large.[209] Thus, already in the first verse of *1 Enoch* 71, the seventh antediluvian hero reports that his "spirit was carried off."[210] Later, in the pivotal moment of the seer's heavenly metamorphosis, we encounter again the title "spirit." In *1 Enoch* 71:11, Enoch reports that when he fell on his face his whole body melted, and his spirit "was transformed and he cried out in a loud voice in 'the spirit of power.'"[211] It is also important that in the *Similitudes* the deity himself is designated as the Lord of Spirits.[212]

Ladder of Jacob

Another principal early Jewish pseudepigraphical account that deals with the notion of Jacob's heavenly identity is the *Ladder of Jacob*. Yet, unlike in the *Prayer of Joseph* where the protagonist's heavenly Self is revealed unambiguously, in the *Ladder* uncovering the possible existence of such concept takes considerable exegetical effort. In part, it is due to the condition of the pseudepigraphon, since the text underwent a long-lasting journey through various linguistic and ideological milieus.

While the *Prayer of Joseph* was preserved in Greek, the main bulk[213] of the *Ladder of Jacob* has survived solely in Slavonic as a part of the so-called *Tolkovaja Paleja*[214] (the *Explanatory Paleia*) where the editors of its various versions reworked[215] and rearranged them. Despite its long life inside the compendium of heterogeneous materials and its long history of transmission in both Greek and Slavonic milieus, the pseudepigraphon seems to have preserved several early traditions that can be safely placed within the Jewish environment of the first century CE. Scholars propose that the Slavonic *Ladder of Jacob* is most likely derived from its Greek variant, which in turn appears to have been translated from Hebrew or Aramaic.

The content of the work is connected with Jacob's dream about the ladder and the interpretation of the vision. In Horace Lund's translation, the text is divided into seven chapters.[216] The first chapter depicts Jacob's dream in which he sees the ladder and receives God's audible revelation about the Promised Land and blessings upon his descendants. The second chapter offers Jacob's lengthy prayer to God in which he uncovers additional details of his dream and asks God to help him interpret the dream. In chapter 3, God sends the angel Sariel to Jacob as an interpreter. In chapter 4, Sariel informs Jacob that his name has been changed to Israel. As one can see, the content of the pseudepigraphon is not confined solely to the ladder account but also accommodates features of Jacob's other visions—namely, the patriarch's acquisition of the new name during the wrestling match at the river Jabbok. The last three chapters of the

Ladder recount Sariel's eschatological interpretations of Jacob's dream in which he reveals the details of future human history to the visionary.

Kavod and *Panim*

It is important for our study that the heavenly counterpart traditions in the *Ladder of Jacob* are surrounded with already familiar *Kavod* symbolism. Moreover, like the authors of previously explored Enochic and Mosaic accounts, the author of the *Ladder* is cognizant of the *panim* imagery as well. It is also possible that here—like in *Hekhalot Rabbati*, *PRE*, and the *piyyutim*—the *panim* imagery serves as a symbolic substitute for the notion of Jacob's *tselem*. In light of their significance for our study, these concepts therefore should be explored more closely.

The symbolism of the divine/angelic faces plays a prominent role, especially in the first chapter of the *Ladder of Jacob*. The text describes Jacob's dream in which he sees a twelve step ladder, fixed on the earth, whose top reaches to heaven with the angels ascending and descending on it. This familiar biblical motif then is expanded further with some new features. *Ladder of Jacob* 1:3–10 offers the following portrayal of the ladder:

> And behold, a ladder was fixed on the earth, whose top reaches to heaven. And the top of the ladder was the face as of a man, carved out of fire.[217] There were twelve steps leading to the top of the ladder, and on each step to the top there were two human faces, on the right and on the left, twenty-four faces (or busts) including their chests. And the face in the middle was higher than all that I saw, the one of fire, including the shoulders and arms, exceedingly terrifying, more than those twenty-four faces. And while I was still looking at it, behold, angels of God ascended and descended on it. And God was standing above its highest face, and he called to me from there, saying, "Jacob, Jacob!" And I said, "Here I am, Lord!" And he said to me, "The land on which you are sleeping, to you will I give it, and to your seed after you. And I will multiply your seed."[218]

As one can see, the story relates that on the ladder Jacob sees twenty-four human faces with their chests, two of them on each step of the ladder. On the top of the ladder, he also beholds another human visage "carved out of fire"[219] with its shoulders and arms.[220] In comparison with the previous countenances, this fiery higher face looks "exceedingly terrifying." The text portrays God standing above this highest countenance and calling Jacob by his name. The depiction leaves the impression that God's voice[221] is hidden behind this fiery terrifying face as a distinct divine manifestation, behind which the deity conveys to Jacob his audible revelation about the Promised Land.

This description of the celestial face as the fiery anthropomorphic extent, which serves as the embodiment of the deity, brings to memory *2 Enoch* in which the theme of the fiery face also looms large. As we remember, *2 Enoch* 22[222] contains an elaborate depiction of God's Visage, which emits light and fire. The salient detail that connects both texts is that the Face in *2 Enoch* is similarly defined as "fiery"[223] and "terrifying."[224] Another parallel is that in both *2 Enoch* and the *Ladder of Jacob* the Face is understood as the luminous divine Form.[225]

It has been previously noted that this fiery extent, labeled in some biblical and intertestamental texts as the "Face," is related to the glorious celestial entity known in theophanic traditions as God's *Kavod*.[226] In these traditions, the Face often serves to designate the radiant façade of the divine *Kavod*.[227] This tendency to equate the *Panim* with the *Kavod* can be found already in some Biblical accounts, including Exodus 33:18–20, where in response to Moses' plea to God to show him his *Glory*, God answers that it is impossible for a human being to see God's *Face*.[228]

The second chapter of the *Ladder of Jacob*, in which the visionary asks God to interpret the dream, provides several additional valid details about the dream that explicitly identify the fiery Face with God's *Kavod*. Here, Jacob offers a prayer in which he discloses further details of his vision of the Face. *Ladder of Jacob* 2:7–19 reads:

> Lord God of Adam your creature and Lord God of Abraham and Isaac my fathers and of all who have walked before you in justice! You who sit firmly on the cherubim and the fiery throne of glory . . . and the many-eyed (ones) I saw in my dream, holding the four-faced cherubim, bearing also the many-eyed seraphim, carrying the whole world under your arm, yet not being borne by anyone; you who have made the skies firm for the glory of your name, stretching out on two heavenly clouds the heaven which gleams under you, that beneath it you may cause the sun to course and conceal it during the night so that it might not seem a god; (you) who made on them a way for the moon and the stars; and you make the moon wax and wane, and destine the stars to pass on so that they too might not seem gods. Before the face of your glory the six-winged seraphim are afraid, and they cover their feet and faces with their wings, while flying with their other (wings), and they sing unceasingly a hymn: . . . whom

I now in sanctifying a new (song) . . . Twelve-topped, twelve-faced, many-named, fiery one! Lightning-eyed holy one! Holy, Holy, Holy, Yao, Yaova, Yaoil, Yao, Kados, Chavod, Savaoth.²²⁹

Several details are eye-catching in this description. Jacob's prayer reveals that his dream about the Face might represent the vision of the Throne of God's Glory. A number of features seem to point to such a possibility.

First, the prayer refers to "his many-eyed ones,"²³⁰ alluding to האופנים, the Wheels, the special class of the Angels of the Throne who are described in Ezekiel 1:18 as the angelic beings "full of eyes." Second, the text describes the deity as seated on the fiery Throne of Glory. Third, the vision contains references to the angelic liturgy and the *Trisagion*. Fourth, the text refers to the fear of the angelic hosts, who stand in the front of the terrifying fiery Face while trying to protect themselves with their wings.²³¹ The motif of protection against the harmful brilliance of God's Throne is typical of theophanic descriptions of the *Kavod* from the earliest attestation found in Isaiah 6:1–4 to the later mystical testimonies reflected in *3 Enoch*, which relates that "in ᶜ*Arabot* there are 660 thousands of myriads of glorious angels, hewn out of flaming fire, standing opposite the throne of glory. The glorious King covers his face, otherwise the heaven of ᶜ*Arabot* would burst open in the middle, because of the glorious brilliance."²³² Fifth, the passage also contains specific terminology associated with the Throne imagery. It has been mentioned earlier that the Slavonic text of the *Ladder* is possibly based on the Semitic original. For example, *Ladder of Jacob* 2:18 contains a non-Slavonic word *Chavod*.²³³ The translator of the text, Horace Lunt, argues that this Slavonic word might represent the transliterated Hebrew term *Kavod*.²³⁴

Finally, the sixth point is that the passage explicitly identifies the fiery Face with God's glory. Thus, from *Ladder of Jacob* 2:15, one learns that "before the face of your glory the six-winged seraphim are afraid."

The apparent similarities between the two Slavonic accounts indicate that the *Ladder of Jacob*, as well as *2 Enoch*, seem to represent a single tradition in which the fiery Face is associated with the *Kavod*.

Additional evidence to support the view that the fiery Face on the ladder in the *Ladder of Jacob* represents God's *Kavod* can be found in the targumic accounts of Jacob's story. *Targ. Ps.-J.* and *Targum Onqelos* both provide numerous references to the Glory of the Lord in their description of Jacob's vision of the ladder. Thus, *Targ. Ps.-J.* to Genesis 28:13–17 reads:

> And, behold, the Glory of the Lord (יקרא דה) stood beside him and said to him, "I am the Lord, the God of your father Abraham and the God of Isaac. The land on which you are lying I will give

to you and to your children" . . . And Jacob awoke from his sleep and said, "In truth the Glory of the Shekinah (יקר שכינתא) of the Lord dwells in this place, and I did not know it." He was afraid and said, "How awesome and glorious is this place! This is not a profane place, but a sanctuary to the name of the Lord; and this is (a place) suitable for prayer, corresponding to the gate of heaven, founded beneath the Throne of Glory (כורסי יקרא)."[235]

Targ. Onq.[236] to Genesis 28:13–16 also reflects the same tradition, which depicts Jacob's encounter as the vision of the divine Glory. In both targumic accounts, the deity's Glory seems topologically located in the place that, in the *Ladder of Jacob*, is occupied by the Face.

Heavenly Counterpart Traditions

Scholars have previously noted that in the *Ladder of Jacob* the fiery Face not only embodies God's Glory but also seems to represent the heavenly counterpart of Jacob.[237] Yet, it also has been noted that the heavenly counterpart traditions in the *Ladder* appear to be garbled by the text's long transmission in multiple ideological and linguistic milieus.[238] The reconstruction of these traditions in the *Ladder of Jacob* requires considerable effort. In their tentative reconstructions, most studies, including ours, must therefore heavily rely on the help of later heavenly counterpart traditions concerning Jacob reflected in targumic, talmudic, and midrashic accounts.[239]

One of the scholars whose studies probably contributed most to the recovery of the heavenly counterpart traditions in the *Ladder of Jacob* is James Kugel. While reflecting on the terminological peculiarities found in the first chapter of the text, he argued that the authors of the text were cognizant of the tradition of Jacob's איקונין installed in heaven. Kugel draws attention to a comment made by a translator of the text, Horace Lunt, who, while speculating about the original language of the text, noted that the word used in the *Ladder* to designate the great "bust" on the ladder is somewhat unusual. Lunt commented that "no other Slavonic text has *lice*, 'face,' used to mean 'statue' or 'bust' (1:5 etc.), and there is no Semitic parallel."[240] Yet, Kugel proposed that such a Semitic parallel might indeed exist. In his opinion, such a term is the Greek loan word into Mishnaic Hebrew—איקונין, which in some rabbinic texts did come to mean "face."[241] Kugel noted that the basic meaning of איקונין as "portrait" or "bust"[242] is preserved in a number of rabbinic usages, including, prominently, in the expression the *'iqonin shel 'aviv* ("His Father's Countenance").[243] In view of these connections, Kugel argued that "there is little doubt that our pseudepigraphon, in seeking to 'translate' the biblical phrase 'his/its head reached to Heaven,' reworded it in Mishnaic Hebrew as 'his [Jacob's] *iqonin* reached Heaven,' and this in turn gave rise to the presence of a heavenly bust or portrait of Jacob on the divine throne."[244]

Jarl Fossum also affirms[245] the presence of the *iqonin* tradition in the *Ladder* by arguing that "in the fiery bust of the terrifying man we are probably correct to see the heavenly 'image' of Jacob."[246] Christfried Böttrich also recently cautiously supported the existence of the doppelganger traditions in the Slavonic pseudepigraphon by arguing that "such an approach to the *Ladder of Jacob* via the idea of a heavenly counterpart opens a further door into Rabbinic Judaism."[247] He brings attention to another decisive detail that might point to the role of the fiery face as Jacob's heavenly identity—namely, to an accentuated distance between this mysterious face and the deity. Reflecting on this feature, Böttrich notes that in the *Ladder* "God is standing 'above its highest face' and seems to speak in hiding from behind it, so that the fiery face does appear only as a divine representation of God himself."[248]

Another important feature of the text supporting the possibility that the fiery face might indeed represent Jacob's heavenly image, his *iqonin*, is the presence of the motif of the hostility of the ascending and descending angels—the theme, which, as we already have learned above, often accompanied the *tselem* traditions in rabbinic accounts concerning Jacob. This theme of angelic hostility unfolds in chapter 5, where the *angelus interpres* explains the seer's vision. Thus, in the fifth chapter of the *Ladder*, the interpreting angel reveals to the patriarch the following meaning of the ladder:

> Thus he [*angelus interpres*] said to me [Jacob]: "You have seen a ladder with twelve steps, each step having two human faces which kept changing their appearance. The ladder is this age, and the twelve steps are the periods of this age. But the twenty-four faces are the kings of the ungodly nations of this age. Under these kings the children of your children and the generations of your sons will be interrogated. These will rise up against the iniquity of your grandsons. And this place will be made desolate by the four ascents . . . through the sins of your grandsons. And around the property of your forefathers a palace will be built, a temple in the name of your God and of (the God) of your fathers, and in the provocations of your children it will become deserted by the four ascents of this age. For you saw the first four busts which were striking against the steps . . . angels ascending and descending, and the busts amid the steps. The Most High will raise up kings from the grandsons of your brother Esau,

and they will receive all the nobles of the tribes of the earth who will have maltreated your seed."²⁴⁹

Here the twelve steps of the ladder represent the twelve periods of "this age," while twenty four "minor" faces embody the twenty-four kings of the ungodly nations. Ascending and descending angels on the ladder are envisioned as the guardian angels belonging to the nations hostile to Jacob and his descendants. The angelic locomotion or "ascents" appear to be construed in the passage as the arrogations against Israel. It has been previously noticed that this historic revelation is influenced by the fourfold scheme of the antagonistic empires reflected in the Book of Daniel through a reference to the "four ascents" and also through the peculiar features of the Danielic empires and specifically the last of the four kingdoms, Rome, represented by Esau.²⁵⁰

Although the description found in the *Ladder* is garbled by the text's long journey in various ideological milieus, a clearer presentation of the same motif can be found in several rabbinic accounts. Kugel notes that several rabbinic passages dealing with Jacob's vision of the ladder attest to the similar motif of the ascending and descending angels as the hostile nations.²⁵¹ Thus, for example, *Lev. Rab.* 29:2 offers the following description:

> R. Nahman opened his discourse with the text, Therefore fear not, O Jacob My servant (Jer 30:10). This speaks of Jacob himself, of whom it is written, And he dreamed, and behold, a ladder set up on the earth . . . and behold the angels of God ascending and descending on it (Gen 28:12). These angels, explained R. Samuel b. Nahman, were the guardian Princes of the nations of the world. For R. Samuel b. Nahman said: This verse teaches us that the Holy One, blessed be He, showed our father Jacob the Prince of Babylon ascending seventy rungs of the ladder, the Prince of Media fifty-two rungs, the Prince of Greece one hundred and eighty, while the Prince of Edom ascended till Jacob did not know how many rungs. Thereupon our father Jacob was afraid. He thought: Is it possible that this one will never be brought down? Said the Holy One, blessed be He, to him: Fear not, O Jacob My servant. Even if he ascend and sit down by Me, I will bring him down from there! Hence it is written, Though you make your nest as high as the eagle, and though you set it among the stars, I will bring you down from there. R. Berekiah and R. Helbo, and R. Simeon b. Yohai in the name of R. Meir said: It teaches that the Holy One, blessed be He, showed Jacob the Prince of Babylon ascending and descending, of Media ascending and descending,

of Greece ascending and descending, and of Edom ascending and descending.[252]

A similar understanding of the descending and ascending angels as political entities that are hostile to Israel is found in *Midrash on Psalms* 78:6: "R. Berechiah, R. Levi, and R. Simeon ben Jose taught in the name of R. Meir that the Holy One, blessed be He, let Jacob see a ladder upon which Babylon climbed up seventy rungs and came down, Media climbed up fifty-two rungs and came down, Greece climbed up a hundred and eighty rungs and came down. But when Edom climbed higher than these, Jacob saw and was afraid. The Holy One, blessed be He, said to him, Therefore fear not, O Jacob My servant (Jer 30:10). Even as the former fell, so will the latter fall."[253]

In these passages, the similarities with the Danielic account are even more apparent than in the *Ladder* since the familiar fourfold structure is now represented by Babylon, Media, Greece, and Edom—the empires that are often associated in the history of interpretation with the four beasts of Daniel 7.[254] Kugel notes that in these materials, like in the *Ladder of Jacob*, "the four beasts [of Daniel's vision] are transformed into 'angels of God' said to go up and down Jacob's ladder."[255]

This peculiar theme of the hostile angels on the ladder that resist Jacob and his progeny by their ascents and descents might provide additional evidence that the authors of the *Ladder* were cognizant of the motif of angelic opposition that performs such a pivotal role in the doppelganger lore. It is also important that the heavenly counterpart imagery in the *Ladder of Jacob* becomes applied to the antagonistic figures when the infamous empires are represented by their angelic "patrons." We already encountered similar conceptual constellations in the Book of Daniel where the heavenly counterpart in the form of the Son of Man is juxtaposed with the upper identities of the hostile nations.

Sariel

There are also some distinctive angelological developments in the *Ladder of Jacob* that are reminiscent of previously explored heavenly counterparts traditions found in the Enochic accounts. One such feature that links Jacob's account in the *Ladder* with the Enochic motifs reflected in *1 Enoch* 71 and *2 Enoch* 22 is a reference to the angel Sariel, who is also known in several Jewish texts as Phanuel and Uriel.[256]

As we recall in *2 Enoch*, Vereveil (Uriel) plays a crucial role in the adept's initiation into his heavenly identity. In *1 Enoch* 71, the same angelic servant, now under the name Phanuel, is also markedly present during the seer's acquisition of his upper Self. Although the *Ladder of Jacob* does not directly refer to the angel named Uriel or Phanuel, it uses another of his names, Sariel, in reference to the angelic being who interprets Jacob's dream and announces to him his new angelic status, depicted symbolically in the text as the changing of the patriarch's name to Israel.

The second chapter of the *Ladder* portrays Jacob asking God in prayer for help in interpreting the dream. The following chapter 3 then relates that God responds to Jacob's prayer by commanding Sariel, "the leader of those who give joy," to make Jacob understand the meaning of the dream. The text further depicts the angelophany of Sariel who comes to the patriarch to inform him about his new angelic name and status.

This reference to Sariel-Uriel-Phanuel as the angel who instructs/wrestles with Jacob and announces to him his new angelic name is documented in several other sources, including *Targ. Neof.* and the *Prayer of Joseph*. In the *Prayer of Joseph*, Jacob attests that "Uriel, the angel of God, came forth and said that 'I [Jacob-Israel] had descended to earth and I had tabernacled among men and that I had been called by the name of Jacob.' He envied me and fought with me and wrestled with me."[257] In targumic and rabbinic accounts, Sariel/Uriel is also depicted as the angel who wrestled with Jacob and announced to him his new angelic name. Thus, *Targ. Neof.* to Genesis 32:25–31 preserves the following tradition:

> And Jacob was left alone; and the angel Sariel (שריאל) wrestled with him in the appearance of a man and he embraced him until the time the dawn arose. When he saw that he could not prevail against him, he touched the hollow of his thigh and the hollow of Jacob's thigh became benumbed in his wrestling with him. And he said: "Let me go because the rise of the dawn has arrived, and because the time of the angels on high to praise has arrived, and I am a chief of those who praise (ואנא ריש למשבחיא)." And he said: "I will not let you go unless you bless me." And he said to him: "What is your name?" And he said: "Jacob." And he said: "Your name shall no longer be called Jacob but Israel, because you have claimed superiority with angels from before the Lord and with men and you have prevailed against them." And Jacob asked and said: "Tell me your name I pray"; and he said: "Why, now, do you ask my name?" And he blessed him there. And Jacob called the name of the place Peniel (פניאל) because: "I have seen *angels from before the Lord face to face* and my life has been spared."[258]

Scholars have previously noted that "in the circles represented by the *Similitudes of Enoch*, Qumran and the *Neofiti* variety of the Palestinian Targum, the angelic adversary of Jacob was recognized as one of the four celestial princes and called alternatively Sariel or Phanuel."[259] It appears that the *Ladder of Jacob* also bears witness to the same conceptual trend.

In *Targ. Neof.* and *Frag. Targ.*[260] to Genesis 32:27, Sariel is defined as "the chief of those who give praise" (ריש למשבחאי). The *Ladder of Jacob* seems to allude to this title. In the *Ladder of Jacob* 3:2, Sariel is described as "*stareishino uslazhdaemych*,"[261] which can be translated as "the chief of those who give joy."[262]

It is possible that in the *Ladder of Jacob*, Uriel-Sariel-Phanuel imagery is influenced by the Enochic tradition even more extensively than in the Targums because in the *Ladder*, the motif of wrestling is completely absent and is substituted by the depiction of Sariel as the interpreter of dreams. It seems that Sariel/Uriel in the *Ladder* assumes the traditional "Enochic" functions of *angelus interpres*.

Princes of the Face

In the *Ladder of Jacob* and the *Prayer of Joseph*, Jacob's identification with his heavenly counterpart, the angel Israel, involves the initiatory encounter with the angel Sariel/Uriel, who in other texts is also known as Phanuel, the angel of the divine Presence or the Face. The same state of events is observable in Enochic materials where Uriel (Vereveil) serves as a principal heavenly guide to another prominent visionary who has also acquired knowledge about his own heavenly counterpart—namely, Enoch-Metatron. As has been already demonstrated, in both traditions, Uriel-Sariel-Phanuel appears as the guide who assists the visionaries in acquiring or identifying with their new celestial identities. Often in the course of these interactions, the human seers are endowed with the roles and functions of these angelic servants of the divine Presence.

In view of these developments, it is possible that the process of the seer's unification with the heavenly counterpart might be reflected in the initiatory procedure of becoming a *Sar ha-Panim*, one of the angelic Princes of the divine Face or Presence, a prominent celestial office, which is often described in detail in various apocalyptic and Merkavah accounts.

The installation of a visionary as *Sar ha-Panim* seems to correlate with the procedure of identifying a visionary with his or her heavenly counterpart. In *2 Enoch* 22:6–10, Enoch's initiation into one of the Princes of the Presence takes place in front of the fiery Face of the Lord. This encounter transforms Enoch into a glorious being. It is noteworthy that after this procedure Enoch observes that he had "become like one of the glorious ones," and "there was no observable difference."²⁶³ The last phrase describes Enoch's transition to his new identity as "one of the glorious ones." This role might refer to his angelic counterpart. It also indicates that Enoch's earthly appearance/face has been radically altered and that the visionary has now acquired a new "face" that mirrors or doubles the divine Visage.²⁶⁴ There is no doubt that one of the features that unifies both "faces" is their luminosity.

As we already learned in this study, *2 Enoch*'s narrative gives evidence that Enoch's face acquired the same qualities of luminosity as the Face of God. In *2 Enoch* 37, the deity calls one of his angels to chill the face of Enoch before his return to earth. The angel, who "appeared frigid," then chilled Enoch's face with his icy hands. Immediately after this procedure, the Lord tells Enoch that if his face had not been chilled in such a way, no human being would be able to look at his face. This chilling procedure indicates that Enoch's metamorphosis near the Face into the *Sar ha-Panim* involves the transformation of the visionary's face into a fiery, perilous entity that now resembles the *Kavod*. We can find a detailed description of this process in another "Enochic" account, *Sefer Hekhalot*—a text already analyzed in our study—that describes the transformation of Enoch-Metatron, the Prince of the divine Presence, into a fiery creature.

It is possible that the reference to the heavenly counterpart of Jacob in the form of his image (engraved) on the Throne of Glory also implies that the heavenly Jacob became one of the servants of the divine Face. This possibility is already hinted at in the biblical account where Jacob is highlighted as one who saw God face-to-face.²⁶⁵ Moreover, in some of Jacob's traditions, he is directly described (in a manner similar to Enoch-Metatron) as the Prince of the divine Face. We learn about this title from the *Prayer of Joseph* 8,²⁶⁶ where Jacob-Israel himself reveals his status as the *Sar*²⁶⁷ *ha-Panim*, proclaiming that he is "the first minister before the Face of God."²⁶⁸

It is also not coincidental that the initiation of Jacob into becoming a celestial being involves another servant of the Face, the angel Sariel whose other name, Phanuel,²⁶⁹ reflects his close proximity to the Face of God. As has been mentioned previously, this initiatory pattern is already observable in the Enochic tradition, where Sariel-Uriel-Phanuel (along with another angel of the Presence, Michael)²⁷⁰ actively participates in the initiation of another prominent servant of the divine Face, Enoch-Metatron.

However, Jacob's identification with a *Sar ha-Panim* seems to be missing one detail that constitutes a distinct feature of the descriptions of visionaries initiated into this office, which is the luminous metamorphosis of an adept's face and body. The *Ladder of Jacob* and the *Prayer of Joseph*, as well as the biblical version of Jacob's vision, are silent about any transformation of Jacob's body and his face. This tradition, however, can be found in another prominent account connected with the Jacob story—namely, *Jos. Asen.*²⁷¹ In this pseudepigraphon, the eyes of Jacob, similar to the eyes of the transformed Enoch-Metatron, are emitting flashes of lighting.

The Son of Man as the Path and the Vessel of the Heavenly Counterparts?

It has been already noted in our study that in the rabbinic materials angels are often depicted as wandering between the two identities of Jacob, heavenly and earthly, thus forming an angelic ladder that links both of his selves. Moreover, in some of these accounts, Jacob himself appears to be envisioned as the ladder that links his earthly and celestial identities. One such interpretation we already encountered is in *Gen. Rab.* 68:12, where one rabbinic authority argued that the angels were ascending and descending on the ladder (בסולם), while the other claimed that they were ascending and descending on Jacob (ביעקב).[272]

Commenting on this rabbinic passage, Jonathan Smith suggests that "R. Yannai's interpretation of בו as ביעקב implies mystical growth of Jacob to cosmic size,[273] a theme present in the Fourth Gospel's allusion to the ladder vision[274] . . . and, perhaps, in the figure of Metatron[275] as the personified ladder of Jacob in late mystical literature."[276]

This tradition, where the seer himself represents the ladder, opens an entirely new chapter in the heavenly counterpart lore and must be explored closely in our study.

Although it is notoriously difficult to date traditions found in rabbinic materials, including the passage from *Gen. Rab.* 68, an additional proof for the antiquity of the motif of Jacob as the cosmic ladder can be found in the Gospel of John, which places this conceptual development no later than the end of the first century—beginning of the second century CE.

It is important for our study that the motif of Jacob's angelic ladder in John 1:51 occurs in the midst of the Son of Man tradition,[277] which, as we already know, represents the prominent mediatorial stream associated with the doppelganger lore in the Jewish pseudepigrapha. The Gospel of John 1:51 reports the following striking utterance of Jesus: "And he [Jesus] said to him, 'Very truly, I tell you, you will see heaven opened and the angels of God ascending and descending upon the Son of Man.'"

In this biblical verse, two portentous conceptual streams dealing with the heavenly counterpart lore, one connected with Jacob traditions and the other tied to the Son of Man traditions, appear to be intertwined, leading the doppelganger speculations into a new symbolic dimension. Even a brief look at the peculiar mold of the Son of Man tradition found in these verses reveals remarkable allusions to the heavenly counterpart currents.

The first significant detail that links John's verses with those developments already explored in this study, specifically connected with the Son of Man in the *Book of the Similitudes*, is a postulated distance between the identity of the protagonist of the story (Jesus) and his heavenly alter ego—the Son of Man figure. Such distance is hinted through Jesus' utterance about the angelic processions. Thus he promises to the disciples not that the angels will be ascending and descending *upon him*, but rather saying that they will be ascending and descending *upon the Son of Man* (ἐπὶ τὸν υἱὸν τοῦ ἀνθρώπου). Such distancing, which might presume that the Son of Man represents the heavenly identity of Jesus,[278] is also discernable in some other Son of Man sayings found in the canonical Gospels where Jesus speaks about the Son of Man in third person.[279] This phenomenon has never been sufficiently explored in its connection with the heavenly counterpart imagery, including the Son of Man tradition found in the *Book of the Similitudes* where the seer, while narrating about the Son of Man's mighty deeds in the early chapters of the text, at its final chapter became suddenly identified with this exalted figure.[280]

The second eye-catching feature is the polemical flavor that overshadows the employment of the Son of Man tradition in the first chapter of John's gospel. It is possible that the Son of Man here is envisioned as a mediator superior to the exalted Jacob. This polemical attitude against Jacob and his exalted status can be detected in other parts of the Gospel as well,[281] including the fourth chapter of the text where the water from Jacob's well is compared to the superior living water of Jesus.[282]

Moreover, such conceptual perspective in which the Son of Man serves as a polemical rival to an exalted patriarch is well known in Second Temple Jewish lore. Thus, it is possible that even the very first appearance of the Son of Man figure in the Book of Daniel was intended to serve as the polemical counterpart to the figure of the exalted Enoch.[283] In the first chapter of the fourth gospel, the Son of Man's exalted status also appears to be overshadowed by the memory of another great patriarchal figure, this time Jacob.

Indeed, it has been ascertained by a large number of ancient[284] and modern interpreters[285] that the passage about the angels ascending and descending on the Son of Man found in John 1:51 is connected with the Jacobite traditions from Genesis 28:12. Reflecting on these influences, Jerome Neyrey noted that "in 1:51, explicit allusion is made to Jacob's theophany in Gen 28:12. Not just Nathanael, but all the disciples are promised a vision like Jacob's vision. Indeed, they are like Jacob, not in guilelessness or cunning, but in virtue of a gratuitous promise made by Jesus that they would see a comparable heavenly vision, a theophany."[286]

Affirming the influences of the Jacob traditions, Neyrey at the same time draws attention to some differences between the biblical account of Jacob's vision and the passage from the Gospel of John. He notes that "in Gen 28:12 three statements are made: (1) a ladder on earth reaches to heaven; (2) angels ascend and descend; and (3) the Lord stands on it and reveals himself. In John 1:51, however, (1) the heavens are opened, but there is no mention of a ladder linking heaven and earth; (2) angels ascend and descend, not on the ladder but on the Son of Man; and (3) he corresponds to the Lord of the theophany."[287]

Summarizing the differences with the Jacob traditions, Neyrey proposes that in John 1:51 "Jesus is apparently not being compared with Jacob. . . . He is not seeing a vision; he is offering one. Rather, the disciples are cast in the role of Jacob, for they will see a heavenly vision just as Jacob did . . . the text apparently sees the disciples of Jesus in the position of Jacob, promising them that they will see a vision just as Jacob did."[288]

One should note that Neyrey's suggestions are valid only if John's account is compared with the biblical version of Jacob's vision, since in some rabbinic accounts Jacob himself is envisioned as the cosmic ladder and the heavenly image and thus becomes the object of the vision. Moreover, in the fourth gospel, Jesus is seen not only offering the vision of the ladder but also reporting to the disciples about its peculiar content.

Nevertheless, Neyrey's observations are important for our study since they allow us again to draw attention to the multidimensional nature of the visionary's situation where the seer is simultaneously able to report a vision and to act in that vision as the crucial mediator. Such a duality in the functions of the seer/the actor have already been registered in our study in respect to Enoch's visionary reports in the *Book of the Watchers* and the *Book of the Similitudes*. The traditions found in the *Book of the Similitudes* where the seer reports about the Son of Man and then becomes identified with this figure in this respect are especially weighty.

Another allegedly "innovative" aspect of the Johannine passage noticed by Neyrey is that in John 1:51 angels ascend and descend not on the ladder but on the Son of Man. Yet, likewise, this motif can be considered as "novel" only in comparison with the biblical rendering of the vision, since as we already learned, the possibility that the angels climbed not on the ladder but instead on the cosmic extent of a mediator is hinted in *Gen. Rab.* 68:12 and possibly in some other accounts.[289] Although the rabbinic testimonies are much later than the Gospel of John, in view of the recognized formative influences of Jacob's conceptual currents, it is most likely that they entered our Gospel from Jewish lore about the patriarch. Neyrey himself later in his study acknowledges the formative influence of such traditions on the Johannine passage by saying that

> in the *Midrash Rabbah* we find several instances of a reading of Gen 28:12 which interpret the vision in an unusual way. The MT says

that when the ladder was set up, the angels ascended and descended "on it" (in) which phrase was interpreted in the midrash to say that the angels ascended/descended "on him," Jacob. This midrash has often been cited apropos of John 1:51, for John says that the angels ascend/descend "on the Son of Man" rather than on a ladder. Following this hint, one would be led to say that Jesus is like Jacob: the angels will ascend and descend on him, just as they did on Jacob.[290]

James Kugel also sees the formative influences of the Jewish traditions as similar to the ones found in *Gen. Rab.* 68:12 on John 1:51. He argues that the expression about the ascending and descending on the Son of Man "belongs to the exegetical school represented by R. Yannai . . . that is, the one that takes, בו in the Genesis text to mean not 'on the ladder' but 'for Jacob.' So here too, בו is being taken as referring to a person, namely, 'upon the Son of Man.' "[291] In relation to the בו terminology, Kugel further observes that although the Gospel of John was presumably composed in Greek, this particular play on words could not work in Greek, since the word for ladder in the Greek Bible is feminine and the only alternative to "on it" would thus be "for her."[292]

As a result of recognizing the formative value of the aforementioned Jacob traditions, a large number of Johannine scholars now accept the hypothesis that in John 1:51 the Son of Man becomes envisioned as the cosmic ladder that links heavenly and earthly realities.[293] Tracing the roots of this hypothesis in the scholarly literature, Raymond Brown notes that "with variations, a theory like this is proposed by Odeberg,[294] Bultmann, Lightfoot,[295] and others."[296] This proposition that came from the greatest minds of twentieth-century biblical scholarship continues to exercise its influence until the present time. Neyrey affirms this scholarly consensus by saying that "commentators who take seriously the allusion to Gen 28:12 suggest that the function of the vision in John is to be understood in terms of some sort of mediation or communion between heaven and earth. . . . According to proponents of these ideas, Jesus is the gate of heaven, the ladder, the mediator."[297]

It should be noted that in attempts to formulate the hypothesis about the Son of Man as the cosmic ladder various scholars too often relied solely on the evidence attested in John 1:51, while the larger context of the passage often has been neglected by scholars. Yet, it appears that the function of Christ as the link between upper and lower realms is reaffirmed by other traditions found in the first chapter of the Gospel through the distinctive arboreal metaphors that might intend to portray the protagonist as the cosmic tree that links upper and lower worlds. We should now explore this arboreal imagery more closely.

The Son of Man as the Arboreal Ladder?

As one remembers, in the verses preceding John 1:51, one curious arboreal metaphor is found. Thus, Gospel of John 1:45–50 reads:

> Philip found Nathanael and said to him, "We have found him about whom Moses in the law and also the prophets wrote, Jesus son of Joseph from Nazareth." Nathanael said to him, "Can anything good come out of Nazareth?" Philip said to him, "Come and see." When Jesus saw Nathanael coming toward him, he said of him, "Here is truly an Israelite in whom there is no deceit!" Nathanael asked him, "Where did you get to know me?" Jesus answered, "I saw you under the fig tree before Philip called you." Nathanael replied, "Rabbi, you are the Son of God! You are the King of Israel!" Jesus answered, "Do you believe because I told you that I saw you under the fig tree? You will see greater things than these."

These verses depict one of the apostles, Nathaniel, under the fig tree. Students of the fourth gospel long have been puzzled by this enigmatic arboreal motif and its possible theological significance.[298] Many hypotheses have been proposed.[299] According to one of them, the symbolism of the fig tree can be tied with the imagery of the Tree of the Knowledge of Good and Evil.[300]

Indeed, several Jewish and Christian sources attempted to identify the Tree of the Knowledge as the fig tree. In relation to this connection, Louis Ginzberg noted that "the fig owes its distinction to the incident that the first pair took hold of the fig leaves after the fall, and this identification is not only found in rabbinic sources, but also in the *Apocalypse of Moses* and in Tertullian."[301]

In the elaboration of the protoplasts' story found in the Greek version of the *Primary Adam Books* 20:4–5, the identification of the Tree of the Knowledge of Good and Evil with the fig tree comes from Eve's lips when the first woman acknowledges that the fig leaves with which she covered her nakedness came from the infamous tree: "And I began to seek, in my nakedness, in my part for leaves to hide my shame, but I found none, for, as soon as I had eaten, the leaves showered down from all the trees in my part, except the fig-tree alone. I took leaves from it and made for myself a girdle [and it was from the same plant of which I had eaten]."[302]

Later patristic and rabbinic sources reaffirm such connection. Thus, for example, Tertullian in *Adversus Marcionem* 2.2 links the arboreal symbol of corruption with the fig tree.[303] Likewise, *Gen. Rab*. 19:6 connects the leaves of the fig tree with the scandalous plant: "And they sewed the leaves of the fig together.

R. Simeon b. Yohai said; That is the leaf which brought the occasion for death—into the world. R. Isaac said: Thou hast acted sinfully: then take thread and sew!"[304]

This motif was not forgotten in later mystical lore. Thus, the *Book of Zohar* I.36b similarly interprets the fig tree as the Tree of the Knowledge of Good and Evil from which the first human couple ate: "And they sewed fig leaves. They strove to cover themselves with the (delusive) images from the tree of which they had eaten, the so-called 'leaves of the tree.' And they made themselves girdles. R. Jose said: 'When they obtained knowledge of this world and attached themselves to it, they observed that it was governed by those "leaves of the tree." They therefore sought in them a stronghold in this world, and so made themselves acquainted with all kinds of magical arts, in order to gird themselves with weapons of those leaves of the tree, for the purpose of self-protection.' "[305]

Another Zoharic passage again underlines such a connection by linking the fig leaves that covered the nakedness of the first humans with the Tree of the Knowledge by interpreting the phrase "sewing fig leaves" as a corruption of humanity with forbidden knowledge.[306]

These testimonies are vital for our study. If the fig tree found in the first chapter of the fourth gospel indeed represents an allusion to the ill-famed paradisal plant, it is possible that the figure of Nathaniel, associated in the gospel's account with this arboreal symbol, might be also overlaid with similar protological allusions. It is therefore possible that Nathaniel can be identified here with the protoplast, who once was corrupted under the infamous tree. If so, could the promise of even greater vision—the vision of angels ascending and descending on the Son of Man—serve here as an allusion to the paradisal counterpart of the ominous Tree of Corruption, namely, the Tree of Life?[307] In this respect, it is noteworthy that the Tree of Life is often portrayed in Jewish lore as an eschatological counterpart that is predestined to restore the fallen nature of humankind to its original prelapsarian condition, which was lost through the Tree of the Knowledge. Several early Jewish apocalyptic accounts appear to entertain such an idea. Thus, for example, in *2 Enoch*, an anointing of the seventh antediluvian patriarch with shining oil or the dew of resurrection from the Tree of Life restores Enoch to the original luminous condition of the protoplast. The same motif is invoked in the *Primary Adam Books* where Eve and Seth are sent to bring the oil of resurrection from the Tree of Life in order to return the dying Adam to the immortality of prelapsarian humanity. In the aforementioned accounts, anointing with the oil coming from the Tree of Life is often understood as being clothed with the eschatological garment of light. Such a clothing metaphor inversely mirrors the ominous dress of fig leaves that the first couple received in the Paradise after their transgression. Here the garments from two paradisal trees again serve as the counterparts of each other.

Another possible interpretation of Nathaniel's figure, especially in light of the already mentioned polemical proclivities of the chapter, is that he might be envisioned as Jacob. The first significant aspect that points to such a possibility is that he is defined in John 1 as "truly an Israelite in whom there is no deceit" (ἀληθῶς Ἰσραηλίτης ἐν ᾧ δόλος οὐκ ἔστιν). This designation might allude to Jacob's story. As we know, Jacob is depicted in the Bible as a trickster who deceives his older brother Esau and his father, Isaac. Later, after his encounters with God, Jacob's character was transformed and perfected. In light of these biblical traditions, Neyrey argues that Nathaniel "is like Jacob, not the devious character who grabbed his brother's heel at birth and stole his birthright and blessing, but the perfect Jacob, the man of wisdom."[308] Neyrey also brings attention to another important feature by noting that "like Jacob, Nathanael comes 'second,' after the founding apostles; he must labor for his reward."[309]

Another significant detail is the peculiar emphasis on the praxis of seeing, a theme that unfolds in the midst of the interactions between Jesus and Nathaniel where Jesus promises this disciple that he will "see" greater things. In relation to these conceptual developments, Camilla von Heijne notices that "a common contemporary interpretation of the name 'Israel' was 'he who sees God.' "[310]

In light of these traditions, it is possible that Nathaniel indeed might be envisioned in the first chapter of our Gospel as Jacob. If so, is it possible that the fig tree under which Nathaniel-Jacob sleeps in its turn can be interpreted as Jacob's arboreal ladder, which in the polemical context of the Gospel, is understood as an entity inferior to the Son of Man's ladder? Such parallelism, if it is indeed present in the Gospel, might again point to the possible arboreal meaning of the Son of Man's ladder that could be envisioned here as the polemical counterpart to the fig tree.

For our study of ladder symbolism in the Gospel of John and its possible association with arboreal imagery, it is important that in some Jewish accounts divine figures are often envisioned as cosmic trees that link upper and lower realms—the plants that are predestined to generate the dew of resurrection for human beings in the eschatological time. Thus, for example, in *PRE* 34, one learns that the reviving dew, a rabbinic metaphor for the oil of the resurrection, will come at the eschatological time from the head of the Holy One:

> Rabbi Tanchum said: On account of the seed of the earth, when it is commanded, (it) discharges the dew for the resurrection of the dead. From what place does it descend? From the head of the Holy One; for the head of the Holy One, is full of the reviving dew. In the future life, the Holy One will shake His head and cause the

quickening dew to descend, as it is said, "I was asleep, but my heart waked . . . for my head is filled with dew, my locks with the drops of the night" (Cant 5:2).³¹¹

In another prominent compendium of Jewish mystical traditions, this motif about the dew of resurrection coming from the head of God is repeated again.³¹² The *Zohar* I:130b–131a reads: "And at the time when the Holy One will raise the dead to life He will cause dew to descend upon them from His head. By means of that dew all will rise from the dust. . . . For the Tree of Life emanates life unceasingly into the universe."³¹³

This understanding of the deity as the Tree of Life, the cosmic plant that links upper and lower realms,³¹⁴ is not merely a later rabbinic invention but a tradition with ancient roots that can be traced to some Mesopotamian motifs in which the cosmic trees are often associated with divine and royal figures.³¹⁵ These early Mesopotamian traditions played a formative role in shaping the arboreal metaphors found in Ezekiel 31³¹⁶ and Daniel 4³¹⁷ where the royal figures also became associated with the cosmic trees.³¹⁸ Scholars have previously noted that the symbolism of the great tree in Ezekiel 31 seems to draw on the Mesopotamian traditions about the Mēsu-Tree, a cosmic plant envisioned in these religious currents as the building material for the divine statues.³¹⁹ Such an association of the Mēsu-Tree with the body of the divine mediators is important for our study of possible arboreal features of the Son of Man's cosmic extent.³²⁰

It is also important that in some Jewish accounts, the cosmic trees, represented by the divine mediators, are often imagined as the "bridges" or the "paths" between upper and lower realms that provide channels for the transition of the souls between heaven and earth and also serve as the repositories or the storages for these souls. In this context, it is not coincidental that even in the biblical portrayals the cosmic trees are depicted as inhabited with various enigmatic creatures including the "birds of air." This motif of the pteromorphic inhabitants of the cosmic trees is found in aforementioned arboreal depictions in Ezekiel 31³²¹ and Daniel 4.³²² A similar tradition is attested in various versions of the so-called Parable of the Mustard Seed found in the Synoptic Gospels, which draws on the Danielic tree imagery.³²³ It is noteworthy that in the Parable, like in the prophetic accounts, the symbolism of the birds of heaven is also placed in the royal context expressed through the formula "kingdom of God."³²⁴

Gershom Scholem points to the conceptual developments found in later Jewish mysticism, and especially in the *Book of Bahir*, where the cosmic tree or the Tree of Life is understood as a channel responsible for the souls' transition between the upper and lower realms.³²⁵ The *Book of Bahir* offers the following depiction of the Tree of Life:

It is I who have planted this "tree" that the whole world may delight in it and with it I have spanned the All, called it "All," for on it depends the All and from it emanates the All; all things need it and look upon it and yearn for it, and it is from it that all souls fly forth. I was alone when I made it and no angel can raise himself above it and say: I was there before thee, for when I spanned my earth, when I planted and rooted this tree and caused them to take delight in each other [the tree and the earth] and myself delighted in them—who was there with me to whom I would have confided this secret?[326]

Here and in some other passages from the *Bahir*, the Tree of Life represents a column or a pillar that links various realms of the created order allowing for the souls' transitions. These souls are often envisioned as the "fruits" of this cosmic tree. In relation to this imagery, Scholem notes that "the idea that this 'column' reached from earth up to heaven can have two meanings. The column can represent the cosmic Tree of Life that grows from earth up to heaven. . . . The souls of the righteous ascend and descend on it. And just as the cosmic tree was also the tree of souls, from which the souls take flight or on which they appear as the fruits."[327]

Scholem also notes that "a vestige of this idea of the Tree of Life as a cosmic tree that grows between the celestial Garden of Eden and the terrestrial paradise and on which the soul of the righteous people ascend and descend as on a ladder has also been preserved in *Midrash Konen*."[328]

Such an understanding of the cosmic trees as the souls' gathering places or the paths that allow the souls' transition between various realms is decisive for our study especially in light of the aforementioned scholarly hypotheses suggesting that in John 1:51 the Son of Man represents a ladder or a path between the lower and the upper regions. If this mediatorial figure indeed is envisioned in the Johannine passage as such a link between the realms, then the angelic processions could be interpreted as the movements of the righteous souls for whom the Son of Man serves as the gate to heaven.

In this respect, it is intriguing that the concept of gathering the chosen represents a recurring theme of the first chapter of the Gospel of John. This process of eschatological collecting appears to be expressed multiple times in the course of the narrative. Thus, such a theme is already hinted in John 1:11–13, the passage that speaks about the elect group of humans who were able to recognize and accept Christ: "He came to what was his own, and his own people did not accept him. But to all who received him, who believed in his name, he gave power to become children of God, who were born, not of blood or of the will of the flesh or of the will of man, but of God." The motif of the gathering of the elect then becomes the leading theme of the rest of the first chapter, which portrays the process of the disciples' gathering done by Jesus.

In view of these developments, it is possible that the overarching idea of the gathering might reach its conceptual crux in the concluding verse of the chapter that depicts the celestial citizens ascending and descending upon the Son of Man. If it is indeed so, it is possible that the vision of the angels ascending and descending on the Son of Man might also pertain to this recurring theme of the eschatological gathering into the Son of Man.

Eschatological Gathering of the Heavenly Counterparts into the Mediator

This concept of the mediator who is envisioned as the "path," the "ladder," or the "vessel" appears not to be unique to the Gospel of John and can be found in some early Jewish pseudepigraphical materials.

The motif of "gathering" into the mediator, who is also envisioned as the heavenly counterpart, can be found in chapter 15 of *Jos. Asen.*, the text that will be explored in depth later in our study. For now, we must draw our attention to a captivating passage from this work, relevant for our current investigation. The passage talks about Aseneth's doppelganger, a mediatorial figure named Metanoia, who is also designated in the text as the "City of Refuge." Such labelling of the mediator as the heavenly metropolis or a celestial gathering place for the elect is relevant for our study since it might represent a conceptual development similar to the Son of Man role found in the first chapter of the Gospel of John. In *Jos. Asen.* 15:7, the seer's celestial guide, the Anthropos, provides the following details about this enigmatic mediatorial entity:

> And your name shall no longer be called Aseneth, but your name shall be City of Refuge, because in you many nations will take refuge with the Lord God, the Most High, and under your wings many peoples trusting in the Lord God will be sheltered, and behind your walls will be guarded those who attach themselves to the Most High God in the name of Repentance. For Repentance—is in the heavens, an exceedingly beautiful and good daughter of the Most High. And she herself entreats the Most High God for you at all times and for all who repent in the name of the Most High God, because he is (the) father of Repentance. And she herself is guardian of all virgins, and loves you very much, and is beseeching the Most High for you at all times and for all who repent she prepared a place of rest in the heavens.[329]

Several features of Metanoia, or the City of Refuge, are noteworthy. First, this entity, similar to the Son of Man figure in John 1:51, is understood as the heavenly counterpart of a human figure. Second, she appears to be envisioned as a heavenly "vessel," whose function is to incorporate and protect the chosen remnant—namely, "those who attach themselves to the Most High God." It appears that in this capacity her role is not limited solely to the function of being Aseneth's celestial alter ego but might incorporate the heavenly identities of other righteous human beings, the role hinted in her peculiar designation as "the guardian of all virgins." Additional proof for Metanoia's function as the vessel for heavenly selves might be implied in her designation as the one who prepares for the repentant humans "a place of rest in the heavens."[330]

Another specimen of this type of tradition in which a personified mediator is understood as the gathering place or the vessel of the adepts' heavenly selves can be found in *2 Enoch* 65 where the souls of the elect are depicted as being gathered at the end of time into a single luminous entity—the eschatological aeon of the righteous.[331] It is noteworthy that the final aeon in the Slavonic apocalypse is envisioned not merely as an unanimated entity—a period or an age—but rather as a mediatorial figure. This understanding of the aeons as personified mediators in *2 Enoch* is hinted already in the narrative about the beginning of creation in chapters 24–25 where such aeons, bearing the distinctive names Adoil and Aruchas, are portrayed as anthropomorphic entities.[332] The second salient detail that points to the idea that the last aeon is envisioned as the personified mediator is the fact that the final consummation of all creation into a single aeon inversely mirrors a protological disintegration of Adoil, who once gave birth to the multiplicity of the created forms.[333] It appears that the righteous, here, are understood as gatherers of the divine light, dispersed during the initial disintegration of Adoil. They are collectors who will assemble the primordial light into a new eschatological vessel.[334]

These traditions about the adept's heavenly counterparts, gathered into personified mediatorial figures, often evoke already familiar concepts of the upper identities as the spirits. Thus, Roelof van der Broek draws attention to the striking pneumatological concepts that are circulated among the Messalians and the Cathars, but in his opinion based on early Jewish and Christian concepts, where the Holy Spirit becomes envisioned as the sum of all individual heavenly spirits—the upper counterpart of the human beings. Van der Broek notes that

> this whole complex of ideas about a heavenly counterpart of man with whom the soul had been united before the Fall and the identification of this spiritual image with the guardian angel and with the Holy Spirit, which makes this Spirit the collective of all spirits,

found acceptance among the Messalians, and from them it must have come to the West. For it is only among the Cathars that we find this same combination of ideas about the Spirit and the soul: the collective notion of the Holy Spirit as the sum of all individual heavenly spirits, which are also seen as the custodians of the human souls to which they originally belonged, and the idea that only he who has received the baptism of the Spirit that is to say, he whose soul is reunited with its heavenly spirit can return to the realm of light.[335]

Another important testimony to this understanding of the eschatological mediator as the path and the vessel of the adepts' heavenly counterparts is the concept of the so-called Last Statue found in the Manichaean materials. Thus, the *Kephalaia of the Teacher* relates that in the eschatological time the righteous remnant will be "sculpted" into the anthropomorphic mediatorial entity[336] named the Last Statue: "Entire universe in it today. Yet, at the end, in the dissolution of the universe, this very counsel of life will gather itself in and sculpt its soul in the Last Statue. Its net is its Living Spirit, because with its Spirit it can hunt after the light and the life that is in all things; and build it upon its body."[337] The main purpose of this eschatological gathering, like in *2 Enoch*, is the unification of the primordial light,[338] gathered by the efforts of the righteous who are predestined to be collected together in a single eschatological entity: "Again, when the sun sinks from the universe and sets, and all people go in to their hiding places and houses and conceal themselves; this also pertains to the mystery of the end, as it presages the consummation of the universe. For, when all the light will be purified and redeemed in the universe at the last, the collector of all things, the Last Statue, will gather in and sculpt itself. It is the last hour of the day, the time when the Last Statue will go up to the aeon of light. (*Keph.* 165)."[339]

It also appears that the Last Statue is sometimes understood as a final gathering point of the righteous souls. Yet, the wicked souls will be banned from this eschatological summit. Thus, *Keph.* 149–150 hints at this process of the banishment of the wicked from the Last Statue:

> The fourth time when they weep is when the Statue will be taken up on the last day, and they will weep for the souls of the liars and blasphemers; for they may give . . . because their limbs have been severed . . . of the darkness. And also those souls, when the Statue will go up and they are left alone, they will weep in that they will remain behind in affliction forever. For they will be cut off and separated

from the Last Statue. And it is a necessity to take these souls who are ready for loss as retribution for the deeds that they have done. They go into this darkness and are bound with the darkness; just as they desired it and loved it, and placed their treasure with it. At that very moment, when the Last Statue rises up, they will weep. And they will scream out loud because they will be severed from the company of this great Statue. And they remain behind forever. This great weeping is terrible, it occurs in front of the souls. . . .[340]

It is also noteworthy that in the concept of the Last Statue one can see familiar parallelism to protological and eschatological symbolism—the imagery discernable also in *2 Enoch* and in the first chapter of the Gospel of John: "From when the First Man went down to the contest, till the time when the Statue comes in . . . this time . . . he appeared. . . . it is the time that occurred from the coming down of the First Man[341] till the going up of the Last Statue. (*Keph.* 71)."[342]

It is intriguing that the gathering of the rescued souls in the Manichaean tradition, like in previously explored accounts, takes the form of an anthropomorphic conduit that will connect earthly and heavenly realms, literally being envisioned as a ladder between earth and heaven. In this respect, it is intriguing that later rabbinic accounts portray Jacob's ladder as the path for righteous souls in the eschatological time. Thus, *Gen. Rab.* 69:7 reads: "'This is none other than the house of gods and this is the gate of heaven' (Gen 28:17). R. Aha said: [God assured him]: This gate will be opened for many righteous men like thyself. . . . 'This is none other than the house of gods and this is the gate of heaven' refers to it rebuilt and firmly established in the Messianic era, as in the verse, For He hath made strong the bars of thy gates (Ps 147:13)."[343]

Sculpting the righteous souls in the eschatological statue or eschatological ladder is known also in later Jewish mysticism where the already familiar image of the cosmic tree or the ladder coincides with the symbolism of the cosmic pillar, which similarly to the Last Statue of the Manichaean tradition will serve as the gathering entity of the righteous souls and shepherd them in the upper realms.

In relation to these traditions, Moshe Idel observes that "in the later layers, one finds a theory of the pillar as a column that connects the two paradises and serves as the mode for the process of continuous ascent and descent of souls from one to the other in privileged moments in time."[344] Moreover, these traditions of the pillar or the vessel of souls are often overlaid with already familiar arboreal symbolism. Thus, already mentioned in this study, *Midrash Konen* explains that "from the Tree of Life rise and descend the souls of the righteous in Paradise, like a man mounting or descending a ladder."[345]

In concluding this section of our study, it should be noted that the hypothesis that in John 1:51 the Son of Man is envisioned as the vessel of souls or heavenly identities of the righteous is not entirely new. Almost one hundred years ago, Hugo Odeberg put forward this proposal by tracing parallels between the peculiar function of the Son of Man in John 1:51 and Metatron's role as the ladder of Jacob.[346] Indeed, in later Jewish mysticism, Metatron is often portrayed as the "guardian" of the upper identities who, like Abatur in the Mandaean tradition, is responsible for the progress of human souls[347] to their final destiny.[348] Both the Babylonian Talmud[349] and Hekhalot literature[350] hint at this mysterious office of Metatron[351] by depicting him as the teacher of Torah to the souls of deceased children.[352]

One can find similar conceptual developments in which the divine mediator is envisioned as Jacob's ladder in Christian authors. Thus the *Akathist Hymn to the Theotokos*,[353] written in the sixth century CE, depicts the Mother of God as the ladder.[354] John of Damascus, in his homilies on the *Dormition of the Holy Mother of God*, identifies Jacob's ladder[355] with the Theotokos.[356]

In later Christian interpretations, the imagery of Jacob's ladder becomes one of the most popular Old Testament *typoi*[357] applied by Christian exegetes to the Holy Virgin.[358]

Conclusion

This chapter of our study has demonstrated that the story of the patriarch Jacob undoubtedly provoked the wealthiest and most sophisticated cluster of heavenly counterpart speculations, which were perpetuated by Jewish and Christian interpreters for millennia. Such attention to the patriarch's story was not coincidental. The biblical account of Jacob's dream regarding a mysterious ladder, which like a bridge linked earthly and heavenly realities, served as an inspiring source for speculations concerning the heavenly identity of the human being. In this respect, the specimens of Jacob's heavenly double traditions, like their equivalents in Enochic and Mosaic lore, remain firmly anchored in biblical imagery.

In this part of our study, we also explored some possible influences of Greco-Roman mythological and philosophical concepts, including the concept of *eidōlon*, on heterodox Christian, Hermetical, and Manichaean traditions of the heavenly doubles. Yet, the question whether these non-Jewish concepts indeed became the originating source for such heavenly counterpart imagery remains open. Thus, our study demonstrated that early biblical and extrabiblical traditions had still exercised a crucial role in later Christian and Manichaean lore regarding heavenly counterparts. As we recall, both in Gnostic and Manichaean accounts, portrayals of the heavenly counterparts of protagonists of these religious movements were predominantly rendered with distinctive theophanic imagery deeply rooted in early biblical materials.

Chapter Four

The Heavenly Counterpart Traditions in *Joseph and Aseneth*

Joseph's Heavenly Double

Early materials associated with another crucial exemplar of the Jewish tradition, the patriarch Joseph, also contain conceptual developments pertaining to the idea of a heavenly counterpart. While we already closely explored the doppelganger motifs in one pseudepigraphon associated with the name of this patriarch—namely, the *Prayer of Joseph*—it is time to draw our attention to another account that deals with the patriarch's story, the text known to us as *Joseph and Aseneth*,[1] an account in which the heavenly counterpart imagery possibly reached its most advanced development in the Jewish pseudepigrapha.[2]

In recent years, this pseudepigraphon has received substantial attention from scholars. One important feature of the text that sets it apart from other early Jewish visionary accounts is that the recipient of the revelation and subsequent metamorphosis is a female seer—Aseneth, who is depicted in the pseudepigraphon as a daughter of an Egyptian priest who becomes the wife of the Jewish patriarch Joseph. In this expansion on the terse biblical story,[3] Aseneth undergoes a conversion and metamorphosis that turns her from a former idolater into a being who will be fed on the heavenly bread of life.

Aseneth's transformation comes to the fore in chapters 14–18 of the pseudepigraphon, which depict her encounter with an angelic visitor, portrayed in the text as Joseph's heavenly double. *Jos. Asen.* 14:2–10 reveals the following depiction of Aseneth's heavenly guest:

> And Aseneth kept looking, and behold, close to the morning star, the heaven was torn apart and great and unutterable light appeared. And Aseneth saw (it) and fell on (her) face on the ashes. And a man came to her from heaven and stood by Aseneth's head. And

he called her and said, "Aseneth, Aseneth." And she said, "Who is he that calls me, because the door of my chamber is closed, and the tower is high, and how then did he come into my chamber?" And the man called her a second time and said, "Aseneth, Aseneth." And she said, "Behold, (here) I (am), Lord. Who are you, tell me." And the man said, "I am the chief of the house of the Lord and commander of the whole host of the Most High. Rise and stand on your feet, and I will tell you what I have to say." And Aseneth raised her head and saw, and behold, (there was) a man in every respect similar to Joseph, by the robe and the crown and the royal staff, except that his face was like lightning, and his eyes like sunshine, and the hairs of his head like a flame of fire of a burning torch, and hands and feet like iron shining forth from a fire, and sparks shot forth from his hands and feet.[4]

In contrast to other accounts explored previously in our study, where the discernment of the heavenly counterpart imagery sometimes required substantial exegetical efforts, in *Jos. Asen.* the tradition of the celestial alter ego is transparent as the heavenly visitor is said to be in the likeness of Joseph. The mysterious guest is not merely Joseph's heavenly correlative, but his celestial double.[5] Some features and attributes of Joseph's doppelganger deserve our close attention. The first detail that catches the eye is that the appearance of the heavenly figure, who is defined in the story as Anthropos,[6] coincides with the appearance of "great and unutterable light" (φῶς μέγα καὶ ἀνεκλάλητον).[7] It is possible that the light here is yet another description for the heavenly visitor who is later portrayed with a face "like lightning" and eyes "like sunshine."

Such a designation recalls Moses' vision in the *Exagoge* where the prophet's heavenly counterpart is also labeled as φῶς/φώς.[8] As has been already noted in our study, the term φῶς/φώς was often used in Jewish theophanic traditions to designate the glorious manifestations of the deity as well as his anthropomorphic human "icons," who radiate the luminosity of their newly acquired celestial bodies. These traditions often play on the ambiguity of the term that, depending on the accent, can designate either "a man" (φώς) or "light" (φῶς), pointing to both the luminous and the anthropomorphic nature of the divine or angelic manifestations.[9] In this respect, it is noteworthy that all major protagonists of the story—the Anthropos, Aseneth, and Joseph—will be portrayed as luminous entities.

Reflecting on the titles and functions of the heavenly man, scholars have noted similarities to the earthly Joseph's offices and roles. As one may recall, *Jos. Asen.* defines the angelic figure as commander in chief of the heavenly armies. Celia Deutsch notices that this position corresponds to the office that "earthly"

Joseph is holding in Pharaoh's court.[10] The wardrobe and the insignia of Joseph's heavenly counterpart also mirror "earthly" Joseph's accoutrement.[11] Thus, the text tells that the celestial man has "the robe and the crown and the royal staff" like Joseph. These peculiar attributes are important, since they evoke the memory of the heavenly counterpart found in the *Exagoge* where the heavenly double transfers a luminous robe, crown, and scepter to the human seer. It is noteworthy that in chapter 18 of *Jos. Asen.* the female seer also receives exactly the same set of the doppelganger's raiment[12]—the luminous robe, the golden crown, and the scepter.[13]

Dale Allison brings attention to some other important parallels between Joseph's angelic double and earthly Joseph by noting that "each character is in charge of his master's kingdom (4:7; 14:8; 15:12; 21:21). Each bears the title *archon* (1:3; 4:7; 14:8; 15:12; 20:9; 21:21). Each appears as a great heavenly light (6:2; 14:2). Each rides a chariot and initially arrives from the east (5:4; 6:1; 17:7). Each, when he appears, causes Aseneth to tremble with fear (6:1; 14:11)."[14]

It is apparent that the celestial figure accommodates features of several mediatorial figures already explored in our study. Thus, it has been previously noted that in the portrayal of Joseph's doppelganger one can detect the influence of the Adamic currents, and possibly the tradition of the protoplast's image, a trend prominent in previously explored accounts of heavenly counterparts. In relation to this, Kraemer notes that "the designation of the angelic double of Joseph as Anthropos may point . . . to his association with the primal Adam, who is himself the Image of the Divine and thus probably closely associated, if not to be identified, with the Name-Bearing Angel."[15]

The symbolism of sun and fire used in the description of the heavenly visitor's appearance evokes the memory of Enochic mediatorial currents as well[16] and, more specifically, the angelological developments found in *2 Enoch*. Kraemer reflects on these angelological parallels, bringing to our attention the descriptions of Enoch's angelic visitors in *2 Enoch* 1:5.[17] There the patriarch's heavenly guests are portrayed with faces like shining sun and eyes like burning lamps.[18] *3 Enoch* 1:6–7 also describes the princes of the Presence, who play a crucial role in the seer's initiation into his heavenly identity with similar symbolism: "Then I entered the seventh palace and he led me to the camp of the *Shekinah* and presented me before the throne of glory so that I might behold the chariot. But as soon as the princes of the chariot looked at me and fiery seraphim fixed their gaze on me, I shrank back trembling and fell down, stunned by the radiant appearance of their eyes and the bright vision of their faces."[19]

The fiery features of Aseneth's guest also bring to memory the fiery transformation of the seventh patriarch into the supreme angel Metatron. Scholars previously reflected on the similarities between Aseneth's celestial visitor and Metatron, who, as we recall, often appears in Jewish lore as a celestial double of a human protagonist.[20] Thus, Kraemer observes that "a careful examination of the attributes of the angelic double of Joseph demonstrates his affinity with numerous ancient angelic figures, particularly, although by no means exclusively, that of Metatron, a complex figure known from orthodox rabbinic sources as well as from various Hekhalot texts."[21] Several scholars have also noticed resemblances between Joseph's double and the archangel Michael,[22] who was responsible for changing Enoch's garments in *2 Enoch* and who is envisioned in some early Jewish and Christian texts as the heavenly double of Melchizedek.

On Earth, Not in Heaven

One distinctive feature of *Jos. Asen.* that sets it apart from some previously explored pseudepigraphical accounts is that the protagonist's acquisition of her heavenly identity and her encounter with an angelic being assisting in this process occur not in heaven but on earth. This simultaneously links *Jos. Asen.* with the aforementioned Christian and Manichaean developments where seers are also initiated, not in heaven, but on earth. One may recall, for instance, that Mani encounters his celestial Self in the earthly realm and, in the heterodox Christian accounts, where the adepts meet their upper identities in the form of Christ or other otherworldly figures on earth as well. Several factors might be responsible for the diverse ways of encountering a doppelganger in different realms.

One of the possible reasons is that the author has perpetuated one of two ancient trajectories already surveyed—one associated with the Enochic tradition and another with Zadokite theology. Scholars previously noticed the distinctive attitudes of these two movements toward the reception of divine revelations. In the latter, the most important disclosures of the deity are given in earthly settings—on mountains, in rivers, or in the desert—while in the former, the utmost mysteries are conveyed in the upper heaven. Thus, while the adepts of the Zadokite trend were obliged to stay on earth, awaiting for the descent of the revealer,[23] the visionaries of the Enochic tradition were forced to bridge the boundaries separating the lower and the upper realms.

Thus, the clearest instances of the doppelganger's acquisition in heaven occur only in compositions related to Enochic tradition—namely, the *Book of the Watchers*, the *Book of the Similitudes*, *2 Enoch*, and *Sefer Hekhalot*.[24] Other pseudepigraphical accounts, which draw on the memory of the prominent "biblical" visionaries, including Moses and Jacob, appear to be more reluctant in depicting their protagonists openly crossing the realms in the search of their doppelgangers and follow the Zadokite tradition.

One decisive factor for determining peculiar locales for the doppelganger's acquisition in various early Jewish and Christian accounts may be their literary forms. Thus, unlike early Enochic works that belong to the genre of the apocalypse, *Jos. Asen.* falls into a different literary category. In this respect, it is noteworthy that clear and unambiguous portrayals of the reception of the upper identity in heaven typically occur only in the apocalyptic compositions, like the *Book of the Similitudes*, *2 Enoch*, and *Sefer Hekhalot*. In the works of other genres, such as the *Exagoge*, *Jubilees*, the *Prayer of Joseph*, or even the *Ladder of Jacob*, the seer's revelations more frequently occur in some earthly location. Thus, for example, in the Mosaic accounts one can see a set of references to the Sinai encounter. In Jacob's narratives, the memories of the specific "earthly" locations, like Bethel, Penuel, or Jabbok, are also explicitly evoked. And although in some of these materials—for example, in the *Exagoge*—Sinai became envisioned as the cosmic mountain, the text still contains a mixture of details pointing to both heavenly and earthly places.

Interaction between the Doppelganger and the Seer

Some details in the peculiar interactions between the celestial visitor and Aseneth recall the communication between angelic guides and humans in the previously explored heavenly counterpart traditions. The first important detail includes the angel's actions during the adept's change of garments.[25] As in other doppelganger accounts, in *Jos. Asen.*, the heavenly double appears to be assisting in changing the garment of the initiate.[26] Thus, in *Jos. Asen.* 14:12–15, the celestial visitor orders the female adept to remove the defied garments of mourning and dress herself in a new linen robe:[27]

> And the man said to her, "Proceed unhindered into your second chamber and put off your black tunic of mourning, and the sackcloth put off your waist, and shake off those ashes from your head, and wash your face and your hands with living water, 'and dress in a new linen robe (as yet) untouched' and distinguished and gird your waist (with) the new twin girdle of your virginity. And come (back) to me, and I will tell you what I have to say." And Aseneth hurried and went into her second chamber where the chests (containing) her ornaments were, and opened her coffer, and took a new linen robe, distinguished (and as yet) untouched, and undressed the black tunic of mourning and put off the sackcloth from her waist, and dressed in her distinguished (and as yet) untouched linen robe, and girded herself with the twin girdle of her virginity, one girdle around her waist, and another girdle upon her breast. And she shook off the ashes from her head, and washed her hands and her face with living

water. And she took an (as yet) untouched and distinguished linen veil and covered her head.[28]

Jos. Asen. 15:10 further elaborates this symbolic change of Aseneth's wardrobe, hinting at the possibility that her new attire might represent the garments of prelapsarian humanity. The angel's words imply such a possibility as he utters the following cryptic statement: "And now listen to me, Aseneth, chaste virgin, and dress in your wedding robe, the ancient and first robe which is laid up in your chamber since eternity."[29] Commenting on these metamorphoses of the adept's attire, Ross Kraemer notes that

> as a result of her encounter with the angelic double of Joseph, Aseneth changes her clothing twice. In the first instance, at the angel's command, she removes the filthy garments of mourning she has worn during her week of penance and replaces them with a "*stolēn kainēn athikton*" (a new, immaculate robe [14.13]). The remainder of her encounter with the angel takes place while she wears this garment. But in 15.10, the angel instructs her to change into a wedding garment, which she only does after the angel departs back up to the heavens. It is this garment that has associations strikingly similar to those of the bridal garment in Ephrem, for it is not just a bridal robe (*stolēn gamou*) but ancient and primordial (*tēn archaian, tēn protēn*).[30]

As one recalls, the change of attires in some heavenly counterpart traditions coincides with the seer's anointing. Thus, for example, in *2 Enoch*, the archangel Michael anoints the seventh antediluvian patriarch with shining oil during the unification with his celestial identity. Although this scene of explicit anointing is absent in *Jos. Asen.*, it is possible that such an event is indeed taking place and that the angel plays some role in the adept's anointing. It has been suggested that, unlike in *2 Enoch* and some other apocalyptic accounts where the angelic guides literally strip the visionary's garments and anoint him, in *Jos. Asen.* the heavenly visitor executes his actions verbally by ordering the seer to perform transformative actions.[31] Kraemer notes that "although the angel never explicitly anoints Aseneth, he announces to her that from this day on, she will 'eat the bread of life and drink the cup of immortality and be anointed with the ointment of incorruptibility.'"[32] She further argues that the angel's statement envisions "Aseneth's transformation as involving anointing with a substance that presumably renders Aseneth's body impervious to the corruption that mortal bodies suffer after death and that appears to confer on her body the same immunity to corruption that angelic bodies by their very nature have."[33]

Another significant detail in the interaction between the celestial visitor and Aseneth that is reminiscent of some other heavenly counterpart traditions is the theme of the angel's right hand with which he embraces the seer during the initiation. *Jos. Asen.* 16:12–13 reads: "And the man smiled at Aseneth's understanding, and called her to himself, and stretched out his right hand (τὴν χεῖρα αὐτοῦ τὴν δεξιὰν), and grasped her head and shook her head with his right hand. And Aseneth was afraid of the man's hand, because sparks shot forth from his hand as from bubbling (melted) iron. And Aseneth looked, gazing with her eyes at the man's hand."[34]

Here, like in the accounts of Enoch's unification with his heavenly double reflected in *2* and *3 Enoch* or Moses' acquisition of the heavenly identity portrayed in the *Exagoge*, Aseneth's heavenly guide also embraces her with his right hand. It is not coincidental that immediately after this significant embrace the Anthropos conveys to the seer that she is now initiated in the utmost mysteries of the universe. Thus, from *Jos. Asen.* 15:13–14, we learn that when Aseneth looked, gazing with her eyes at the man's hand, he saw (it) and with a smile said, "Happy are you, Aseneth, because the ineffable mysteries of the Most High have been revealed to you."[35]

During Aseneth's initiation, the heavenly visitor also feeds the adept with the mysterious honeycomb that has been miraculously discovered in the maiden's storehouse. It is noteworthy that the seer's nourishment with this heavenly food that grants her transformation is also executed by the right hand of the heavenly visitor. Thus, *Jos. Asen.* 16:15 relates the following words about this interaction: "And the man stretched out his right hand[36] and broke a small portion off the comb, and he himself ate and what was left he put with his hand into Aseneth's mouth, and said to her, 'Eat.' And she ate."[37]

Becoming a "Male"

Although it has been previously suggested that Aseneth might acquire her own celestial identity in the form of the heavenly figure called "Metanoia," it is clear that the acquisition of the upper Self in the case of a female adept is not entirely conventional and straightforward like in previous heavenly counterpart traditions. One might say that it represents a novel chapter in the history of the doppelganger lore.

One notable feature that assists our understanding of the novel mechanics of Aseneth's acquisition of the heavenly double is a statement her heavenly visitor makes in chapter 15 where he tells the Egyptian virgin that she can remove the veil from her head because her head is now as a young man's (ἡ κεφαλή σού ἐστιν ὡς ἀνδρὸς νεανίσκου).³⁸ *Jos. Asen.* 15:1–2 reads: "And she went to the man into her first chamber and stood before him. And the man said to her, 'Remove the veil from your head, and for what purpose did you do this? For you are a chaste virgin today, and your head is like that of a young man.' And Aseneth removed the veil from her head."³⁹

Before we proceed to a close analysis of this newly acquired "maleness" of Aseneth, several words must be said about the youth imagery found in the passage from chapter 15. The heavenly visitor tells the female seer that he is not just a man but a *young* man.⁴⁰ It has been already demonstrated in our study that an endowment with the juvenile identity is a standard feature of many Jewish and Christian accounts in which humans are predestined to encounter their upper Self in the form of a celestial "Youth."

But how is the newly acquired "maleness" of Aseneth related to the doppelganger lore? It is possible that the transition to the identity of a male person signifies here the seer's acquisition of the heavenly identity. In this respect, it is instructive that in some heterodox Christian materials, the heavenly Self or guardian angel of a human being was envisioned as a "male" while its earthly counterpart was understood as a "female." Peter Brown points out that in these conceptual developments "the spirit of each individual was male to the random, female soul. But even the spirit was female to the dominant guardian angel that hovered, as yet undiscovered, close to it. Redemption took the form of a reunion with that guardian angel . . . [reestablishing] . . . the severed link between the conscious person and its angel, a being that stood for the latent, truest self."⁴¹ One of the specimens of such understanding can be found in Clement of Alexandria's *Excerpta ex Theodoto* 21:1, a passage that unveils the following Valentinian tradition:

> The Valentinians say that the finest emanation of Wisdom is spoken of in "He created them in the image of God, male and female created he them." Now the males from this emanation are the "election," but the females are the "calling" and they call the male: beings angelic, and the females themselves, the superior seed. So also, in the case of Adam, the male remained in him but all the female seed was taken from him and became Eve, from whom the females are derived, as the males are from him. Therefore the males are drawn together with the Logos, but the females, becoming men, are united to the angels and pass into the Pleroma. Therefore the woman is said to be changed into a man, and the church here on earth into angels.⁴²

This understanding is reaffirmed by some heterodox Christian accounts, already mentioned in our study, where the heavenly counterparts of the female characters appeared as "males."

Nonetheless, the concept of Aseneth's doppelganger in our pseudepigraphon appears to be not as straightforward as in the aforementioned Christian traditions with their tendencies to envision the humans' upper selves as male figures. As one may recall, despite Aseneth's paradoxal acquisition of a novel male identity, her heavenly alter ego in the form of Metanoia will be clearly envisioned in our pseudepigraphon as a female figure. It is also significant that, unlike with some other heavenly counterpart accounts where embodied alter egos are present at the seers' initiations, Metanoia herself is markedly absent at the scene of initiation, and instead Aseneth receives knowledge about her female upper Self from the mouth of a male doppelganger.

This acquisition of paradoxal maleness[43] by the female seer also appears to have profound anthropological significance, as it might hint at a peculiar way in which the eschatological restoration of fallen humanity will inversely mirror its protological fall. Such an understanding relies on Jewish and Christian traditions in which the division of the primordial androgynous humankind into two genders was understood as the "fall."[44] These theories also postulate that in the eschatological time this original androgynous humanity again will be restored and the human being will no longer be divided into a male and a female.[45] Early Jewish and Christian traditions often understand this process of restoration as inversely mirroring the fall of androgynous humankind—namely, as in the protological act, when Eve was literally taken from Adam in the eschatological time, she will be reversely incorporated into him[46] again, thus becoming the "male."[47] Eschatology in such perspective, like in so many early Jewish accounts, is predestined to mirror protology. One of the specimens of such anthropological understanding can be found in Logion 114 of the *Gos. Thom.*, where Jesus tells Simon Peter that he will make Mary a male: "Simon Peter said to them, 'Let Mary leave us, for women are not worthy of life.' Jesus said 'I myself shall lead her in order to make her male, so that she too may become a living spirit resembling you males. For every woman who will make herself male will enter the kingdom of heaven.' "[48]

Reflecting on this passage, April DeConick notes that "Thomas seems to be referring to the Genesis story in Logion 114 where Jesus states that woman must become 'male' in order to enter the Kingdom. Since Eve was taken from Adam's side, so she must reenter him and become 'male' in order to return to the prelapsarian state of Adam before the gender division."[49] In view of such understanding, the female adept's incorporation into the Anthropos, represented here by Christ, brings her condition into the original protological mold thus reversing the gender separation of fallen humanity.[50]

It appears that in *Jos. Asen.*, one can discern a very similar dynamic of the unification of the female adept with the heavenly Anthropos, who is portrayed in the text as the heavenly double of Joseph. Here, the heavenly Joseph and his earthly bride, in the form of Aseneth, are predestined to become a new Adam and a new Eve who will restore humanity to their prelapsarian and possibly even pregendered unified state. Ross Kraemer rightly observes that "the divine couple of Joseph and Aseneth restore the damage done by Adam and Eve, affording human beings a means to return to their original angelic state and, indeed, acquiring precisely the immortality that God feared Adam and Eve might acquire had they remained in Eden (Gen 3:22–24)."[51]

It is also significant that the unification of the primordial couple here is executed through the process of a nourishment overlaid with erotic overtones, when Aseneth's heavenly visitor feeds the seer with a mysterious honeycomb. The new Adam thus nourishes the new Eve with the food of angels. I have argued elsewhere that such feeding with the heavenly food must be seen as a redeeming reversal of the nourishment with the forbidden food by which the primordial couple lost its heavenly state.[52] Kraemer, similarly, observes that

> Genesis 3.1–5 and following may be read (and, indeed, has been so read) to imply that Eve learned of the forbidden fruit not from God directly but rather from Adam, and therefore, it is Eve's disobedience to her husband that leads to their shared mortality. By contrast, it is Aseneth's obedience to the angelic double of her husband, Joseph that obtains immortality for her. And although the masculine figure also eats, thus formally reversing the actions of Adam and Eve, he is already an angelic being, and it is hardly necessary for him to eat angelic food in order to receive immortality.[53]

We should now explore the account of the seer's nourishment more closely.

Nourishment from the Heavenly Counterpart

In *Jos. Asen.*, the protagonist's unification with her doppelganger is executed in part through the act of nourishment portrayed as her consumption of the mysterious honeycomb offered by the heavenly Anthropos. This constellation of motifs where nourishment coincides with an acquisition of a celestial double appears to be hinted at in some Christian texts as well. In Logion 108 of the *Gospel of Thomas*, Jesus utters the following, saying: "He who will drink from my mouth will become like me. I myself shall become he."[54]

This Thomasine passage is significant since it is reminiscent of a type of nourishment where the angelic food seems to be come from the mouth of the heavenly initiator. It is manifested in *Jos. Asen.* through Aseneth's repeated affirmations about the provenance of the honeycomb from the mouth of the celestial visitor.⁵⁵ *Jos. Asen.* 16:8–10, for instance, reads: "And the comb was big and white as snow and full of honey. And that honey was like dew from heaven and its exhalation like breath of life. And Aseneth wondered and said in herself, Did then this comb come out of the man's mouth, because its exhalation is like the breath of this man's mouth?"⁵⁶ Also, *Jos. Asen.* 16:11 provides a reference to a similar origin of the angelic food: "And Aseneth was afraid and said, 'Lord, I did not have a honeycomb in my storeroom at any time, but you spoke and it came into being. Surely this came out of your mouth, because its exhalation is like breath of your mouth.'"⁵⁷

Other scholars suggest that the provenance of the angelic food in *Jos. Asen.*, coming from the mouth of the celestial being, has roots in the biblical manna traditions. Andrea Lieber observes: "The association of the honeycomb with mannah is explicit: it was like dew from heaven, white like snow, containing the breath of life. Indeed the honeycomb, like mannah, is identified with the 'word' of the angel—the *anthropos* spoke and the comb came from his angelic mouth."⁵⁸ In the Book of Deuteronomy, already, the manna tradition has been reformulated in terms of an oral paradigm when the symbolism of heavenly nourishment is juxtaposed with imagery of the word coming from the deity's mouth. Thus, in Deuteronomy 8:3, we find the following tradition: "He humbled you by letting you hunger, then by feeding you with manna, with which neither you nor your ancestors were acquainted, in order to make you understand that one does not live by bread alone, but by every word that comes from the mouth of the Lord."⁵⁹

The unusual means of nourishment seem to be closely tied to the nature and the function of Aseneth's heavenly guide who is portrayed in our text as the Angel of the Name. Thus, Kraemer argues that "it is particularly in the longer text that the angelic figure is more closely aligned with the figure developed in other sources as the Name-Bearing Angel—the virtual double of God."⁶⁰

It appears that the metamorphosis of the Egyptian maiden is profoundly affected by these means of nourishment. In fact, the text demonstrates that the nature of the female seer was figuratively reconstituted by the ingestion of the divine Name. It is not coincidental that such transformation is executed orally—that is to say, from the mouth of the angel of the Name to the mouth of an earthly creature. As we remember, the heavenly man, who bears some characteristics of the Angel of the Name, puts the angelic food that originated from his mouth into the mouth of the female seer.

If in *Jos. Asen.* the human seer is indeed transformed by means of her ingestion of the divine Name, such initiatory practice points to an important ancient trajectory. Other scholars have noted, for example, that Aseneth's partaking of the celestial food is reminiscent of certain ritual practices, through which cultic images are given life by placing the divine Name in their mouths.⁶¹ These rituals are rooted in ancient Mesopotamian and Egyptian⁶² animation ceremonies of cultic statues known as the rite of the "washing of the mouth" (*mīs pî*) and the "opening of the mouth" (*pīt pî*).⁶³ Some scholars have argued that these trends exercised a formative influence on some later Hermetic⁶⁴ traditions and Kabbalistic stories about the creation of the artificial humanoid.⁶⁵

Returning to the pseudepigraphical account about Joseph and Aseneth, we see that the peculiar metamorphosis effected through the mouth of the celestial being is replete with protological symbolism. These transformational accounts replicate the paradigmatic event of the creation of humankind when the spirit of life was blown from the mouth of the deity into the mouth of the lifeless human body molded from the dust of the earth.⁶⁶ Such protological connections are highlighted in *Jos. Asen.* when the angelic food, the honeycomb, is compared with the spirit of life. Through the ingestion of the divine Name, then, the protagonist of *Jos. Asen.* becomes a "new Protoplast," returning to the prelapsarian condition of humanity.⁶⁷ Such "vivifications" of the seers bring to mind later Jewish Golem legends in which the lifeless body of the artificial humanoid becomes alive when God's name is inserted into his mouth.⁶⁸

The Hypostasized Name as the Heavenly Counterpart of the Visionary

The depiction of the heavenly counterpart of Joseph as the Angel of the Name might also reveal a deliberate conceptual tendency in the doppelganger lore. The Anthropos' peculiar nourishing routines—evocative of the gift of heavenly manna, a motif that is closely connected in various biblical passages with the Angel of the Lord imagery—offers an additional support for the likely association of the heavenly visitor with the divine Name in *Jos. Asen.* In view of a possible connection between Joseph's doppelganger and the Tetragrammaton, we should explore whether other heavenly counterpart trends, tied to other exalted patriarchs and prophets, likewise attempt to portray their seers' upper identities as the possessors or even the embodiments of the divine Name.

Jacob's Identification with the Divine Name

It is important for our study that in early Jewish materials the divine Name became envisioned as a hypostasis or even as a celestial figure. Scholars previously noted that in some biblical accounts the divine Name is already envisioned as a quasi-independent instrument through which God was acting in the world.⁶⁹ In this respect, the figure of the Angel of the Lord, or the Angel of YHWH, became an important conceptual nexus of the onomatological ideology that exercised its lasting influence on later pseudepigraphical materials. We already noticed the influence of the divine Name's angelic manifestation and his peculiar offices in the depiction of Aseneth's heavenly visitor. It also appears that the Jacob pseudepigrapha have been influenced by the Angel of the Lord traditions. The impact of these conceptual currents is implicitly present in the *Prayer of Joseph*. There, one may recall, Jacob-Israel, while arguing with the archangel Uriel about his superior heavenly status, utters the following cryptic statement: "I told him his name and what rank he held among the sons of God. 'Are you not Uriel, the eighth after me? And I, Israel, the archangel of the power of the Lord and the chief captain among the sons of God? Am I not Israel, the first minister before the face of God? And I called upon my God by the inextinguishable name (καὶ ἐπεκαλεσάμην ἐν ὀνόματι ἀσβέστῳ τὸν θεόν μου).'"[70]

An important feature of this account is that Jacob-Israel is portrayed as the first minister before the deity's face who calls upon God by his inextinguishable Name. This peculiar routine is reminiscent of the duties of another distinguished *Sar ha-Panim*—Metatron, who, because of his unique role as the Lesser YHWH, is often portrayed as invoking the Tetragrammaton during the heavenly liturgy.[71] In view of these connections, scholars entertain the possibility that in the *Prayer of Joseph* Jacob-Israel might be envisioned not merely as a possessor of the divine Name but even as its embodiment—the Angel of YHWH. Thus, reflecting on the text's onomatological traditions, Fossum observes that in the *Prayer of Joseph* "we find a pre-existent angel called 'Jacob' and 'Israel,' who claims superiority over the angel Uriel on the basis of his victory in personal combat where he availed himself of the Divine Name. The angelic name 'Israel,' explained as אִישׁ רָאָה אֵל, is among the names of the many-named intermediary in Philo's works,[72] and, in one of the passages where Philo presents this name as one of the designations of the intermediacy, he also says that the 'Name of God' is among the appellations of this being."[73]

Fossum further suggests that in some Jewish and Christian circles "Israel" apparently was one of the names of the Angel of the Lord. He notes that Justin Martyr was possibly cognizant of such an identification when he mentions the name "Israel" as one of the names of the Son as he appeared under the old dispensation.[74] Fossum also notes that another passage from Justin Martyr's *Dialogue with Trypho* 75:2[75] identifies the Angel of the Lord in Exodus 23:20 as Jesus and mentions that he was also called "Israel" as he bestowed this name on Jacob.[76]

Likewise, analyzing the divine Name traditions in the *Prayer of Joseph*, Alan Segal argues that "here it is an archangel of the power of the people of God who is called Israel and is also identified with the patriarch Jacob. He was created before all the works of creation and claims ascendancy over Uriel on the basis of his victory in personal combat by which he ostensibly possesses the divine name."[77] In light of Fossum's and Segal's suggestions, Charles Gieschen proposes that the evidence found in the *Prayer* "leads to the conclusion that this angel was understood to be the Angel of the Lord and more specifically the Divine Name Angel of Exod 23:20."[78]

Metatron's Identification with the Divine Name

We already learned in our study that Enoch's celestial alter ego, the supreme angel Metatron, was often depicted in the Hekhalot and *Shiʿur Qomah* materials as a very distinguished operator or even as the embodiment of the divine Name, the office that is briefly and accurately summed up in his striking title יהוה הקטן, the Lesser YHWH. This designation occurs with abbreviations several times in *Sefer Hekhalot*, including passages found in *3 Enoch* 12:2; 48C:7;[79] and 48D:1. Thus, *3 Enoch* 12–13 offers the following revelation of the great angel:

> R. Ishmael said: Metatron, Prince of the Divine Presence, said to me: Out of the love which he had for me, more than for all the denizens of the heights, the Holy One, blessed be he, fashioned for me a majestic robe, in which all kinds of luminaries were set, and he clothed me in it. He fashioned for me a glorious cloak in which brightness, brilliance, splendor, and luster of every kind were fixed, and he wrapped me in it. He fashioned for me a kingly crown in which refulgent stones were placed, each like the sun's orb, and its brilliance shone into the four quarters of the heaven of ʿArabot, into the seven heavens, and into the four quarters of the world. He set it upon my head and he called me, the lesser YHWH (יי הקטן) in the presence of his whole household in the height as it is written, "My name is in him." R. Ishmael said: The angel Metatron, Prince of the Divine Presence, the glory of highest heaven, said to me: Out of the abundant love and great compassion wherewith the Holy One, blessed be he, loved and cherished me more than all the denizens of the heights, he wrote with his finger, as with a pen of flame, upon the crown which was on my head, the letters by which heaven and earth were created; the letters by which seas and rivers were created; the letters by which mountains and hills were created; the letters by which stars and constellations, lightning hurricane and tempest were created; the letters by which all the necessities of the world and all the orders of creation were created. Each letter flashed time after

time like lightnings, time after time like torches, time after time like flames, time after time like the rising of the sun, moon, and stars.[80]

Like some other Jewish accounts, this passage attempts to connect Metatron's duties as the bearer of the divine Name with the biblical figure of the Angel of the Lord through the invocation of the prominent phrase "My name is in him" applied to the Angel of YHWH in Exodus 23:21.

In *3 Enoch* 48D:1, Metatron's name "lesser YHWH" is also mentioned, again with an allusion to Exodus 23:21, this time, however, among the seventy names of Metatron.[81] Jarl Fossum suggests that the references to the seventy names of Metatron might indirectly point to the function of the exalted angel as the bearer of the "ultimate" Name of God, since these seventy names might just represent various aspects of God's "main" Name. Elucidating such a connection, Fossum points to *3 Enoch* 3:2, where Metatron tells R. Ishmael that his seventy names "are based on the name of the King of kings of kings," and to *3 Enoch* 48D:5, which informs that "these seventy names are a reflection of the Explicit Name upon the Merkavah which is engraved upon the Throne of Glory."[82] Fossum suggests that these seventy names originally belonged to God himself and only later were transferred to Metatron.[83]

It is also important for our study that in some Jewish mystical accounts the exalted agents endowed with the divine Name are put in charge of the celestial alter egos. It has been already mentioned in our study that in rabbinic literature Metatron is often envisioned as such an entity who is put in charge of "heavenly identities" of human beings.[84]

Michael's Identification with the Divine Name

Our study already demonstrated the important role that Michael plays in the doppelganger legends, where he often serves as the celestial double of various protological characters, including Melchizedek and Isaac. For our ongoing investigation, it is important that in some early Jewish materials this angelic figure is closely associated with the divine Name as well.[85] For example, the *Book of the Similitudes* portrays the archangel Michael as the possessor of the divine Name. *1 Enoch* 69:13–15 reads:

> And this is the task of Kesbeel, the chief of the oath, who showed (the oath) to the holy ones when he dwelt on high in glory, and its name (is) Beqa. And this one told the holy Michael that he should show him the secret name, that they might mention it in the oath, so that those who showed the sons of men everything which is secret

trembled before that name and oath. And this (is) the power of this oath, for it is powerful and strong; and he placed this oath Akae in the charge of the holy Michael.[86]

Although the aforementioned passage does not directly designate the mysterious oath as the Tetragrammaton, the verses that follow it affirm the connections between the oath and the divine Name. From *1 Enoch* 69:16–20, we learn the following about the powers of the oath:

> And these are the secrets of this oath and they are strong through his oath, and heaven was suspended before the world was created and for ever. And through it the earth was founded upon the water, and from the hidden (recesses) of the mountains come beautiful waters from the creation of the world and for ever. And through that oath the sea was created, and as its foundation, for the time of anger, he placed for it the sand, and it does not go beyond (it) from the creation of the world and for ever. And through that oath the deeps were made firm, and they stand and do not move from their place from (the creation of) the world and forever. And through that oath the sun and the moon complete their course and do not transgress their command from (the creation of) the world and for ever.[87]

Here the oath is described as an instrument of creation with which the deity once fashioned the heaven and earth.[88] It is noteworthy that in other parts of the *Book of the Similitudes*—namely, in *1 Enoch* 41—this demiurgic oath[89] is used interchangeably with the divine Name.[90] Later rabbinic accounts deliberate extensively on the demiurgic functions of the Tetragrammaton[91] and its letters,[92] often interpreting them as the instruments through which the world came into existence.[93] These traditions often construe God's command יהי at the creation of the world as an abbreviation of the divine Name.[94] In view of these traditions, Darrell Hannah observes that "this passage indicates that Michael was viewed by the author of the *Similitudes* as the angel of the Name, for into the 'hand of Michael' the secret of the oath, that is the Divine Name, had been entrusted."[95]

Moses' Investiture with the Divine Name

Although the story of Moses' reception of the divine Name[96] was attested already in the biblical accounts, the later Jewish and Samaritan traditions further elevate this event by depicting it as the prophet's investiture with the Name.[97]

We have already seen that in some heavenly counterpart accounts, the reception of the garment is envisioned as an acquisition of the upper identity.

It is in light of this phenomenon that the motif of Moses' investiture with the Name should be explored more closely. The theme of the prophet's clothing with the divine Name received its most extensive elaboration in the Samaritan materials, including the compilation known to us as *Memar Marqah*.[98] In the very first chapter of this document, one learns that the deity himself announced to the great prophet that he will be vested with the divine Name.[99] Several other passages of *Memar Marqah* further affirm this striking clothing metaphor.[100]

It is significant that the investiture with the Tetragrammaton in the Samaritan materials, similar to the Metatron lore, entails a ritual of "crowning" with the divine Name.[101] Thus, *Memar Marqah* 1:9 unveils the following actions of the deity:

> On the first day I created heaven and earth; on the second day I spread out the firmament on high; on the third day I prepared a dish and gathered into it all kinds of good things; on the fourth day I established signs, fixing times, completing my greatness; on the fifth day I revealed many marvels from the waters; on the sixth day I caused to come up out of the ground various living creatures; on the seventh day I perfected holiness. I rested in it in my own glory. I made it my special portion. I was glorious in it. I established your name then also—my name and yours therein as one, for I established it and you are crowned with it.[102]

In this passage, the endowment of Moses with a crown, like the aforementioned crowning of Metatron, is given a creational significance when the letters on both headdresses are depicted as demiurgic tools, by means of which heaven and earth came into existence. Similarly, *3 Enoch* 13 tells that the deity wrote with his finger, as with a pen of flame, upon Metatron's crown the letters by which heaven and earth were created. Such crowning with the demiurgic instruments, represented by the letters of the divine Name, gives its recipients power to understand the utmost mysteries of creation or even to control the entire creation.

In light of this imagery, it is possible that the motif of the investiture with the divine Name is also present in another Mosaic account—the *Exagoge* of Ezekiel the Tragedian. Recall that there Moses receives a mysterious crown and that immediately thereafter he is suddenly able to permeate the secrets of creation and even control the created order. The *Exagoge* 75–80 relates: "Then he gave me a royal crown and got up from the throne. I beheld the whole earth all around and saw beneath the earth and above the heavens. A multitude of stars fell before my knees and I counted them all."[103] Here, crowned, Moses suddenly has immediate access to all created realms, "beneath the earth and above the heaven," and the stars are now kneeling before a newly initiated demiurgic agent. Although the divine Name is not mentioned in this Mosaic narrative, it is possible in light of other peculiar features that the seer's encounter with his doppelganger coincides with this endowment of the divine Name.

It is also important that in some Samaritan sources, Moses' clothing with the Name is set parallel with Adam's endowment with the image. Thus, Fossum suggests[104] that in *Memar Marqah*, Moses' investiture with the Name appears to be also understood as vestment with the image.[105] Such a confluence of motifs once again points to the possibility that the hypostasized Name is envisioned as the heavenly Self in ways similar to how the image is portrayed as Jacob's doppelganger in the rabbinic lore.

Jesus' Clothing with the Divine Name

In their analysis of Jewish onomatological traditions, Fossum and Quispel also draw attention to another important case of the investiture with the Name, present in early Christian heterodox materials, where Jesus' clothing with the divine Name in his baptism was understood as an acquisition of his upper identity.[106] They suggest that the *Gospel of Philip* from the Nag Hammadi library postulates that the Son "vested" himself with the Name of the Father.[107] *Gos. Phil.* 54:5–13 (*Nag Hammadi Codex* II, 3, 54:5–13) reads: "One single name is not uttered in the world, the name which the father gave to the son; it is the name above all things: the name of the father. For the son would not become father unless he wore the name of the father. Those who have this name know it, but they do not speak it. But those who do not have it do not know it."[108] Analyzing this and similar Valentinian traditions, Quispel proposed that Jesus' investiture with the Name of God might have occurred at the time of his baptism in the Jordan, "for the Valentinians thought that at that moment the Name of God descended upon Jesus."[109] This association between the investiture with the Name and the baptism in the Jordan is significant since this event is often interpreted as the revelation of Jesus' upper Self.

It is also significant that in some Christian traditions baptism of the believers was associated both with the acquisition of the guardian angel and reception of the divine Name. Thus, a passage from Clement of Alexandria's *Excerpta ex Theodoto* 22:5[110] details the following baptismal tradition:

> And when the Apostle said, "Else what shall they do who are baptized for the dead?" . . . For, he says, the angels of whom we are portions were baptized for us. But we are dead, who are deadened by this existence, but the males are alive who did not participate in this existence. "If the dead rise not why, then, are we baptized?"

Therefore we are raised up "equal to angels," and restored to unity with the males, member for member. Now they say "those who are baptized for us, the dead," are the angels who are baptized for us, in order that when we, too, have the Name, we may not be hindered and kept back by the Limit and the Cross from entering the Pleroma. Wherefore, at the laying on of hands they say at the end, "for the angelic redemption" that is, for the one which the angels also have, in order that the person who has received the redemption may be baptized in the same Name in which his angel had been baptized before him. Now the angels were baptized in the beginning, in the redemption of the Name which descended upon Jesus in the dove and redeemed him. And redemption was necessary even for Jesus, in order that, approaching through Wisdom, he might not be detained by the Notion of the Deficiency in which he was inserted, as Theodotus says.[111]

This passage tells that the Christians who imitate Jesus' baptism at the Jordan by their own immersions are predestined to obtain both the divine Name and guardian angel. This striking constellation of concepts related to the heavenly double and the divine Name again reaffirms the possibility that in some Jewish and Christian circles the divine Name was closely associated with the adept's heavenly identity.

The Ritual of the Bridal Chamber

After our excursus into the divine Name traditions, we now return to *Jos. Asen.* The striking intimate routines, overlaid with erotic overtones, which occurred during the initiation of the seer by her angelic visitor, bring us to another important symbolic dimension of Aseneth's metamorphosis—the concept of the bridal chamber.[112] It is significant that Aseneth's conversion and transformation unfold in the midst of her preparation to become Joseph's bride.[113] And yet, while the marriage between the Jewish patriarch and the Egyptian maiden is not yet consummated,[114] the interaction between Aseneth and Joseph's heavenly double is laden with the peculiar actions usually only allowed to take place between married partners. Thus, the heavenly Anthropos orders the female seer to be undressed and redressed, grasps her head with his hand, speaks about her anointment,[115] removes her veil, and later places the food from his mouth into the seer's mouth. It is also significant that the celestial Anthropos, in his own words, is in love with Aseneth's heavenly counterpart—Metanoia. All these actions of the angelic visitor suggest that although the physical consummation between Aseneth and Joseph has not yet taken place, the spiritual counterpart of such an act is already unfolding in the form of the heavenly union between the female seer and Joseph's heavenly counterpart.[116] It is therefore possible that here the earthly person and the heavenly being are forming a so-called "*syzygia*, the *mysterium conjunctionis* between a human being and his [or her] angel or transcendental Self."[117] Although the concept of the bridal chamber has been preserved in its most articulated form in early heterodox Christian materials, *Jos. Asen.* provides a possible proof that the origins of this concept might be rooted in early Jewish accounts.

It is important for our study that in early Christian testimonies dealing with the bridal chamber's imagery, one of the members of the *syzygia* is often envisioned as a heavenly double of a human being. Thus, analyzing the Valentinian notion of the *syzygia* or the *mysterium conjunctionis* between a human being and his angel, Quispel suggested that this angel was "conceived as image and counterpart (*iqonin*) both in Judaism and primitive Christianity."[118]

The presence of the bridal chamber imagery in *Jos. Asen.* has been previously acknowledged by several scholars.[119] Ross Kraemer also notices some connections between Aseneth's transformation into a "male" and the bridal chamber imagery found in the *Acts of Thomas*.[120] She observes that

> in this same vein, we might also consider a narrative in the *Acts of Thomas* concerning a newly married young royal couple. The night of their wedding, Jesus, in the form of his twin brother, the apostle Judas Thomas, appears in their bridal chamber before they can consummate the marriage and dissuades them from doing so, persuading them instead to adopt permanent chastity. The next morning, the bride is found sitting uncovered. Her mother, seeing her this way, asks why she sits with her husband, unashamed, as though long-married, an inquiry seconded by her father. The bride responds: "That I do not veil myself is because the mirror of shame has been taken away from me: I am no longer ashamed or abashed, since the work of shame and bashfulness has been removed from me."[121]

Kraemer further argues that "here, as in *Aseneth* 15.1, where the angelic figure instructs Aseneth to remove her head covering, sexuality and covering are clearly linked; the unveiled woman is 'asexual.'"[122] It is also noteworthy that in both accounts, the female seer's anthropological metamorphosis coincides with the apparition of the doppelganger. This union between the heavenly and the earthly is laden therefore with profound changes in the nature and social behavior of the initiated.

Although our analysis of the bridal chamber traditions has been mainly executed through the spectacles of later heterodox Christian developments, it is significant that the authors or transmitters of the text themselves were applying this technical terminology to the conceptual developments found in the text. Thus, some manuscripts of the shorter version[123] specifically mention that Aseneth's heavenly counterpart, Metanoia, has prepared a *heavenly bridal chamber* (νυμφῶνα οὐράνιον)[124] for those who love her.[125] It again demonstrates that in the minds of the authors (or handlers) of the text, the details of Aseneth's transformation and the acquisition of her heavenly identity were closely associated with the imagery of the bridal chamber.

Heavenly Counterpart of Aseneth

Aseneth's figure can be viewed as a very complex and enigmatic nexus of heavenly counterpart traditions. As has been already noticed, her attributes imitate both descriptions of the earthly Joseph and his heavenly double. Thus, her heavenly identity is closely tied to the heavenly identity of Joseph with whom she forms the *mysterium conjunctionis*.

This complex web of conceptual developments in which the female seer is identified with the upper correlative of Joseph becomes even more complicated through the imagery of Aseneth's own heavenly counterpart in the form of Metanoia.

Scholars previously noted that *Jos. Asen.*'s account offers a unique constellation of the heavenly counterpart motifs. Not only is the initiating angel portrayed as the heavenly alter ego of Joseph, but Aseneth herself, in the course of initiation, receives knowledge about her own doppelganger under the name of Repentance (Μετάνοια). In *Jos. Asen.* 15:7–8, the heavenly Anthropos relates to the seer the following:

> And your name shall no longer be called Aseneth, but your name shall be City of Refuge, because in you many nations will take refuge with the Lord God, the Most High, and under your wings many peoples trusting in the Lord God will be sheltered, and behind your walls will be guarded those who attach themselves to the Most High God in the name of Repentance. For Repentance is in the heavens, an exceedingly beautiful and good daughter of the Most High. And she herself entreats the Most High God for you at all times and for all who repent in the name of the Most High God, because he is (the) father of Repentance. And she herself is guardian of all virgins,

and loves you very much, and is beseeching the Most High for you at all times and for all who repent she prepared a place of rest in the heavens. And she will renew all who repent, and wait on them herself for ever (and) ever. And Repentance is exceedingly beautiful, a virgin pure and laughing always, and she is gentle and meek. And, therefore, the Most High Father loves her, and all the angels stand in awe of her. And I, too, love her exceedingly, because she is also my sister. And because she loves you virgins, I love you, too.[126]

In respect to this conceptual development, Ross Kraemer observes that as the angel is the celestial double of Joseph, so Aseneth also has a celestial alter ego named Metanoia. The uniqueness of this pseudepigraphical account in comparison with previously explored materials is that here one celestial double conveys to the seer the revelation about the second one. It is also intriguing that the Anthropos and Metanoia are envisioned as siblings, since the Heavenly Man tells Aseneth that Metanoia is his sister. Such relationships mirror a paradoxal bond between earthly Joseph and Aseneth who are repeatedly identified in the text as brother and sister.[127]

Kraemer draws her attention to the differences in features and functions of Aseneth's heavenly double in longer and shorter versions.[128] Thus, in her opinion, the longer version revises "the portrait of Metanoia to conform to Wisdom[129] traditions more closely."[130] The identification of Aseneth's doppelganger with the mediatorial figure of the hypostasized Sophia is not coincidental. Our study has already demonstrated that various mediatorial figures become envisioned as the divine mirrors, in whom human adepts are predestined to encounter their own upper identities. Such a function of the hypostasized Sophia as a mirror of the deity is already hinted in early descriptions of this important mediatorial figure. Thus, from Wisdom of Solomon 7:25–26, one learns that "she [Wisdom] is a reflection of eternal light, a spotless mirror (ἔσοπτρον ἀκηλίδωτον) of the working of God, and an image (εἰκών) of his goodness." This striking passage can serve as a good illustration of the doppelganger's proclivities of this distinguished sapiential mediator, since Wisdom here is portrayed not only as the mirror (ἔσοπτρον) of God but also as his image (εἰκών)—the concept that, as we already witnessed, became so important in several heavenly counterpart accounts where the celestial image became synonymous with the adept's upper Self.[131]

Kraemer notes that the figure of Aseneth's heavenly double in fact is much more enigmatic than the persona of Joseph's heavenly identity since ancient Jewish sources very rarely envision an explicitly female angel in the heavenly cosmology.[132]

It is also intriguing that some functions of Aseneth's celestial alter ego in the form of Metanoia appear reminiscent of the roles of another prominent heavenly counterpart already explored in this study—namely, Metatron. Thus, Kraemer notes that both characters share certain attributes and features—namely, "both are intercessory figures, mediating between the human and the divine.[133] Both are described as exceedingly beautiful."[134]

Kraemer also draws attention to one of Metatron's titles, "Beloved."[135] This title is closely connected with the title of the seventh antediluvian hero, who already in Mesopotamian lore became designated as "the beloved of gods."[136] In respect to these traditions, Kraemer suggests that "just as Metanoia is beloved by God in heaven (and in the longer version, by the angel as well), so also Metatron is said in some texts to be much loved in heaven."[137]

It is also noteworthy that in the case of Aseneth-Metanoia, the functions of the heavenly and earthly identity appear to be strictly delineated in such a way that might point to the simultaneous existence of Aseneth and her heavenly double in their respective realms—the condition that has been already noted in other mediatorial currents connected with the heavenly counterpart lore. Thus, Kraemer notes that "on earth, Aseneth will henceforth shelter those who devote themselves to God through repentance [*metanoia*], while in heaven, Metanoia herself continually petitions God on behalf of all those who repent."[138]

Celia Deutsch also reflects on these similar, but yet delineated, functions of the seer's celestial and earthly counterparts. She observes that in her new identity, Aseneth becomes a heavenly/earthly being. She will assume a role correspondent to that of the angel Repentance or Metanoia, exercising a corresponding earthly role on behalf of all those who repent.[139]

Deutsch also brings attention to Aseneth's heavenly counterpart's endowment with scribal duties, the office that we already encountered in various doppelganger accounts. Deutsch observes that Aseneth "is transformed in Lady Wisdom's image.... The association with personified Wisdom indicates that her new role will also have a scribal element, something that will be confirmed by her association with Levi as the narrative progresses."[140]

As in the case of Joseph's heavenly correlative who emulates the features and attributes of the earthly Joseph, Aseneth's heavenly counterpart bears some traits of the earthly protagonist. In this respect, Kraemer notes that to the extent that Metanoia is Aseneth's divine double, Metanoia's traits are also those of Aseneth. She also notes that these common attributes are expanded and given more explicit expression in the longer text.[141]

Transformation in the Mirror

After Aseneth's interaction with the celestial visitor, an encounter laden with profound anthropological and spiritual metamorphoses, the story unveils another striking account of transformation, this time involving changes of Aseneth's face. *Jos. Asen.* 18:3–11 offers the following description:

> And her foster-father saw her, and behold, her face had fallen from the affliction and the weeping and the fasting of the seven days, and he was distressed and wept, and he took her right hand and kissed it and said, "What have you, my child, because your face has fallen so (much)?" And Aseneth said to him, "My head is stricken with heavy pain, and the sleep kept away from my eyes and therefore my face has fallen." And her foster-father went away and prepared the house and the dinner . . . And Aseneth remembered the words of her foster-father, because he had said to her, "Your face has fallen." And she sighed and was much distressed and said, "Woe is me, the humble, because my face has fallen. Joseph will see me and despise me." And she said to her foster-sister, "Bring me pure water from the spring, and I will wash my face." And she brought her pure water from the spring and poured it into the basin. And Aseneth leaned (over) to wash her face and saw her face in the water. And it was like the sun and her eyes (were) like a rising morning star, and her cheeks like fields of the Most High and on her cheeks (there was) red (color) like a son of man's blood and her lips (were) like a rose of life coming out of its foliage, and her teeth like fighting men lined up for a fight and the hair of her head (was) like a vine in the paradise of God prospering in its fruits and her neck like an all-variegated cypress, and her breasts (were) like the mountains of the Most High God. And when Aseneth saw herself in the water, she was amazed at the sight and rejoiced with great joy, and did not wash her face, for she said, "Perhaps I (will) wash off this great beauty." And her foster-father came to say to her, "Everything is prepared as you have commanded." And when he saw her he was alarmed and stood speechless for a long (time) and was filled with great fear and fell at her feet and said, "What is this, my mistress, and what is this great and wonderful beauty? At last the Lord God of heaven has chosen you as a bride for his firstborn son, Joseph?"[142]

This portentous motif of the seer's transformation in the watery mirror deserves our close attention, since it brings to memory some familiar themes already encountered in our analysis of the heavenly counterpart traditions in the Enochic, Mosaic, and Jacobite lore.

The important features of the narrative are the *tropheus*' statements, manifested at the beginning and at the end of the account. These reactions attempt to draw attention to the pivotal theme of the passage—namely, the striking metamorphosis of Aseneth's face.[143] We learn that in the beginning the *tropheus* is unimpressed with Aseneth's appearance and notices that Aseneth's face "has fallen." Yet, at the end of the narrative, when he sees her again after she gazed into the mirror of the "pure water,"[144] he is speechless and filled with fear and falls at her feet.[145] Such a peculiar set of human reactions is reminiscent of the Jewish theophanic accounts in which human visionaries encounter angelic and divine manifestations, including the anthropomorphic *Kavod*, often labelled in these accounts as the "Face." Moreover, as has been previously noted, the *tropheus*' response mirrors Aseneth's own earlier reaction to her celestial visitor.[146] It is clear that the vision of the "face" in the water dramatically altered the maiden's countenance.[147] Reflecting on this dramatic change, Christoph Burchard suggested that "she comes close to being an angelic creature."[148]

Philonenko, Burchard, and some other scholars tried to link the motif of Aseneth's vision in the water to the magical rites, which flourished in the Greco-Roman environment, seeing in this peculiar action of gazing into water a lecanomancy ritual.[149] While connections with Hellenistic magic were duly acknowledged in previous studies, possible ties to some Jewish mystical accounts of theophanic encounters through water have often been forgotten in these attempts to clarify the background of Aseneth's metamorphosis. Previously, some scholars drew attention to the importance of the water rituals in Merkavah and Hekhalot mysticism.[150] In light of the aforementioned parallels between *Jos. Asen.* and the Merkavah tradition, these motifs deserve to be explored more closely.

Martti Nissinen argued that "in the Hekhalot literature, water not only appears as a ritual precondition for divine revelation, but also as the site where revelation takes place, and, most notably, as a medium for inducing the altered state of consciousness."[151] Moreover, in the Hekhalot accounts, the vision of water or its "likeness" often serves as a test for a visionary when the adept enters the sixth celestial palace.[152]

The possibility of theophanic vision in the water might be already present in the earliest formative account of the Merkavah lore—the first chapter of the Book of Ezekiel. Thus, some Jewish mystical accounts attempt to interpret Ezekiel's revelation as a vision received in the mirror of waters—namely, the waters of the river Chebar.[153] In one such mystical interpretation, reflected in the text known to us as the *Visions of Ezekiel*, the following striking explanation can be found:

> While Ezekiel was watching, God opened to him seven firmaments, and he saw the Power. They coined a parable. To what may the matter be likened? To a man who went to a barber shop, got a haircut, and was given a mirror to look into. While he was looking into the

mirror, the king passed by. He saw the king and his forces through the doorway. The barber turned and said to him, "Turn around and see the king." He said, "I have already seen the mirror." So Ezekiel stood by the river Chebar and looked into the water, and the seven firmaments were opened to him and he saw God's glory, and the *hayyot*, angels, troops, seraphim, and sparkling-winged ones joined to the *merkavah*. They passed by in the heavens and Ezekiel saw them in the water. So it is written: At the river Chebar (Ezek 1:1).[154]

Reflecting on this passage, David Halperin observes that "looking into the river Chebar, Ezekiel sees the primordial waters, and the *Hayyot* and other merkavah beings in them (understood to mean, reflected in them)."[155] Some scholars argue that such a practice of seeing the *Kavod* in bodies of water possibly became a mystical ritual, known to Jewish apocalypticists and mystics. Thus, Halperin argues that the passage from the *Visions of Ezekiel* is "a reflection of the actual practice of early Jewish visionaries, who used natural bodies of water as mirrors in which they could see supernatural beings appear in the sky. Water-divination of this sort, using a vessel filled with water (often with oil added) as a mirror in which the medium can see divine images, seems to have been common enough in the ancient world."[156] Halperin argued that such a ritual allowed a mystic to bridge realms since "when the merkavah appears in the waters, the upper realms are merged into the lower."[157]

It is noteworthy that *Leviticus Rabbah* 1:14[158] and *Zohar* II.82b[159] make a connection between the revelation on the river Chebar and Moses' vision of the *Kavod* reflected in a mirror. In this study, we encountered a very similar development in the Mosaic currents with their extensive application of the mirror's imagery in relation to the heavenly identities of human seers. It is not coincidental that this theme also appears in *Jos. Asen.*, where the heavenly counterpart traditions come to their conceptual apex.

Let us look more closely at some peculiar details of Aseneth's vision in water. One intriguing feature of *Jos. Asen.* 18 is that the seer's visage is first depicted as "fallen"[160] and then as luminous.[161] It appears that such a transition might entail an anthropological significance. It brings to memory two conditions of the Protoplast—the radiant one before the transgression in the Garden of Eden and the dimmed one afterward. Here Aseneth appears to undergo a reverse metamorphosis that restores the human condition to the prelapsarian state by regaining the full manifestation of the divine image. In this respect, it is intriguing that Aseneth's reflection in the water is portrayed not merely as her "face" but rather as her "bust"[162] (with her neck and breasts), which brings to memory a peculiar symbolism found in the *Ladder of Jacob* where such "bust" signifies Jacob's *iqonin*.

In light of the aforementioned Enochic, Mosaic, and Jacobite accounts, where the *panim* and the *tselem* imagery is often closely interrelated and even interchangeable, it is possible that in *Jos. Asen.* the portrayal of Aseneth's "face"/"bust" is connected with the concept of the divine image.¹⁶³ If it is indeed so, the praxis of the eschatological restoration of the divine image through gazing into water evokes a memory of Jewish and Christian protological accounts where the mediators of the divine image are portrayed as gazing into the water. Thus, for example, in *Corp. Herm.* 1:14, the primordial Anthropos, who is understood in this text as the embodiment of the divine image¹⁶⁴ (τὴν τοῦ πατρὸς εἰκόνα ἔχων),¹⁶⁵ is portrayed as staring into the water, giving existence to its lower material counterpart:

> Having all authority over the cosmos of mortals and unreasoning animals, the man broke through the vault and stooped to look through the cosmic framework, thus displaying to lower nature the fair form of god. Nature smiled for love when she saw him whose fairness brings no surfeit (and) who holds in himself all the energy of the governors and the form of god, for in the water she saw the shape of the man's fairest form and upon the earth its shadow. When the man saw in the water the form like himself as it was in nature, he loved it and wished to inhabit it; wish and action came in the same moment, and he inhabited the unreasoning form. Nature took hold of her beloved, hugged him all about and embraced him, for they were lovers.¹⁶⁶

It is intriguing that the very next verse of the *Corpus Hermeticum* (1:15) appears to postulate the existence of the human being's doppelganger based on this pivotal primordial act of looking into the water: "Because of this, unlike any other living thing on earth, mankind is twofold—in the body mortal but immortal in the essential man."¹⁶⁷ This tradition, in which the divine image is reflected in the water, appears to be widespread in early Christian literature. Analyzing this motif in the heterodox Christian materials, Gedaliahu Stroumsa notes that "as in the *Poimandres*, also in some of the other texts the image of God is said to appear in the water. Thus, in the *Apocryphon of John*, the Son of Man reveals upon the water the appearance in human (ἀνδρέος) form (τύπος) of Anthropos, the invisible Father of the All. In the *Hypostasis of the Archons*, the image of Incorruptibility revealed upon the water is explicitly called the image of God. In the *Origin of the World*, it is Pistis who reveals the likeness of her greatness upon the water."¹⁶⁸

It is also noteworthy that in some already mentioned Manichaean texts where the doppelganger traditions arguably came to their conceptual pinnacle, one can also encounter some references to a peculiar ritual of encountering a heavenly double as the divine form or image in water. Thus, in the section of the *Cologne Mani Codex* (11–12) where Mani speaks about his early encounters with his heavenly twin or *syzygos*, a cryptic statement can be found in which the Mesopotamian mystic says that "from the spring of the waters (ἐκ τῆς πηγῆς τῶν ὑδάτων) there appeared to me a human form (εἶδος ἀνθρώπου) which showed me by hand the 'rest' so that I might not sin and bring distress on him."[169] Although the *CMC* 11–12 does not openly connect this apparition in the water with Mani's *syzygos*, in his recent study, Charles Stang entertains a possibility that this vision is related to the heavenly counterpart traditions.[170] Stang also brings attention to another episode of gazing into water found in *CMC* 94–96 where the leader of the baptismal sect, Alchasai, similarly encounters "an image of man" in the waters. *CMC* 94–96 reads:

> For Elkhasai, the founder of your law, indicates (this): for when he was going to wash in the waters, an image of a man (εἰκὼν ἀνδρὸς) appeared to him from the spring of water. . . . And again, after a long time, he wished to wash in the waters and he ordered his disciples to [look out] for a place that did not [have much] water so that he might wash. [His] disciples [found] the place for him. But when he [was about to] wash, again for a second time, an image of a man (εἰκὼν ἀνδρὸς) appeared to him out of that spring.[171]

Stang suggests that in this episode the image in the water "is not of Alchasai himself, and thus raises the question of whether this image too is the *syzygos*, the divine companion to the Apostle of Light, who is here visiting not one of the apostles proper (e.g., Buddha, Zoroaster, Jesus), but instead visiting and guiding the figure, Alchasai, who will establish the law of the baptists in whose midst Mani will be raised."[172]

These traditions in which the divine image is described as reflected in the water might constitute the conceptual background of the eschatological restoration of Aseneth's *panim*, which in the doppelganger lore is often associated with the divine image.

Furthermore, Aseneth's final metamorphosis in the watery mirror might also be informed by some conceptual currents, similar to the one found in 2 Corinthians 3:15, where the transformation into the image is tied to the vision of the divine glory reflected in a mirror. In light of these testimonies, it is possible that Aseneth's vision represents the final stage of the process of acquisition of her heavenly identity when the seer's face becomes a mirror of the divine *Kavod* also known as God's *Panim*.

The transformation of the seer's face also brings to memory another theophanic account—namely, the metamorphosis of Enoch's face in *2 Enoch*, which, as we remember, occurred immediately after his acquisition of his heavenly identity, a procurement that has just occurred in Aseneth's story as well. As one recalls, in both stories, their transformed protagonists also undergo the transition from the "heavenly" transformed identities to their "normal" earthly selves. In this respect, it is intriguing that in both accounts these portentous transitions are marked by the metamorphosis of the adepts' visages. The transformations of the protagonists in *2 Enoch* and *Jos. Asen.*, however, are strikingly different: while Enoch's face prior to his trip to the earth was subdued by the "frigid" angel, Aseneth's countenance, on the contrary, was accentuated. It is almost like some sort of veil was removed from her face by means of the mysterious watery mirror, finally revealing her novel transformed visage.

Although both stories are informed by the Mosaic conceptual currents, the motif of Aseneth's transformed face appears to be closer to the traditional biblical rendering of Exodus where the great prophet veils his transformed countenance. Reflecting on Aseneth's transformation attested in *Jos. Asen.* 20:6,[173] Ross Kraemer draws attention to the Mosaic background of her transformation by arguing that

> it may also allude to the transformation of Moses in Exodus 34:29–34, which says that when Moses came down from Sinai, he did not know that his face shone because he had been talking to God. After this experience, Moses veils his face before the Israelites except when he goes to speak with God. This lends the veiling of Aseneth an interpretation alternative to the view that it reflects her status as a respectable woman. In subsequent Jewish mystical traditions, Moses' face was believed to shine with the reflection of God's glory. Aseneth's veiling may be analogous to that of Moses: just as Moses spoke with God face to face and beheld an aspect of God, so Aseneth has conversed with God, or at least God's manifestation in the form of the angel. Therefore, like Moses, her face shines and requires a veil to protect others from the brilliance of her face.[174]

The episode of Aseneth's transformation also invokes some memories of extrabiblical Mosaic traditions, especially those found in the *Exagoge*, where Moses' father-in-law, Jethro, calls him "stranger" (ξένος)—an epithet, which as we previously suggested, might point to the possibility of Moses' transformation. It is also noteworthy that in both accounts (the *Exagoge* and *Jos. Asen.*) it is the members of the seers' household who bring readers' and the protagonists' attention to their facial metamorphoses. In this respect, the reaction of Aseneth's *tropheus* and later Joseph himself[175] can be compared to the reaction of Moses' father-in-law.

In concluding this section of our study, we must acknowledge that the seer's vision in the watery mirror serves as a climax of the heavenly counterpart ideology, the conceptual trend so essential for the theological universe of *Jos. Asen.* In this perspective, all major protagonists of the story—the Anthropos, Joseph, and Aseneth—appear to be envisioned as "mirrors" of each other as they are portrayed again and again with similar theophanic attributes and features that provoke similar reactions from their beholders. Such imagery of embodied "mirrors" plays a paramount role in the conceptual framework of the text where all major characters are predestined to emulate, in their own paradoxal way, the mirror of the divine *Kavod*.

Conclusion

In conclusion of our study of the heavenly counterpart imagery found in the Jewish pseudepigrapha, it is time to return to the question about the conceptual roots of these striking developments. Our study of the doppelganger traditions found in the Jewish pseudepigrapha demonstrated that these theological currents are closely connected with theophanic imagery manifested in the biblical accounts. Thus, almost all major accounts of divine apparitions found in the Hebrew Bible became crucial conceptual nexuses for unfolding the heavenly counterpart speculations in the Jewish pseudepigraphical accounts.

Already in the *Book of the Watchers* and the *Book of the Similitudes*, two formative theophanic *loci* of the Hebrew Bible—the vision of the divine *Kavod* found in Ezekiel 1 and the appearance of the Son of Man in Daniel 7—became the main conceptual playgrounds for unfolding speculations about Enoch's heavenly identity. This reliance on biblical visions of the deity and the memories of their distinguished seers will continue to exercise its influence on the later speculations about the patriarch's heavenly Self reflected in *2 Enoch* and *Sefer Hekhalot* where the encounter with the divine Face by another prominent visionary of the Hebrew Bible, Moses, will become a locus of intense theological deliberations. This appropriation of the Mosaic biblical theophanic traditions by the Enochic lore will become eventually reflected in the symbolism of the radiant faces of Enoch and Metatron, whose visages come to be strikingly reminiscent of the luminosity of the son of Amram's countenance.

In the Mosaic pseudepigrapha, once again we find traces of the distinctive memories of the biblical encounters with the deity and the angels that occurred in the peculiar locations, represented among others by Mount Sinai, which has now become envisioned as the heavenly abode. The account found in the *Exagoge* waives a panoply of these familiar biblical Sinai motifs into the distinctive settings of the doppelganger lore. Furthermore, the symbolism of the divine *Panim* and its retinue, outlined already in Exodus and developed further in Enochic pseudepigrapha, will continue to exercise its prominent influence during

Moses' acquisition of his heavenly identity in the form of the angelic servant of the divine Face in the *Book of Jubilees*. Moreover, in later Jewish and Christian accounts, the divine Face will become portrayed as the mirror that is intended to reflect the seer's heavenly alter ego.

In the pseudepigraphical accounts devoted to the patriarch Jacob, his biblical encounters with the divine and angelic beings at Bethel and Jabbok again will come to be the crucial narrative vehicles for unfolding the speculations about the patriarch's heavenly identity. Both the *Prayer of Joseph* and the *Ladder of Jacob* take the patriarch's ordeals at Bethel and Penuel as the starting points of their doppelganger speculations. In the heavenly counterpart speculations about Jacob's heavenly image, one can also detect the formative influence of another biblical theophanic trend pertaining to the protoplast's figure, who according to Genesis 1:27 was created in the likeness of God's image.

The distinctive markers of the protoplast story will continue to exercise their formative influences also in *Jos. Asen.*, another Jewish pseudepigraphical account, deeply affected by the various molds of biblical theophanic imagery. There, the female seer, through her transformation, which has culminated in the consumption of the mysterious honeycomb, will be predestined to reverse the fall of the first protological couple in the Garden of Eden, who there once consumed the forbidden fruit from the Tree of the Knowledge of Good and Evil.

All these memories of the biblical theophanic accounts, so formative in shaping the pseudepigraphical doppelganger speculations, provide us with new evidence for the possible conceptual origins of the heavenly counterpart imagery in early Jewish and Christian lore. They point to the possibility that the complex symbolism of the heavenly double, found in the early Jewish pseudepigraphical materials, takes its inspiration not from the Greco-Roman or the "Iranian" mythologies, as has been previously suggested by Gilles Quispel and Henry Corbin, but instead represent an authentic Jewish phenomenon deeply rooted in the theophanic traditions of the Hebrew Bible.

Moreover, the heavenly counterpart traditions attested in the Jewish pseudepigrapha can be seen as an important stage in the developments of these biblical theophanic currents. They lead the symbolism of the divine and angelic encounters found in the Hebrew Bible into a new theophanic dimension. This novel mold, in which the ancient epiphanies become enriched with the doppelganger symbolism, play a formative role in shaping the later rabbinic and Hekhalot speculations about the heavenly identities of the exalted patriarchs and prophets. These will include the traditions about the celestial Self of Enoch in the form of the supreme angel Metatron and the rabbinic stories about the upper identity of Jacob in the form of his engraved or enthroned image—developments that will become crucial theophanic *loci* in later Jewish mysticism.

Furthermore, the heavenly counterpart traditions, with their keen attention to the details of the protagonists' transformations, the metamorphoses that are turning human adepts into celestial citizens, provide a unique insight into the murky and mysterious transition from Jewish apocalypticism, where the visionaries' heavenly identities are often envisioned as angelic manifestations, to early Jewish mysticism, where the seers' heavenly alter egos become paradoxically divinized.

Notes

Preface

1. A. Orlov, *The Enoch-Metatron Tradition* (TSAJ, 107; Tübingen: Mohr/Siebeck, 2005), 165ff.

2. A. Orlov, "The Face as the Heavenly Counterpart of the Visionary in the Slavonic Ladder of Jacob," in *Of Scribes and Sages: Early Jewish Interpretation and Transmission of Scripture* (2 vols.; ed. C. A. Evans; SSEJC, 9; London: T&T Clark, 2004), 2.59–76; idem, "Moses' Heavenly Counterpart in the Book of Jubilees and the Exagoge of Ezekiel the Tragedian," *Biblica* 88 (2007): 153–173; idem, "In the Mirror of the Divine Face: The Enochic Features of the Exagoge of Ezekiel the Tragedian," in *The Significance of Sinai: Traditions about Sinai and Divine Revelation in Judaism and Christianity* (ed. G. Brooks, H. Najman, L. Stuckenbruck; TBN, 12; Leiden: Brill, 2008), 183–199.

3. A. Orlov, *Dark Mirrors: Azazel and Satanael in Early Jewish Demonology* (Albany, NY: SUNY Press, 2011); idem, *Divine Scapegoats: Demonic Mimesis in Early Jewish Mysticism* (Albany, NY: SUNY Press, 2015).

Introduction

1. "I was gazing at my familiar with my eyes of light." *Manichaean Texts from the Roman Empire* (ed. I. Gardner and S. N. C. Lieu; Cambridge: Cambridge University Press, 2004), 101.

2. See *Keph.* 14:4–7; *Keph.* 14:27–15:3; *Keph.* 15:19–24; *Keph.* 16:19–21 in I. Gardner, *The Kephalaia of the Teacher: The Edited Coptic Manichaean Texts in Translation with Commentary* (NHMS, 37; Leiden: Brill, 1995), 20–22.

3. In modern times, there have been several studies attempting to apply the concept of a double to an interpretation of human experience and human development. One of the most influential applications has emerged from the psychoanalytical approach. Charles Stang notices that Sigmund Freud, for example, used the concept of a double, symbolized by the figure of Narcissus, for developing his theory of selfhood. For Freud, "narcissism" was a necessary developmental stage that must be surpassed on the way to proper adult selfhood. Stang demonstrates that Freud regarded the double, in its benign

and malevolent versions, as a developmental stage that ultimately supported his theory of repression and his explanation for the emergence of the superego. C. M. Stang, *Our Divine Double* (Cambridge, MA: Harvard University Press, 2016), 11–12.

4. Henry Corbin once defined the Eranos Seminar as "the meeting of acting, autonomous individualities, each in complete freedom revealing and expressing his original and personal way of thinking and being outside of all dogmatism and all academicism." H. Corbin, "The Time of Eranos," in *Man and Time: Papers from the Eranos Yearbooks* (ed. J. Campbell; Princeton: Princeton University Press, 1957), xx. On the history of the Eranos Seminar, see H. T. Hakl, *Eranos: An Alternative Intellectual History of the Twentieth Century* (trans. C. McIntosh; London: Routledge, 2014).

5. H. Corbin, *The Man of Light in Iranian Sufism* (trans. N. Pearson; New Lebanon, NY: Omega, 1971), 28–37; idem, *Avicenna and the Visionary Recital* (trans. W. R. Trask; Bollingen Series, 66; Princeton: Princeton University Press, 1986), 20–24; idem, *Spiritual Body and Celestial Earth: From Mazdean Iran to Shīʿite Iran* (trans. N. Pearson; Princeton: Princeton University Press, 1989), 9–10.

6. G. Quispel, "Das ewige Ebenbild des Menschen: Zur Begegnung mit dem Selbst in der Gnosis," *Eranos-Jahrbuch* 36 (1967): 9–30; idem, "Genius and Spirit," in *Gnostica, Judaica, Catholica: Collected Essays of Gilles Quispel* (ed. J. van Oort; NHMS, 55; Leiden: Brill, 2008), 103–118.

7. G. Scholem, *On the Mystical Shape of the Godhead* (New York: Schocken, 1976).

8. A. DeConick, *Seek to See Him: Ascent and Vision Mysticism in the Gospel of Thomas* (SVC, 33; Leiden: Brill, 1996), 150–151. In his recent book, Charles Stang reiterates this hypothesis about the formative influences of the concept of *daimon* on some early heavenly counterpart traditions. Stang's study follows the already familiar row of Christian and Manichaean sources, previously traversed by Quispel, including Tatian's *Oratio ad Graecos*, Clement of Alexandria's *Excerpta ex Theodoto*, the *Gospel of Thomas*, the *Acts of Thomas*, the *Book of Thomas the Contender*, the *Gospel of Philip*, the *Cologne Mani Codex*, and the *Kephalaia of the Teacher*. Similar to Quispel, Stang also does not deal at all with Jewish pseudepigraphical texts and traditions while recognizing that "there are undoubtedly other witnesses to the divine double from these same centuries, including not only other Christian sources but also Jewish, Hermetic, and Sethian sources." Stang, *Our Divine Double*, 143.

9. DeConick, *Seek to See Him*, 151.

10. Corbin, *The Man of Light in Iranian Sufism*, 28–33. On the Iranian imagery of the heavenly counterparts, see also M. Boyce, "Fravaši," *Encyclopedia Iranica* (ed. E. Yarshater; 16 vols.; Costa Mesa: Mazda, 2001), 10.195–199; idem, "The Absorption of the Fravašis into Zoroastrianism," *AOASH* 48.1–2 (1995): 26; C. Colpe, "Daēnā, Lichtjungfrau, Zweite Gestalt: Verbindungen und Unterschiede zwischen zarathustrischer und manichäischer Selbst-Anschauung," in *Studies in Gnosticism and Hellenistic Religions, presented to Gilles Quispel on the Occasion of His 65th Birthday* (EPRO, 91; ed. R. van den Broek and M. J. Vermaseren; Leiden: Brill, 1981), 58–77; F.-T. Lankarny, *Daēnā in Avesta: Eine Semantische Untersuchung* (SII, 10: Reinbek: Verlag für Orientalistische Fachpublikationen, 1985); M. Molé, "Daēnā, Le Pont Činvat et l'initiation dans le Mazdéisme," *RHR* 157 (1960): 155–185; J. H. Moulton "'It Is His Angel,'" *JTS* 3 (1902): 514–527; idem,

"Fravashi," in *Encyclopaedia of Religion and Ethics* (ed. J. Hastings; 12 vols.; Edinburgh: Charles Scribner's Sons, 1913), 5.116–118; idem, *Early Zoroastrianism: Lectures Delivered at Oxford and in London February to May 1912* (London: Constable & Company, 1926), 254–285; S. Shaked, *Dualism in Transformation: Varieties of Religion in Sasanian Iran* (Jordan Lectures; London: School of Oriental and African Studies, 1994), 146–147; A. F. von Gall, *Basileia tou theou: Eine religionsgeschichtliche Studie zur vorkirchlichen Eschatologie* (Heidelberg: Carl Winter, 1926), 99–102, 111–115.

Chapter One: The Heavenly Counterpart Traditions in the Enochic Pseudepigrapha

1. In relation to this enigmatic priestly group, Gabriele Boccaccini observes that

after the Babylonian exile and the end of the Davidic monarchy, the leadership of the Jewish people was provided by the Zadokites. They claimed descent from Zadok, according to the ancient Jewish historiography a priest and companion of David (2 Sam 8:17), who supported Solomon as the legitimate heir and anointed him king (1 Kgs 1:32–46). For around 350 years, the high priesthood in Jerusalem was held by individuals who asserted themselves, and were recognized by their subjects, as members of a single family line. From the construction of the Second Temple to the eve of the Maccabean Revolt, Flavius Josephus gives a list of 14 names. . . . Whether the list is accurate and complete, and whether the continuity of blood was never broken, are matters of scholarly debate, yet there are no doubts about the historicity of Zadokite supremacy.

G. Boccaccini, *Roots of Rabbinic Judaism: An Intellectual History from Ezekiel to Daniel* (Grand Rapids, MI: Eerdmans, 2002), 43.

2. G. Boccaccini, *Beyond the Essene Hypothesis: The Parting of the Ways between Qumran and Enochic Judaism* (Grand Rapids, MI: Eerdmans, 1998), 71.

3. On the heavenly temple and heavenly priesthood traditions, see J. L. Angel, *Otherworldly and Eschatological Priesthood in the Dead Sea Scrolls* (STDJ, 86; Leiden: Brill, 2010); V. Aptowitzer, "The Celestial Temple as Viewed in the Aggadah," in *Binah: Studies in Jewish Thought* (ed. J. Dan; Binah: Studies in Jewish History, Thought, and Culture, 2; New York: Praeger, 1989), 1–29; M. Barker, *The Gate of Heaven: The History and Symbolism of the Temple in Jerusalem* (London: SPCK, 1991); J. J. Collins, "A Throne in the Heavens: Apotheosis in Pre-Christian Judaism," in *Death, Ecstasy, and Other Worldly Journeys* (ed. J. J. Collins and M. Fishbane; Albany, NY: SUNY Press, 1995), 43–57; B. Ego, *"Im Himmel wie auf Erden"* (WUNT, 2.34; Tübingen: Mohr/Siebeck, 1989); R. Elior, "From Earthly Temple to Heavenly Shrines: Prayer and Sacred Song in the Hekhalot Literature and its Relation to Temple Traditions," *JSQ* 4 (1997): 217–267; D. N. Freedman, "Temple Without Hands," in *Temples and High Places in Biblical Times: Proceedings of the Colloquium in Honor of the Centennial of Hebrew Union College-*

Jewish Institute of Religion, Jerusalem, 14–16 March 1977 (ed. A. Biran; Jerusalem: Hebrew Union College–Jewish Institute of Religion, 1981), 21–30; I. Gruenwald, *Apocalyptic and Merkavah Mysticism* (2nd ed.; Leiden: Brill, 2014); D. Halperin, *The Faces of the Chariot: Early Jewish Response to Ezekiel's Vision* (TSAJ, 16; Tübingen: Mohr/Siebeck, 1988); idem, "Heavenly Ascension in Ancient Judaism: The Nature of the Experience," *SBLSP* 26 (1987): 218–231; R. G. Hamerton-Kelly, "The Temple and the Origins of Jewish Apocalyptic," *VT* 20 (1970): 1–15; M. Himmelfarb, "From Prophecy to Apocalypse: The Book of the Watchers and Tours of Heaven," in *Jewish Spirituality: From the Bible through the Middle Ages* (ed. A. Green; New York: Crossroad, 1986), 145–165; idem, "Apocalyptic Ascent and the Heavenly Temple," *SBLSP* 26 (1987): 210–217; idem, *Ascent to Heaven in Jewish and Christian Apocalypses* (New York: Oxford University Press, 1993); idem, "The Practice of Ascent in the Ancient Mediterranean World," in *Death, Ecstasy, and Other Worldly Journeys* (ed. J. J. Collins and M. Fishbane; Albany, NY: SUNY Press, 1995), 123–137; C. R. Koester, *The Dwelling of God: The Tabernacle in the Old Testament, Intertestamental Jewish Literature and the New Testament* (CBQMS, 22; Washington, DC: Catholic Biblical Association of America, 1989); J. D. Levenson, "The Temple and the World," *JR* 64 (1984): 275–298; idem, "The Jerusalem Temple in Devotional and Visionary Experience," in *Jewish Spirituality: From the Bible through the Middle Ages* (ed. A. Green; New York: Crossroad, 1987), 32–59; A. J. McNicol, "The Heavenly Sanctuary in Judaism: A Model for Tracing the Origin of the Apocalypse," *JRelS* 13 (1987): 66–94; C. R. A. Morray-Jones, "Transformational Mysticism in the Apocalyptic-Merkabah Tradition," *JJS* 43 (1992): 1–31; idem, "The Temple Within: The Embodied Divine Image and Its Worship in the Dead Sea Scrolls and Other Jewish and Christian Sources," *SBLSP* 37 (1998): 400–431; C. Newsom " 'He Has Established for Himself Priests': Human and Angelic Priesthood in the Qumran Sabbath Shirot," in *Archaeology and History in the Dead Sea Scrolls: The New York University Conference in Memory of Yigael Yadin* (ed. L. H. Schiffman; JSPSS, 8; Sheffield: JSOT Press, 1990), 101–120; G. W. E. Nickelsburg, "The Apocalyptic Construction of Reality in 1 Enoch," in *Mysteries and Revelations: Apocalyptic Studies since the Uppsala Colloquium* (ed. J. J. Collins; JSPSS, 9; Sheffield: JSOT Press, 1991), 51–64; R. Patai, *Man and Temple in Ancient Jewish Myth and Ritual* (New York: Ktav, 1967); C. Rowland, "The Visions of God in Apocalyptic Literature," *JSJ* 10 (1979): 137–154; idem, *The Open Heaven: A Study of Apocalyptic in Judaism and Early Christianity* (London: SPCK, 1982); A. F. Segal, "Heavenly Ascent in Hellenistic Judaism, Early Christianity and Their Environment," *ANRW* II/23.2 (1980): 1333–1394; M. S. Smith, "Biblical and Canaanite Notes to the Songs of the Sabbath Sacrifice from Qumran," *RevQ* 12 (1987): 585–588.

 4. See Exod 25:8–9: "And have them make me a sanctuary, so that I may dwell among them. In accordance with all that I show you concerning the pattern of the tabernacle and of all its furniture, so you shall make it." Exod 25:40: "And see that you make them according to the pattern for them, which is being shown you on the mountain." Exod 26:30: "Then you shall erect the tabernacle according to the plan for it that you were shown on the mountain." Exod 27:8: "You shall make it hollow, with boards. They shall be made just as you were shown on the mountain." Num 8:4: "Now this was how the lampstand was made, out of hammered work of gold. From its base to its flowers,

it was hammered work; according to the pattern that the Lord had shown Moses, so he made the lampstand." All biblical quotations are taken from the New Revised Standard Version (NRSV) unless otherwise indicated. Cf. also *Bereshit Rabbah* 69:7: "R. Simeon b. Yohai said: The celestial Temple is higher than the terrestrial one only by eighteen miles." H. Freedman and M. Simon, *Midrash Rabbah* (10 vols.; London: Soncino, 1961), 2.634.

5. G. Beale, *The Temple and the Church's Mission* (NSBT, 17; Downers Grove, IL: InterVarsity Press, 2004), 32. Beale and Ego also drew attention to the later rabbinic elaborations of this idea of correspondence between the earthly and heavenly sanctuary found in *Targ. Onq.* on 2 Chr 6:2; *Targ. Ps.-J.* on Exod 15:17; *Num. Rab.* 4:13; 12:12; Midrash on Psalms 30:1. See Beale, *The Temple and the Church's Mission*, 32, n. 7; Ego, "Im Himmel wie auf Erden."

6. 1 Chr 28:19: "All this, in writing at the Lord's direction, he made clear to me—the plan of all the works."

7. Gabriele Boccaccini observes that "as the temple so closely mirrors the divine order of heaven, 'to enter the Temple and take part in the Temple cult is therefore to participate in some degree in the unceasing worship going on in heaven.'" Boccaccini, *Roots of Rabbinic Judaism*, 80. On this, see also J. Blenkinsopp, *Sage, Priest, Prophet: Religious and Intellectual Leadership in Ancient Israel* (Louisville, KY: Westminster John Knox, 1995), 113.

8. J. M. Scott, *On Earth as in Heaven: The Restoration of Sacred Time and Sacred Space in the Book of Jubilees* (JSJSS, 91; Leiden: Brill, 2005), 217.

9. On Mesopotamian traditions of the heavenly sanctuaries, see Smith, "Biblical and Canaanite Notes to the Songs of the Sabbath Sacrifice from Qumran," 585–588.

10. Beale, *The Temple and the Church's Mission*, 32, n. 5.

11. The *Book of the Watchers* represents a multilayered composition, of which the earliest strata are usually dated to the third century BCE. On the date of the *Book of the Watchers*, see J. H. Charlesworth, "A Rare Consensus among Enoch Specialists: The Date of the Earliest Enoch Books," *Henoch* 24 (2002): 255–234; J. J. Collins, *The Apocalyptic Imagination: An Introduction to Jewish Apocalyptic Literature* (2nd ed.; Grand Rapids, MI: Eerdmans, 1998), 44; T. M. Erho and L. T. Stuckenbruck, "A Manuscript History of Ethiopic Enoch," *JSP* 23 (2013): 87–133; G. W. E. Nickelsburg, *1 Enoch 1: A Commentary on the Book of 1 Enoch; Chapters 1–36; 81–108* (Hermeneia; Minneapolis: Fortress, 2001); M. E. Stone, "The Book of Enoch and Judaism in the Third Century B.C.E.," *CBQ* 40 (1978): 479–492 at 484.

12. M. Knibb, *The Ethiopic Book of Enoch: A New Edition in the Light of the Aramaic Dead Sea Fragments* (2 vols.; Oxford: Clarendon, 1978), 2.98–99.

13. Himmelfarb, "Apocalyptic Ascent," 210.

14. Himmelfarb, "Apocalyptic Ascent," 211.

15. Other pseudepigraphical accounts (*Jubilees, Aramaic Levi Document*) and some Qumran materials (*Songs of the Sabbath Sacrifice, 4QInstruction, 4QVisions of Amram, 11QMelchizedek*) also develop the concept of the heavenly temple and associate it with the notion of the heavenly priesthood.

16. G. W. E. Nickelsburg, "Enoch, Levi, and Peter: Recipients of Revelation in Upper Galilee," *JBL* 100 (1981): 575–600, esp. 579.

17. David Halperin's research also stresses the "apocalyptic" priestly function of Enoch in the *Book of the Watchers*. He observes that "Daniel and Enoch share an image, perhaps drawn from the hymnic tradition of merkavah exegesis (think of the Angelic liturgy), of God surrounded by multitudes of angels. But, in the Holy of Holies, God sits alone. . . . The angels, barred from the inner house, are the priests of Enoch's heavenly Temple. The high priest must be Enoch himself, who appears in the celestial Holy of Holies to procure forgiveness for holy beings." Halperin, *Faces of the Chariot*, 81–82. Helge Kvanvig also argues for Enoch's priestly role in *1 Enoch* 14. On this, see H. Kvanvig, "The Son of Man in the Parables of Enoch," in *Enoch and the Messiah Son of Man: Revisiting the Book of Parables* (ed. G. Boccaccini; Grand Rapids, MI: Eerdmans, 2007), 182–183. For the criticism of this position, see J. Collins, "Enoch and the Son of Man: A Response to Sabino Chialà and Helge Kvanvig," in *Enoch and the Messiah Son of Man*, 219.

18. Himmelfarb, "Apocalyptic Ascent," 213.

19. Enoch's sacerdotal duties in the *Book of the Watchers* also involve his intercession on behalf of the Watchers and transmission of the judgment against Asael. Crispin Fletcher-Louis observes that "Enoch's intercession and transmission of the judgment against Asael is thoroughly priestly and related closely to that of the high priest on the Day of Atonement whose ministry involves the sending of a scapegoat into the wilderness to Azazel (Lev 16)." C. Fletcher-Louis, *All the Glory of Adam: Liturgical Anthropology in the Dead Sea Scrolls* (STDJ, 42; Leiden: Brill, 2002), 40.

20. Himmelfarb, "Apocalyptic Ascent," 212.

21. Kvanvig, "The Son of Man in the Parables of Enoch," 181.

22. Kvanvig, "The Son of Man in the Parables of Enoch," 182. For the criticism of this position, see Collins, "Enoch and the Son of Man," 218.

23. Both James VanderKam and Helge Kvanvig have argued that "Enoch sees the Son of Man in visions of the future, not in disclosures of the present. He is seeing what he will become." Kvanvig, "The Son of Man in the Parables of Enoch," 201.

24. Kvanvig, "The Son of Man in the Parables of Enoch," 181.

25. The *Animal Apocalypse* is usually dated to the second century BCE. In relation to the date of the text, Daniel Olson notes that

> fragments of the *An. Apoc.* from Qumran provide a *terminus ad quem* before 100 B.C.E., but greater precision is possible since the allegory appears to describe the ascendancy of Judas Maccabee (90:9), but says nothing about his death (90:12). Based on this, most scholars agree that the *An. Apoc.* was written between 165–160 B.C.E., and they further agree that the author was probably a member of or a sympathizer with the reform group described in 90:6–9 and a supporter of the Maccabean revolt when it broke out, expecting it to evolve into earth's final battle, God's direct intervention in history, and the inauguration of the eschatological age (90:9–20). If this is correct, one may suppose that one reason the *An. Apoc.* was published was to encourage readers to back the Maccabean revolt.

D. Olson, *A New Reading of the Animal Apocalypse of 1 Enoch: "All Nations Shall be Blessed"* (SVTP, 24; Leiden: Brill, 2013), 85–86. See also D. Assefa, *L'Apocalypse des animaux (1Hen 85–90): Une propagande militaire? Approches narrative, historico-critique, perspectives théologiques* (JSJSS, 120; Leiden: Brill, 2007), 220–232.

26. Thus, for example, *1 Enoch* 89:36 depicts Moses as the one who was transformed from a sheep into a man at Sinai. In the metaphorical language of the *Animal Apocalypse*, where angels are portrayed as anthropomorphic and humans as zoomorphic creatures, the transition from the sheep to a man unambiguously indicates that the character has acquired an angelic form and status.

27. See J. VanderKam, "Righteous One, Messiah, Chosen One, and Son of Man in 1 Enoch 37–71," in *The Messiah: Developments in Earliest Judaism and Christianity; The First Princeton Symposium on Judaism and Christian Origins* (ed. J. H. Charlesworth, et al.; Minneapolis: Fortress, 1992), 182–183; M. Knibb, "Messianism in the Pseudepigrapha in the Light of the Scrolls," *DSD* 2 (1995): 177–180; J. Fossum, *The Image of the Invisible God: Essays on the Influence of Jewish Mysticism on Early Christology* (NTOA, 30; Fribourg: Universitätsverlag Freiburg Schweiz. Göttingen: Vanderhoeck & Ruprecht, 1995), 144–145; C. H. T. Fletcher-Louis, *Luke–Acts: Angels, Christology and Soteriology* (WUNT, 2.94; Tübingen: Mohr/Siebeck, 1997), 151; A. Orlov, *The Enoch-Metatron Tradition* (TSAJ, 107; Tübingen: Mohr/Siebeck, 2005), 167–168.

28. In his conclusion to the Enoch Seminar's volume devoted to the *Similitudes*, Paolo Sacchi writes: "In sum, we may observe that those scholars who have directly addressed the problem of dating the Parables all agree on a date around the time of Herod. Other participants of the conference not addressing the problem directly nevertheless agree with this conclusion." P. Sacchi, "The 2005 Camaldoli Seminar on the Parables of Enoch: Summary and Prospects for Future Research," in *Enoch and the Messiah Son of Man*, 510. See also D. Suter, "Enoch in Sheol: Updating the Dating of the Book of Parables," in *Enoch and the Messiah Son of Man*, 415–443; G. W. E. Nickelsburg and J. C. VanderKam, *1 Enoch 2: A Commentary on the Book of 1 Enoch. Chapters 37–82* (Hermeneia; Minneapolis: Fortress, 2012), 58–63.

29. Knibb, *Ethiopic Book of Enoch*, 2.165–167.

30. Crispin Fletcher-Louis argues that "the identification of Enoch with the Son of Man is intended throughout [the text], and thus chapter 71 is the climax of the whole . . . already in 37:1 the Ethiopic of Enoch's genealogy presents him as the 'walda henos, walda 'adam, both of which mean 'son of man.'" Fletcher-Louis, *Luke-Acts*, 151.

31. VanderKam, "Righteous One," 182–183.

32. VanderKam, "Righteous One," 182–183. Jacob's developments will be explored in detail later in our study.

33. Michael Knibb supports VanderKam's hypothesis by stating the following:

> I would therefore still argue in favor of the view that a real identification is made between Enoch and the pre-existent son of man in 71:14, and I would also argue that the awkwardness of this identification combined with the literary evidence makes it very likely that chapters 70–71 are secondary. Perhaps no more need be said than this. But the awkwardness still remains at the redactional level, and here the idea, to which VanderKam has drawn attention, that a human being could have a heavenly double or counterpart is of relevance in helping to explain the awkwardness. One of the texts to

which VanderKam refers, *Prayer of Joseph* Fragment A is the most important. Here Jacob states: "I, Jacob, who is speaking to you, am also Israel, an angel of God and a ruling spirit. Abraham and Isaac were created before any work. But, I, Jacob, who men call Jacob but whose name is Israel am he who God called Israel which means, a man seeing God, because I am the firstborn of every living thing to whom God gives life." Here Jacob the man identifies himself as also being the angel Israel, and it is particularly significant that the angel Israel is conceived of as being preexistent.

Knibb, "Messianism in the Pseudepigrapha in the Light of the Scrolls," 180.

34. In relation to this tradition, James Charlesworth observes that "chapter 71:5 continues to clarify that Enoch is the one who speaks in the first person and 'in the heaven of heavens.' The conclusion seems to evolve: the 'Son of Man' relates to Enoch himself. This title does not focus on Enoch as a human being; he is someone being singled out or set apart for a special purpose. Perhaps the early Jew who composed this masterpiece imagined that the human Enoch finally perceives his heavenly counterpart, his eternal Self and his God-given task to serve as eschatological Judge." J. Charlesworth, "The Date and Provenience of the Parables of Enoch," in *Parables of Enoch: A Paradigm Shift* (ed. D. Bock and J. Charlesworth; London: T&T Clark, 2013), 37–57 at 42.

35. VanderKam, "Righteous One," 183.

36. A notable detail in the description is that during his ascension Enoch, in a manner similar to Jacob's vision of the ladder, sees the angelic movements and the angelic faces. In *1 Enoch* 71:1, he reports about "the sons of the holy angels treading upon flames of fire, and their garments (were) white, and their clothing, and the light of their face (was) like snow." Knibb, *Ethiopic Book of Enoch*, 2.165.

37. Knibb, *Ethiopic Book of Enoch*, 2.166.

38. In the *Book of the Watchers* (*1 Enoch* 14:18–19), the Throne of Glory is also described as a crystal structure surrounded by rivers of fire. The reference to a "crystal" structure also recalls the depiction of the Throne in Ezek 1:26, where it is portrayed as a throne of sapphire (ספיר).

39. *1 Enoch* 71:7: "And round about (were) the Seraphim, and the Cherubim, and the Ophannim; these are they who do not sleep, but keep watch over the throne of his glory." Knibb, *Ethiopic Book of Enoch*, 2.166.

40. In relation to the concept of the doppelganger, Collins notes that

> the Son of Man is not a personification of the righteous community, but is conceived, in mythological fashion, as its heavenly *Doppelgänger*. Now it is characteristic of mythological thinking that such a *Doppelgänger* is conceived to be more real and permanent than its earthly counterpart and prior to it in the order of being. From a modern critical perspective, the reverse is true. It "is a question of men before it is a question of angels." The human community is the datum of our experience and knowledge. The heavenly counterpart is posited on the basis of this datum. While the Son of Man is conceived as a real being, he symbolizes the destiny of the righteous community both in its present hiddenness and future manifestation.

Collins, *The Apocalyptic Imagination*, 187. Collins also observes that the "close connection between the individual Son of Man and the community of the righteous has led some scholars to invoke the allegedly Hebrew conception of corporate personality. This idea has rightly been criticized insofar as it implies 'psychical unity' and rests on outdated anthropological theories that have been widely discredited." Collins, *The Apocalyptic Imagination*, 185. See also J. J. Collins, *Daniel: A Commentary on the Book of Daniel* (Hermeneia; Minneapolis: Fortress, 1993), 82, 310.

41. It is possible that such correspondences can be encountered even in the *Book of the Similitudes*. Thus, Daniel Olson argues that "the Son of Man in the *Parables*, also called the 'Chosen One' and the 'Righteous One,' has his earthly counterpart in the congregation of 'the chosen,' 'the righteous,' and 'the holy' (38:1; 41:2; 45:1; 46:8; 53:6; 62:8)." Olson, *A New Reading*, 96.

42. J. J. Collins, "The Heavenly Representative: The 'Son of Man' in the Similitudes of Enoch," in *Ideal Figures in Ancient Judaism: Profiles and Paradigms* (ed. J. Collins and G. Nickelsburg; SBLSCS, 12; Missoula, MO: Scholars, 1980), 114. See also J. J. Collins, *The Apocalyptic Vision of the Book of Daniel* (HSM, 16; Missoula, MO: Scholars, 1977), 144–146.

43. A similar pattern where the Son of Man becomes juxtaposed with the heavenly correlatives of social entities can be found in Rev 1 with its portrayal of the Son of Man figure and seven angelic patrons of seven Christian churches. On this, see D. E. Aune, *Revelation 1–5* (WBC, 52A; Nashville: Thomas Nelson, 1997), 109–111.

44. See Darrell Hannah's research on heavenly representatives of the nations, both positive and demonic, in D. Hannah, "Guardian Angels and Angelic National Patrons in Second Temple Judaism and Early Christianity," in *Angels: The Concept of Celestial Beings; Origins, Development and Reception* (ed. F. V. Reiterer, T. Nicklas, K. Schöpflin; Deuterocanonical and Cognate Literature Yearbook; Berlin: Walter de Gruyter, 2007), 413–435.

45. D. C. Allison Jr., *Constructing Jesus: Memory, Imagination, and History* (Grand Rapids, MI: Baker Academic, 2010), 300. See also Klaus Koch's paper, "Questions Regarding the So-Called Son of Man in the Parables of Enoch: A Response to Sabino Chialà and Helge Kvanvig," in *Enoch and the Messiah Son of Man*, 237 n. 24.

46. D. Catchpole, "The Angelic Son of Man in Luke 12:8," *NovT* 24 (1982): 255–265. On this tradition, see also B. Chilton, "(The) Son of (the) Man, and Jesus," in *Authenticating the Words of Jesus* (ed. B. Chilton and C. A. Evans; Leiden: Brill, 1999), 259–288; S. J. Gathercole, *The Preexistent Son: Recovering the Christologies of Matthew, Mark, and Luke* (Grand Rapids, MI: Eerdmans, 2006), 267–268.

47. Allison, *Constructing Jesus*, 300.

48. Allison, *Constructing Jesus*, 300.

49. If Luke 12:8–9 indeed speaks about the heavenly counterpart of Jesus in the form of the Son of Man, verse 10, which immediately follows this passage, also appears to be important. There Jesus claims that "everyone who speaks a word against the Son of Man will be forgiven; but whoever blasphemes against the Holy Spirit will not be forgiven." As will be shown in our study, in some Christian and Manichaean traditions, the heavenly identity of a human being was often identified with the Holy Spirit.

50. Catchpole, "The Angelic Son of Man," 260.

51. Catchpole, "The Angelic Son of Man," 260.

52. Catchpole, "The Angelic Son of Man," 260.

53. Scrutinizing Catchpole's hypothesis, Crispin Fletcher-Louis observes that "there are a couple of interrelated weaknesses in Catchpole's reading. First, he has too rigid a distinction between Jesus and his angelic counterpart, which conflicts with the Son of Man concept we have found elsewhere. Secondly, he fails to provide an example of a text where the distinction between angelic guardian and human being is expressed by means of alternative names or titles." Fletcher-Louis, *Luke-Acts*, 235–236.

54. Fletcher-Louis, *Luke-Acts*, 236. Fletcher-Louis also notes that Catchpole's comparison with Mt 18:10 poses a risk of reducing the Son of Man to the mere heavenly Self of one individual, i.e. Jesus. In Fletcher-Louis' opinion

> sight should not be lost of the fact that the Son of Man holds a very specific office in the heavenly realm, particularly as judge and intercessor. It is by no means self-evident that Jesus could have said, on analogy with Mt 18:10, "whoever confesses one of these little ones on earth, their angelic guardians will confess them before (the other) angels of God. . . ." That confession and denial take place before the angels of God, suggests that the Son of Man is set over against those angels. That Jesus/Son of Man is in fact more than angelic in this saying is indicated by an important connection with the *Similitudes*, hitherto ignored.

Fletcher-Louis, *Luke-Acts*, 237. In his recent book, Fletcher-Louis reaffirms his position by saying that in Luke 12:8–9 "Jesus' present heavenly identity . . . stands behind his empirical earthly identity." Fletcher-Louis argues that in Luke 12:8–9 "the Son of Man can be taken as a way of talking about Jesus' true, heavenly identity, which is unrecognized on earth. On analogy to Jesus' view that disciples have an angelic Self or counterpart in heaven—the most likely import of Matt 18:10, Jesus really is, already in the present, the heavenly Son of Man of apocalyptic tradition. On earth his Son of Man identity goes unrecognized and he is even reviled by some (Luke 12:10), but in heaven his witness is decisive in the divine courtroom (cf. Dan 7:9–14)." C. Fletcher-Louis, *Jesus Monotheism: Volume 1; Christological Origins: The Emerging Consensus and Beyond* (Eugene, OR: Cascade Books, 2015), 103.

55. Reflecting on these traditions, Jarl Fossum observes,

> Finally coming back to John 1.51, we now have to ask if the Gospel contains the idea that Jesus, like Jacob-Israel, is both in heaven and on earth at the same time. It would seem that this actually is an aspect of John's Christology which has gone rather unappreciated. John 1.18 says: "No one has ever seen God; the Only-Begotten, the one being in the bosom of the Father (ὁ ὢν εἰς τὸν κόλπον τοῦ πατρός), has revealed him." It is not improbable that ὢν denotes the continuous timeless existence of the revealer with God: even when he is on earth and brings the revelation, the Son is in the Father's bosom. The original text of 3.13 would seem to have read: "No one has gone up into heaven except the one having come down from heaven, the Son

of Man, *who is in heaven* (ὁ ὢν ἐν τῷ οὐρανῷ)." In this statement, which is uttered by Jesus, we again find the suggestion of the revealer's timeless existence with God.

Fossum, *Image of the Invisible God*, 149.

56. On the Son of Man as Jesus' heavenly counterpart in the Gospel of John, see C. F. Burney, *The Aramaic Origin of the Fourth Gospel* (Oxford: Clarendon, 1922), 115; C. H. Dodd, *The Interpretation of the Fourth Gospel* (Cambridge: Cambridge University Press, 1953), 245ff.; H. Odeberg, *The Fourth Gospel: Interpreted in Its Relation to Contemporaneous Religious Currents in Palestine and the Hellenistic-Oriental World* (Uppsala: Almqvist & Wiksell, 1929; repr. Chicago: Argonaut, 1968), 33–42; C. Rowland, "John 1.51, Jewish Apocalyptic and Targumic Tradition," *NTS* 30 (1984): 498–507; Fossum, *Image of the Invisible God*, 135–151.

57. On the date of *2 Enoch*, see R. H. Charles, and W. R. Morfill, *The Book of the Secrets of Enoch* (Oxford: Clarendon, 1896), xxvi; R. H. Charles and N. Forbes, "The Book of the Secrets of Enoch," in *The Apocrypha and Pseudepigrapha of the Old Testament* (2 vols.; ed. R. H. Charles; Oxford: Clarendon, 1913), 2.429; J. T. Milik, *The Books of Enoch* (Oxford: Clarendon, 1976), 114; C. Böttrich, *Das slavische Henochbuch* (JSHRZ, 5; Gütersloh: Gütersloher Verlaghaus, 1995), 813; Orlov, *The Enoch-Metatron Tradition*, 323–328; idem, "The Sacerdotal Traditions of 2 Enoch and the Date of the Text," in *New Perspectives on 2 Enoch: No Longer Slavonic Only* (ed. A. Orlov, G. Boccaccini, J. Zurawski; SJS, 4; Leiden: Brill, 2012), 103–116.

58. *Yalkut Shimoni* depicts the divine Face looking at thousands of visionaries. For this tradition, see M. Idel, *Old Worlds, New Mirrors: On Jewish Mysticism and Twentieth-Century Thought* (Philadelphia: University of Pennsylvania Press, 2010), 45.

59. F. Andersen, "2 (Slavonic Apocalypse of) Enoch," in *The Old Testament Pseudepigrapha* (ed. J. H. Charlesworth; 2 vols.; New York: Doubleday, 1983–1985), 1.163.

60. The exploration of heavenly counterpart imagery often reveals a paradoxical fluidity of this symbolism. Sometimes a translated figure is depicted on earth and then in heaven. Sometimes the same figure is on earth and in heaven at the same time, while the two selves are not yet merged. Sometimes the two identities are merged and become one. One can see these perplexing variations in the correspondences between earthly and heavenly versions of the protagonists again and again in our study. At first look, it appears that we might have here different concepts of the heavenly counterpart that should be treated separately. Yet, a closer look at these phenomena indicates that the aforementioned variations in "correspondences," in fact, often simply represent various stages in the acquisition of the heavenly identity. Thus, in the initial stages of the heavenly counterpart's procurement, the heavenly and the earthly "identities" of the protagonist are often depicted as separate entities. Later, during the adept's unification with his or her heavenly counterpart, the two selves are often merged. Then, at the end of the process, we often only have one identity postulated, while the other is no longer mentioned.

61. *2 Enoch* 36:3. Andersen, "2 Enoch," 1.161.

62. W. F. Stinespring, "Testament of Isaac," in *The Old Testament Pseudepigrapha*, 1.905.

63. *Targ. Neof.* to Gen 28:12: "And behold, the angels from before the Lord ascended and descended and observed him [Jacob]." *Targum Neofiti 1: Genesis* (trans. M. McNamara, MSC; ArBib, 1A; Collegeville, MN: Liturgical Press, 1992), 140; *Gen. Rab.* 68:12: "They ascended on high and saw his features and they descended below and found him sleeping." Freedman and Simon, *Midrash Rabbah*, 2.626.

64. J. Z. Smith, "Prayer of Joseph," in *The Old Testament Pseudepigrapha*, 2.699–714 at 705. See also J. Z. Smith, "The Prayer of Joseph," in *Religions in Antiquity: Essays in Memory of Erwin Ramsdell Goodenough* (ed. J. Neusner; SHR, 14; Leiden: Brill, 1968), 253–294 at 290–291.

65. *2 Enoch* 33:3–10 (the shorter recension). Andersen, "2 Enoch," 1.157.

66. See *2 Enoch* 23:6: "I wrote everything accurately. And I wrote 366 books." Andersen, "2 Enoch," 1.140.

67. See *Jub.* 6:22 and 30:12. On the blurred boundaries between the angel of the Presence and the deity in *Jubilees*, see J. C. VanderKam, "The Angel of the Presence in the Book of Jubilees," *DSD* 7 (2000): 378–393 at 390–392. It should be noted that the tendency to identify the seer's heavenly identity with the deity or his anthropomorphic extent (known as his *Kavod* or the Face) is discernable in all accounts dealing with the heavenly counterpart.

68. Although the text undoubtedly contains early pseudepigraphical traditions, the final composition of the macroform is usually dated to the ninth or tenth centuries CE. Peter Schäfer notes that the text belongs to the late phase of the Hekhalot literature. He considers that the redaction of the Babylonian Talmud should be taken as the *terminus post quem* of the text and a quotation from §§71–80 by the Karaite Kirkisani as its *terminus ante quem*, which provides a time frame from ca. 700 CE until ca. 900 CE for the final redaction of *3 Enoch*. P. Schäfer, *The Origins of Jewish Mysticism* (Tübingen: Mohr/Siebeck, 2009), 315–316. See also P. S. Alexander, "The Historical Setting of the Hebrew Book of Enoch," *JJS* 28 (1977): 156–180.

69. Fletcher-Louis, *Luke-Acts*, 156. See also M. Himmelfarb, "The Experience of the Visionary and Genre in the Ascension of Isaiah 6–11 and the Apocalypse of Paul," in *Early Christian Apocalypticism: Genre and Social Setting* (ed. A. Y. Collins; Semeia, 36; Decatur, GA: Scholars, 1986), 97–111, esp. 102.

70. A. F. Segal, *Two Powers in Heaven: Early Rabbinic Reports about Christianity and Gnosticism* (Leiden: Brill, 1977), 65.

71. G. Scholem, *Jewish Gnosticism, Merkabah Mysticism, and Talmudic Tradition* (New York: Jewish Theological Seminary of America, [1960] 1965), 51.

72. For an in-depth analysis of these roles, see Orlov, *The Enoch-Metatron Tradition*, 121–146.

73. *3 Enoch* 15. P. Alexander, "3 (Hebrew Apocalypse of) Enoch," in *The Old Testament Pseudepigrapha*, 1.267; P. Schäfer, with M. Schlüter and H. G. von Mutius, *Synopse zur Hekhaloth-Literatur* (TSAJ, 2; Tübingen: Mohr/Siebeck, 1981), 10–11.

74. In *Synopse* §6 (*3 Enoch* 4:5–10), the following tradition about Metatron's title "Youth" can be found:

> And the Holy One, blessed be he, appointed me (Enoch) in the height as a prince and a ruler among the ministering angels. Then three of ministering angels, ʿUzzah, ʿAzzah, and ʿAzaʾel, came and laid charges against me in the

heavenly height. They said before the Holy One, blessed be he, "Lord of the Universe, did not the primeval ones give you good advice when they said, do not create man!" The Holy One, blessed be he, replied, "I have made and I will sustain him; I will carry and I will deliver him." When they saw me they said before him, "Lord of the Universe, what right has this one to ascend to the height of heights? Is he not descended from those who perished in the waters of the Flood? What right has he to be in heaven?" Again the Holy One, blessed be he, replied and said to them, "What right have you to interrupt me? I have chosen this one in preference to all of you, to be a prince and a ruler over you in the heavenly heights." At once they all arose and went to meet me and prostrated themselves before me, saying, "Happy are you, and happy your parents, because your Creator has favored you." Because I am young in their company and a mere youth among them in days and months and years—therefore they call me "Youth" (נער).

Alexander, "3 Enoch," 1.258–259; Schäfer et al., *Synopse*, 6–7.

75. *3 Enoch* 48C:1. Alexander, "3 Enoch," 1.311. Schäfer et al., *Synopse*, 36–37.

76. M. Idel, "Enoch is Metatron," *Imm* 24/25 (1990): 220–240 at 226–227.

77. As we will see later, the similar angelological constellations can be found in another early account of the heavenly counterpart—the *Ladder of Jacob*, which also refers to three classes of angels—ophanim (many-eyed ones), cherubim, and seraphim—right after the remark about the Throne: "The fiery throne of glory . . . and the many-eyed (ones) just as I saw in my dream, holding the four-faced cherubim, bearing also the many-eyed seraphim." H. G. Lunt, "Ladder of Jacob," in *Old Testament Pseudepigrapha*, 2.408.

78. Fletcher-Louis, *Luke-Acts*, 154. The same feature is also observable in the *Ladder of Jacob* 2:15–18.

79. *1 Enoch* 71:11: "And I fell upon my face." Knibb, *Ethiopic Book of Enoch*, 2.166. *2 Enoch* 21:2: "I fell on my face." Andersen, "2 Enoch," 1.135.

80. *1 Enoch* 71:14–15: "You are the Son of Man who was born to righteousness, and righteousness remains over you . . . and so you will have it forever and for ever and ever." Knibb, *Ethiopic Book of Enoch*, 2.166–167. *2 Enoch* 22:5–6: "Be brave, Enoch! Don't be frightened! Stand up, and stand in front of my face forever." Andersen, "2 Enoch," 1.138–139.

81. As has already been noted, the beginning of this tradition can be found in the *Astronomical Book* (*1 Enoch* 74:2), where Enoch writes the instructions of the angel Uriel regarding the secrets of heavenly bodies and their movements. Knibb, *Ethiopic Book of Enoch*, 2.173.

82. Vereveil's dictation of the book to Enoch is intriguing in light of later Manichaean traditions of the heavenly counterpart that claim that the inspiration for Manichaean books was by Mani's celestial twin. On this, see L. J. R. Ort, *Mani: A Religio-Historical Description of His Personality* (Leiden: Brill, 1957), 86 ff.

83. In relation to the angel's identity, Daniel Olson notes that

> the angel who informs Enoch that he is the Son of Man in *1 Enoch* 71:14 is not identified, but there is a hint that Michael, Gabriel, Raphael, and

Phanuel go into the house of God in 71:8, but only Michael, Gabriel, and Raphael emerge in 71:9, according to most of the best manuscripts. Why has Phanuel been separated from the group? Whatever the reason, by verse 13 Phanuel has rejoined the foursome, and in the next verse "that one" or "that angel" approaches Enoch and tells him his heavenly identity. Since the angel (Phanuel?) who gives Jacob the name "Israel" refuses to divulge his own name (Gen 32:28–29), it may be that the anonymity of Enoch's angelic counterpart (also Phanuel?) is another example of the same motif.

Olson, *A New Reading of the Animal Apocalypse of 1 Enoch*, 48.

84. Geza Vermes observes that at Qumran "Sariel becomes one of the four chief angels, replacing Uriel, the traditional fourth archangel in the Greek Enoch and midrashic literature. . . . He also appears in an Aramaic fragment of 4QEnoch 9:1." G. Vermes, "The Impact of the Dead Sea Scrolls on Jewish Studies," *JJS* 26 (1975): 13.

85. *Hekhalot Rabbati* (*Synopse* §108) refers to the angel Suria/Suriel as the Prince of the Face: סוריאל/סוריא שר הפנים. Schäfer, et al., *Synopse zur Hekhaloth-Literatur*, 52. On the identification of Sariel with the Prince of the Presence, see H. Odeberg, *3 Enoch or the Hebrew Book of Enoch* (New York: Ktav, 1973), 99ff; Smith, "Prayer of Joseph," 2.709.

86. Geza Vermes suggests that the angelic name "Phanuel" "is dependent on the Peniel/Penuel of Genesis 32." Vermes, "The Impact of the Dead Sea Scrolls on Jewish Studies," 13. Jonathan Smith supports Vermes' position. In his opinion, "it is most likely that the name Phanuel is to be derived from the place name Peniel/Penuel (the face of God) in Genesis 32:30, and therefore may be related to the title 'a man seeing God.'" Smith, "Prayer of Joseph," 2.709. Saul Olyan also argues that "the angel Penuel was either derived from texts such as Exod 13:14–15 and Deut 4:37, where the divine Presence is given figurative treatment, or it emerged from the exegesis of Gen 32:25–33." S. Olyan, *A Thousand Thousands Served Him: Exegesis and the Naming of Angels in Ancient Judaism* (TSAJ, 36; Tübingen: Mohr/Siebeck, 1993), 108–109.

87. Smith, "Prayer of Joseph," 2.713.

88. *2 Enoch* 21:3: "And the Lord sent one of his glorious ones, the archangel Gabriel. And he said to me, 'Be brave, Enoch! Don't be frightened! Stand up, and come with me and stand in front of the face of the Lord forever.'" *2 Enoch* 22:6: "And the Lord said to his servants, sounding them out, 'Let Enoch join in and stand in front of my face forever!'" *2 Enoch* 36:3: "Because a place has been prepared for you, and you will be in front of my face from now and forever." Andersen, "2 Enoch," 1.136, 1.138, 1.161.

89. According to Isaiah Tishby, this term is the most popular title of Metatron. He explains, "Metatron is known by many names and titles, but his regular designation, found even in the earlier literature, is נער–'boy' or 'lad.'" I. Tishby, *The Wisdom of the Zohar* (3 vols.; London: Littman Library of Jewish Civilization, 1994), 2.628.

90. On Jesus' polymorphism, see I. Czachesz, *The Grotesque Body in Early Christian Discourse: Hell, Scatology, and Metamorphosis* (New York: Equinox, 2012); P. Foster, "Polymorphic Christology: Its Origins and Development in Early Christianity," *JTS* 58 (2007): 66–99; H. Garcia, "La polymorphie du Christ dans le christianisme ancien: Remarques sur quelques définitions et quelques enjeux," *Apocrypha* 10 (1999): 16–55; E.

Junod, "Polymorphie du Dieu sauver," in *Gnosticisme et monde hellénistique* (ed. J. Ries et al.; Publications de l'Institut orientaliste de Louvain, 27; Louvain-la-Neuve: Université Catholique de Louvain, Institut orientaliste, 1982), 38–46. On the connection between Jesus' polymorphism and the doppelganger traditions, see D. R. Cartlidge, "Transfigurations of Metamorphosis Traditions in the Acts of John, Thomas, and Peter," in *The Apocryphal Acts of the Apostles* (ed. D. MacDonald; Semeia, 38; Decatur, GA: Scholars, 1986), 53–66.

91. *Acts of John* 87 reads: "In particular they were perplexed at Drusiana's statement, 'The Lord appeared to me when I was in the tomb. He resembled John and resembled a youth (νεανίσκος).'" R. I. Pervo, *The Acts of John* (ed. J. V. Hills; Salem, OR: Polebridge Press, 2015), 38; E. Junod and J.-D. Kaestli, *Acta Iohannis* (2 vols.; Corpus Christianorum, Series Apocryphorum, 1–2; Turnhout: Brepols, 1983), 1.191.

92. *Acts of John* 88–89 reads:

> After he had chosen Peter and Andrew, two brothers, he approached my brother James and me and said, "I have need of you. Come to me." My brother heard this and asked, "John, what does this child (τὸ παιδίον τοῦτο) who is calling to us from the shore want?" "What child (παιδίον)?" "The one gesturing to us." "We've spent too much time out on the water. You can't see straight, James. Don't you see a man, well-built, handsome, and cheerful-looking?" "I don't. But let's go and see what this is about." As we brought the boat to shore, we observed that he helped us get it securely beached. After we had left that spot, determined to follow him, he appeared to me still differently: almost bald, with a thick, flowing beard, but to James as a youth (νεανίσκος) whose beard had just begun to come in. We were both confused about the meaning of this apparition; and as we kept following, we became more and more confused in our struggle to comprehend what had happened.

Pervo, *The Acts of John*, 38–39; Junod and Kaestli, *Acta Iohannis*, 1.191–193.

93. *Acts of Andrew and Matthias* 18 reads: "When Andrew heard this he was exuberant that his disciples had been considered worthy to see these marvels. Andrew looked up into heaven and said, 'Appear to me, Lord Jesus Christ, for I know you are not far from your servants. Forgive me, for I beheld you on the boat as a human and spoke with you as with a human. Therefore, O Lord, reveal yourself now to me in this place.' After Andrew had said these things, Jesus came to him appearing like a most beautiful *small child* (μικρῷ παιδίῳ) and said, 'Greetings, our Andrew.'" D. R. MacDonald, *The Acts of Andrew and the Acts of Andrew and Matthias in the City of the Cannibals* (Texts and Translations, 33; Christian Apocrypha, 1; Atlanta: Scholars, 1990), 109.

94. *Acts of Andrew and Matthias* 33 reads: "The Lord Jesus, having become like a beautiful *small child* (μικρῷ παιδίῳ), descended and greeted Andrew saying, 'Andrew, why do you depart leaving them fruitless, and why do you have no compassion on the children following after you and on the men who implore, stay with us a few days'? Their cry and weeping rose to heaven.'" MacDonald, *The Acts of Andrew*, 164–167.

95. *Acts of Peter* 21 reads:

> "Now, Lord let your sweet and holy name come to the aid of these women! Touch their eyes—for you are able—that they may see by their own light!" When everyone had prayed, the dining room where they were shone with bright light as when the dawn comes, and with such a light as is usually seen only in the clouds. Yet it was not like the light of the day, but an ineffable, invisible light which no one can describe, a light which illuminated us so that we were beside ourselves with bewilderment and called out to the Lord, "Lord, have mercy on us, your servants. Give us, Lord, what we are able to bear, for this we can neither see nor bear." As we lay there, only those widows who were blind stood up. The bright light which appeared to us entered into their eyes and made them see." Peter said to them, "Tell what you saw!" They said, "We saw an old man whose beauty we cannot describe to you." Others said, "A young man in adolescence." Others said, "We saw a boy gently touching our eyes. That's how our eyes were opened."

R. F. Stoops Jr., *The Acts of Peter* (ed. by J. V. Hills; Salem, OR: Polebridge Press, 2012), 71. Cf. also *Acts of Peter* 5: "Then, in the spot where Theon was baptized, a youth with radiant beauty appeared and said to them, 'Peace be with you!'" Stoops, *The Acts of Peter*, 51.

96. "And when they had come up out of the water, a youth appeared to them, and he was holding a lighted taper; and the light of the lamps became pale through its light. And when they had gone forth, he became invisible to them." A. F. J. Klijn, *The Acts of Thomas: Introduction, Text, and Commentary* (2nd ed.; Leiden: Brill, 2003), 77. On Christ as the Child in this passage from the *Acts of Thomas*, see Klijn, *The Acts of Thomas*, 83.

97. "He began to speak with them about the mysteries beyond this world and what would take place at the end. Often he did not appear to his disciples as himself, but he was found among them as a child." *The Gospel of Judas from Codex Tchacos* (ed. R. Kasser, M. Meyer, G. Wurst; Washington, DC: National Geographic Society, 2006), 22–23. On Jesus as the Child in the *Gospel of Judas*, see E. Albrile, "Shining like a Star Man: Iranian Elements in the Gospel of Judas," in *The Gospel of Judas in Context: Proceedings of the First International Conference on the Gospel of Judas* (ed. M. Scopello; NHMS, 62; Leiden: Brill, 2008), 277–292. Lance Jenott recently affirms the "child" terminology in the *Gospel of Judas* by noting that it is "the most plausible translation, since it does not require emendation or hypothetical metathesis." L. Jenott, *The Gospel of Judas* (STAC, 64; Tübingen: Mohr/Siebeck, 2011), 190. Jenott also notes that

> traditions about Jesus' appearing as a child are found in other ancient Christian writings. In the *Gospel of the Savior*, Jesus ambiguously declares to his disciples that "I am in your midst as the little children" (107:57–60, ed. Hedrick & Mireki). In the *Apocryphon of John*, Jesus first appears to John as a child, then as an old man, in order to demonstrate his complex divine nature that spans the heavenly trinity of Father, Mother, and Son. However,

there is no indication that Judas uses child imagery for the same purpose: nowhere else in this Gospel does he appear in other forms, nor does Judas include such a trinitarian theology as found in the *Apocryphon of John*.

Jenott, *The Gospel of Judas*, 190.

98. *Apocryphon of John* (BG 21:3–4) reads: "I was afraid and [I looked], and behold, a child appeared to me"; *Apocryphon of John* (*NHC* II, 2:1–2) reads: "[I] saw in the [light a child who stood] by me." *The Apocryphon of John: Synopsis of Nag Hammadi Codices 11,1; 111,1 and IV, 1 with Papyrus Berolinensis 8502,2* (ed. M. Waldstein and F. Wisse; Leiden: Brill, 1995), 16–17.

99. *The Concept of Our Great Power* 44:32–33 (*NHC* VI, 4, 44:32–33) reads: "Then the time came until the child would grow up." *Nag Hammadi Codices V, 2–5 and VI with Papyrus Berolinensis 8502, 1 and 4* (ed. D. M. Parrott; NHS, 11; Leiden: Brill, 1979), 315.

100. *Apocalypse of Paul* 18:3–22 (*NHC* V, 2, 18:3–22) reads:

the road. And [he spoke to him], saying, "[By which] road [shall I go] up to [Jerusalem]?" The little child [replied, saying], "Say your name, so that [I may show] you the road." [The little child] knew [who Paul was]. He wished to make conversation with him through his words [in order that] he might find an excuse for speaking with him. The little child spoke, saying, "I know who you are, Paul. You are he who was blessed from his mother's womb. For I have [come] to you that you may [go up to Jerusalem] to your fellow [apostles. And] for this reason [you were called. And] I am the [Spirit who accompanies] you."

Parrott, *Nag Hammadi Codices V, 2–5 and VI with Papyrus Berolinensis 8502, 1 and 4*, 51–53. Analyzing this passage, some commentators suggested that "the little child who meets Paul on the mountain and gives him revelation most naturally suggest an epiphany of the risen Christ, who is sometimes described as a small child." G. W. MacRae and W. R. Murdock, "The Apocalypse of Paul," in *Nag Hammadi Codices V, 2–5 and VI with Papyrus Berolinensis 8502, 1 and 4*, 48. For criticism of such connection with Christ, see M. Kaler and J.-M. Rosenstiehl, *L'Apocalypse de Paul* (Québec, Presses de l'Université Laval, 2005), 177–181.

101. Hippolytus, *Ref.* 6.42.2 reads: "For Valentinus says (that) he saw a small child, newly born, and asked him who he was, and he answered that he was the Logos." W. Foerster, *Gnosis: A Selection of Gnostic Texts* (2 vols.; Oxford: Clarendon, 1972), 1.243. Stroumsa notes that the imagery of the Child also appears in the *Pistis Sophia*, where it is identified with the "twin savior," a figure probably related to Mani's conception of his own "spiritual twin." G. G. Stroumsa, *Another Seed: Studies in Gnostic Mythology* (Brill, Leiden, 1984), 78.

102. Foster, "Polymorphic Christology: Its Origins and Development in Early Christianity," 83. Further in his article, Foster argues along the same lines by noting that "in this sense it was used to highlight a transcendence of the physical by the purer spiritual manifestation of Christ. Such a tendency is most fully exemplified in the *Acts of*

John where polymorphic events prior to the resurrection illustrate a separation between Christ and the earthly domain." Foster, "Polymorphic Christology," 98.

103. On this figure, see E. Rose, *Die Manichäische Christologie* (SOR, 5; Wiesbaden: Harrassowitz, 1979), 103–109, M. Franzmann, *Jesus in the Manichaean Writings* (London: T&T Clark, 2003), 119–124, and E. B. Smagina, *Maniheistvo po rannim istochnikam* (Moscow: Vostochnaja Literatura, 2011), 189–190.

104. Thus, for example, *Keph.* 35.27–34 tells the following about Jesus the Youth: "The third power is / [the Y]outh, the gre[at . . .] light in his two pers/ons, in [. . .], I am speaking about that which has been established [i]n the summons [and] the obedience. [He] too [stood] with his fa[ther/ the] king [. . .] the savio[ur . . .] seen, as he tells / [. . .] I, what I have seen with my Father, / [I tell to] you. For yourselves, what you have seen / [with your fath]er, do that." I. Gardner, *The Kephalaia of the Teacher: The Edited Coptic Manichaean Texts in Translation with Commentary* (NHMS, 37; Leiden: Brill, 1995), 40. Majella Franzmann notes that in this passage " 'the Youth' is called forth by Jesus the Splendour from himself." Franzmann, *Jesus in the Manichaean Writings*, 119. In another passage from *Keph.* 61.26–28, Jesus the Youth again represents one of the identities of Jesus since Jesus the Splendour is clearly distinguished there from Jesus the Youth:

> [Th]e fourth s[av]ing is that of Jesus [the Splendour, since whe/n he was] re[ve]aled in the zone he displayed [his im]/age in front of the firmaments and purified [the light] that is above. He established the first righteous o[ne . . . / . . .] all the churches. He took the likeness [. . . / . . .] he made himself like the angels in [. . .] un/til he travelled and descended to the form of flesh. He set in order / [t]he earths and all the fastenings. He also loosen[ed . . .] light without measure in the entire structure. He gave / [the s]ummons and the obedience to the elements, he formed [J]esus the Youth. He as[ce]n[d]ed and rested himself in the/light [land].

Gardner, *The Kephalaia of the Teacher*, 64–66.

105. Mk 14:51–52: "A certain young man was following him, wearing nothing but a linen cloth. They caught hold of him, but he left the linen cloth and ran off naked."

106. Mk 16:5: "As they entered the tomb, they saw a young man, dressed in a white robe, sitting on the right side; and they were alarmed."

107. H. Fleddermann, "The Flight of a Naked Young Man (Mark 14:51–52)," *CBQ* 41 (1979): 412–418 at 413. See also J. Knox, "A Note on Mark 14:51–52," in *The Joy of Study: Papers on New Testament and Related Subjects Presented to Honor Frederick Clifton Grant* (ed. S. Johnson; New York: Macmillan, 1951), 27–30; A. Vanhoye, "La fuite du jeune homme nu (Mc 14,51–52)," *Biblica* 52 (1971): 401–406 at 404–405.

108. R. Brown, *The Death of the Messiah: From Gethsemane to the Grave; A Commentary on the Passion Narratives in the Four Gospels* (2 vols.; New Haven: Yale University Press, 1998), 1.301.

109. Brown, *The Death of the Messiah*, 1.301.

110. Some researchers also draw their attention to the parallels between the young man in Mark and the patriarch Joseph, a character who in *Joseph and Aseneth* become

a locus of intense doppelganger speculations. Thus, for example, Herman Waetjen, reflecting on the youth's clothing routines, argues that the "contrast between the fleeing Joseph, who leaves behind his clothes and is unjustly disgraced on the one hand, with the exalted Joseph, who wears splendid garments and is exalted to vice-regent on the other, is matched and reproduced by Mark 14, 51f. and 16, 5." H. Waetjen, "The Ending of Mark and the Gospel's Shift in Eschatology," *ASTI* 4 (1968): 116–120 at 120.

111. Cf. Matt 28:1–3: "After the sabbath, as the first day of the week was dawning, Mary Magdalene and the other Mary went to see the tomb. And suddenly there was a great earthquake; for an angel of the Lord (ἄγγελος γὰρ κυρίου), descending from heaven, came and rolled back the stone and sat on it. His appearance was like lightning, and his clothing white as snow." Luke 24:4–5: "While they were perplexed about this, suddenly two men in dazzling clothes stood beside them. The women were terrified and bowed their faces to the ground." John 20:11–12: "But Mary stood weeping outside the tomb. As she wept, she bent over to look into the tomb; and she saw two angels (δύο ἀγγέλους) in white, sitting where the body of Jesus had been lying, one at the head and the other at the feet." It is noteworthy that in the Lukan, Matthean, and Johannine passages the distinctive clothing metaphors are also present. Moreover, the presence of the Angel of the Lord figure in Matthew, a figure prominent in various heavenly counterpart traditions, serves as an important conceptual marker.

112. *Acts of Thomas* 154 reads:

> And Judas said to Vizan: "Go before us and prepare for us what is needful for our service." Vizan says to him: "Who will open for us the doors of the prison? For, see, they have closed them all and the keepers are asleep." Judas says to him: "Believe in Jesus and doubt not and you shall go and find the doors open and turned on their hinges." And when he had gone out, he went before them and all (the rest) of them were coming after Judas. And when they had gone half-way, Manashar, the wife of Vizan met them, coming to the prison. And she knew him and says to him: "My brother Vizan?" And she says to her: "Yes and you my sister Manashar?" She says to him: "Yes." He says to her: "Where do you go at this time alone? And how were you able to arise from the bed?" She says to him: "This youth laid his hand on me and I was healed. And I saw in my dream that I should go to the stranger where he is imprisoned that I might be quite healed." Vizan says to her: "Where is the youth who was with you?" And he says to him: "Do you not see him? For, see, he is holding my right hand and supporting me."

Klijn, *The Acts of Thomas*, 238.

113. The Syriac text of the *Acts of Thomas* 108–112 reads:

> When I was a little child and dwelling in my kingdom, in my father's house, and was content with the wealth and the luxuries of my nourishers, from the East our home.... And they took off from me the glittering robe.... And because I did not remember its fashion—for in my childhood I had left it in

> my father's house—on a sudden, when I received it, the garment seemed to me to become like a mirror of myself. I saw it all in all, and I too received all in it, for we were two in distinction and yet again one in one likeness. And the treasurers too, who brought it to me, I saw in like manner to be two (and yet) one likeness.

Klijn, *The Acts of Thomas*, 182–185. The Greek version of this passage reads: "And I was not able to remember my splendour (clothing), for I was still a child (παῖς) and also very young (κομιδῇ νέος) when I had left it in my father's palace." J. Ferreira, *The Hymn of the Pearl: The Syriac and Greek Texts with Introduction, Translations, and Notes* (Sydney: St. Pauls Publications, 2002), 90–91.

114. In relation to this passage, Moulton observes that

> the "angels" of individuals appear twice in the New Testament. In Acts 12:15 Peter's angel is imagined to have spoken to the girl Rhoda who answers the door. We cannot deduce much from this, except that the incredulous Christians, if they meant Peter's ghost, must have thought of a "phantasm of the living," for there is no suggestion that they supposed he was dead without their having heard of it. The conditions are best satisfied with the assumption that they imagined Peter's angel or heavenly counterpart to have taken his shape and appeared as his "double." Incomparably more important, of course, is the saying of our Lord, reported in Matt 18:10, in which it seems to me clear that He meant to set His seal upon the doctrine now under consideration. That doctrine is not, however, the existence of "guardian angels." The importance of the *debita pueris reverentia* is not especially inculcated by the statement that angels charged with their care are always near the Throne; we should rather expect to find them "encamping around" their charges. Substitute the idea of the heavenly counterpart, and we get at once a profound reason for their presence nearest to the Father. They represent those who have not yet learned to sin, despite the potentialities which time will develop. The "angels of the little ones" are nearest to God for the same reason that their earthly counterparts are typical members of the kingdom of heaven. As sin asserts its power over the child, its angel must correspondingly lose its privilege, to be regained only when stern conflict has forever slain the primal enemy.

Moulton, " 'It Is His Angel,' " 516–517.

115. On Seth's identity as "youth," see Stroumsa, *Another Seed*, 77–80. Seth's identity as "youth" is important in view of his association with the image of God in some Adamic accounts. As will be shown later in our study, in some heavenly counterpart traditions, the divine image will become envisioned as the heavenly identity of a human being.

116. Odeberg, *3 Enoch*, 1.119.

117. "It is the mystery of the boy who reaches old age and then reverts to his youth as at the beginning." Tishby, *The Wisdom of the Zohar*, 2.628.

118. According to the current consensus, the earliest rabbinic reference to the title "Youth" is *b. Yebam.* 16b, which also attests to him as the Prince of the World. Metatron is not mentioned, but the conjunction makes it plausible. Metatron, the Youth, and the Prince of the World are identified with each other in *Synopse* §959. Among pre-mishnaic Jewish texts, two documents must be mentioned. First, Charles Mopsik draws attention to the passage in Zech 2 in which an angel, described as a measurer responsible for the measuring of Jerusalem, is also designated in 2:4 as "youth" (נער). Mopsik points to the fact that the Merkavah tradition, similar to Zech 2, also often describes Metatron both as the "youth" and the "measurer." C. Mopsik, *Le Livre hébreu d'Hénoch ou Livre des palais* (Paris: Verdier, 1989), 48–49. Second, the *Wisdom of Solomon* 4:10–16 might refer to Enoch as the "youth." The text reads: "There were some who pleased God and were loved by him, and while living among sinners were taken up . . . and youth that is quickly perfected will condemn the prolonged old age of the unrighteous." On the title "youth" in Hekhalot literature, see J. Davila, "Melchizedek, the 'Youth,' and Jesus," in *The Dead Sea Scrolls as Background to Postbiblical Judaism and Early Christianity: Papers from an International Conference at St. Andrews in 2001* (ed. J. R. Davila; STDJ, 46; Leiden: Brill, 2003), 248–274 at 254; Halperin, *Faces of the Chariot*, 491–494.

119. Alexander, "3 Enoch," 1.257; Schäfer et al., *Synopse*, 4–5.

120. On the Adamic motif of the angelic opposition and its appropriation in early Enochic materials, including *2 Enoch*, see M. E. Stone, "The Fall of Satan and Adam's Penance: Three Notes on the *Books of Adam and Eve*," in *Literature on Adam and Eve: Collected Essays* (ed. G. Anderson, M. Stone, J. Tromp; SVTP, 15; Leiden: Brill, 2000), 43–56.

121. Ms. V, fol. 308; Ms. B in M. I. Sokolov, "Materialy i zametki po starinnoj slavjanskoj literature. Vypusk tretij. VII. Slavjanskaja Kniga Enoha Pravednogo. Teksty, latinskij perevod i izsledovanie. Posmertnyj trud avtora prigotovil k izdaniju M. Speranskij," *COIDR* 4 (1910): 1–167 at 83.

122. Sreznevskij's dictionary equates this Slavonic word with Greek νεανίσκος. I. Sreznevskij, *Slovar' drevnerusskogo jazyka* (3 vols.; Moscow: Kniga, 1989), 2.1627–1628.

123. Sokolov, "Materialy i zametki po starinnoj slavjanskoj literature," 85.

124. Andersen, "2 Enoch," 1.119.

125. Sokolov, "Materialy i zametki po starinnoj slavjanskoj literature," 90–91.

126. It is not coincidental that the "youth" identity of Enoch receives its articulation in *2 Enoch* 22 where the patriarch is transformed with the shining dew from the Tree of Life. In this respect, it is intriguing that in the Manichaean Bema Psalm 167:54 the figure of "youth" is described as the "son of the dew." On this tradition, see Franzmann, *Jesus in the Manichaean Writings*, 120.

127. Ms. V, fol. 317.

128. *1 Enoch* 15:11: "And he answered me and said to me with his voice: 'Hear! Do not be afraid, Enoch, (you) righteous man and scribe of righteousness.'" Knibb, *Ethiopic Book of Enoch*, 2.100.

129. *1 Enoch* 12:3–4: "And I, Enoch, was blessing the Great Lord and the King of Eternity, and behold the Watchers called to me, Enoch the scribe, and said to me: 'Enoch, scribe of righteousness, go, inform the Watchers of heaven.'" Knibb, *Ethiopic Book of Enoch*, 2.92.

130. C. Burchard, "Joseph and Aseneth," in *Old Testament Pseudepigrapha*, 2.177–247 at 2.225–226.

131. *Jos. Asen.* 22:7:

And Aseneth saw him and was amazed at his beauty, because Jacob was exceedingly beautiful to look at, and his old age (was) like the youth of a handsome (young) man, and his head was all white as snow, and the hairs of his head were all exceedingly close and thick like (those) of an Ethiopian and his beard (was) white reaching down to his breast, and his eyes (were) flashing and darting (flashes of) lightning, and his sinews and his shoulders and his arms were like (those) of an angel, and his thighs and his calves and his feet like (those) of a giant.

Burchard, "Joseph and Aseneth," 2.238.

132. *Joseph und Aseneth kritisch herausgegeben von Christoph Burchard mit Unterstützung von Carsten Burfeind & Uta Barbara Fink* (PVTG, 5; Leiden: Brill, 2003), 272.

133. On early Noachic traditions, see M. Bernstein, "Noah and the Flood at Qumran," in *The Provo International Conference on the Dead Sea Scrolls: Technological Innovations, New Texts, and Reformulated Issues* (ed. D. W. Parry and E. Ulrich; STDJ, 30; Leiden: Brill, 1999), 199–231; D. Dimant, "Noah in Early Jewish Literature," in *Biblical Figures Outside the Bible* (ed. M. E. Stone and T. A. Bergren; Harrisburg, PA: Trinity Press International, 1998), 123–150; Fletcher-Louis, *All the Glory of Adam*, 33–54; F. García Martínez, *Qumran and Apocalyptic* (STDJ, 9; Leiden: Brill, 1992), 24–44; F. García Martínez, "Interpretation of the Flood in the Dead Sea Scrolls," in *Interpretations of the Flood* (ed. F. García Martínez and G. P. Luttikhuizen; TBN, 1; Leiden: Brill, 1998), 86–108; H. Kvanvig, *Roots of Apocalyptic: The Mesopotamian Background of the Enoch Figure and the Son of Man* (WMANT, 61; Neukirchen-Vluyn: Neukirchener Verlag, 1988), 242–254; J. Lewis, *A Study of the Interpretation of Noah and the Flood in Jewish and Christian Literature* (Leiden: Brill, 1968); *Noah and His Book(s)* (ed. M. Stone, A. Amihay, V. Hillel; Atlanta: Scholars, 2010); D. M. Peters, *Noah Traditions in the Dead Sea Scrolls: Conversations and Controversies of Antiquity* (Atlanta: Scholars, 2008); J. Reeves, "Utnapishtim in the Book of Giants?," *JBL* 12 (1993): 110–115; J. M. Scott, "Geographic Aspects of Noachic Materials in the Scrolls of Qumran," in *The Scrolls and the Scriptures: Qumran Fifty Years After* (ed. S. E. Porter and C. E. Evans; JSPSS, 26; Sheffield: Sheffield Academic Press, 1997), 368–381; R. C. Steiner, "The Heading of the Book of the Words of Noah on a Fragment of the Genesis Apocryphon: New Light on a 'Lost' Work," *DSD* 2 (1995): 66–71; M. Stone, "The Axis of History at Qumran," in *Pseudepigraphic Perspectives: The Apocrypha and the Pseudepigrapha in Light of the Dead Sea Scrolls* (ed. E. Chazon and M. E. Stone; STDJ, 31; Leiden: Brill, 1999), 133–149; M. Stone, "Noah, Books of," *Encyclopaedia Judaica* (Jerusalem: Keter, 1971), 12.1198; J. VanderKam, "The Righteousness of Noah," in *Ideal Figures in Ancient Judaism: Profiles and Paradigms* (ed. J. J. Collins and G. W. E. Nickelsburg; SBLSCS, 12; Chico: Scholars, 1980), 13–32; J. VanderKam, "The Birth of Noah," in *Intertestamental Essays in Honor of Józef Tadeusz Milik* (ed. Z. J. Kapera; QM, 6; Krakow: Enigma Press, 1992), 213–231; C. Werman, "Qumran and the

Book of Noah," in *Pseudepigraphic Perspectives: The Apocrypha and the Pseudepigrapha in Light of the Dead Sea Scrolls* (ed. E. Chazon and M. E. Stone; STDJ, 31; Leiden: Brill, 1999), 171–181.

134. *1 Enoch* 106:5: "His eyes (are) like the rays of the sun, and his face glorious." Knibb, *Ethiopic Book of Enoch*, 2.244–245.

135. *1QapGen* 5:12–13: "His face has been lifted to me and his eyes shine like [the] s[un . . .] of this boy is flame and he." *The Dead Sea Scrolls Study Edition* (ed. F. García Martínez and E. J. C. Tigchelaar; 2 vols.; Leiden: Brill, 1997), 1.31.

136. A similar tradition is reflected in *1Q19*. *1Q19* 3 reads: "were aston[ished . . .] [. . . (not like the children of men) the fir]st-born is born, but the glorious ones [. . .] [. . .] his father, and when Lamech saw [. . .] [. . .] the chambers of the house like the beams of the sun [. . .] to frighten the [. . .]." *1Q19* 13 reads: "[. . .] because the glory of your face [. . .] for the glory of God in [. . .] [. . . he will] be exalted in the splendor of the glory and the beauty [. . .] he will be honored in the midst of [. . .]." García Martínez and Tigchelaar, *Dead Sea Scrolls Study Edition*, 1.27.

137. Later rabbinic materials, possibly cognizant of the Noachic "youth" traditions, also provide almost identical details about the miraculous birth of Moses. Thus, according to *Pirke de Rabbi Eliezer* 48, at birth Moses' body was like an angel of God. *b. Sotah* 12a tells that the house was filled with light. According to *Deut. Rab.* 11:10, a young prophet who is only one day old was able to speak and at four months—to prophesy. See also *Exod. Rab.* 1:20 and *Zohar* II.11b.

138. Fletcher-Louis, *All the Glory of Adam*, 33ff.

139. Crispin Fletcher-Louis notes parallels between this scene and the description of the ideal high priest from Sirach 50. He argues that "in Sirach 50 the liturgical procession through Simon's various ministrations climaxes with Aaron's blessings of the people (50:20, cf. Numbers 6) and a call for all the readers of Sirach's work 'to bless the God of all who everywhere works greater wonders, who fosters our growth from birth and deals with us according to his mercy' (50:22). So, too, in *1 Enoch* 106:3 the infant Noah rises from the hands of the midwife and, already able to speak as an adult, 'he opened his mouth and blessed the Lord.'" Fletcher-Louis, *All the Glory of Adam*, 47. Fletcher-Louis concludes that "the staging for [Noah's] birth and the behavior of the child have strong priestly resonances." Fletcher-Louis, *All the Glory of Adam*, 46.

140. See M. Delcor, "Melchizedek from Genesis to the Qumran Texts and the Epistle to the Hebrews," *JSJ* 2 (1971): 129; idem, "La naissance merveilleuse de Melchisédeq d'après l'Hénoch slave," in *Kecharitomene: Mélanges René Laurentin* (ed. C. Augustin et al.; Paris: Desclée, 1990), 217–229; A. de Santos Otero, "Libro de los secretos de Henoc (Henoc eslavo)," in *Apócrifos del Antiguo Testamento* (ed. A. Díez Macho; Madrid: Ediciones Christiandad, 1984), 4.199; R. Stichel, *Die Namen Noes, seines Bruders und seiner Frau. Ein Beitrag zum Nachleben jüdischer Überlieferungen in der außerkanonischen und gnostischen Literatur und in Denkmälern der Kunst* (AAWG, 3; Folge 112; Göttingen: Vandenhoeck & Ruprecht, 1979), 42–54.

141. The content of the story is connected with the family of Nir, who is defined in the Slavonic pseudepigraphon as Noah's brother. Sothonim, the wife of Nir, gave birth to a miraculous child "in her old age," right "on the day of her death." She conceived

the child, "being sterile" and "without having slept with her husband." The book explains that Nir, envisioned in the story as a priest, had not slept with her from the day that the Lord had appointed him before the face of the people. Therefore, Sothonim hid herself during all the days of her pregnancy. On the day she was to give birth, Nir remembered his wife and called her to himself in the temple. She came to him, and he saw that she was pregnant. Nir, filled with shame, wanted to cast her from him, but she died at his feet. Melchizedek was born from Sothonim's corpse. When Nir and Noah came in to bury Sothonim, they saw the child sitting beside the corpse with his clothing on him. According to the story, they were terrified because the child was fully developed physically. The child spoke with his lips and he blessed the Lord. The unusual child was marked by the sign of priesthood. The story describes how "the badge of priesthood" was on his chest, glorious in appearance. Nir and Noah dressed the child in the garments of the priesthood and fed him the holy bread. They decided to hide him, fearing that the people would have him put to death. Finally, the Lord commanded his archangel Michael to take the child and place him in the paradise Eden, so that he might become the high priest after the Flood. The final passages of the short recension describe the ascent of Melchizedek on the wings of Michael to the paradise Eden.

142. At least nine points should be mentioned: 1. Both Noah and Melchizedek belonged to the circle of Enoch's family. 2. Both characters are attested to as "survivors" of the Flood. 3. Both characters have an important mission in the postdiluvian era. 4. Both characters are pictured as glorious wonder children. 5. Immediately after their birth, both characters spoke to the Lord. 6. Both characters were suspected of divine/angelic lineage/parentage. 7. Their fathers were suspicious of the conception of their sons and the faithfulness of their wives. 8. Their mothers were ashamed and tried to defend themselves against the accusation of their husbands. 9. Their fathers were eventually comforted by the special revelation about the prominent future role of their sons in the postdiluvian era. It is noteworthy that this information is given in both cases in the context of the revelation about the destruction of the earth by the Flood.

143. A. Orlov, "'Noah's Younger Brother': Anti-Noachic Polemics in 2 Enoch," *Henoch* 22 (2000): 259–273; idem, "Noah's Younger Brother Revisited: Anti-Noachic Polemics and the Date of 2 (Slavonic) Enoch," *Henoch* 26 (2004): 172–187.

144. *b. Sotah* 12a: "He was born circumcised; and the Sages declare, At the time when Moses was born, the whole house was filled with light—as it is written here, 'And she saw him that he was good' (Exod 2:2), and elsewhere it is written, 'And God saw the light that it was good' (Gen 1:4)." Epstein, *The Babylonian Talmud*, Sotah, 12a; *Exod. Rab.* 1:20: "She saw that the Shechinah was with him; that is, the 'it' refers to the Shechinah which was with the child." Freedman and Simon, *Midrash Rabbah*, 3.29–30; *Deut. Rab.* 11:10: "Moses replied: 'I am the son of Amram, and came out from my mother's womb without prepuce, and had no need to be circumcised; and on the very day on which I was born I found myself able to speak and was able to walk and to converse with my father and mother . . . when I was three months old I prophesied and declared that I was destined to receive the law from the midst of flames of fire.'" Freedman and Simon, *Midrash Rabbah*, 7.185; *PRE* 48: "Rabbi Nathaniel said: the parents of Moses saw the child, for his form was like that of an angel of God. They circumcised him on the eight day and they called his name Jekuthiel." Friedlander, *Pirke de Rabbi Eliezer*, 378;

Zohar II.11b: "She saw the light of the Shekinah playing around him: for when he was born this light filled the whole house, the word 'good' here having the same reference as in the verse 'and God saw the light that it was good' (Gen 1:4)." Sperling and Simon, *The Zohar*, 3.35. See also Samaritan *Molad Mosheh*: "She became pregnant with Moses and was great with child, and the light was present." *Samaritan Documents Relating to Their History, Religion and Life* (trans. J. Bowman; Pittsburgh: Pickwick, 1977), 287. On Moses' birth in Artapanus' *On the Jews*, the *Exagoge* of Ezekiel the Tragedian, the *Book of Jubilees*, Philo's *Life of Moses*, Josephus' *Jewish Antiquities*, and Pseudo-Philo's *Book of Biblical Antiquities*, see A. Pinnick, *The Birth of Moses in Jewish Literature of the Second Temple Period* (PhD diss.; Harvard University, 1996).

145. It is intriguing that in the *Genesis Apocryphon* Methuselah is traversing realms, making a journey to a mysterious, possibly heavenly, location called Parvain to ask Enoch about the miraculous child Noah. It is not clear if here and in *1 Enoch* 106 Methuselah serves as a bridge between the two identities of the seventh antediluvian hero. On the tradition about Parvain, see J. R. Davila, "Heavenly Ascents in the Dead Sea Scrolls," in *The Dead Sea Scrolls After Fifty Years: A Comprehensive Assessment* (ed. P. W. Flint and J. C. VanderKam; 2 vols.; Leiden: Brill, 1998–1999), 2.469ff; L. T. Stuckenbruck, "The Lamech Narrative in the Genesis Apocryphon (1QapGen) and Birth of Noah (4QEnoch^c ar): A Tradition-Historical Study," in *Aramaica Qumranica* (ed. K. Berthelot and D. Stökl Ben Ezra; STDJ, 94; Leiden: Brill, 2010), 253–271.

146. Thus, Helge Kvanvig points out that in the Noachic traditions Noah and Enoch often appear in the same roles. Kvanvig, *Roots of Apocalyptic*, 117.

147. Horton also notes that "functions assigned to Melchizedek in the *11QMelch* are elsewhere either assigned to God or to other figures such as Michael." F. L. Horton, *The Melchizedek Tradition: A Critical Examination of the Sources to the Fifth Century A.D. and in the Epistle to the Hebrews* (SNTSMS, 30; Cambridge: Cambridge University Press, 1976), 81.

148. *1QM* XVII 6–7. In the *Songs of the Sabbath Sacrifice* (*4Q401* 11.1–3 and 22:1–3), Melchizedek appears to be envisioned among the angels in the heavenly sanctuary.

149. F. García Martínez, *Qumranica Minora II: Thematic Studies on the Dead Sea Scrolls* (ed. E. Tigchelaar; Leiden: Brill, 2007), 99. Paul Kobelski notes that this conceptual trajectory was continued in later Jewish developments. He points out that

> the archangel Michael is described as a heavenly high-priest in the Babylonian Talmud (see *Hag.* 12b, *Zebah.* 62a, and *Menah.* 110a), and in a medieval Jewish text (*Yalqut had.* f. 115, col. 3, no. 19) he is identified with Melchizedek, who is called by his biblical title "priest of El Elyon." Though this last text is late, it may be based on earlier traditions such as those cited above that viewed Michael as a high priest in heaven and Melchizedek as an angelic being who exercised a priestly ministry in heaven; or it may represent a development or conflation of such ideas.

P. J. Kobelski, *Melchizedek and Melchireša^c* (CBQMS, 10; Washington: Catholic Biblical Association of America, 1981), 65–66. On the identification of Melchizedek with

Michael in medieval rabbinic texts, see also M. de Jonge and A. S. van der Woude, "11QMelchizedek and the New Testament," *NTS* 12 (1966): 301–326 at 305.

150. D. Frankfurter, "The Legacy of Jewish Apocalypses in Early Christianity: Regional Trajectories," in *The Jewish Apocalyptic Heritage in Early Christianity* (ed. J. C. VanderKam and W. Adler; CRINT, 3.4; Assen: Van Gorcum, 1996), 183. On the identification of Michael with Melchizedek, see also J. R. Davila, "Melchizedek, Michael, and War in Heaven," *SBLSP* 35 (1996): 259–272; D. D. Hannah, *Michael and Christ: Michael Traditions and Angel Christology in Early Christianity* (WUNT, 2.109; Tübingen: Mohr/Siebeck, 1999), 70–74.

151. J. Dunn, *Christology in the Making: A New Testament Inquiry into the Origins of the Doctrine of the Incarnation* (Grand Rapids, MI: Eerdmans, 1996), 153. It is also noteworthy that, in his interpretation of the connections between Melchizedek and Michael, Dunn brings as an illustration some angelological developments found in the *Prayer of Joseph*, a document already mentioned in our study, where the identification between Jacob and his angelic counterpart is made explicit. Thus, Dunn argues that "it is certainly the case that such an exalted being could be conceptualized as an angel (see again particularly the *Prayer of Joseph*; and cf. the description of Melchizedek in 11QMelch. and of the Son of Man in the *Similitudes of Enoch—1 Enoch* 46:1; 61:10)." Dunn, *Christology in the Making*, 155.

152. Knibb, "Messianism in Pseudepigrapha," 177.

153. Dunn, *Christology in the Making*, 153. In view of connections between Melchizedek, Michael, and Metatron, it is noteworthy that Philip Alexander entertains some conceptual links between Michael and Metatron. He argues that

> Metatron is, in a number of respects, similar to the archangel Michael: Both angels were known as "the Great Prince"; both were said to serve in the heavenly sanctuary; both were guardian angels of Israel; what is said in one text about Michael is said in another about Metatron. A possible explanation of these similarities would be that originally Metatron and Michael were one and the same angel: Michael was the angel's common name, Metatron one of his esoteric, magical names. At some point, however, the connection between Metatron and Michael was obscured, and a new, independent archangel with many of Michael's powers came into being.

Alexander, "3 Enoch," 1.243–244.

154. I am thankful to Michael Stone for bringing my attention to these traditions.

155. *2 Enoch* 72:1–10 reads: "And when the child had been 40 days in Nir's tent, the Lord said to Michael, 'Go down onto the earth to Nir the priest, and take my child Melkisedek, who is with him, and place him in the paradise of Eden for preservation. For the time is approaching, and I will pour out all the water onto the earth, and everything that is on the earth will perish.' . . . And Michael took the child on the same night on which he had come down; and he took him on his wings, and he placed him in the paradise of Eden." Andersen, "2 Enoch," 1.210.

156. N. Rubin and A. Kosman, "The Clothing of the Primordial Adam as a Symbol of Apocalyptic Time in the Midrashic Sources," *HTR* 90 (1997): 155–174 at 163–164.

157. Andersen, "2 Enoch," 1.138.

158. Martha Himmelfarb observes that "the combination of clothing and anointing suggests that the process by which Enoch becomes an angel is a heavenly version of priestly investiture." Himmelfarb, *Ascent to Heaven*, 40. Similarly, Crispin Fletcher-Louis notes that

> Enoch's transformation in *2 Enoch* is greatly indebted to priestly practice and its understanding of investiture. The myrrh fragrance of the oil of Enoch's anointing recalls the sacred oil of anointing prescribed by Moses for the tabernacle in Exodus 30:22–23. The comparison of the oil with sweet dew is perhaps a reflection of Psalm 133:2–3 where there is a parallelism between the oil running down the head of Aaron and the dew of Mount Hermon. The reference to the glittering rays of the sun is yet one more witness to the theme of priestly luminescence. The specific comparison of the oil of anointing with the sun's rays is ultimately dependent on the priestly tradition within the Pentateuch since there the oil of anointing is placed in God's fourth speech to Moses in Exodus 25–31 as a parallel within the Tabernacle instructions to the creation of the sun, moon, and stars on the fourth day of creation (Genesis 1:14–19). In general terms, Enoch's investiture is indebted to the scene in Zechariah 3 where the high priest's old clothes are removed and replaced with new ones. In that scene too the priest is attended by angels, just as Michael acts as Enoch's attendant in *2 Enoch* (see *T. Levi* 8). In *2 Enoch* 22:6 Enoch is granted permanent access to God's throne room, just as Joshua is given rights of access to the heavenly realm in Zechariah 3:7. The concluding chapters of *2 Enoch* (chs. 69–73) are devoted to the priestly succession after Enoch's ascension.

Fletcher-Louis, *All the Glory of Adam*, 23–24.

159. See *3 Enoch* 15.

160. Alexander, "3 Enoch," 1.265.

161. Fossum, "Ascensio, Metamorphosis: The 'Transfiguration' of Jesus in the Synoptic Gospels," in *Image of the Invisible God*, 83.

162. Burchard, "Joseph and Aseneth," 2.225.

163. R. Kraemer, *When Aseneth Met Joseph: A Late Antique Tale of the Biblical Patriarch and His Egyptian Wife, Reconsidered* (New York: Oxford University Press, 1998), 266.

164. Moshe Idel suggested that Enoch's luminous metamorphosis in *2 Enoch* 22 might belong to the tradition that views Enoch as the one who regained Adam's lost status and radiance. He observed that, to the best of his knowledge, "Enoch is the only living person for whom . . . luminous garments, reminiscent of Adam's lost garments of light, were made." Idel, "Enoch is Metatron," 224.

165. For discussions about the luminous "garments" of the protoplast, see D. H. Aaron, "Shedding Light on God's Body in Rabbinic Midrashim: Reflections on the Theory of a Luminous Adam," *HTR* 90 (1997): 299-314; S. Brock, "Clothing Metaphors as a Means of Theological Expression in Syriac Tradition," in *Typus, Symbol, Allegorie bei den östlichen Vätern und ihren Parallelen im Mittelalter* (ed. M. Schmidt; EB, 4; Regensburg: Friedrich Pustet, 1982), 11-40; A. D. DeConick and J. Fossum, "Stripped before God: A New Interpretation of Logion 37 in the Gospel of Thomas," *VC* 45 (1991): 123-150 at 141; N. A. Dahl and D. Hellholm, "Garment Metaphors: The Old and the New Human Being," in *Antiquity and Humanity: Essays on Ancient Religion and Philosophy: Presented to Hans Dieter Betz on His Seventieth Birthday* (ed. A. Yarbro Collins and M. M. Mitchell; Tübingen: Mohr/Siebeck, 2001), 139-158; A. Goshen-Gottstein, "The Body as Image of God in Rabbinic Literature," *HTR* 87 (1994): 171-195; B. Murmelstein, "Adam, ein Beitrag zur Messiaslehre," *WZKM* 35 (1928): 242-275 at 255; Rubin and Kosman, "The Clothing of the Primordial Adam as a Symbol of Apocalyptic Time in the Midrashic Sources," 155-174; J. Z. Smith, "The Garments of Shame," *HR* 5 (1965/1966): 217-238.

166. Aaron, "Shedding Light on God's Body," 303.

167. See, for example, Ezek 1; Ps 101:1; Job 40:10.

168. Brock, "Clothing Metaphors," 14.

169. The Qumran materials appear to be aware of the motif of the glorious condition of Adam. Thus several texts invoke the tradition of the glory of the protoplast: *1QS* 4:15-22-23 reads: "For those God has chosen for an everlasting covenant and to them shall belong all the glory of Adam (כבוד אדם)." *1QH* 4:9 15 reads: "Giving them as a legacy all the glory of Adam (כבוד אדם)." *CD-A* 3:20 reads: "Those who remained steadfast in it will acquire eternal life, and all the glory of Adam (כבוד אדם) is for them." García-Martínes and Tigchelaar, *The Dead Sea Scrolls Study Edition*, 78-79; 148-149; 554-555.

170. G. Anderson and M. Stone, *A Synopsis of the Books of Adam and Eve: Second Revised Edition* (EJL, 17; Atlanta: Scholars, 1999), 58E. Cf. also the Armenian *LAE* 10:1, "When Eve came forth from the water, her flesh was like withered grass, for her flesh had been changed from the water, but the form of her glory remained brilliant." Anderson and Stone, *A Synopsis of the Books of Adam and Eve*, 12E. On the Armenian version of the *Primary Adam Books*, see also M. E. Stone, *The Penitence of Adam* (CSCO, 429-430; Louvain: Peeters, 1981); idem, *Texts and Concordances of the Armenian Adam Literature* (EJL, 12; Atlanta: Scholars, 1996), 70-81.

171. It is noteworthy that the concept of stripping the heavenly "garments" in the process of the character's demotion is also reaffirmed in the *Primary Adam Books* in the destiny of Satan.

172. See also the Armenian version of the *Primary Adam Books* [44] 21:2-5: "Then Adam came to me with his great glory . . . and I gave him to eat of the fruit, and I made him like me." Anderson and Stone, *A Synopsis of the Books of Adam and Eve*, 60E-61E. Later rabbinic traditions also speak about the loss of Adam's glory after the Fall. *Gen. Rab.* 12:6 contains the following elaboration: "The six things . . . were taken away from Adam, viz. his lustre, his immortality . . . Adam did not retain his glory for a night . . . He deprived him of his splendor and expelled him from the Garden of Eden." Freedman and Simon, *Midrash Rabbah*, 1.91.

173. Marinus de Jonge and Johannes Tromp noted that in the Greek version of the *Primary Adam Books* the

> promise of the eschatological restoration to glory does not postpone the divine grace to the end of times. Immediately after Adam's death, the angels and the sun and the moon offer incenses and prayers to God, that he may have mercy on Adam (33:4–36:1). Their efforts succeed, and trumpets announce the favorable outcome of God's gracious verdict on Adam (37:1–2). A Seraph washes Adam in the Acherusian Lake (37:3), a ritual known from Greek mythology as the post mortem cleansing from guilt. Then God hands him over to Michael, who is to bring Adam to the third heaven, where he is to remain until the day of visitation (37:4–6).

M. de Jonge and J. Tromp, *The Life of Adam and Eve and Related Literature* (GAP; Sheffield: Sheffield Academic Press, 1997), 51.

174. *A Synopsis of the Books of Adam and Eve*, 86E–87E (Armenian version). See also the *Primary Adam Books*: "They seized three folded shrouds of [cloth] and God told Michael and Gabriel, 'Unfold these shrouds and envelop Adam's body and take the ointment from the olive tree and pour it upon him.' And three angels dressed him (in it) and when they had dressed Adam's body (in it)." Anderson and Stone, *A Synopsis of the Books of Adam and Eve*, 87E.

175. In *Targ. Ps.-J.* on Gen 3:21, the following tradition can be found: "And the Lord God made garments of glory for Adam and for his wife from the skin which the serpent had cast off (to be worn) on the skin of their (garments of) fingernails of which they had been stripped, and he clothed them." Maher, *Targum Pseudo-Jonathan: Genesis*, 29. *Targ. Neof.* on Gen 3:21 reveals a similar tradition: "And the Lord God made for Adam and for his wife *garments of glory* (לבושין דיקר), for the skin of their flesh, and he clothed them." McNamara, *Targum Neofiti 1: Genesis*, 62–63; A. Díez Macho, *Neophiti 1: Targum Palestinense MS de la Biblioteca Vaticana* (Madrid: Consejo Superior de Investigaciones Científicas, 1968), 1.19. The *Frg. Targ.* on Gen 3:21 also uses the imagery of the glorious garments: "And He made: And the *memra* of the Lord God created for Adam and his wife *precious garments* (לבושין דיקר) [for] the skin of their flesh, and He clothed them." M. L. Klein, *The Fragment-Targums of the Pentateuch According to Their Extant Sources* (2 vols.; AnBib, 76; Rome: Biblical Institute Press, 1980), 1.46; 2.7.

176. *Targ. Onq.* on Gen 3:21 reads: "And the Lord God made for Adam and his wife *garments of honor for the skin of their flesh* (לבושין דיקר על משך בסרהון), and He clothed them." Grossfeld, *The Targum Onqelos to Genesis*, 46; *The Bible in Aramaic Based on Old Manuscripts and Printed Texts* (5 vols.; ed. A. Sperber; Leiden: Brill, 1959), 1.5.

177. Freedman and Simon, *Midrash Rabbah*, 1.171.

178. *Pirke de Rabbi Eliezer* (trans. G. Friedländer; New York: Hermon Press, 1965), 98. Other midrashic passages also speak about the luminosity of Adam's body. Thus, for example, in *Leviticus Rabbah* 20.2, the following tradition is found: "Resh Lakish, in the name of R. Simeon the son of Menasya, said: The apple of Adam's heel outshone the globe of the sun; how much more so the brightness of his face!" Freedman and Simon, *Midrash Rabbah*, 4.252. *Ecclesiastes Rabbah* 8:1 reads: "R. Levi said: 'The ball of Adam's

heel outshone the sun . . . so was it not right that the ball of his heel should outshine the sun, and how much more so the beauty of his face!'" Freedman and Simon, *Midrash Rabbah*, 8.213–214. A similar tradition is also found in *b. Baba Batra* 58a.

179. Sperling and Simon, *The Zohar*, 1.136.

180. Klijn, *The Acts of Thomas*, 182–185.

181. Ross Kraemer notices the similarities in clothing metaphors found in the *Hymn of the Pearl* and in *Jos. Asen.*, the texts where the heavenly counterpart traditions loom large. She observes that

> the so-called Hymn of the Pearl, within Thomas, also recalls the imagery of Aseneth with its extended emphasis on the royal garment. As Aseneth's identity is repeatedly symbolized in her garments, from her initial royal but idolatrous clothing, to the mourning garments of her symbolic death, to the new garments that mark her new existence, to the primordial wedding garment that may point to her true identity as the pristine human, so does the Hymn employ the image of the royal garment in the journey of the protagonist (usually assumed by scholars to represent the Soul). As Aseneth first appears clothed in royal garments embroidered in gold and encrusted with gems, so, too, the protagonist first has a "garment set with gems and spangled with gold" (108.9) that his royal parents take from him, as they send him on his appointed journey in search of the pearl in Egypt. Instead, the protagonist clothes himself in ordinary, dirty clothing that he removes as he journeys home, having finally found the pearl. Only then does he see the image of his garment before him in which he recognizes his true self, in a scene reminiscent of Aseneth's moment of recognition when she looks in the bowl of spring water and sees her transformed self.

Kraemer, *When Aseneth Met Joseph*, 262. Kraemer further reflects on general similarities between *Jos. Asen.* and the *Hymn of the Pearl*:

> Numerous other elements in the Hymn recall Aseneth, from the general theme of the aristocratic or royal child to the more specific feature of alienation from the parents, followed by reconciliation. As I have noted earlier, this is a particular feature of the longer, but not the shorter, version of Aseneth. In the extended speech in chapter 12, Aseneth proclaims her desolate state as an orphan abandoned by her parents and prays instead to God as Father to protect her. In the end of the longer version, Aseneth is reconciled to her parents, who themselves praise God (20.6–8). Both tales are set in Egypt, although perhaps for differing reasons, and feature a ferocious animal enemy: the savage lion in Aseneth, the devouring serpent in the Hymn. Both Aseneth and the unnamed protagonist of the Hymn are named in the Book of Life.

Kraemer, *When Aseneth Met Joseph*, 262.

182. G. Luttikhuizen, "The Hymn of Jude Thomas, the Apostle, in the Country of the Indians," in *Apocryphal Acts of Thomas* (ed. J. N. Bremmer; Leiden: Brill, 2001), 113.
183. W. Foerster, *Gnosis: A Selection of Gnostic Texts* (2 vols.; Oxford: Clarendon, 1972), 2.255; M. Lidzbarski, *Ginza, der Schatz oder das große Buch der Mandäer* (Göttingen: Vandenhoeck & Ruprecht, 1925), 461.
184. Scholem, *On the Mystical Shape of the Godhead*, 264.
185. Anderson and Stone, *A Synopsis of the Books of Adam and Eve*, 15–18E.
186. Anderson and Stone, *A Synopsis of the Books of Adam and Eve*, 18–18E.
187. Andersen, "2 Enoch," 1.160; G. Macaskill, *The Slavonic Texts of 2 Enoch* (SJS, 6; Leiden: Brill, 2013), 142. The shorter recension of *2 Enoch* 37:1–2 provides a very similar description: "But the Lord called (one) of his senior angels, *a terrifying one* (*grozna*), and he made him stand with me. And the appearance of that angel (was) snow, and his hands ice, and he refreshed my face, because I could not endure the terror of the burning of the fire. And it is thus that the Lord spoke to me all his words." Andersen, "2 Enoch," 1.161; Macaskill, *The Slavonic Texts*, 143.
188. On these traditions, see J. VanderKam, *Enoch and the Growth of an Apocalyptic Tradition* (CBQMS, 16; Washington, DC: Catholic Biblical Association of America, 1984); Kvanvig, *Roots of Apocalyptic*.

Chapter Two: The Heavenly Counterpart Traditions in the Mosaic Pseudeipgrapha

1. On the *Exagoge* of Ezekiel the Tragedian, see S. N. Bunta, *Moses, Adam and the Glory of the Lord in Ezekiel the Tragedian: On the Roots of a Merkabah Text* (PhD diss.; Milwaukee, WI: Marquette University, 2005); J. J. Collins, *Between Athens and Jerusalem. Jewish Identity in the Hellenistic Diaspora* (2nd ed.; Grand Rapids, MI: Eerdmans, 2000), 224–225; Y. Gutman, *The Beginnings of Jewish-Hellenistic Literature* (2 vols.; Jerusalem: Mosad Bialik, 1958–1963), 2.43 [in Hebrew]; M. Hadas, *Hellenistic Culture: Fusion and Diffusion* (Morningside Heights, NY: Columbia University Press, 1959), 99; J. Heath, "Homer or Moses? A Hellenistic Perspective on Moses' Throne Vision in Ezekiel Tragicus," *JJS* 58 (2007): 1–18; C. R. Holladay, "The Portrait of Moses in Ezekiel the Tragedian," *SBLSP* 10 (1976): 447–452; idem, *Fragments from Hellenistic Jewish Authors* (3 vols.; SBLTT, 30; Pseudepigrapha Series 12; Atlanta: Scholars, 1989), 2.439–449; P. W. van der Horst, "De Joodse toneelschrijver Ezechiël," *NedTT* 36 (1982): 97–112; idem, "Moses' Throne Vision in Ezekiel the Dramatist," *JJS* 34 (1983): 21–29; idem, "Some Notes on the *Exagoge* of Ezekiel," *Mnemosyne* 37 (1984): 364–365; L. Hurtado, *One God, One Lord: Early Christian Devotion and Ancient Jewish Monotheism* (Philadelphia: Fortress Press, 1988), 58ff; H. Jacobson, "Mysticism and Apocalyptic in Ezekiel's Exagoge," *ICS* 6 (1981): 273–293; idem, *The Exagoge of Ezekiel* (Cambridge: Cambridge University Press, 1983); K. Kuiper, "De Ezekiele Poeta Iudaeo," *Mnemosyne* 28 (1900): 237–280; idem, "Le poète juif Ezéchiel," *REJ* 46 (1903): 48–73, 161–177; P. Lanfranchi, *L'Exagoge d'Ezéchiel le Tragique: Introduction, texte, traduction et commentaire* (SVTP, 21; Leiden: Brill, 2006); W. A. Meeks, "Moses as God and King," in *Religions in Antiquity: Essays in Memory of Erwin*

Ramsdell Goodenough (ed. J. Neusner; SHR, 14; Leiden: Brill, 1968), 354–371; idem, *The Prophet-King: Moses Traditions and the Johannine Christology* (NovTSup, 14; Leiden: Brill, 1967); Orlov, *The Enoch-Metatron Tradition*, 262–268; R. G. Robertson, "Ezekiel the Tragedian," *The Old Testament Pseudepigrapha*, 2.803–819; K. Ruffatto, "Polemics with Enochic Traditions in the *Exagoge* of Ezekiel the Tragedian," *JSP* 15 (2006): 195–210; idem, "Raguel as Interpreter of Moses' Throne Vision: The Transcendent Identity of Raguel in the Exagoge of Ezekiel the Tragedian," *JSP* 17 (2008): 121–139; E. Starobinski-Safran, "Un poète judéo-hellénistique: Ezéchiel le Tragique," *MH* 3 (1974): 216–224; J. VanderKam and D. Boesenberg, "Moses and Enoch in Second Temple Jewish Texts," in *Parables of Enoch: A Paradigm Shift* (ed. D. Bock and J. Charlesworth; London: T&T Clark, 2013), 124–158 at 145–148; E. Vogt, *Tragiker Ezechiel* (JSHRZ, 4.3; Gütersloh: Mohn, 1983); J. Wieneke, *Ezechielis Judaei poetae Alexandrini fabulae quae inscribitur Exagoge fragmenta* (Münster: Monasterii Westfalorum, 1931); R. Van De Water, "Moses' Exaltation: Pre-Christian?," *JSP* 21 (2000): 59–69.

2. The Greek text of the passage was published in several editions, including A.-M. Denis, *Fragmenta pseudepigraphorum quae supersunt graeca* (PVTG, 3; Leiden: Brill, 1970), 210; B. Snell, *Tragicorum graecorum fragmenta I* (Göttingen: Vandenhoeck & Ruprecht, 1971), 288–301; Jacobson, *The Exagoge of Ezekiel*, 54; Holladay, *Fragments*, 2.362–366.

3. Jacobson, *The Exagoge of Ezekiel*, 54–55.

4. Meeks, *The Prophet-King*, 149. See also Holladay, *Fragments*, 2.308–312.

5. On the Enochic motifs in the *Exagoge*, see van der Horst, "Moses' Throne Vision," 21–29; Orlov, *The Enoch-Metatron Tradition*, 262–268; Ruffatto, "Polemics with Enochic Traditions," 195–210.

6. van der Horst, "Some Notes on the *Exagoge*," 364. Contrary to van der Horst's opinion, Richard Bauckham argues that, although *Exagoge* 67–90 depicts Moses quite literally as God, "the meaning of the dream is not its literal meaning." Its literal meaning, in Bauckham's opinion, is to illustrate "the scriptural use of the word 'God' for Moses as a metaphor for Moses' rule over Israel." Thus, Bauckham sees Moses' enthronement not as a "real" occupation of the divine Seat, nor as the prophet's identification with his heavenly counterpart, but instead as a "symbolic" representation of Moses' role as the leader of the Israelites. God thus symbolically "vacates his throne" by commissioning Moses to take leadership over his people. See R. J. Bauckham, "The Throne of God and the Worship of Jesus," in *Jewish Roots of Christological Monotheism: Papers from the St. Andrews Conference on the Historical Origins of the Worship of Jesus* (ed. C. C. Newman, J. Davila, G. Lewis; Leiden: Brill, 1999), 43–69 at 57. I disagree with Bauckham's interpretation, since it neglects the complex nature of the *Exagoge*'s theophanic imagery by reducing it to a single speculative dimension, an aspect that might indeed be present among so many other significant agendas of the passage.

7. van der Horst, "Moses' Throne Vision," 25; Holladay, *Fragments*, 444.

8. On the heavenly counterpart traditions in the *Exagoge*, see VanderKam and Boesenberg, "Moses and Enoch in Second Temple Jewish Texts," 146; L. Gallusz, *The Throne Motif in the Book of Revelation* (London: Bloomsbury, 2014), 62; W. van Peursen, "Who Was Standing on the Mountain? The Portrait of Moses in 4Q377," in *Moses in*

Biblical and Extra-Biblical Traditions (ed. A. Graupner and M. Wolter; BZAW, 372; Berlin: Walter de Gruyter, 2007), 99–114.

9. It is noteworthy that the heavenly counterpart of Joseph in *Jos. Asen.* is also decorated with the crown and holding a staff in his hand. We will explore this imagery later in our study. Henry Corbin discusses the peculiar attributes of the angelic double by noting that "this wise guide is the Form of light which is manifested in extremis to the Elect, 'the image of light in the semblance of the soul,' the angel bearing the 'diadem and crown.'" Corbin, *The Man of Light*, 35.

10. See *Targ. Ps.-J.*, *Targ. Neof.*, and *Frg. Targ.* to Gen 28:12.

11. Jacobson, *The Exagoge of Ezekiel*, 91.

12. C. Rowland and C. R. A. Morray-Jones, *The Mystery of God: Early Jewish Mysticism and the New Testament* (CRINT, 12; Leiden: Brill, 2009), 70.

13. *1 Enoch* 71:11.

14. Robertson points to this possibility. See Robertson, "Ezekiel the Tragedian," 812, n. d2.

15. H. Jacobson, *A Commentary on Pseudo-Philo's Liber Antiquitatum Biblicarum with Latin Text and English Translation* (AGAJU, 31; 2 vols.; Leiden: Brill, 1996), 1.110.

16. In *2 Enoch*, the motif of the luminous face of the seer was transferred for the first time to the seventh antediluvian patriarch. The text explains that the vision of the divine Face had dramatic consequences for Enoch's appearance. His body endured radical changes as it became covered with the divine light. In Enoch's radiant metamorphosis before the divine Countenance, an important detail can be found that links Enoch's transformation with Moses' account in the Book of Exodus. In *2 Enoch* 37, one learns about the unusual procedure performed on Enoch's face at the final stage of his encounter with the Lord. The text informs us that the Lord called one of his senior angels to chill the face of Enoch. The text says that the angel was "terrifying and frightful" and appeared frozen; he was as white as snow, and his hands were as cold as ice. With these cold hands, he then chilled the patriarch's face. Right after this chilling procedure, the Lord informs Enoch that if his face had not been chilled here, no human being would have been able to look at him. This reference to the dangerous radiance of Enoch's face after his encounter with the Lord is an apparent parallel to the incandescent face of Moses after the Sinai experience in Exodus 34.

17. *Synopse* §19 (*3 Enoch* 15:1) depicts the radiant metamorphosis of Enoch-Metatron's face.

18. *3 Enoch* 15B:5. Alexander, "3 Enoch," 1.304.

19. Scholars have observed that in the Merkavah tradition Metatron is explicitly identified as the hypostatic Face of God. On Metatron as the hypostatic Face of God, see A. DeConick, "Heavenly Temple Traditions and Valentinian Worship: A Case for First-Century Christology in the Second Century," in *The Jewish Roots of Christological Monotheism* (ed. C. C. Newman, J. R. Davila, G. S. Lewis; JSJSS, 63; Leiden: Brill, 1999), 329; Halperin, *The Faces of the Chariot*, 424–425.

20. See *2 Enoch* 22:6: "And the Lord said to his servants, sounding them out: 'Let Enoch join in and stand in front of my face forever!'"; *2 Enoch* 36:3: "Because a place has been prepared for you, and you will be in front of my face from now and forever." Andersen, "2 Enoch," 1.138 and 1.161.

21. Moses' standing here does not contradict his enthronement. The same situation is discernible in *2 Enoch*, where the hero, who was promised a place to stand in front of God's Face for eternity, is placed on the seat next to the deity.

22. Jacobson, *The Exagoge of Ezekiel*, 54.

23. Fletcher-Louis, *All the Glory of Adam*, 146–147; J. Fossum, *The Name of God and the Angel of the Lord: Samaritan and Jewish Concepts of Intermediation and the Origin of Gnosticism* (WUNT, 36; Tübingen: Mohr/Siebeck, 1985), 121; J. A. Montgomery, *The Samaritans* (New York: Ktav, 1968), 215.

24. Fossum, *Name of God*, 56–58.

25. García Martínez and Tigchelaar, *The Dead Sea Scrolls Study Edition*, 2.745.

26. H. Najman, "Angels at Sinai: Exegesis, Theology, and Interpretive Authority," *DSD* 7 (2000): 313–333 at 319.

27. The idioms of standing in connection with the protagonist's heavenly identity also seem to be assumed in Jacob's traditions. Thus, in the *Prayer of Joseph*, Jacob is linked to the office of the angel of the Presence. We will explore this tradition later in our study.

28. This emphasis on mediation is important, since mediating the divine Presence is one of the pivotal functions of the princes of the Face.

29. *2 Enoch* 39:5. Andersen, "2 Enoch," 1.162.

30. Jacobson, *The Exagoge of Ezekiel*, 54.

31. *Synopse* §384.

32. "The Holy One, blessed be he, laid his hand on me and blessed me with 1,365,000 blessings. I was enlarged and increased in size until I matched the world in length and breadth." Alexander, "3 Enoch," 1.263.

33. Burchard, "Joseph and Aseneth," 2.228.

34. *Hekhalot Rabbati* §164: "You see Me—what I do to the visage of the face of Jacob your father which is engraved for Me upon the throne of My glory. For in the hour that you say before Me 'Holy,' I kneel on it and embrace it and kiss it and hug it and My hands are on its arms three times, corresponding to the three times that you say before Me, 'Holy,' according to the word that is said, Holy, Holy, Holy (Isa 6:3)." J. R. Davila, *Hekhalot Literature in Translation: Major Texts of Merkavah Mysticism* (SJJTP, 20; Leiden: Brill, 2013), 86.

35. In the *Cologne Mani Codex* 11–12, which offers the portrayal of Mani's heavenly counterpart in the spring of the waters, the doppelganger's hand is again mentioned: "from the spring of the waters there appeared to me a human form which showed me by hand (διὰ τῆς χειρὸς) the 'rest' so that I might not sin and bring distress on him." *Der Kölner Mani-Kodex: Über das Werden seines Leibes; Kritische Edition* (ed. L. Koenen and C. Römer; Papyrologica Coloniensia, 14; Opladen: Westdeutscher Verlag, 1988), 8; Gardner and Lieu, *Manichaean Texts from the Roman Empire*, 49.

36. *Pistis Sophia* (ed. C. Schmidt and V. MacDermot; NHS, 9; Leiden: Brill, 1978), 243–245. In another important early Christian text, the *Acts of Thomas*, the celestial "youth" is depicted as putting his hand on a human protagonist. Thus, the *Acts of Thomas* 154 reads: "He says to her: 'Where do you go at this time alone? And how were you able to arise from the bed?' She says to him: '*This youth laid his hand on me* and I was healed. And I say in my dream that I should go to the stranger where he is imprisoned

that I might be quite healed.' Vizan says to her: 'Where is the youth who was with you?' And he says to him: 'Do you not see him? For, see, *he is holding my right hand* and supporting me.'" Klijn, *The Acts of Thomas*, 238.

37. Quispel "Genius and Spirit," 110.

38. Scholarly consensus dates *Jubilees* to the second century BCE somewhere between 170 and 150 BCE. On the date of *Jubilees*, see J. C. VanderKam, *Textual and Historical Studies in the Book of Jubilees* (HSM, 14; Missoula, MO: Scholars, 1977), 207–285; idem, "The Origins and Purposes of the Book of Jubilees," in *Studies in the Book of Jubilees* (ed. M. Albani, J. Frey, and A. Lange; TSAJ, 65; Tübingen: Mohr/Siebeck, 1997), 3–24 at 4–16; M. Segal, *The Book of Jubilees: Rewritten Bible, Redaction, Ideology and Theology* (JSJSS, 117; Leiden: Brill, 2007), 35–41.

39. Scott, *On Earth as in Heaven*, 212. In his other book, James Scott notes that "the juxtaposition of *Urzeit* and *Endzeit*—the beginning of the nations and their cataclysmic end—occurs not only in *Jubilees* 8–9 itself, but also in Dan 12:1 and the *War Rule*." J. M. Scott, *Geography in Early Judaism and Christianity: The Book of Jubilees* (SNTSMS, 113; Cambridge: Cambridge University Press, 2002), 227.

40. Scott, *On Earth as in Heaven*, 217.

41. Scott notes that

> the ultimate goal of history for *Jubilees* is the complete restoration of sacred time and sacred space, so that what is done in the earthly cultus in the Land of Israel exactly corresponds to the way that things are already done in the heavenly cultus, that is, in accordance with the will of God from creation as inscribed on the heavenly tablets. There is, therefore, a strong sense in *Jubilees* not only that earth should perfectly mirror heaven, but that *Endzeit* should completely recapitulate *Urzeit*, that is, restore the world to its original, pristine condition before the fall of Adam. This rigorous symmetry between the temporal and spatial axes in the space-time continuum is an important hallmark of the book.

Scott, *On Earth as in Heaven*, 8.

42. VanderKam, "The Angel of the Presence in the Book of Jubilees," 390. Michael Segal observes that "in certain instances, an angel or angels in *Jubilees* come in the place of God in the Pentateuch. The most conspicuous case of the replacement of God by an angel is the narrative frame of the entire book, in which the angel of the presence speaks to Moses at Sinai, and dictates to him from the Heavenly Tablets. The general effect of the insertion of the angels into the stories is the distancing of God from the everyday events of the world, transforming him into a transcendental deity." Segal, *The Book of Jubilees*, 9–10.

43. J. C. VanderKam, *The Book of Jubilees* (2 vols.; CSCO, 510–511, Scriptores Aethiopici, 87–88; Leuven: Peeters, 1989), 2.40.

44. VanderKam, "The Angel of the Presence," 391.

45. VanderKam, "The Angel of the Presence," 391.

46. VanderKam, *The Book of Jubilees*, 2.195.

47. The scribal office of Moses is reaffirmed throughout the text. Already in the beginning (*Jub.* 1:5; 7; 26), he receives a chain of commands to write down the revelation dictated by the angel.

48. On the angelology of the *Book of Jubilees*, see R. H. Charles, *The Book of Jubilees or the Little Genesis* (London: Black, 1902) lvi–lviii; M. Testuz, *Les idées religieuses du livre des Jubilés* (Geneva: Droz, 1960), 75–92; K. Berger, *Das Buch der Jubiläen* (JSHRZ, 2.3; Gütersloh: Gütersloher Verlaghaus Gerd Nohn, 1981), 322–324; D. Dimant, "The Sons of Heaven: The Theory of the Angels in the Book of Jubilees in Light of the Writings of the Qumran Community," in *A Tribute to Sarah: Studies in Jewish Philosophy and Cabala Presented to Professor Sara A. Heller-Wilensky* (ed. M. Idel, D. Dimant, and S. Rosenberg; Jerusalem: Magnes, 1994), 97–118 [in Hebrew]; VanderKam, "The Angel of the Presence in the Book of Jubilees," 378–393; Najman, "Angels at Sinai: Exegesis, Theology and Interpretive Authority," 313–333; J. L. Kugel, *A Walk through Jubilees: Studies in the Book of Jubilees and the World of its Creation* (JSJSS, 156; Leiden: Brill, 2012), 26–28.

49. See *Jub.* 1:27: "Then he said to an angel of the presence: 'Dictate to Moses (starting) from the beginning of the creation until the time when my temple is built among them throughout the ages of eternity.'" VanderKam, *Jubilees*, 2.6. *Jub.* 2:1–2: "On the Lord's orders the angel of the presence said to Moses: 'Write all the words about the creation—how in six days the Lord God completed all his works, everything that he had created, and kept sabbath on the seventh day. He sanctified it for all ages and set it as a sign for all his works. For on the first day he created the heavens that are above, the earth, the waters, and all the spirits who serve before him, namely: the angels of the presence; the angels of holiness.'" VanderKam, *Jubilees*, 2.7.

50. VanderKam, *Jubilees*, 2.235–236.

51. VanderKam, *Jubilees*, 2.12.

52. Cf. *Jub.* 31:13–14: "He [Isaac] turned to Levi first and began to bless him first. He said to him: 'May the Lord of everything—he is the Lord of all ages—bless you and your sons throughout all ages. May the Lord give you and your descendants extremely great honor; may he make you and your descendants (alone) out of all humanity approach him to serve in his temple like the angels of the presence and like the holy ones." VanderKam, *Jubilees*, 2.203–204. Reflecting on this passage, James Scott notes that "here we learn that Levi and his descendants were elected out of all humanity, including the rest of Israel, to serve as priests in the earthly Temple and to do so in correspondence to the heavenly priests, the angels, who serve before the very presence of God in heaven." Scott, *On Earth as in Heaven*, 4.

53. *Jub.* 15:26–28:

> Anyone who is born, the flesh of whose private parts has not been circumcised by the eighth day does not belong to the people of the pact which the Lord made with Abraham but to the people (meant for) destruction. Moreover, there is no sign on him that he belongs to the Lord, but (he is meant) for destruction, for being destroyed from the earth, and for being uprooted from the earth because he has violated the covenant of the Lord our God. For this is what the nature of all the angels of the presence and

all the angels of holiness was like from the day of their creation. In front of the angels of the presence and the angels of holiness he sanctified Israel to be with him and his holy angels. Now you command the Israelites to keep the sign of this covenant throughout their history as an eternal ordinance so that they may not be uprooted from the earth.

VanderKam, *Jubilees*, 2.92–93. On this tradition, see also Scott, *On Earth as in Heaven*, 3–4; Segal, *The Book of Jubilees*, 236–8; J. T. A. G. M. van Ruiten, *Abraham in the Book of Jubilees: The Rewriting of Genesis 11:26–25:10 in the Book of Jubilees 11:14–23:8* (JSJSS, 161; Leiden: Brill, 2012), 158; A. Kim Harkins, *Reading with an "I" to the Heavens: Looking at the Qumran Hodayot through the Lens of Visionary Traditions* (Ekstasis: Religious Experience from Antiquity to the Middle Ages, 3; Berlin: Walter de Gruyter, 2012), 221.

54. G. Brooke, "Men and Women as Angels in Joseph and Aseneth," *JSP* 14 (2005): 161. On this, see also D. Dimant, "Men as Angels: The Self-Image of the Qumran Community," in *Religion and Politics in the Ancient Near East* (ed. A. Berlin; STJHC, 1; Bethesda: University Press of Maryland, 1996), 93–103; B. Ego, "Heilige Zeit—heiliger Raum—heiliger Mensch: Beobachtungen zur Struktur der Gesetzesbegründung in der Schöpfungs- und Paradiesgeschichte des Jubiläenbuches," in *Studies in the Book of Jubilees* (ed. M. Albani, J. Frey, and A. Lange; TSAJ, 65; Tübingen: Mohr/Siebeck, 1997), 207–219.

55. In *Jos. Asen.* 18:3–6, the transformed seer is also endowed with a luminous robe, a golden crown, and a scepter—the attributes of her heavenly initiator.

56. On Metatron's office of the celestial scribe, see Orlov, *The Enoch-Metatron Tradition*, 97–101.

57. *2 Enoch* 22:10–11 (the shorter recension): "The Lord summoned Vereveil, one of his archangels, who was wise, who records all the Lord's deeds. And the Lord said to Vereveil, 'Bring out the books from storehouses, and give a pen to Enoch and read him the books.' And Vereveil hurried and brought me the books mottled with myrrh. And he gave me the pen from his hand." Andersen, "2 Enoch," 1.141.

58. This "intermediate" authoritative stand is often further reinforced by the authority of the deity himself through the identification of the heavenly counterparts with the divine Form. On this process, see our previous discussion about the blurring of the boundaries between the doppelganger and the deity.

59. About the inspiration of Manichaean books by the Twin, see Ort, *Mani: A Religio-historical Description of His Personality*, 86 ff.

60. Thus, Thomas Dozeman suggests that already in the biblical accounts Moses' face serves as a mirror of the divine Face—*Kavod*. T. B. Dozeman, *God on the Mountain* (Atlanta: Scholars, 1989), 172, n. 58.

61. *Synopse* §§396–397: "The Lord of all the worlds warned Moses that he should beware of his face. So it is written, 'Beware of his face.' This is the prince who is called Metatron."

62. Some scholars argue that the designation of the angelic servants of the divine Face—*Sar ha-Panim*—can be translated as the "prince who is the face [of God]." On this, see N. Deutsch, *Guardians of the Gate: Angelic Vice Regency in Late Antiquity* (BSJS,

22; Leiden: Brill, 1999), 43; idem, *The Gnostic Imagination: Gnosticism, Mandaeism, and Merkabah Mysticism* (Leiden: Brill, 1995); R. S. Boustan, *From Martyr to Mystic: Rabbinic Martyrology and the Making of Merkavah Mysticism* (TSAJ, 112; Tübingen: Mohr/Siebeck, 2005), 118–121; R. Neis, "Embracing Icons: The Face of Jacob on the Throne of God," *Images: A Journal of Jewish Art and Visual Culture* 1 (2007): 36–54 at 42.

63. Orlov, *The Enoch-Metatron Tradition*, 165–176; idem, "The Face as the Heavenly Counterpart," 2.59–76.

64. See the section on the angelic princes of the Face earlier in our study.

65. As I previously suggested, the metaphor of "engraving" on the *Kavod* might signify that the seer's identity became reflected in the divine Face, as in a mirror. On this, see A. Orlov, *Selected Studies in the Slavonic Pseudepigrapha* (SVTP, 23; Leiden: Brill, 2009), 176. The tradition about Jacob's image engraved on the divine Face will be explored in detail later in our study.

66. P. Schäfer, *The Hidden and Manifest God: Some Major Themes in Early Jewish Mysticism* (Albany, NY: SUNY Press, 1992), 18. This motif recalls *2 Enoch*, in which the description of the Face and the statement about the impossibility of enduring its vision are combined.

67. This theme looms large in the Hekhalot tradition where one can often find the "danger motif" applied to the Face imagery. On this, see Schäfer, *The Hidden and Manifest God*, 17; *Synopse* §§102, 159, 183, 189, 356.

68. Schäfer, *The Hidden and Manifest God*, 18.

69. Schäfer, *The Hidden and Manifest God*, 18.

70. For discussion of this rabbinic passage, see M. Fishbane, "Through the Looking-Glass: Reflections on Ezek. 43.4, Num. 12.8 and 1 Cor. 13.8," *HAR* 10 (1986): 63–75 at 71; M. D. Litwa, "Transformation through a Mirror: Moses in 2 Cor. 3.18," *JSNT* 34 (2012): 286–297 at 291.

71. Cf. *b. Yeb.* 49b: "[Do not] the contradictions between the Scriptural texts, however, still remain?—'I saw the Lord,' [is to be understood] in accordance with what was taught: All the prophets looked into a dim glass, but Moses looked through a clear glass." Epstein, *The Babylonian Talmud. Yebamot*, 49b. Gershom Scholem draws attention to the passage from R. Moses Isseries of Cracow, who is reflecting on the talmudic passage from *b. Yeb.* 49b that offers the following comment:

> For in truth, it is fitting to describe Him by this parable and metaphor, for light is found with Him [Dan 2:22], and in Him all those who gaze see, and each one sees Him like one gazing in a mirror. For the coarse matter that is in man stands opposite the prophet or the one who contemplates, behind the clear light that is in the soul, which is like a mirror for him, and he sees in it, in an inner vision, his own form. For this reason the prophets compared the divine glory (*Kavod*) to a human image, for they saw their own form. But Moses our teacher, because he had removed from himself all corporeality, and there was none of the dark matter from without left within him, saw naught but the brilliant light itself, and there was no [reflected] image, but he saw only the clear aspect. . . . And let not this reason be a small thing

in your eyes, for it strikes me as being the truth concerning the prophetic visions: that they saw the *Kavod* (the divine glory) in human shape, which was the shape of the prophet himself. And for this reason our rabbis said: "Great is the power of the prophets, who made the form to resemble the Former." That is to say, they transferred their own form that they saw to the Creator. And this is the literal meaning of this saying, according to this way [of interpretation]. Similarly, the [author of] *Minhath Yehudah* wrote, in his Commentary to *Maʿarekheth ha-Elohuth*, as follows: "The lower Adam is a throne for the upper Adam; for the physical limbs in him allude to the spiritual limbs up above, and they are divine potencies. And not for naught did He say, 'Let us make man in our image' [Gen 1:26]. But this image is the image of the supernal, spiritual man, and the prophet is the physical man, who at the moment of prophecy becomes spiritual, and whose external senses nearly depart from him; therefore, if he sees the image of a man, it is as if he sees his own image in a glass mirror."

Scholem, *On the Mystical Shape of the Godhead*, 258–259.

72. See also *Zohar* I.170b: "For Moses gazed into the clear mirror of prophecy, whereas all the other prophets looked into a hazy mirror." Sperling and Simon, *The Zohar*, 2.153. *Zohar* I.183a: "Now all the prophets drew their inspiration from one side, from the midst of two certain grades which they beheld in a 'dull mirror,' as it says: 'I do make myself known unto him in a vision,' the word 'vision' denoting, as has been explained, a medium reflecting a variety of colours; and this is the 'dull mirror.'" Sperling and Simon, *The Zohar*, 2.199. *Zohar* II.82b:

Why, then, did Isaiah not give a detailed account of his visions, like Ezekiel? According to R. Jose, it was necessary that Ezekiel should speak in a detailed manner in order to impress the people in exile with the fact that the Holy One loved them, and that the *Shekinah* and Her Chariots had gone down into exile also, to be present with them. R. Hiya asked, why did the *Shekinah* reveal Herself in "the land of the Chaldeans" (Ezek 1:3), of which it says: "Behold the land of the Chaldeans, a people which is not" (Isa 23:13, i.e. degraded)? If it was for Israel's sake, surely She could have been present among them without manifesting Herself in that inauspicious place? However, had She not revealed Herself the people would not have known that She was with them. Besides, the revelation took place "by the river Chebar" (Ezek 1:3), by undefiled waters where impurity has no abode, that river being one of the four which issued from the Garden of Eden. It was there, and nowhere else, then, that "the hand of the Lord was upon him," as is directly stated. R. Hiya also expounded, in accordance with the esoteric teaching, Ezekiel's vision: "Out of the midst thereof came the likeness of four living creatures, and this was their appearance, they had the likeness of a man," saying that there is a sacred Hall in which dwell four living Creatures, which are the most ancient celestial beings ministering to the Holy Ancient, and which constitute the essence of the Supernal Name; and that Ezekiel saw only the likeness of the supernal Chariots, because his beholding was from a region which was not very bright. He furthermore said that there are lower beings corresponding to these upper ones, and so throughout, and they are all linked one with another. Our teachers have laid down that Moses derived his prophetic vision from a bright mirror, whereas the other prophets derived their vision from a dull mirror. So it is written concerning Ezekiel: "I saw visions of God," whereas in connection with the difference between Moses and all other prophets it says: "If there is a prophet among you, I the Lord will make Myself known to him in a vision. . . . My servant Moses is not so, who is faithful in all my house: and with him I will speak mouth to mouth" (Num 12:7-8). R. Jose remarked that all the prophets are in comparison with Moses like females in comparison with males. The Lord did not speak to him in "riddles," but showed him everything clearly. Blessed, indeed, was the generation in whose midst this prophet lived!

Sperling and Simon, *The Zohar*, 3.274.

73. Reflecting on this phrase, Jan Lambrecht suggests that "it is obvious that Philo thinks here of 'seeing in a mirror.'" J. Lambrecht, "Transformation in 2 Cor 3,18," *Biblica* 64 (1983): 243–254 at 248.

74. For Philo, a mirror clearly reflects the original. Cf. *Somn.* 2.31 §206: "Yet we need little thought in our quest of him, for the dreamer's vision is the closest possible reproduction of his image, and through careful study of the dream we shall see him reflected as it were in a mirror." *Philo* (trans. F. H. Colson and G. H. Whitaker; 10 vols.; LCL; Cambridge, MA: Harvard University Press, 1929-1964), 5.535–537; *Decal.* 21 §105: "But nothing so much assures its predominance as that through it is best given the revelation of the Father and Maker of all, for in it, as in a mirror, the mind has a vision of God as acting and creating the world and controlling all that is." Colson and Whitaker, *Philo*, 7.61.

75. Colson and Whitaker, *Philo*, 1.369–371. This tradition is also found in later interpretations of Jacob's story—a trend that will be explored in our study. For example, *Zohar* I.149b reflects on Jacob's vision: "A 'vision' (*mar'eh* = vision, or mirror) is so called because it is like a mirror, in which all images are reflected. Thus we read: 'And I appeared . . . as El Shaddai' (Exod 6:2), this grade being like a mirror which showed another form, since all supernal forms are reflected in it." Sperling and Simon, *The Zohar*, 2.79. *Zohar* I.168a unveils the following tradition: "Hence it is that when the children of Jacob are oppressed, God looks at the image of Jacob and is filled with pity for the world. This is hinted in the passage: 'Then will I remember my covenant with Jacob' (Lev 26:42), where the name Jacob is spelt *plene*, with a *vau*, which is itself the image of Jacob. To look at Jacob was like looking at the 'clear mirror.'" Sperling and Simon, *The Zohar*, 2.144.

76. Scholars also noted influences from the formative Ezekelian account. Thus, Alan Segal argues that

in 2 Cor 3:18, Paul says that believers will be changed into Christ's likeness from one degree of glory to another. . . . Paul's term the Glory of the Lord must be taken both as a reference to Christ and as a technical term for the *kavod*, the human form of God appearing in biblical visions. In 2 Cor 3:18, Paul says that Christians behold the Glory of the Lord as in a mirror and are transformed into his image. . . . The use of the mirror here is also a magico-mystical theme, which can be traced to the word עין occurring in Ezek 1. Although it is sometimes translated otherwise, עין probably refers to a mirror even there, and possibly refers to some unexplained technique for achieving ecstasy. The mystic bowls of the magical papyri and Talmudic times were filled with water and oil to reflect light and stimulate trance.

A. Segal, "The Afterlife as Mirror of the Self," in *Experientia: Volume 1; Inquiry into Religious Experience in Early Judaism and Christianity* (ed. F. Flannery, C. Shantz, and R. A. Werline; SBLSS, 40; Atlanta: SBL, 2008), 26.

77. See Litwa, "Transformation through a Mirror," 286–297.

78. Alan Segal notes that

Paul's use of the language of transformation often goes unappreciated. In 2 Cor 3:18, Paul says that believers will be changed into Christ's likeness from one degree of glory to another. He refers to Moses' encounter with the angel of the Lord in Exodus 33–34. Earlier in the Exodus passage, the angel of the Lord is described as carrying the name of God. Moses sees the Glory of the Lord, makes a covenant, receives the commandments on the two tables of the law, and when he comes down from the mount, the skin of his face shines with light (Exod 34:29–35). Moses thereafter must wear a veil except when he is in the presence of the Lord. Paul assumes that Moses made an ascension to the presence of the Lord, was transformed by that encounter, and that his shining face is a reflection of the encounter. . . . Paul's phrase the "Glory of the Lord" must be taken both as a reference to Christ and as a technical term for the *Kavod*, the human form of God appearing in biblical visions. In 2 Cor 3:18, Paul says that Christians behold the Glory of the Lord (*ten doxan kyriou*) as in a mirror and are transformed into his image (*ten auten eikōna*). For Paul, as for the earliest Jewish mystics, to be privileged to see the *Kavod* or Glory (*doxa*) of God is a prologue to transformation into his image (*eikōn*).

A. Segal, *Paul the Convert: The Apostolate and Apostasy of Saul the Pharisee* (New Haven: Yale University Press, 1990), 60.

79. It is intriguing that a passage from *Zohar* I.168a connects the tradition of Jacob's heavenly identity in the form of an image with the mirror symbolism: "Hence it is that when the children of Jacob are oppressed, God looks at the image of Jacob and is filled with pity for the world. This is hinted in the passage: 'Then will I remember my covenant

with Jacob' (Lev 26:42), where the name Jacob is spelt *plene*, with a *vau*, which is itself the image of Jacob. To look at Jacob was like looking at the 'clear mirror.'" Sperling and Simon, *The Zohar*, 2.144.

80. *Lev. Rab.* 1:14, mentioned above, in which Moses receives his revelation through the mirror, also evokes the terminology of "image": "R. Phinehas said in the name of R. Hosha'iah: This may be compared to a king who allowed himself to be seen by his intimate friend [only] by means of his image. In this world the *Shekhinah* manifests itself only to chosen individuals; in the Time to Come, however, the glory of the Lord shall be revealed, and all the flesh shall see it together; for the mouth of the Lord hath spoken it (Isa 40:5)." Reflecting on this passage, David Litwa observes that "in context, this interpretation indicates that at Sinai Moses was looking at God's image, and that this foreshadows the eschatological age when all people will recapitulate this experience. It is important to note that the mirror Moses looks at in the previous two interpretations has become an image. Second, Moses looking at God's 'image' is functionally equivalent to the 'glory' seen by everyone in the world to come. The semantic associations of 'glory' and 'image' as well as 'image' and 'mirror' indicate that we are close to the kind of interpretation we see in 2 Cor. 3:18." Litwa, "Transformation through a Mirror," 292. Moshe Idel notes that in some rabbinic texts and, in a different manner, in Hasidei Ashkenaz and in some Kabbalistic sources the biblical "image" *tselem* is understood as "face." M. Idel, "Panim: On Facial Re-Presentations in Jewish Thought: Some Correlational Instances," in *On Interpretation in the Arts: Interdisciplinary Studies in the Honor of Moshe Lazar* (ed. N. Yaari; Tel Aviv: Tel Aviv University, 2000), 21–56 at 24. From later Jewish mystical testimonies, one learns that through his or her reflection/shadow a person can access and manipulate his or her heavenly counterpart represented by his or her image. Thus, *Zohar* III.43a reads:

> if someone wishes to indulge in sorcery of the Left Side and immerse himself in it, he should stand in the light of a lamp, or in another place where his own images can be seen, and say the words prescribed for this kind of sorcery, and summon these unclean powers by their unclean names. He should then commit his images on oath to those he has summoned, and say that he is of his own free will prepared to obey their command. Such a man leaves the authority of his Creator and assigns his trust to the power of uncleanness. And with these words of sorcery which he pronounces and [with which] he adjures the images, two spirits are revealed, and they are embodied in his images in human form, and they give him information both for good and evil purposes for particular occasions. These two spirits that were not comprised within a body are now comprised in these images and are embodied in them.

Tishby, *The Wisdom of the Zohar*, 2.788.

81. In relation to these traditions, Concetta Principe observes that

> there is a tradition of the mirror in the first century period, Segal notes, adapted from Moses experience of God, by Paul and his contemporaries:

"Philo believed that people do not see God directly but through a mirror (*On Flight*, 213)." The pure water in Aseneth's story becomes a mirror in which the *doxa* of God is reflected back in her face as her converted self. This reflection does not signify a magic practice, Burchard notes, but a mystical transformation: "She comes close to being an angelic figure" echoing Moses and Paul's experience with God's *doxa* and paralleled by 2 Corinthians 3:18. I would add that there are parallels to the glory Paul claims that can be found in the human face as defined in 2 Corinthians 3:16 to 4:6.

C. V. Principe, *Secular Messiahs and the Return of Paul's "Real": A Lacanian Approach* (New York: Palgrave Macmillan, 2015), 129.

82. Emphasis is mine. Segal, "The Afterlife as Mirror of the Self," 20.

83. Segal, "The Afterlife as Mirror of the Self," 24.

84. Emphasis is mine. A. DeConick, *Voices of the Mystics: Early Christian Discourse in the Gospels of John and Thomas and Other Ancient Christian Literature* (London: T&T Clark, 2001), 65–66.

85. Emphasis is mine. DeConick, *Voices of the Mystics*, 65–66.

86. A. DeConick, *Recovering the Original Gospel of Thomas: A History of the Gospel and Its Growth* (London: T&T Clark, 2005), 205.

87. The similar conceptual constellations of image and mirror play a prominent role in the Mandaean tradition where lower mediatorial figures, like Ptahil, are also portrayed both as an image and as a reflection or a mirror of the upper mediatorial figures, including Abatur. In relation to these developments, Gilles Quispel observes that

> the first Idea, God's Wisdom looks down on the Chaos below, and the primeval waters mirror her shadowy image: that is the demiurge who orders unorganized matter. So the world originates from the projecting activity of the great Goddess Barbelo. Even today we find the same among the Mandaeans, the only Gnostics in this world who can boast an uninterrupted continuity of the ancient Gnostics: according to them . . . at the commandment of God ("Life") the heavenly weighmaster, Abatur, looks down from above into that black water; at the same moment his image was formed in the black water, the demiurge, Gabriel or Ptahil, took shape and ascended to the borderland (on high near heaven, near the realm of light). Or, again, this holy Motherfather reveals herself to the demonic powers of this world through her luminous image in the primordial waters.

G. Quispel, "Gnosis and Psychology," in *The Rediscovery of Gnosticism* (ed. B. Layton; 2 vols.; SHR, 41; Leiden: Brill, 1981), 1.29.

88. Emphasis is mine. Lambrecht, "Transformation in 2 Cor 3,18," 249.

89. In *CMC* 17, Mani's heavenly counterpart is labeled as the "greatest mirror-image" (μέγιστον κάτοπτρον). Koenen and Römer, *Der Kölner Mani-Kodex*, 10. The similar imagery is applied to the upper Self in *Acts of Thomas* 112: "When I received it, the garment seemed to me to become like a mirror of myself. I saw it all in all, and I too received all in it." Klijn, *Acts of Thomas*, 185. For a discussion of these passages, see

A. Henrichs, H. Henrichs, and L. Koenen, "Der Kölner Mani-Kodex (P. Colon. inv. nr. 4780)," *ZPE* 19 (1975): 1–85 at 79, n. 41; I. Gruenwald, *From Apocalypticism to Gnosticism: Studies in Apocalypticism, Merkavah Mysticism and Gnosticism* (BEATAJ, 14; Frankfurt am Main: Lang, 1988), 256; J. C. Reeves, *Heralds of that Good Realm: Syro-Mesopotamian Gnosis and Jewish Traditions* (NHMS, 41, Leiden: Brill, 1996), 91–92, n. 18.

90. It is intriguing that in later Jewish mystical lore some patriarchical figures are envisioned as "mirrors." As one remembers, *Zohar* I.168a says that "to look at Jacob was like looking at the 'clear mirror.'" Sperling and Simon, *The Zohar*, 2.144.

91. On the Logos as the intermediate mirror of God, see Philo's *Her.* 230–231: "One is the archetypal Logos above us, the other the copy of it which we possess. Moses calls the first the 'image of God,' the second the cast of that image. For God, he says, made man not 'the image of God' but 'after the image' (Gen 1:27)." Colson and Whitaker, *Philo*, 4.399.

92. Litwa, "Transformation through a Mirror," 293.

93. Litwa, "Transformation through a Mirror," 294.

94. Nathaniel Deutsch notes that

> it also appears that some sources understood Metatron to be the hypostatic embodiment of a particular part of the divine form, most notably the face of God. As I have argued elsewhere, it is likely that this tradition underlies the title *Sar ha-Panim*, which is associated with Metatron. Rather than "prince of the face [of God]," this title is better understood as "prince who is the face [of God]." Indeed, at least one Merkabah passage explicitly identifies Metatron as the hypostatic face of God: "Moses said to the Lord of all the worlds: 'If your face does not go [with us], do not bring me up from here.' [Exod 33:15]. The Lord of all the worlds warned Moses that he should beware of that face of his. So it is written, 'Beware of his face.' [Exod 23:21]. This is he who is written with the one letter by which heaven and earth were created, and was sealed with the seal of 'I am that I am' [Exod 3:14]. . . . This is the prince who is called Yofiel Yah-dariel . . . he is called Metatron." *Synopse* §§396–397.

Deutsch, *Guardians of the Gate*, 43.

95. Some early Jewish and Christian accounts provide hints to these hierarchies of mediatorial "faces" that, depending on their powers, are able differently to "light up" the countenance of a seer. One such testimony can be found in the *Ascension of Isaiah* 7:19–25:

> And [I saw there, as] in the first heaven, angels on the right and on the left, and a throne in the middle, and the praise of the angels who (were) in the second heaven; and the one who sat on the throne in the second heaven had more glory than all (the rest). . . . And he took me up into the third heaven, and in the same way I saw those who (were) on the right and on the left, and there also (there was) a throne in the middle and one who sat (on it), but no mention of this world was made there. And I said to the

angel who (was) with me, for the glory of my face was being transformed as I went up from heaven to heaven.

M. A. Knibb, "Martyrdom and Ascension of Isaiah," in *The Old Testament Pseudepigrapha*, 2.166–167. In relation to this passage, Peter Schäfer observes that "in the third heaven Isaiah notices that the gradual increase of glory in each heaven is mirrored in his own physical transformation: the higher he gets, the brighter becomes his face (7:25)." Schäfer, *Origins of Jewish Mysticism*, 96.

96. It should be noted that this concept of multiple divine "faces" was affirmed by later Jewish mystical lore that postulates that the deity possesses several "faces," each of them fashioned according to the identity of the seer. Moshe Idel notes that such conceptual traits attempt to emphasize the dynamic aspect of the divinity by "opting for a variety of divine faces, each expressing what is conceived of as real, namely not imaginable aspect of the divine being." Idel, "Panim: On Facial Re-Presentations in Jewish Thought," 25. Idel draws his attention to a rabbinic tradition circulated in the name of a third century Palestinian master R. Levi. Thus, *Pesiqta de-Rav Kahana* reads: "The Holy One, blessed be He, has shown Himself to them like this icon that is showing its faces in all the directions. A thousand people are looking at it and it looks to each of them. So does the Holy One, blessed be He, when He was speaking each and every one of Israel was saying the speech was with me. 'I am God, your Lord' is not written, but I am God, your Lord. Rabbi Yossei bar Hanina said: according to the strength of each and every one, the (divine) speech was speaking." *Pesikta de Rav Kahana According to an Oxford Manuscript, with Variants from All Known Manuscripts and Genizoth Fragments and Parallel Passages* (ed. B. Mandelbaum; 2 vols.; New York: Jewish Theological Seminary of America, 1962), 1.224. Reflecting on this passage, Idel suggests that

> the divine face, just as an icon as described above, is not a totally determined entity; just as the voice is open to a variety of auditory experiences each of which is conceived of as real. . . . Important for some other Midrashic discussions is the reference in this passage to many divine faces. Though the above text does not express this multiplicity in an explicit manner, such a multiplicity is conveyed by the term *panim* in the context of the icon which is the parable for the manner in which the divine face operates. In Hebrew the very term for face, *panim*, has a plural form, but there can be no doubt that it is not the grammatical plural form, but it is the concept of multiplicity of faces that transpires in this passage.

Idel, "Panim: On Facial Re-Presentations in Jewish Thought," 25. In other midrashic composition, *Pesiqta Rabbati*, to R. Levi is attributed another reflection about multiple faces of the deity: "The Holy One, Blessed be he, revealed Himself to them with many faces: with an angry face, with a downcast face, with a dour face, with a joyful face, with a smiling face, and with a radiant face. How? When he showed them the punishment (awaiting) the wicked, he did so with an angry, downcast, dour face. But when He showed them the reward (awaiting) the just in the World to come, it was with a happy, (smiling), radiant face." Idel, "Panim: On Facial Re-Presentations in Jewish Thought," 26. A similar tradition is found in *Zohar* II.86b–87a: "We know that the Holy One has many aspects (faces) in His manifestations to men: He manifests to some a beaming face, to others a gloomy one; to some a distant face, to others one that is very near; to some an external, to others an inner, hidden aspect; to some from the right side, to others from the left." Sperling and Simon, *The Zohar*, 3.264. Cf. also a passage from *Pesiqta de-Rav Kahana*: " 'I am your Lord'—Rabbi Hanina bar Papa said: the Holy One, blessed be He, has shown to them a face of anger, a face of welcoming, a moderate face, and a laughing face. A face of anger—[corresponds to] the Bible, because when a person teaches the Bible to his son, he has to teach him with awe. A moderate face—to the Mishnah. A face of welcoming—to the Talmud. A laughing face—to the Aggadah. The Holy One, blessed be He, said to them: despite you have seen all these appearances, 'I am your Lord.' " Mandelbaum, *Pesikta de Rav Kahana*, 1.223–224. Idel notes that "if the first quote of R. Levi deals with concomitant revelations that are diversified by the various human capacities, in the last quote the different countenances of the divine face, or the faces, reflect different parts of the divine revelation, or different verses in the Bible; some dealing with retribution and some with punishment. When pronouncing those different verses, the divine face changes accordingly, or accommodates itself. It is as if the divine face uses different masks attuned to the content of the text recited." Idel also points out that although "the divine faces do not correspond to the human faces, but to the literary corpora, since those corpora are intended to be studied by people, ultimately this is another form of correlational theology. Those passages are part of a broader Midrashic theory of multiple revelations based on the assumption that God accommodates Himself to the specific situation in which the revelation is taking place." Idel, "Panim: On Facial Re-Presentations in Jewish Thought," 27–28.

97. The traditions about Jacob as a hypostatic divine Face will be explored in the next chapter of our study. It is possible that this tradition is connected with the Metatron lore. Thus, Nathaniel Deutsch suggests that "the possibility that Metatron was actually identified as the hypostatic face of God is strengthened by a complex set of associations linking Metatron with the face of Jacob engraved on the throne of God." Deutsch, *Gnostic Imagination*, 106.

98. On Christ as the hypostatic Face of God, see Clement of Alexandria's *Excerpta ex Theodoto* 10:6: "But they 'always behold the face of the Father' and the face of the Father is the Son, through whom the Father is known." Casey, *The Excerpta ex Theodoto of Clement of Alexandria*, 49.

99. Cf. *Odes of Solomon* 13:1–2: "Behold, the Lord is our mirror. Open [your] eyes and see them in him. And learn the manner of your face, then announce praises to his Spirit. And wipe the paint from your face, and love his holiness and put it on. Then you will be unblemished at all times with him." J. H. Charlesworth, "Odes of Solomon," in *The Old Testament Pseudepigrapha*, 2.747.

100. See *2 Enoch* 64:4–5: "O our father, Enoch! May you be blessed by the Lord, the eternal king! And now, bless your [sons], and all the people, so that we may be glorified in front of your face today. For you will be glorified in front of the face [of the Lord for eternity], because you are the one whom the Lord chose in preference to all the people

upon the earth; and he appointed you to be the one who makes a written record of all his creation, visible and invisible, and the one who carried away the sin of mankind." Andersen, "2 Enoch," 1.190.

101. On Moses' face as a divine hypostatic entity in later Jewish mysticism, see Moshe Idel's chapter "Moses' Face as a Divine Hypostasis in Ecstatic Kabbalah," in *Moshe Idel: Representing God* (ed. H. Tirosh-Samuelson and A. W. Hughes; LCJP, 8; Leiden: Brill, 2014), 103–122 at 114–117.

102. B. Britt, *Rewriting Moses: The Narrative Eclipse of the Text* (JSOTSS, 402; London: T&T Clark, 2004), 85.

Chapter Three: The Heavenly Counterpart Traditions in the Pseudepigrapha about Jacob

1. *Targum Pseudo-Jonathan: Genesis* (trans. M. Maher, MSC; ArBib, 1B; Collegeville, MN: Liturgical Press, 1992), 99–100. In other parts of this targum, the idea of the heavenly counterpart or the guardian angel can be found. Thus, *Targ. Ps.-J.* on Gen 33:10 reads: "And Jacob said, 'Do not speak thus, I pray; if now I have found mercy in your eyes, you must accept my gift from my hand; because it is for this I have seen your countenance, and it seems to me like seeing the face of your angel; and behold, you have received me favorably.'" Maher, *Targum Pseudo-Jonathan: Genesis*, 116. *Targ. Ps.-J.* on Gen 48:16: "May it be pleasing before you that the angel whom you assigned to me to redeem me from all evil, bless the boys; and let my name be recalled in them, and the name of my fathers Abraham and Isaac." Maher, *Targum Pseudo-Jonathan: Genesis*, 156.

2. McNamara, *Targum Neofiti 1: Genesis*, 140.

3. Klein, *Fragment-Targums of the Pentateuch*, 1.57 and 2.20.

4. Fossum, *Image of the Invisible God*, 140–141.

5. Fossum notes that this tradition is already observable in some versions of the *Fragmentary Targum* that do not contain the verb "engraved" or "fixed." Fossum, *Image of the Invisible God*, 141. He also points to a certain baraita (*b. Hul.* 91b) that seems to attests to the same tradition. Fossum, *Image of the Invisible God*, 139–140.

6. Rowland, "Jewish Apocalyptic and Targumic Tradition," 504.

7. Halperin notes that

> targumic Tosefta to Ezekiel 1:26 introduces a striking interpretation of that verse at the same time that it sidesteps its anthropomorphism. According to the Hebrew text, the prophet sees the form of a sapphire throne, "and upon the form of the throne a form like the appearance of a human being, upon it from above." Most Targum manuscripts leave "the appearance of a human being" in Hebrew; *Codex Reuchlinianus* and the printed editions translate it literally. But one manuscript (Montefiore H.116) records a variant: "the form of Jacob our father upon it from above." When we read Ezekiel 1:26 we normally assume that the appearance of a "human being" is sitting on the throne. But it is just as possible to understand the Hebrew to mean that it

is engraved on the throne. Both Palestinian and Babylonian rabbinic sources (*Gen. Rab.* 68:12; *b. Hull.* 91b) speak of Jacob's image as being engraved on God's throne, but do not give any satisfactory exegetical basis for it. This Tosefta suggests that the idea derives from an anti-anthropomorphic interpretation of Ezekiel 1:26, developed in the synagogue. Of course, we still do not know why the "form" is identified as Jacob's; this is probably connected with the belief that a celestial embodiment of Israel (Jacob) is perpetually in God's sight. An Aramaic hymn for *Shabuʿot*, of uncertain date, connects Jacob's image with a heavenly ascension: Moses sees "the image of Jacob rising up opposite him" when he ascends to receive the Torah.

Halperin, *The Faces of the Chariot*, 121. In relation to these traditions, Wolfson observes that "this notion too is clearly reflected in the *piyyut* literature, for example, the *qerovah* of Qallir." E. Wolfson, "The Image of Jacob Engraved upon the Throne," in idem, *Along the Path: Studies in Kabbalistic Myth, Symbolism, and Hermeneutics* (Albany, NY: SUNY Press, 1995), 1–62 at 8. See also *Zohar* I.72a: "'As the appearance of a man' refers to the image of Jacob, who sits on it." Sperling and Simon, *The Zohar*, 1.242.

8. Fossum, *Image of the Invisible God*, 142.
9. Fossum, *Image of the Invisible God*, 142.
10. In relation to this theme in the rabbinic materials, James Kugel notes that

this particular motif is widely distributed in rabbinic texts. Thus, for example, in *Numbers Rabba* (*Bemidbar* 4:1) the verse from Isaiah 43:4, "Because you are precious in my eyes, you have been honored . . ." is explained: "God said to Jacob: Jacob, you are so precious in my eyes that I have, as it were, fixed your portrait (*iqonin*) on the heavenly throne." Similarly, one reads concerning the opening verse of chapter 2 of Lamentations: "How the Lord in his anger has beclouded . . ." Said God to Israel: "Do you truly aggravate me? It is only the fact that the portrait (*iqonin*) of Jacob is engraved on my throne. Here then, take it! And he threw it in their faces." And likewise in *Genesis Rabbah* 78:3, on the verse "For you have wrestled with God and with men and have prevailed" (Gen 32:28) we read: "You are the one whose portrait is engraved on high."

J. Kugel, *In Potiphar's House: The Interpretive Life of Biblical Texts* (San Francisco: Harper Collins, 1990), 113. For an in-depth discussion about the traditions of Jacob's image engraved on the Throne in rabbinic literature, see Wolfson, "The Image of Jacob Engraved," 1–62; 111–186.

11. Neis, "Embracing Icons: The Face of Jacob on the Throne of God," 46.
12. Freedman and Simon, *Midrash Rabbah*, 2.752.
13. Freedman and Simon, *Midrash Rabbah*, 7.151.
14. Neis, "Embracing Icons: The Face of Jacob on the Throne of God," 45.
15. Freedman and Simon, *Midrash Rabbah*, 5.94.
16. Freedman and Simon, *Midrash Rabbah*, 2.626.

17. I. Epstein, *The Babylonian Talmud. Hullin* (London: Soncino, 1935–1952), 91b.
18. Wolfson, "The Image of Jacob Engraved," 4.
19. Wolfson, "The Image of Jacob Engraved," 4.
20. Davila, *Hekhalot Literature in Translation*, 86; Schäfer et al., *Synopse*, 72.
21. Reflecting on this obscure term, Rachel Neis observes that "the word *qlaster* in rabbinic texts describes the identity facial features (e.g. Isaac's and Abraham's). Jastrow views the expression *qlaster panim* as analogous to the term דיו איקונין [radiance of icon], which is used to mean 'features of face,' in cases of verisimilitude." Neis, "Embracing Icons: The Face of Jacob on the Throne of God," 42.
22. Louis Ginzberg also suggests that "the legend about the man in the moon, who is identified with Jacob, is perhaps connected with the old legend concerning Jacob's countenance in the divine throne." L. Ginzberg, *The Legends of the Jews* (7 vols.; Baltimore: John Hopkins University Press, 1998), 5.291. On these traditions, see also E. R. Wolfson, "The Face of Jacob in the Moon: Mystical Transformations of an Aggadic Myth," in *The Seductiveness of Jewish Myth* (ed. S. D. Breslaur; Albany, NY: SUNY Press, 1997), 235–270.
23. Neis, "Embracing Icons," 46.
24. Neis, "Embracing Icons," 46.
25. In the Hekhalot literature, one of the Living Creatures of the Throne bears the name Israel. On this tradition, see *Synopse* §406; Scholem, *Major Trends*, 62; Wolfson, "The Image of Jacob Engraved," 7.
26. Friedländer, *Pirke de Rabbi Eliezer*, 265.
27. *2 Enoch* 39: "You, my children, you see my face, a human being created just like yourselves; I am one who has seen the face of the Lord, like iron made burning hot by a fire, emitting sparks." Andersen, "2 Enoch," 1.163.
28. The *Ladder of Jacob* 1:3–4 reads: "And behold, a ladder was fixed on the earth, whose top reached to heaven. And the top of the ladder was the face as of a man, carved out of fire." Lunt, "Ladder of Jacob," 2.407. The *Prayer of Joseph* also affirms Jacob's connection with the divine Face, defining him as the *Sar ha-Panim*.
29. Sperling and Simon, *The Zohar*, 1.242.
30. Sperling and Simon, *The Zohar*, 4.319.
31. Sperling and Simon, *The Zohar*, 2.144.
32. *Targum Neofiti 1 and Pseudo-Jonathan: Exodus* (ed. M. J. McNamara, R. Hayward, and M. Maher, ArBib, 2; Collegeville, MN: Liturgical Press, 1994), 260.
33. McNamara et al., *Targum Neofiti 1 and Pseudo-Jonathan: Exodus*, 261.
34. McNamara et al., *Targum Neofiti 1 and Pseudo-Jonathan: Exodus*, 261.
35. Such an understanding of Moses' shining face as the luminous *tselem* is also hinted at in the midrashim where the protoplast's glorious image is put in conspicuous parallel with the radiant *panim* of the great prophet. Thus, *Deut. Rab.* 11:3 reads: "Adam said to Moses: 'I am greater than you because I have been created in the image of God.' Whence this? For it is said, And God created man in His own image (Gen 1:27). Moses replied to him: 'I am far superior to you, for the honour which was given to you has been taken away from you, as it is said, But man (Adam) abideth not in honour (Ps 49:13); but as for me, the radiant countenance which God gave me still remains with me.'" Freedman and Simon, *Midrash Rabbah*, 7.173. See also *Midrash Tadshe* 4: "In the

likeness of the creation of the world the Holy One blessed be He performed miracles for Israel when they came out of Egypt. . . . In the beginning: 'and God created man in his image,' and in the desert: 'and Moshe knew not that the skin of his face shone.'" A. Goshen Gottstein, "The Body as Image of God in Rabbinic Literature," *HTR* 87 (1994): 183.

36. Scholem, *On the Mystical Shape of the Godhead*, 260–261.

37. Scholem, *On the Mystical Shape of the Godhead*, 261.

38. Sperling and Simon, *The Zohar*, 2.227. See also *Zohar* II.86b: "Said R. Jose: 'Therefore the graving and painting of all forms is permitted, except the human figure.' Said R. Isaac: 'The reason is, because when a human figure is represented in sculpture or painting, it is not only the body which is fashioned in the image of the person, but as it were the wholeness of the man is being reproduced, his inner form, namely his spirit, as well as his outer bodily form.'" Sperling and Simon, *The Zohar*, 3.261.

39. Such conceptual constellations, in which the motif of the protecting angels coincides with the motif of the *tselem*, are widespread in rabbinic literature. Thus, for example, *Deuteronomy Rabbah* 4:4 reads: "And who are they? The angels who guard man. R. Joshua b. Levi said: A procession [of angels] pass before man and the heralds proclaim before him saying: 'Make room for the image of God.' See [says the Torah] how many watchmen guard you." Freedman and Simon, *Midrash Rabbah*, 7.92. Similarly *Midrash Tehillim* 17:8 details the following tradition: "so that wherever a man reaches, his hand is in the midst of demons,—and yet the Holy One, blessed be He, protects him. R. Joshua ben Levi said: When a man walks on the highway, a company of angels goes before him, crying out and saying: 'Make way for the image of the Holy One, blessed be He.'" W. G. Braude, *The Midrash on Psalms* (2 vols.; YJS, 13; New Haven: Yale University Press, 1959), 1.212. See also *Midrash Tehillim* 55:3: "R. Joshua ben Levi taught: What do the words He hath delivered my soul in peace, etc. mean? That a company of angels goes before a man, and these heavenly beings cry out, saying: 'Make way for the likeness of the Lord!'" Braude, *The Midrash on Psalms*, 1.493; *Zohar* II.129a: "An angel appears who is the storekeeper of the celestial figures of the righteous, and this angel's name is Jehudiam because of his office ('over the people of the Jews') and he is crowned with a crown on which is engraved the Holy Name . . . for there is no righteous person in the world whose image is not engraved in heaven under the authority of that angel." Sperling and Simon, *The Zohar*, 3.367.

40. In relation to this tradition, Scholem observes that "the angel is thus the primal image of man himself, which frightens all the beasts because it is made in the image of God; the *tselem* of the righteous man is identical with the angel which protects him." Scholem, *On the Mystical Shape of the Godhead*, 269.

41. Scholem, *On the Mystical Shape of the Godhead*, 261.

42. Scholem, *On the Mystical Shape of the Godhead*, 261.

43. Scholem argues that

> the *Zohar* connects the notion of the *tselem* as an astral body with that of the garments worn by the soul prior to birth, which it again dons in Paradise after death. The fine-material ether, which is the air of Paradise, is parallel to the fine-material garment, identical to the holy, ethereal body in

which the blissful spirits are clothed.... The earliest Kabbalistic writings speak only of a garment put on by the soul after death, or of the garments assumed by the transfigured Enoch or Elijah when they ascended to heaven. Only after the souls "cast off" the filth of their earthly bodies can they put on "the body that radiates brilliance."

Scholem, *On the Mystical Shape of the Godhead*, 270.
44. Scholem, *On the Mystical Shape of the Godhead*, 261.
45. Sperling and Simon, *The Zohar*, 2.326.
46. *Zohar* III.104a:

R. Simeon quoted here the verse: "Every one that is called by my name, for my glory I have created him, I have formed him, yea I have made him." "Every one that is called by my name": this is man whom God has created in His likeness and whom He calls by His own name when he does truth and justice, as it is written, "Thou shalt not revile the judges." "I have formed him, yea I have made him": as has been explained, the words "Let us make man in our image, after our likeness" refer to the time of wedlock, namely, the union of "image" and "likeness," so that man issued from Male and Female.

Sperling and Simon, *The Zohar*, 5.137.
47. Scholem, *On the Mystical Shape of the Godhead*, 262–263.
48. Scholem notes that in some Zoharic passages the *tselem* is not described as a garment of the soul but as something that "stands" or "floats" over it; in other passages (in which, to be sure, the term *tselem* does not expressly appear), such a function is ascribed to the garment of the soul. Scholem, *On the Mystical Shape of the Godhead*, 264.
49. Scholem, *On the Mystical Shape of the Godhead*, 262. Cf. *Zohar* II.217b: "For when I saw you and looked well at your inward forms, I saw that you were stamped with the mystical impress of Adam, and so I knew that your image is stationed on high." Sperling and Simon, *The Zohar*, 4.239.
50. D. Matt, *The Zohar: Pritzker Edition* (12 vols.; Palo Alto, CA: Stanford University Press, 2003), 7.264.
51. *Zohar* III.13a–b reads:

R. Jose said: "For so we have learnt, that when the Holy One, blessed be He, draws forth a soul to send it down to earth, He impresses upon it many warnings and threatens to keep His commandments, and He also takes it through a thousand and eight worlds to see the glory of those who have devoted themselves to the Torah, and who now stand before the King in a robe of splendor in the form which they possessed in this world, beholding the glory of the King and crowned with many diadems. When its time comes to descend to earth, it makes its abode in the terrestrial Paradise for thirty days to see the glory of the Master of the righteous, and then ascends to their abode above and afterwards comes down to earth. Before it enters into the body of a man, the holy King crowns it with seven crowns. If it sins in this world and walks in darkness, the Torah is grieved for it and says, All this honor and all this perfection has the holy King delivered to the soul, and she has sinned before Him! And what if she does sin? We learn the answer," continued R. Jose, "from the verse which says, 'Until the day be cool and the shadows flee away.' 'Until the day be cool': this is a warning to the soul to repent and purify itself before the day of this world shall cool off and be followed by that awful day on which God shall call her to account when she departs from this world. 'And the shadows flee away': this refers to the secret known to the Companions, that when a man's time comes to leave this world, his shadow deserts him. R. Eleazar says that man has two shadows, one larger and one smaller, and when they are together, then he is truly himself. Therefore a man should review his actions and rectify them before his Master and confess his sins, because God is called merciful and gracious, and He receives those who return to Him. Hence he should repent before the shadows flee away, for if he only does so when he is already under arrest, this is indeed repentance, but not so acceptable."

Sperling and Simon, *The Zohar*, 4.349–350.
52. Scholem, *On the Mystical Shape of the Godhead*, 262.
53. Scholem, *On the Mystical Shape of the Godhead*, 264.
54. Sperling and Simon, *The Zohar*, 5.137–138.
55. Scholem, *On the Mystical Shape of the Godhead*, 266.
56. Scholem, *On the Mystical Shape of the Godhead*, 266. In this respect, it is noteworthy that some Kabbalistic authorities entertained the possibility that the heavenly counterpart in the form of *tselem* can be encountered in a human's lifetime. Thus, for example, R. Moses Cordovero in his *Pardes Rimmonim*, while dealing with the doctrine of the *tselem* as the astral body, argued that "some of the pious achieve the observation of their image even in this world." Also R. Hayim Vital, a main exponent of R. Isaac Luria's teaching, wrote that "the ethereal body of them [the righteous] is [contained] in the secret of the *tselem*, which is perceived by those who have purified vision." Scholem, *On the Mystical Shape of the Godhead*, 266.
57. Matt, *The Zohar*, 7.264–265.
58. Moshe Idel brings attention to some other rabbinic testimonies in which the shadows appear to be understood as the counterparts of the human being. On these traditions, see Idel, "Panim: On Facial Re-Presentations in Jewish Thought," 28–29.
59. Scholem, *On the Mystical Shape of the Godhead*, 268.
60. Scholem, *On the Mystical Shape of the Godhead*, 263. Daniel Matt's research also underlines this terminological connection. Reflecting on *Zohar* III.43a, he notes that "here the צולמא (*tsulma*), 'image,' is associated with a person's צל (*tsel*), 'shadow,' which likewise disappears shortly prior to death. The final word, 'two,' refers to the notion of two images (which appears elsewhere in the *Zohar*). The link between *tsulma*, 'image,'

and *tsel*, 'shadow,' is accentuated by the fact that the Hebrew equivalent of *tsulma*—צל (*tselem*) actually means 'shadow' in the verse in Psalms: אך בצלם (*Akh be-tselem*), As a mere shadow [or phantom], a human goes about." Matt, *The Zohar*, 7.264.

61. Scholem, *On the Mystical Shape of the Godhead*, 263.

62. *A Greek-English Lexicon with a Revised Supplement* (ed. H. G. Liddell, R. Scott, H. S. Jones, and R. McKenzie; Oxford: Clarendon, 1996), 483.

63. In relation to these terminological distinctions, Jean-Pierre Vernant observes that

> like a phantom, the Homeric *psychē* belongs to other phenomena that enter, as it does, into the category of what the Greeks in the archaic period call *eidōla*, a word that should be translated not as "images" but rather as "doubles." . . . A double is a wholly different thing from an image. It is not a "natural" object, but it is also not a product of the imagination: neither an imitation of a real object, nor an illusion of the mind, nor a creation of thought. The double is a reality external to the subject and is inscribed in the visible world. Yet even in its conformity with what it simulates, its unusual character ensures its substantial difference from familiar objects and the ordinary setting of daily life. The double plays on two contrasting levels at the same time: at the moment when it shows itself to be present, it also reveals itself as not being of this world but rather as belonging to an inaccessible elsewhere.

J.-P. Vernant, "Psuche: Simulacrum of the Body or Image of the Divine?," in idem, *Mortals and Immortals* (ed. F. I. Zeitlin; Princeton: Princeton University Press, 1991), 186–187. On these traditions, see also J.-P. Vernant, "The Figuration of the Invisible and the Psychological Category of the Double: The Kolossos," in idem, *Myth and Thought among the Greeks* (New York: Zone Books, 2005), 321–332. I am thankful to David Litwa for bringing my attention to Vernant's reflections.

64. *Homer, The Odyssey* (ed. A. T. Murray; LCL; 2 vols.; Cambridge, MA: Harvard University Press, 1945), 1.164–165.

65. Unlike in the previously explored traditions where the twin of a person resides in the heavenly realms, in the *Odyssey*, the "phantoms or images of the deceased (*eidōla*) reside in Hades." Jan Bremmer notes that during his visit to Hades Odysseus spoke with the *eidōlon* of his friend Elpenor (11.83). And after the bloody end of the suitors, the seer Theoclymenos saw the doorway to the court filled with *eidōla* (20.355). J. N. Bremmer, *The Early Greek Concept of the Soul* (Princeton: Princeton University Press, 1983), 79.

66. Murray, *Homer, The Odyssey*, 2.428–429.

67. Bremmer notes that

> the *psychē* leaves the body at the moment of death and begins an afterlife. After death, however, the deceased is presented not only as *psychē* but also as an *eidōlon* or compared to shadows. . . . It is the physical attributes of the

soul that have some importance for the Greeks rather than the psychological. The descriptions of the *eidōlon* suggests that the Greeks believed the dead soul looked like the living being. And they described the physical actions of the souls of the dead in two opposite ways: they believed both that the dead souls moved and spoke like the living and that the soul of the dead could not move or speak but instead flitted and squeaked.

Bremmer, *The Early Greek Concept of the Soul*, 73.
68. *Iliad* 5.550 reads:

On this wise spake they one to the other; but Diomedes, good at the warcry, leapt upon Aeneas, though well he knew that Apollo himself held forth his arms above him; yet had he no awe even of the great god, but was still eager to slay Aeneas and strip from him his glorious armour. Thrice then he leapt upon him, furiously fain to slay him, and thrice did Apollo beat back his shining shield. But when for the fourth time he rushed upon him like a god, then with a terrible cry spake to him Apollo that worketh afar: "Bethink thee, son of Tydeus, and give place, neither be thou minded to be like of spirit with the gods; seeing in no wise of like sort is the race of immortal gods and that of men who walk upon the earth," So spake he, and the son of Tydeus gave ground a scant space backward, avoiding the wrath of Apollo that smiteth afar, Aeneas then did Apollo set apart from the throng in sacred Pergamus where was his temple builded. There Leto and the archer Artemis healed him in the great sanctuary, and glorified him; but Apollo of the silver bow fashioned a wraith in the likeness (εἴδωλον) of Aeneas' self and in armour like to his.

Homer, *The Iliad* (ed. A. T. Murray; LCL; 2 vols.; Cambridge, MA: Harvard University Press, 1924), 1.226–227.

69. *Iliad* 23.100–107 reads: "So saying he reached forth with his hands, yet clasped him not; but the spirit like a vapour was gone beneath the earth, gibbering faintly. And seized with amazement Achilles sprang up, and smote his hands together, and spake a word of wailing: 'Look you now, even in the house of Hades is the spirit and phantom (εἴδωλον) somewhat, albeit the mind be not anywise therein; for the whole night long hath the spirit of hapless Patroclus stood over me, weeping and wailing, and gave me charge concerning each thing, and was wondrously like his very self.'" Murray, *Homer, The Iliad*, 2.501–503.

70. Bremmer, *The Early Greek Concept of the Soul*, 79.
71. Bremmer, *The Early Greek Concept of the Soul*, 79.
72. Jarl Fossum draws attention to a specimen of this conceptual development found in Plutarch's *On the Sign of Socrates* 585E, where the tradition about *eidōlon* as a double of either a dead or living person is ascribed to the Pythagoreans:

Theanor smiled at this and said: "It would appear, Simmias, that Lysis is attached to his present abode, since, thanks to Epameinondas, he lacks no honorable provision. For a certain special rite is performed at the burials of Pythagoreans, and without it we do not feel in full possession of the blessed end that is proper to our sect. And so, when we learned from our dreams of Lysis' death (we tell by a certain token appearing in our sleep whether the apparition [εἴδωλον] is of the dead or of the living) it occurred to many that Lysis had been improperly buried in a foreign land and that we must remove him so that over there he might have the benefit of our customary rites."

Plutarch's Moralia (ed. P. H. De Lacy and B. Einarson; LCL; Cambridge, MA: Harvard University Press, 1959), 7.435–437. In relation to this passage, Jarl Fossum observes that "the Pythagoreans called the guardian spirit εἴδωλον, 'image.' . . . [and]. . . . the Pythagoreans knew if a person's εἴδωλον appearing in a dream belonged to a dead or living person: if the 'image' did not cast a shadow or wink the person was dead." Fossum, "The Son of Man's Alter Ego," 145–147.

73. Vernant, *Mortals and Immortals*, 190.

74. Vernant, *Mortals and Immortals*, 190. Both Vernant and Bremmer noticed that such a paradigm shift in understanding the *eidōlon* is already manifest in Pindar. Pindar's fragment 131b reads: "And all men's bodies follow the call of overpowering death. And yet there still will linger behind a living image of life (αἰῶνος εἴδωλον), for this alone has come from the gods. It sleeps while the members are active; but to those who sleep themselves it reveals in myriad visions the fateful approach of adversities or delights." W. Jaeger, *The Theology of the Early Greek Philosophers* (Oxford: Clarendon, 1947), 75; *Pindari carmina cum fragmentis: Pars I Epinicia* (ed. B. Snell and H. Maehler; Leipzig: B. G. Teubner, 1980), 111.

75. Vernant, *Mortals and Immortals*, 190.

76. Vernant, *Mortals and Immortals*, 190.

77. Vernant, *Mortals and Immortals*, 190.

78. On this, see also T. Griffith, "Eidolon as 'Idol' in Non-Jewish and Non-Christian Greek," *JTS* 53 (2002): 95–101 at 99.

79. Vernant, *Mortals and Immortals*, 190.

80. Vernant, *Mortals and Immortals*, 190.

81. Vernant notes that

for Plotinus, the One, or God, eternally immobile in its complete perfection, produces "images" by a radiation comparable to the light that emanates from the sun. Insofar as these images express the One, they are inferior to it. Dependent on it, engendered from it, these images draw their existence from the link they must preserve with their source and model (*Enn.* 5.1.6.25ff.). The One produces as its first image *nous*, or intelligence. On the next level, the soul arises as the *eidōlon nou*, the reflection of intelligence, an image that is already obscured, a simulacrum of this *nous* from which it cannot be separated. Like the *eidōlon* of that which has engendered it, the soul is inferior to the *nous*. It revolves around intelligence; it is the light that radiates from *nous*, its trace of the world beyond. On the one hand, the soul remains merged with intelligence, is filled with it, and takes pleasure from it; the *psychē* takes part in it and itself has the power to think. But on the other hand, it is in contact with what follows, or rather, the *psychē* also engenders beings that are necessarily inferior to it (*Enn.* 5.1.7.36–47). What does it mean, asks Plotinus, to descend into Hades (*Enn.* 6.4.16.37ff.)? If Hades designates the world below, the inferior place, does the expression mean that our soul, our *psychē*, is found in the same place as our bodies? But what if the body no longer exists? Since the soul is not separable from its *eidōlon* (from this body whose reflection or simulacrum it is), how could it not be in the same place where its body-reflection (*eidōlon*) can be found? Yet, even so, a turning of the soul toward Intelligence and the One is always possible. "If philosophy were to free us entirely, only the *eidōlon* [the body-reflection of the soul] would descend into the lower regions. The soul would live purely in the intelligible world without being separated in any way from it" (*Enn.* 6.4.16.41–43). To be a philosopher would therefore mean to turn oneself away from the body-simulacrum of the soul to return to that of which the soul is also the simulacrum and from which it remains separated as long as it is content to reflect it instead of being identified with it. The idea is that the soul would lose itself there to find itself again, no longer as an image, a double, similar to the exterior model, but as a single and authentic being in the full coincidence of the self with the self through an assimilation to the god who is the All.

Vernant, *Mortals and Immortals*, 192.

82. A. H. Armstrong, *Plotinus: Enneads* (7 vols.; Cambridge, MA: Harvard University Press, 1966–1988), 1.256–257. Reflecting on this passage, Charles Stang notes that "curiously, the word Plotinus uses, *eidōlon* (here rendered 'reflection'), is the word Plato uses when he has Socrates tell Alcibiades what we see when we look into the pupil of another's eye, that is, a miniature mirror-image or *eidōlon* (*Alcibiades* I.132e). For Plato, this serves as an analogy for how we come to know ourselves: one looks into another's soul and sees one's *eidōlon* or reflection and this allows for mutual cultivation and deification. I do not think Plotinus's choice of words here is a coincidence." Stang, *Our Divine Double*, 216–217.

83. It has been also previously suggested that the Manichaean concept of the heavenly doppelganger was shaped by the Platonic concepts. On this, see L. Koenen, "Augustine and Manichaeism in Light of the Cologne Mani Codex," *ICS* 3 (1978): 154–195; L. Sweeney, "Mani's Twin and Plotinus: Questions on 'Self,'" in *Neoplatonism and Gnosticism* (ed. R. T. Wallis and J. Bregman; Albany, NY: SUNY Press, 1992), 381–424; W. Fauth, "Syzygos und Eikon," in *Gnosis und Philosophie: Miscellanea* (ed. R. Berlinger and W. Schrader; Elementa, 59; Amsterdam: Rodopi, 1994), 115–139.

84. Reflecting on the presence of the *eidōlon* terminology in the Nag Hammadi materials, Gilles Quispel observes that

> the Gnostics, who were the friends of Plotinus and attended his courses for years until he wrote his treatise against them, had in their library

non-Christian books, like the *Apocalypses of Zoroaster* and *Zostrianos* and *Nikotheos* and *Allogenes* and *Messos*, which in part turned up at Nag Hammadi. They taught that the world-soul and Wisdom (Sophia) had inclined towards the lower regions of the world, though she has not come down, but has only illuminated, so that an image (*eidōlon*) was made in the matter. From that image, they say, comes another image, which is the Demiurge who removed himself from his mother and made a world which consists of images only; they say this in order to blame the Demiurge, who made this picture (2.9).

Quispel, "Valentinian Gnosis and the Apocryphon of John," in *Gnostica, Judaica, Catholica*, 368.

85. E. S. Drower and R. Macuch, *A Mandaic Dictionary* (Oxford: Clarendon, 1963), 111–112.

86. On the connection between *dmuta* and *tselem/iqonin*, see G. Quispel, "Jewish Gnosis and Mandaean Gnosticism," in *Les textes de Nag Hammadi* (ed. J.-É. Ménard; NHS, 7; Leiden: Brill, 1975), 82–122 at 115–116.

87. E. S. Drower, *The Secret Adam* (Oxford: Oxford University Press, 1960), 40.

88. J. J. Buckley, *The Mandaeans: Ancient Texts and Modern People* (Oxford: Oxford University Press, 2002), 37. For discussion of the *dmuta*, see also J. J. Buckley, "The Mandaean Sitil as an Example of 'The Image Above and Below,'" *Numen* 26 (1979): 185–191; idem, "Two Female Gnostic Revealers," *HR* 19 (1980): 259–269; idem, "A Rehabilitation of Spirit Ruha in Mandaean Religion," *HR* 21 (1982): 60–84; Corbin, *The Man of Light in Iranian Sufism*, 33; Deutsch, *Guardians of the Gate*, 133, 139.

89. R. Foltz, *Religions of Iran: From Prehistory to the Present* (London: Oneworld, 2013), 128.

90. *Left Ginza* II.5: "I shall take you out of the world and cause you to ascend. I shall take you out of it and cause you to ascend and shall leave all behind. I shall leave all, they shall all die and disappear. You are my counterpart (*dmuta*), I shall cause you to ascend and keep you safe in my garment. In my garment, which the Great (Life) gave to me, and in the pure fragrance which is entrusted to me." Foerster, *Gnosis*, 2.255; Lidzbarski, *Ginza*, 461.

91. *Left Ginza* II.5: "Wherefore am I stripped of my radiance, brought and cast into the bodily garment? I am cast into the bodily garment, which he put on and took off. I am angry and tormented in the bodily garment, into which I was brought and cast. How many times must I take it off, how many times must I put it on!" Foerster, *Gnosis*, 2.255; Lidzbarski, *Ginza*, 461.

92. Gardner, *The Kephalaia of the Teacher*, 20.

93. Stang, *Our Divine Double*, 162–163.

94. Gardner, *The Kephalaia of the Teacher*, 40.

95. Stang, *Our Divine Double*, 180–181.

96. Koenen and Römer, *Der Kölner Mani-Kodex*, 66; E. B. Aitken, "The Cologne Mani Codex," in *Religions of Late Antiquity in Practice* (ed. R. Valantasis; Princeton Readings in Religions; Princeton: Princeton University Press, 2000), 168.

97. Thus, Charles Stang notes that in this episode the image in the water "is not of Alchasai himself, and thus raises the question of whether this image too is the *syzygos*, the divine companion to the Apostle of Light." Stang, *Our Divine Double*, 284. Manichaean Coptic prayer from Kellis (*T. Kell. Copt.* 2, text a 5) also unveils the concept of the heavenly counterpart as the image: "The image of my counterpart came unto me, with her three angels. She gave to me the garment and the crown and the palm and the victory.... I came to rest in the kingdom of the household (?); for the Father of the Lights has revealed to me his image." Gardner and Lieu, *Manichaean Texts from the Roman Empire*, 257–258.

98. It is possible that such a concept of the image as the upper Self is already present in the New Testament materials where in Col 1:15 Christ is identified as "the image of the invisible God" (εἰκὼν τοῦ θεοῦ τοῦ ἀοράτου). On the possible connection between Col 1:15 and the doppelganger traditions, see Fossum, "The Image of the Invisible God: Colossians 1:15–18a in the Light of Jewish Mysticism and Gnosticism," in *Image of the Invisible God*, 13–39. In 2 Cor 3:18, the heavenly counterpart symbolism is also closely tied to the *eikōn* terminology.

99. In view of these conceptual developments, Gilles Quispel suggests that the notion of the image as the heavenly correlative "was already known in Edessa at a very early date, if we accept that the *Gospel of Thomas* was written there about 140 A.D." Quispel, "Genius and Spirit," 107.

100. *Nag Hammadi Codex II, 2–7 together with XIII, 2,* Brit. Lib. Or. 4926(I), and P. Oxy. I, 654, 655* (ed. B. Layton; NHS, 20; Leiden: Brill, 1989), 1.85.

101. In contrast, in the *Gospel of Philip*, the symbolism of "image" is applied not to the heavenly but to the human part of the *syzygia*. *Gos. Phil.* 58:11–14 reads: "You who have joined the perfect light with the holy spirit, unite the angels with us also, as being the images." Layton, *Nag Hammadi Codex II, 2–7*, 1.157. Commenting on this passage, Charles Stang observes that "for the *Gospel of Philip*, it is we who are the images, and the angels who are, as it were, our archetypes." Stang, *Our Divine Double*, 115.

102. DeConick, *Seek to See Him*, 149.

103. H.-Ch. Puech, "Doctrines ésotériques et thèmes gnostiques dans L'Évangile selon Thomas," *ACF* 62 (1962): 199–213.

104. Quispel, "Genius and Spirit," 107.

105. Layton, *Nag Hammadi Codex II, 2–7*, 1.85.

106. Klijn, *The Acts of Thomas*, 186.

107. In relation to these pneumatological developments, Roelof van der Broek notes that the *Macarian Homilies* offer intense speculations about the relationship between the Holy Spirit and the spirit of man. These reflections are also overlaid with the peculiar symbolism of the "image." He observes that

> in *Homily* 30.3, Macarius expounds his theory that the soul without the Spirit is dead. It has to be born out of the Spirit and in that way become Spirit itself: "All angels and holy powers rejoice in the soul which has been born out of the Spirit and has become Spirit itself." The soul is the image of the Holy Spirit. Christ, the heavenly painter, paints after his own image

"a heavenly man" in the believer who constantly looks at him: "Out of his own Spirit, out of his substance, the ineffable light, he paints a heavenly image and presents that to the soul as its noble and good bridegroom" (*Hom.* 30.4). . . . this "image of the heavenly Spirit," as it is called, is identified with Christ and with the Holy Spirit. The soul that does not possess "the heavenly image of the divine light, which is the life of the soul," is useless and completely reprehensible: "Just as in this world the soul is the life of the body, so in the eternal, heavenly world it is the Spirit of Divinity which is the life of the soul" (*Hom.* 30.5).

R. van den Broek, "The Cathars: Medieval Gnostics?," in *Gnosis and Hermeticism from Antiquity to Modern Times* (ed. R. van den Broek and W. J. Hanegraaff; SUNY Series in Western Esoteric Traditions; Albany, NY: SUNY Press, 1997), 100. For the author of the *Macarian Homilies*, therefore,

it is absolutely necessary to obtain this life of the soul, the Spirit, in this earthly existence, for otherwise the soul will be unable to enter the Kingdom of Heaven and will end in hell (*Hom.* 30.6). Before the Fall, Adam possessed this heavenly image, which meant that he was in possession of the Holy Spirit; he lost it when he fell (*Hom.* 12.6). Christ, "who had formed body and soul," comes to bring the works of the Evil One to an end: "[H]e renews and gives shape to the heavenly image and makes a new soul, so that Adam [i.e., man] can become king of death and lord of the creatures again" (*Hom.* 11.6) . . . "the heavenly man unites with your [earthly] man, resulting in one communion" (*Hom.* 12.18).

van den Broek, "The Cathars: Medieval Gnostics?," 100.
108. Pseudo-Macarius, *The Fifty Spiritual Homilies and the Great Letter* (trans. G. A. Maloney; New York: Paulist Press, 1992), 97. H. Dörries et al. *Die 50 Geistlichen Homilien des Makarios* (PTS, 4; Berlin: Walter de Gruyter, 1964), 110.
109. Quispel, "Genius and Spirit," 108.
110. Another important witness to the tradition of the doppelganger as an image is Tatian's *Oratio ad Graecos* 12, a text that also belongs to the second century CE. *Oratio* 12 reads: "We have knowledge of two different kinds of spirits, one of which is called soul, *but the other is greater than the soul; it is the image (εἰκών) and likeness of God*. The first men were endowed with both, so that they might be part of the material world, and at the same time above it. This is how things are." M. Whittaker, *Tatian, Oratio ad Graecos and Fragments* (Oxford: Clarendon, 1982), 22–23. In relation to this tradition, Charles Stang observes that "humans have now only their own soul as a spirit; the second spirit, the one greater than soul, has abandoned them. This other spirit is the image and likeness of God (like the 'image' in §84 of the *Gospel of Thomas*), and so without it humans are bereft of the divine, or nearly so." Stang, *Our Divine Double*, 110.
111. C. Osiek, *Shepherd of Hermas* (Hermeneia; Minneapolis: Fortress, 1999), 98.
112. Quispel, "Genius and Spirit," 109.

113. See M. Dibelius, *Der Hirt des Hermas* (HNT; Die Apostolischen Väter, 4; Tübingen: Mohr/Siebeck, 1923), 495; W. Bousset, *Die Religion des Judentums in späthellenistischen Zeitalter* (3rd ed.; HNT, 21; Tübingen: Mohr/Siebeck, 1926), 324; H. Conzelmann, *Acts of the Apostles* (Hermeneia; Philadelphia: Fortress, 1987), 95. For criticism of this hypothesis, see G. Snyder, *The Shepherd of Hermas* (ed. R. M. Grant; Apostolic Fathers, 6; Camden, NJ: Nelson, 1969), 61–62; Osiek, *Shepherd of Hermas*, 100.

114. The connection between the likeness (or the image) and the *Sar ha-Panim* that serves as the designation of the seer's heavenly identity can also be found in the *Apocalypse of Paul* 19, the text that unveils the following tradition:

> And I followed the angel and he lifted me up to the third heaven and he set me at the door of a gate. . . . And I asked the angel and said: Sir, tell me, for what reason are these letters set on those tables? The angel answered and said to me: Those are the names of the righteous who while they dwell on earth serve God with a whole heart. And again I said: Are then their names written in heaven while they are still on earth? And he said: Not only their names but also their faces are written, and the likeness of those who serve God is in heaven, and the servants of God, who serve him with a whole heart are known to the angels before they leave the world.

New Testament Apocrypha (ed. E. Hennecke and W. Schneemelcher; 2 vols.; Louisville, KY: Westminster John Knox, 2003), 2.724–725. In the *Apocalypse of Paul* 7, the motif of heavenly representatives of human beings is again conflated with the theme of the image of God: "When then the sun has set at the first hour of the night, in the same hour (comes) the angel of each people and the angel of each man and woman, (the angels) which protect and preserve them, because man is the image of God." Hennecke and Schneemelcher, *New Testament Apocrypha*, 2.718.

115. *Testament of Our Lord* (ed. J. Cooper and A. J. Maclean; Edinburgh: T&T Clark, 1902), 96; I. E. Rahmani, *Testamentum Domini Nostri Jesu Christi* (Moguntiae: F. Kirchheim, 1899), 96–97.

116. Quispel, "Genius and Spirit," 107.

117. Quispel, "Genius and Spirit," 107.

118. Quispel, "Genius and Spirit," 107.

119. Kugel, *In Potiphar's House*, 250.

120. On this connection, see Ginzberg, *The Legends of the Jews*, 5.290, n. 134; A. Altmann, "The Gnostic Background of the Rabbinic Adam Legends," *JQR* 35 (1945): 371–391; Wolfson, "The Image of Jacob Engraved," 4. Wolfson points to the fact that in some rabbinic materials the beauty of Jacob has been often compared with the beauty of Adam. See, for example, *Zohar* I.168a: "According to tradition, the beauty of Jacob was equal to that of Adam, the first man." Sperling and Simon, *The Zohar*, 2.144.

121. One of the early occurrences of the motif of the angelic veneration of Adam is possibly hinted at in *4Q381*. See Fletcher-Louis, *All the Glory of Adam*, 98–100. The motif of the angelic veneration is also present in the temptation narrative of the Synoptic Gospels. On this, see A. Orlov, "The Veneration Motif in the Temptation Narrative of the Gospel of Matthew: Lessons from the Enochic Tradition," in *Divine Scapegoats*, 153–166.

122. On the angelic veneration, see C. Fletcher-Louis, "The Worship of Divine Humanity as God's Image and the Worship of Jesus," in *The Jewish Roots of Christological Monotheism: Papers from the St. Andrews Conference on the Historical Origins of the Worship of Jesus* (ed. C. Newman et al.; JSJSS, 63; Leiden: Brill, 1999): 112–128 at 125–128; idem, *All the Glory of Adam*, 101–102.

123. The Latin version of the *Primary Adam Books* 13:2 reads: "When God blew into you the breath of life and your countenance and likeness were made in the image of God, Michael led you and made you worship in the sight of God." The Armenian version of the *Primary Adam Books* 13:2 reads: "When God breathed his spirit into you, you received the likeness of his image. Thereupon, Michael came and made you bow down before God." Anderson and Stone, *A Synopsis of the Books of Adam and Eve*, 16E.

124. The Latin version of the *Primary Adam Books* 13:2–14:1 reads: "The Lord God then said: 'Behold, Adam, I have made you in our image and likeness.' Having gone forth Michael called all the angels saying: 'Worship the image of the Lord God, just as the Lord God has commanded.'" The Armenian version of the *Primary Adam Books* 13:2–14:1 reads: "God said to Michael, 'Behold I have made Adam in the likeness of my image.' Then Michael summoned all the angels, and God said to them, 'Come, bow down to god whom I made.'" Anderson and Stone, *A Synopsis of the Books of Adam and Eve*, 16E.

125. The Latin version of the *Primary Adam Books* 14:2–15:1 reads: "Michael himself worshipped first then he called me and said: 'Worship the image of God Jehovah.' I answered: 'I do not have it within me to worship Adam.' When Michael compelled me to worship, I said to him: 'Why do you compel me? I will not worship him who is lower and later than me. I am prior to that creature. Before he was made, I had already been made. He ought to worship me.' Hearing this, other angels who were under me were unwilling to worship him." The Armenian version of the *Primary Adam Books* 14:2–15:1 reads: "Michael bowed first He called me and said 'You too, bow down to Adam.' I said, Go away, Michael! I shall not bow [down] to him who is posterior to me, for I am former. Why is it proper [for me] to bow down to him? The other angels, too, who were with me, heard this, and my words seemed pleasing to them and they did not prostrate themselves to you, Adam." Anderson and Stone, *A Synopsis of the Books of Adam and Eve*, 16E–17E.

126. Andersen, "2 Enoch," 1.138. The tradition of the angelic veneration of Enoch is found in both recensions of *2 Enoch*. *2 Enoch* 22:6–7 in Ms. J (longer recension) reads: "And the Lord said to his servants, sounding them out, 'Let Enoch join in and stand in front of my face forever!' And the Lord's glorious ones did obeisance and said, 'Let Enoch yield in accordance with your word, O Lord!'" Andersen, "2 Enoch," 1.138. *2 Enoch* 22:6–7 in Ms. A (shorter recension) reads: "The Lord said, 'Let Enoch come up and stand in front of my face forever!' And the glorious ones did obeisance and said, 'Let him come up!'" Andersen, "2 Enoch," 1.139.

127. Slav. "*iskushaja ih.*" Macaskill, *The Slavonic Texts of 2 Enoch*, 100.

128. R. H. Charles and W. R. Morfill, *The Book of the Secrets of Enoch* (Oxford: Oxford University Press, 1896), 28.

129. Stone, "The Fall of Satan and Adam's Penance," 47.

130. Stone, "The Fall of Satan and Adam's Penance," 48.

131. See Ms. V (VL 125) [Nr. 3], fol. 317: "And the Lord with his own mouth called me [Enoch] and said: Be brave, Youth! Do not be frightened! Stand up in front

of my face forever. And Michael, the Lord's archistratig, brought me in the front of the Lord's face. And the Lord tempted his servants and said to them: 'Let Enoch come up and stand in the front of my face forever.' And the glorious ones bowed down and said: 'Let him come up!'"

132. Jacobson, *The Exagoge of Ezekiel*, 54–55.

133. John Collins notes that "the stars had long been identified with the angelic host in Israelite tradition. . . . Ultimately this tradition can be traced back to Canaanite mythology where the stars appear as members of the divine council in the Ugaritic texts." Collins, *Apocalyptic Vision*, 136. See, for example, Judg 5:20: "The stars fought from heaven, from their courses they fought against Sisera"; Job 38:7: "When the morning stars sang together and all the heavenly beings shouted for joy?"; Dan 8:10: "It grew as high as the host of heaven. It threw down to the earth some of the host and some of the stars, and trampled on them"; *1 Enoch* 86:3–4: "And again I saw in the vision and looked at heaven, and behold, I saw many stars, how they came down and were thrown down from heaven to that first star, and amongst those heifers and bulls; they were with them, pasturing amongst them. And I looked at them and saw, and behold, all of them let out their private parts like horses and began to mount the cows of the bulls, and they all became pregnant and bore elephants and camels and asses." Knibb, *Ethiopic Book of Enoch*, 2.197; *1 Enoch* 88:1: "And I saw one of those four who had come out first, how he took hold of that first star which had fallen from heaven, and bound it by its hands and its feet, and threw it into an abyss; and that abyss was narrow, and deep, and horrible, and dark." Knibb, *Ethiopic Book of Enoch*, 2.198; *1 Enoch* 90:24: "And the judgment was held first on the stars, and they were judged and found guilty; and they went to the place of damnation, and were thrown into a deep (place), full of fire, burning and full of pillars of fire." Knibb, *Ethiopic Book of Enoch*, 2.215.

134. Alexander, "3 Enoch," 1.258–259.

135. G. Anderson, "The Exaltation of Adam and the Fall of Satan," in *Literature on Adam and Eve: Collected Essays* (ed. G. Anderson, M. Stone, and J. Tromp; SVTP, 15; Leiden: Brill, 2000), 107.

136. Anderson, "The Exaltation of Adam and the Fall of Satan," 108.

137. Andersen, "2 Enoch," 1.170.

138. In relation to this passage, Nathaniel Deutsch notes that

> the key to understanding this passage has been provided by F.I. Andersen, who notes in his edition of *2 Enoch*, that its form imitates that of Gen 1:27, which states that "God created man in His image, in the image of God he created him, male and female he created them." Instead of the "image" of God, in *2 Enoch* we find God's "face," and in place of "male and female He created them," we read "small and great the Lord created." In light of the Jewish, Gnostic, and Mandaean traditions which treated the image of God in Gen 1:27 hypostatically, often identifying it with the Cosmic Adam, the substitution of the divine image in Gen 1:27 with the divine face is early evidence that God's face was perceived hypostatically, as well.

Deutsch, *Gnostic Imagination*, 102.

139. Andersen, "2 Enoch," 1.171, note b. As has been already indicated, some scholars point to the fact that in some Jewish materials the concept of the divine image is often rendered through the symbolism of the divine Face. On this, see Idel, "The Changing Faces of God," 103–122.

140. Idel, "The Changing Faces of God," 103–122.

141. A total of nine Greek sentences of this pseudepigraphon were preserved in the writings of Origen (c. 185–c. 254 CE). Fragment A is quoted in Origen's *In Ioannem* II. 31.25. Fragment B, a single sentence, is cited in St. Basil the Great and St. Gregory Nazianzen's compilation of Origen, the *Philokalia*. This fragment is also quoted in Eusebius, *The Preparation of the Gospel* and in the Latin *Commentary on Genesis* by Procopius of Gaza. Fragment C, which is found also from the *Philokalia*, quotes Fragment B and paraphrases Fragment A. Smith, "Prayer of Joseph," 2.699. Pieter van der Horst and Judith Newman note that "according to the ancient *Stichometry* of Nicephorus, the text originally contained 1100 lines. The extant portions totaling only nine Greek sentences or 164 words thus reflect a small fraction of the original composition." *Early Jewish Prayers in Greek* (CEJL; ed. P. W. van der Horst and J. H. Newman; Berlin: Walter de Gruyter, 2008), 249.

142. Smith, "Prayer of Joseph," 255.

143. Smith, "Prayer of Joseph," 2.701. Van der Horst and Newman observe that "the composition must likely have been in circulation for a good period for Origen to have recognized it by title." Van der Horst and Newman, *Early Jewish Prayers in Greek*, 249.

144. Wolfson observes that "the notion of an angel named Jacob-Israel is also known from Jewish Christian texts, as reported mainly by Justin, and appears as well in Gnostic works such as the Nag Hammadi treatise *On the Origin of the World*, and in Manichaean texts." He further suggests that "such a tradition, perhaps through the intermediary of Philo, passed into Christian sources wherein the celestial Jacob or Israel was identified with Jesus who is depicted as the Logos and Son of God." Wolfson, "The Image of Jacob Engraved," 5.

145. The authors of *Book of Jubilees* appear to be also cognizant of the heavenly identity of Jacob. Thus, *Jubilees* 35:17 reads: "Now you are not to be afraid for Jacob because Jacob's guardian is greater and more powerful, glorious, and praiseworthy than Esau's guardian." VanderKam, *Jubilees*, 2.235–236. On this tradition, see also *Targ. Ps.-J.* on Gen 33:10: "And Jacob said, 'Do not speak thus, I pray; if now I have found mercy in your eyes, you must accept my gift from my hand; because it is for this I have seen your countenance, and it seems to me like seeing the face of your angel; and behold, you have received me favorably.'" Maher, *Targum Pseudo-Jonathan: Genesis*, 116.

146. This verse appears to be pointing to the demiurgic role of Jacob-Israel. Wolfson argues that references to the demiurgic quality of Jacob may also be found in a number of rabbinic passages, including *Leviticus Rabbah* 36:4 and *Genesis Rabbah* 98:3. Wolfson, "The Image of Jacob Engraved," 5. These passages unveil the following traditions: *Gen. Rab.* 98:3: "R. Phinehas interpreted it: Your father Israel is as a god: as God creates worlds, so does your father create worlds; as God distributes worlds, so does your father distribute worlds." Freedman and Simon, *Midrash Rabbah*, 2.947–948. *Lev. Rab.* 36:4: "R. Phinehas in the name of R. Reuben explains this to mean that the Holy One, blessed be He, said to His world: 'O My world, My world! Shall I tell thee who created thee, who formed thee? Jacob has created thee, Jacob has formed thee'; as is proved by

the text, 'He that created thee is Jacob and he that formed thee is Israel.'" Freedman and Simon, *Midrash Rabbah*, 4.460.

147. Smith, "Prayer of Joseph," 2.713–714. For the primary texts, see Denis, *Fragmenta pseudepigraphorum quae supersunt graeca*, 61–64; A. Resch, *Agrapha: Aussercanonische Schriftfragmente* (Leipzig: J. C. Hinrichs, 1906), 295–298; Origène, *Commentaire sur Saint Jean: Tome I (Livres I-V)* (ed. C. Blanc; SC, 120; Paris: Cerf, 1966), 334–337; Origen, *Philocalia* (ed. J. A. Robinson; Cambridge: Cambridge University Press, 1893); *Eusebius, Praeparatio Evangelica* (ed. K. Mras; GCS, 43:1–2; Leipzig: J. C. Hinrichs, 1954–1956).

148. M. R. James, *The Lost Apocrypha of the Old Testament: Their Titles and Fragments* (Eugene, OR: Wipf and Stock, 2007), 30. James Dunn draws attention to the complexity of the angelological developments found in the *Prayer of Joseph*. He observes that

> somewhere in the second century . . . we have the *Prayer of Joseph* with Jacob presented as "an angel of God and a ruling spirit," indeed as "the archangel of the power of God and supreme commander among the sons of God" (in rank far above the angel Uriel), who "had descended to earth and had tabernacled among men and had been called by the name Jacob." However esoteric these documents, the fact that they could appear within Jewish circles shows just how much Jewish thought could accommodate— from angels which are merely personifications of God's will coming to effect, through personalized divine beings whose functions are distinct from and over against those of God, to archangels who bear the name of God, to a supreme angel that became incarnate as a historical individual.

Dunn, *Christology in the Making*, 153–154.

149. Allison, *Constructing Jesus*, 299.
150. Allison, *Constructing Jesus*, 299.
151. Striking parallels between Enochic and Jacobite accounts of the heavenly counterparts have been noted before. Thus, Daniel Olson observes that "perhaps Enoch and Jacob were even seen as sharing an identity in some mysterious sense, as if the earthly Enoch and Jacob were two iterations of the same heavenly being." Olson, *A New Reading*, 37. Olson further observes that "the *An. Apoc.*'s willingness to defer to an over-arching Israelite identity in Jacob may represent either an earlier or a variant Enochic theology, or perhaps it is to be explained by an understanding of the two men as avatars of the same heavenly personality and therefore in no competition with each other." Olson, *A New Reading*, 96.

152. "Being reminded of it by the archangel Uriel." Smith, "Prayer of Joseph," 2.713.
153. On this, see Smith, "Prayer of Joseph," 705.
154. In relation to this, John Ashton notes that although some words in the *Prayer* have a "docetic ring," "it is doubtful if the writer intends to question the full humanity of Jacob. True, both passages imply a double role, one in heaven, which has at least a priority in time, and one on earth. But the question of *ontological* priority is harder to answer. Is the 'real' Jacob the heavenly one, who descends to earth for a particular purpose only to re-ascend after his work there is done? At first sight it would appear so." J. Ashton, *Understanding the Fourth Gospel* (Oxford: Oxford University Press, 1991), 344–345.

155. "I [Jacob-Israel] had descended to earth and I had tabernacled among men." Smith, "Prayer of Joseph," 2.713.

156. Denis, *Fragmenta pseudepigraphorum quae supersunt graeca*, 61.

157. Thus, for example, Jonathan Smith in relation to this title observes that it represents "a general term in astrological and angelological materials to which no special significance may be attached." Smith, "Prayer of Joseph," 2.703. Yet, recently Bogdan Bucur drew his attention to this designation by noting its distinctive connection with Jewish pneumatological lore. Bucur notes that "according to the *Prayer* of Joseph, dated to the first century C.E., Israel is a heavenly being—called indistinctly both ἄγγελος θεοῦ and πνεῦμα ἀρχικόν—who ranks higher than the seven archangels, as chief captain and first minister before the face of God." B. G. Bucur, *Angelomorphic Pneumatology: Clement of Alexandria and Other Early Christian Witnesses* (SVC, 95; Leiden: Brill, 2009), 39.

158. Scholars often argue for the formative influences of the doppelganger traditions found in such texts as the *Acts of Thomas* on the Manichaean symbolism of the heavenly counterpart. Thus, for example, Drijvers observes that

> the idea of the heavenly twin, which dominates the *Acts of Thomas* and the picture of the apostle Judas Thomas as the representative of a theological idea, exercised a profound influence on Mani's self-understanding as is clearly shown by the *Cologne Mani Codex* [. . .]. The Coptic Manichaean texts show acquaintance with the Thomas legend and with the martyrdom of the apostle [. . .], although they have taken over only the legend and not the gnosticising elements [. . .]. It has often been assumed that the *Acts of Thomas* has preserved traces of a Manichaean revision [. . .], and that the *Hymn of the Pearl* in particular was soon transferred to Mani and provided with individual features from his Vita. It is certainly possible that the Manichaeans recognized in the king's son of the Hymn and in his life elements of the *Vita of the Apostle of Light*, but the differences are too great to make a Manichaean revision credible. Rather, the figure of the apostle Judas Thomas as the twin brother of Jesus was a decisive influence upon Mani's consciousness of mission, and it is also to be assumed that individual motifs from the *Acts of Thomas* were accepted into the legendary *Vita of Mani*.

Drijvers, "The Acts of Thomas," in *New Testament Apocrypha*, 2.338. On the connections between Manichaeism and the *Hymn of the Pearl*, see also W. Bousset, "Manichäisches in den Thomasakten: Ein Beitrag zur Frage nach den christlichen Elementen im Manichäismus," ZNW 18 (1917/18): 1–39; P. Nagel, "Die apokryphen Apostelakten des 2. und 3. Jahrhunderts in der manichäischen Literatur: Ein Beitrag zur Frage nach den christlichen Elementen im Manichäismus," in *Gnosis und Neues Testament: Studien aus Religionswissenschaft und Theologie* (ed. K.-W. Tröger; Gütersloh: Mohn, 1973), 149–182 at 172; P.-H. Poirier, "L'Hymne de la Perle et le manichéisme à la lumière du Codex manichéen de Cologne," in *Codex Manichaicus Coloniensis: Atti del Simposio Internazionale (Rende-Amantea 3–7 settembre 1984); Università degli studi della Calabria, Centro interdipartimentale di science religiose* (ed. L. Cirillo; Studi e ricerche, 4; Cosenza: Marra, 1986), 235–248.

159. On Mani's heavenly Twin, see A. Henrichs and L. Koenen, "Ein griechischer Mani-Codex (P. Colon. inv. nr. 4780)," *ZPE* 5 (1970): 97–216 esp. 161–189; A. Henrichs, H. Henrichs, and L. Koenen, "Der Kölner Mani-Kodex (P. Colon. inv. nr. 4780)," *ZPE* 19 (1975): 1–85; W. Fauth, "Manis anderes Ich: Gestalthafte Metaphysik in Kölner Mani-Kodex," in *Gnosis und Philosophie: Miscellanea* (ed. R. Berlinger and W. Schrader; Elementa, 59; Amsterdam: Rodopi, 1994), 75–114; G. G. Stroumsa and P. Fredriksen, "The Two Souls and the Divided Will," in *Self, Soul, and Body in Religious Experience* (ed. A. I. Baumgarten et al; Leiden: Brill, 1998), 198–208; F. de Blois, "Manes' 'Twin' in Iranian and non-Iranian Texts," in *Religious Themes and Texts of Pre-Islamic Iran and Central Asia: Studies in Honour of Professor Gherardo Gnoli on the Occasion of His 65th Birthday on 6th December 2002* (ed. C. G. Cereti, M. Maggi, and E. Provasi; BI, 24; Wiesbaden: Ludwig Reichert, 2003), 7–16.

160. *CMC* 18 reads: "(When) I was twenty (four) years old, in the year in which Dariadaxar, the king of Persia, conquered the city of Hatra, and in which his son King Sapores assumed the mighty diadem, in the month Pharmouthi, on the eighth day according to the moon, the most blessed lord had compassion on me and called me to his grace and sent to me (my) *Syzygos* (who) in great (glory)." Gardner and Lieu, *Manichaean Texts from the Roman Empire*, 50.

161. *CMC* 20–21 reads:

> He (the *Syzygos*) conveyed to me the noblest (hope and) redemption for the long-suffering, and the truest counsels and judgements and the laying on of hands which comes from our Father. Therefore, when he came, he released me and separated me and drew me away from the midst of that rule in which I was brought up. In this way he called me and chose me and drew me and separated me from their midst. He drew (me away to one) side . . . and (showed me) who I am and what my body is, in what way I came and how my coming into this world happened, and who I have become among those who are most distinguished in pre-eminence, and how I was born into this fleshly body, or through what woman I was brought to birth and delivered into this flesh, and by whom I was begotten.

Gardner and Lieu, *Manichaean Texts from the Roman Empire*, 50.

162. Ort, *Mani: A Religio-historical Description of His Personality*, 92–93.

163. In the Manichaean *Bema-Psalm* 241, the Twin-Spirit of Mani is named as Christ. On this, see Ort, *Mani: A Religio-historical Description of His Personality*, 89–90.

164. *CMC* 4 reads: "Very many are the visions and very great the marvels which he showed me throughout all that period of my youth." Gardner and Lieu, *Manichaean Texts from the Roman Empire*, 48.

165. Ort, *Mani: A Religio-historical Description of His Personality*, 89.

166. Ort, *Mani: A Religio-historical Description of His Personality*, 89.

167. "I was gazing at my familiar with my eyes of light." Gardner and Lieu, *Manichaean Texts from the Roman Empire*, 101.

168. Gardner, *The Kephalaia of the Teacher*, xi.

169. Gardner, *The Kephalaia of the Teacher*, 20.
170. Gardner, *The Kephalaia of the Teacher*, 20. See also *Keph*. 15:19–24: "This is how everything th[at] has ha[pp]ened and that will happen was unveiled to me by the Paraclete; [. . .] /everything the eye shall see, and the ear hear, and the th/ought think, a[n]d the [. . .] I have understood by him e/verything. I have seen the totality through him! I have become a single body/with a single Spirit!" Gardner, *The Kephalaia of the Teacher*, 21. *Keph*. 16:19–21: "[. . .] about which you questioned me. S/[ince the] Spirit is of the Paraclete, the one who was sent to me from [the greatness; what has] happened and what will happen [has been]/unveiled to me." Gardner, *The Kephalaia of the Teacher*, 22.
171. J. van Oort, "Mani and the Origins of a New Church," in *The Apostolic Age in Patristic Thought* (ed. A. Hilhorst; SVC, 70; Leiden: Brill, 2004), 139–157 at 155.
172. John Reeves affirms that "the Manichaean concept of the Paraclete as it is exhibited in western sources such as the Coptic *Kephalaia* and the *Cologne Mani Codex* is also visible in Middle Iranian Manichaean texts emanating from central Asia, thus confirming the likely centrality of this notion for the earliest strata of tradition." J. C. Reeves, *Prolegomena to a History of Islamicate Manichaeism* (Comparative Islamic Studies; Sheffield: Equinox, 2011), 80. On the Paraclete in the Manichaean tradition, see also P. Nagel, "Der Parakletenspruch des Mani (Keph. 14,7–11) und die altsyrische Evangelienübersetzung," in *Festschrift zum 150-jährigen Bestehen des Berliner Ägyptischen Museums* (MAS, 8; Berlin: Akademie-Verlag, 1974), 303–313; W. Sundermann, "Der Paraklet in der ostmanichäischen Überlieferung," in *Manichaean Studies: Proceedings of the First International Conference on Manichaeism, August 5–9, 1987* (ed. P. Bryder; LSAAR, 1; Lund: Plus Ultra, 1988), 201–212.
173. van Oort, "Origins of a New Church," 154. On Mani as the Paraclete, see Reeves, *Prolegomena to a History*, 50–62, 68, 80.
174. "Of this sending of the spirit of the Paraclete, and having turned away say that those men alone wrote about the rapture of their teacher in order to boast." Gardner and Lieu, *Manichaean Texts from the Roman Empire*, 54.
175. "For we know, brethren, the exceeding greatness of his wisdom towards us through this coming (of the) Paraclete of (truth)." Gardner and Lieu, *Manichaean Texts from the Roman Empire*, 57.
176. "In the books of our father there are very many other extraordinary events similar to these, which make known his revelation and the rapture of his mission. For great is this magnificent coming which comes to (us) through the Paraclete, the spirit of truth." Gardner and Lieu, *Manichaean Texts from the Roman Empire*, 58. See also *Fihrist of al-Nadīm*: "Mani asserted that he was the paraclete about whom Jesus, for whom may there be peace, preached." B. Dodge, *The Fihrist of al-Nadīm: A Tenth-Century Survey of Muslim Culture* (New York: Columbia University Press, 1970), 776.
177. van Oort, "Origins of a New Church," 154.
178. van Oort, "Origins of a New Church," 155. Charles Stang in his recent study reaffirms this position by arguing that "strictly speaking, Mani's undescended Nous and his companion are two faces of the same divine agent. Once the companion (Paraclete) has visited the incarnate Mani to awaken him to his apostolate, then he (Mani) can also be said to be the Paraclete, precisely insofar as the companion has been conjoined to

its counterpart, the now-embodied Apostle of Light. Thus, the resolution to the 'seeming contradiction' reinforces the essential, doubled nature of Mani's selfhood, once he is visited by (and so becomes) the Paraclete." Stang, *Our Divine Double*, 161–162.

179. van Oort, "Origins of a New Church," 155–156.

180. Gardner, *The Kephalaia of the Teacher*, xxxi.

181. K. Valavanolickal, *Aphrahat, Demonstrations I* (Kerala: SEERI, 2005), 154.

182. The idea of the Holy Spirit as the heavenly counterpart is found in the already mentioned passage from the *Macarian Homilies* where the Protoplast's heavenly image is identified with the Holy Spirit. Roelof van der Broek argues that the pneumatological ideas found in the *Macarian Homilies* can be traced back to the second century. He notes that already

> the apologist Tatian (ca. 170 C.E.) taught that with the transgression of man "the more powerful spirit departed from him," so that man became mortal (*Orat.* 7.3). Before that, man had two different kinds of spirits, the soul and the "image and likeness of God," which is identical with that more powerful spirit (*Orat.* 12.1). Of itself, the soul is mortal, it dies with the flesh (*Orat.* 13.1). Only if the soul obtains knowledge of God is it reunited with the divine Spirit, who is called the soul's companion (*syndiaitos*) (*Orat.* 13.2). This spirit-companion of the soul, who helps it to find the way back to God, is identified with the Holy Spirit. We have to search for what we once lost; we have to link our soul to the Holy Spirit and busy ourselves with the God-willed union (*syzygia*) (*Orat.* 15.1).

Van den Broek, "The Cathars: Medieval Gnostics?," 101. Gilles Quispel similarly argues that in Tatian's *Oratio ad Graecos* "the Spirit forms a *syzygia* with the soul and so leads her to heaven." Quispel, "Genius and Spirit," 116–117. On this tradition, see also Stang, *Our Divine Double*, 110–113. Tatian's *Oratio ad Graecos* 13 unveils the following tradition:

> The soul, men of Greece, is not in itself immortal but mortal; yet it also has the power to escape death. For if it is ignorant of the truth it dies and is dissolved with the body, but rises later at the end of the world along with the body, to suffer death by immortal punishment; on the other hand it does not die, even if it is dissolved for a time, if it has obtained knowledge of God. In itself it is dark and there is no light in it, and so the saying goes "The dark does not comprehend the light." For the soul did not itself preserve the spirit, but was preserved by it. The light comprehended the dark, in that the light of God is Word, but the ignorant soul is darkness. Because of this if it lives alone it inclines down towards matter and dies with the flesh, but if it gains union with the divine spirit it is not unaided, but mounts to the realms above where the spirit leads it; for the spirit's home is above, but the soul's birth is below. So the spirit became originally the soul's companion, but gave it up when the soul was unwilling to follow it. The soul

kept a spark, as it were, of the spirit's power, yet because of its separation it could no longer see things that are perfect, and so in its search for God went astray and fashioned a multitude of gods, following the demons and their hostile devices. God's spirit is not given to all, but dwelling among some who behaved justly and being intimately connected with the soul it revealed by predictions to the other souls what had been hidden. The souls which were obedient to wisdom attracted to themselves the kindred spirit, but those which were disobedient and rejected the servant of the suffering God were clearly shown to be enemies of God rather than his worshippers.

Whittaker, *Tatian, Oratio ad Graecos and Fragments*, 28–29.

183. Quispel, "Genius and Spirit," 108.

184. For the use of Matt 18:10 in Clement's *Strom.* 5.14.91; *Exc.* 10.6; 11:1; 23:4; *Quis div.* 31.1, see Bucur, *Angelomorphic Pneumatology*, 63ff.

185. The conceptual currents about seven celestial beings in Clement appears to be drawing on some biblical passages including Rev 1:4–5 where the seven Spirits are situated before the divine throne. Yet this development is deeply rooted in Jewish angelology. On the angelic heptad in Second Temple Judaism and later Jewish developments, see W. F. Smelik, "On Mystical Transformation of the Righteous into Light in Judaism," *JSJ* 26 (1995): 131–141; R. Elior, *The Three Temples: On the Emergence of Jewish Mysticism* (Oxford: Littman Library of Jewish Civilization, 2005), 77–81; Bucur, *Angelomorphic Pneumatology*, 39ff.

186. Matt 18:10.

187. Matt 18:10.

188. *The Excerpta ex Theodoto of Clement of Alexandria* (ed. R. P. Casey; London: Christophers, 1934), 49.

189. Bucur, *Angelomorphic Pneumatology*, 62.

190. Quispel, "Genius and Spirit," 112.

191. Kevin Sullivan also sees in Jacob's designation in the *Prayer of Joseph* a reference to the role of the angelic servant. He observes that the expression "the first minister before the face of God . . . is similar to what we find in *Targum Onqelos* and *Targum Neofiti* where the angels are said to be 'before the face of God.' This once again suggests that Jacob/Israel has seen God, since he ministers before his countenance." K. P. Sullivan, *Wrestling with Angels: A Study of the Relationship between Angels and Humans in Ancient Jewish Literature and the New Testament* (AGAJU, 55; Leiden: Brill, 2004), 101.

192. Despite some striking similarities with the Christian understanding of "spirit" as the seer's heavenly identity, one can detect a striking conceptual difference between the heavenly state of the *Protoktistoi* of the Christian accounts and Jacob's celestial stand in the *Prayer*. While the seven angels are first-created, similar to Abraham and Isaac who "were created before any work," Jacob's heavenly Self is born. The difference between the celestial origins of Abraham and Isaac on the one hand and Jacob on the other is noteworthy since it might point to some polemical developments.

193. Peter van der Horst and Judith Newman note that "the word used for 'precreated,' προεκτίσθησαν, is a prefixed form of the more frequently appearing κτίζω. The

word is used to emphasize the idea that Jacob existed before the creation of the world and its order. The Greek term is found in later Christian literature to refer to the status of Christ as pre-existent, yet the idea resonates with rabbinic traditions that posit the preexistence of certain items before creation, variously among them the Torah, the temple, the heavenly throne, repentance, and wisdom." Van der Horst and Newman, *Early Jewish Prayers in Greek*, 250–251.

194. Van der Horst and Newman note that "the LXX of Exod 4:22 speaks of Israel as God's πρωτότοκος, 'first-born son.' This word is not found elsewhere in scripture, but Philo uses the term to refer both to the Logos (*Conf*. 63, 146; *Somn*. I. 215) and to Israel as a first-born (*Post*. 63; *Fug*. 208), or to Israel in the character of the Logos (*Agr*. 51). This idea of Jacob being 'the firstborn' is also mentioned in the *Prayer of Joseph* in which Jacob is . . . the 'firstborn of all living.'" Van der Horst and Newman, *Early Jewish Prayers in Greek*, 256.

195. Richard Hayward notes that "Philo uses this word only six times in his writings, always to speak of the Logos (*De Conf. Ling*. 63, 146; *De Som*. I. 215), Israel as a first-born (*De Post*. 63; *De Fuga* 208), or Israel in the character of the Logos (*De Agr*. 51)." C. T. R. Hayward, *Interpretations of the Name Israel in Ancient Judaism and Some Early Christian Writings* (Oxford: Oxford University Press, 2005), 200. He further notes that "when Philo calls Israel πρωτόγονος therefore, it may be that he has in mind once again a being who belongs both on earth and in heaven." Hayward, *Interpretations of the Name*, 200.

196. H. Schwartz, *Tree of Souls: The Mythology of Judaism* (Oxford: Oxford University Press, 2004), 366.

197. H. Windisch, "Die göttliche Weisheit der Juden und die paulinische Christologie," in *Neutestamentliche Studien für G. Heinrici* (ed. A. Deissmann and H. Windisch; UNT, 6; Leipzig: J. C. Heinrichs, 1914), 225, n. 1.

198. Fossum, *Image of the Invisible God*, 24.

199. "He envied me and fought with me and wrestled with me saying that his name and the name that is before every angel was to be above mine." Smith, "Prayer of Joseph," 2.713.

200. Hayward, *Interpretations of the Name*, 205.

201. The Latin version of the *Primary Adam Books* 12:1: "Groaning, the Devil said: 'O Adam, all my enmity, jealousy, and resentment is towards you, since on account of you I was expelled and alienated from my glory, which I had in heaven in the midst of the angels. On account of you I was cast out upon the earth.'" Anderson and Stone, *A Synopsis of the Books of Adam and Eve*, 15E.

202. See the Latin and the Armenian versions of the *Primary Adam Books* 14:2–15:1.

203. Quispel, "Genius and Spirit," 109. Quispel traces a similar development in other principal materials associated with the Syrian milieu, including the *Macarian Homilies* where the symbolism of the Spirit and the Image are conflated. See *Homily* II.12.6: "Since Adam lost his own image and also that heavenly image, therefore, if he shared in the heavenly image, did he have the Holy Spirit?" Maloney, *Pseudo-Macarius, The Fifty Spiritual Homilies and the Great Letter*, 97. The confluence of the spirit and the image as a human being's heavenly identity is also present in the already mentioned passage from *Zohar* III.43a–b:

And the Holy One, blessed be He, directs an emissary who is in charge of human embryos, and assigns to him this particular spirit, and indicates to him the place to which it should be entrusted. This is the meaning of "The night said, a man-child has been conceived" (Job 3:3). "The night said" to this particular emissary, "a man-child has been conceived" by so-and-so. And the Holy One, blessed be He, then gives this spirit all the commands that He wishes to give, and they have already explained this. Then the spirit descends together with the image, the one in whose likeness [the spirit] existed above. With this image [man] grows; with this image he moves through the world. This is the meaning of "Surely man walks with an image" (Ps 39:7).

Tishby, *The Wisdom of the Zohar*, 2.787–789.
204. Quispel, "Genius and Spirit," 109. Quispel also draws attention to another passage in the *Shepherd of Hermas* (*Mand.* 11) where the heavenly counterpart of a human being seems to be identified with the Holy Spirit. *Mand.* 11:9 reads: "So when the person who has the spirit of God enters the assembly of just men who believe in the divine spirit, and prayer is made to God by the assembly of those men, then the angel of the prophetic spirit that rests upon that person fills the person, who, being filled with the holy spirit, speaks to the whole crowd as the Lord wishes." Osiek, *Shepherd of Hermas*, 139. Quispel argues that in this passage "the 'angel of the prophetic spirit' is the Holy Spirit and at the same time a guardian angel." Quispel, "Genius and Spirit," 110.
205. *Pistis Sophia* 61:11 reads:

When thou wast small, before the Spirit came upon thee, while thou wast in a vineyard with Joseph, the Spirit came forth from the height, he came to me into my house, he resembled thee. And I did not recognize him and I thought that he was thou. And the Spirit said to me: "Where is Jesus, my brother, that I meet him?" And when he said these things to me, I was confused and I thought that he was a phantom to tempt me. But I took him, I bound him to the leg of the bed in my house, until I came out to you in the field, thou and Joseph, and I found you in the vineyard, as Joseph was hedging the vineyard with reeds. Now it happened, when thou didst hear me speaking the word to Joseph, thou didst understand the word and thou didst rejoice. And thou didst say: "Where is he that I may see him? Or else I await him in this place." But it happened when Joseph heard thee saying these words, he was agitated and we came up at the same time, we went into the house. We found the Spirit bound to the bed. And we looked at thee with him, we found thee like him. And he that was bound to the bed was released, he embraced thee, he kissed thee. And thou also, thou didst kiss him and you became one.

Schmidt and MacDermot, *Pistis Sophia*, 243–245.
206. Quispel, "Genius and Spirit," 110.
207. Quispel, "Genius and Spirit," 110.

208. It is also important that Enoch's heavenly counterpart, the Son of Man (also known in the text as the Chosen One), is also defined in the *Similitudes* with various pneumatological titles. See, for example, *1 Enoch* 49:3 "And in him dwells the spirit of wisdom, and the spirit which gives understanding, and the spirit of knowledge and of power, and the spirit of those who sleep in righteousness." Knibb, *Ethiopic Book of Enoch*, 2.135; *1 Enoch* 62:2: "And the Lord of Spirits sat on the throne of his glory, and the spirit of righteousness was poured out on him." Knibb, *Ethiopic Book of Enoch*, 2.150.

209. Klaus Koch notes that "the Book of Parables teaches a sophisticated pneumatology that is not restricted to a holy spirit within the community of believers, but further reckons with a background force sustaining the cosmos as God's good creation." K. Koch, "Questions Regarding the So-Called Son of Man," in *Enoch and the Messiah Son of Man*, 233.

210. Knibb, *Ethiopic Book of Enoch*, 2.165.

211. Knibb, *Ethiopic Book of Enoch*, 2.166. Matthew Black traces the expression "the spirit of power" to Isa 11:2: רוח עצה וגבורה. M. Black, *The Book of Enoch or 1 Enoch* (SVTP, 7; Leiden: Brill, 1985), 251.

212. *1 Enoch* 71:2: "And I fell upon my face before the Lord of Spirits." Knibb, *Ethiopic Book of Enoch*, 2.165. On this title, see Olson, *Enoch: A New Translation; The Ethiopic Book of Enoch, or 1 Enoch* (North Richland Hills, TX: Bibal Press, 2004), 136.

213. Jacob's prayer found in chapter 2 of the *Ladder* has been identified by Reimund Leicht among a collection of prayers in an eleventh-century codex from the Cairo Genizah published by Peter Schäfer and Shaul Shaked. See R. Leicht, "Qedushah and Prayer to Helios: A New Hebrew Version of an Apocryphal Prayer of Jacob," *JSQ* 6 (1999): 140–176. For the Hebrew text of the prayer, see P. Schäfer and S. Shaked, *Magische Texte aus der Kairoer Geniza* (TSAJ, 64; Tübingen: Mohr/Siebeck, 1997), 2.27–78. In their recent study on early Jewish prayers, van der Horst and Newman affirm the identification by arguing that

> the prayer from the Cairo Genizah appears to be a version of the composition in the first century *Ladder of Jacob* (*Lad. Jac.* 2:6–22). The fact that a prayer imbedded in a longer narrative appears in modified version as part of a collection of independent prayers points to an artificial divide often made by scholars between "narrative prayers" and "liturgical prayers" especially if the latter are thought to preclude forms of worship, whether public or private, communal or individual, other than a fixed liturgical cycle for daily or festival use. . . . The prayer found in the *Ladder of Jacob* and its later Cairo Genizah cousin contain similarities to the *Prayer of Jacob* of *PGM* XXIIb at a number of points which will be addressed in the commentary.

Van der Horst and Newman, *Early Jewish Prayers in Greek*, 218–219.

214. On *Explanatory Paleja*, see V. P. Adrianova, *K literaturnoj istorii Tolkovoj Palei* (Kiev: Petr Barskij, 1910); C. Böttrich, "Palaea/Paleja. Ein byzantinisch-slavischer Beitrag zu den europäischen Historienbibeln," in *Fragmentarisches Wörterbuch: Beiträge zur biblischen Exegese und christlichen Theologie; Horst Balz zum 70. Geburtstag* (ed. K. Schiffner, K. Wengst, and W. Zager; Stuttgart: W. Kohlhammer, 2007), 304–313. A. de

Santos Otero, "Alttestamentliche Pseudepigrapha und die sogenannte 'Tolkovaja Paleja' [TP]," in *Oecumenica et Patristica: FS für W. Schneemelcher zum 75. Geburtstag* (ed. D. Papandreou, W. A. Bienert, and K. Schäferdieck; Stuttgart: W. Kohlhammer, 1989), 107–122; V. M. Istrin, "Zamechanie o sostave Tolkovoj Palei," *IORJS* 2.1 (1897): 175–209; idem, "Redakcii Tolkovoj Palei," *IORJS* 10.4 (1905): 150–151; A. M. Kamchatnov, "Paleja Tolkovaja," in *Idejnye techenija russkoj mysli* (ed. M. N. Gromov and V. V. Mil'kov; St. Petersburg: RHGI, 1999), 571–677; idem, "Paleja Tolkovaja," in *Filosofskie i bogoslovskie idei v pamjatnikah drevnerusskoj mysli* (ed. M. N. Gromov and V. V. Mil'kov; Moscow: Nauka, 2000), 114–169; A. V. Mihajlov, "Obshij obzor sostava, redakcij i literaturnyh istochnikov Tolkovoj Palei," *VUI* 7 (1895): 1–21; P. P. Novickij, *Tolkovaja paleja 1477 goda: Vosproizvedenie Sinodal'noj Rukopisi No 210* (St. Petersburg: Tipografia Imperatorskoj Akademii Nauk, 1892); *Paleja tolkovaja po spisku sdelannomu v gorode Kolomne v 1406 g. Trud uchenikov N.S. Tihonravova* (Moscow: Gerbek, 1892); I. Ja. Porfir'ev, *Apokrificheskie skazanija o vethozavetnyh licah i sobytijah po rukopisjam soloveckoj biblioteki* (SORJS, 17.1; St. Petersburg: Tipografija Imperatorskoj Academii Nauk, 1877), 11–12; O. V. Tvorogov, "Paleja Tolkovaja," in *Slovar' knizhnikov i knizhnosti Drevnei Rusi (XI—pervaja polovina XIV v.)* (ed. D. S. Lihachev; Leningrad: Nauka, 1987), 285–288; V. M. Uspenskij, *Tolkovaja Paleja* (Kazan', 1876); E. G. Vodolazkin, "O Tolkovoj Palee, Zlatoj Matice i 'estestvenno nauchnyh' compiljacijah," *TODRL* 51 (1999): 80–90; idem, *Vsemirnaja istorija v literature Drevnej Rusi (na materiale hronograficheskogo i palejnogo povestvovanija XI-XV vekov)* (SSS, 26; München: Sagner, 2000).

215. Horace Lunt observes that the seventh chapter of the *Ladder* is a later Christian addition juxtaposed to the story by a Slavic (possibly, Russian) editor of *Paleja*. Lunt, "Ladder of Jacob," 2.404–405.

216. In this study, I follow Horace Lunt's division of chapters and verses. The Slavonic citations are drawn from the following publications of the MSS:

Recension A:

MS S (Sinodal'naja Paleja. Sin. 210) published in *Tolkovaja paleja 1477 goda*, 100a–107b.

MS R (Rumjancevskaja Paleja. Rum. 455) published in A. N. Pypin, *Lozhnye i otrechennye knigi russkoj stariny* (Pamjatniki starinnoj russkoj literatury, izdavaemye Grafom Grigoriem Kushelevym-Bezborodko, 3; St. Petersburg: Kulish, 1862), 27–32.

MS F (Krehivskaja Paleja) published in I. Franko, *Apokrifi i legendi z ukrains'kih rukopisiv* (Monumenta Linguae Necon Litterarum Ukraino-Russicarum [Ruthenicarum]; 5 vols.; L'vov: Shevchenka, 1896–1910), 1.108–120.

Recension B:

MS K (Kolomenskaja Paleja. Tr.-Serg. 38) published in N. S. Tihonravov, *Pamjatniki otrechennoj russkoj literatury* (2 vols; St. Petersburg: Obshestvennaja Pol'za, 1863), 1.91–95 and in *Paleja tolkovaja po spisku sdelannomu v g. Kolomne v 1406 g. Trud uchenikov N.S. Tihonravova*, 153–166.

MS P (Soloveckaja Paleja. Sol. 653) published in *Apokrificheskie skazanija*, 138–149.

217. Reflecting on this verse, James Kugel notes that

> anyone who knows the Hebrew text of Gen 28:12 will immediately recognize the source of this image. For though the Bible says that in his dream

Jacob saw a ladder whose top reached to the Heavens, the word for "top," in Hebrew, *rosh*, is the same word normally used for "head." And so our Slavonic text—or, rather, the Hebrew text that underlies it—apparently takes the biblical reference to the ladder's "head" as a suggestion that the ladder indeed had a head, a man's head, at its very top. The fact, then, of this biblical text's wording—"a ladder set up on the earth, and its head reached to heaven"—engendered the heavenly "head" in our pseudepigraphon.

Kugel, *In Potiphar's House*, 118.
218. Lunt, "Ladder of Jacob," 2.407.
219. Lunt, "Ladder of Jacob," 2.406.
220. Elliot Wolfson points to the possible connection of this imagery to the conceptual developments found in the targumim. He notes that "it is worthwhile to compare the targumic and midrashic explanation of Gen 28:12 to the words of the apocryphal text the *Ladder of Jacob* . . . 'And the top of the ladder was the face as of a man, carved out of fire.'" Wolfson, "The Image of Jacob Engraved," 114.
221. James Charlesworth notes that in the *Ladder of Jacob*, as "in some of other pseudepigrapha, the voice has ceased to be something heard and has become a hypostatic creature." See Charlesworth's comment in Lunt, "Ladder of Jacob," 2.406.
222. *2 Enoch* 22:1–4 (the longer recension):

> I saw the view of the face of the Lord, like iron made burning hot in a fire and brought out, and it emits sparks and is incandescent. Thus even I saw the face of the Lord. But the face of the Lord is not to be talked about, it is so very marvelous and supremely awesome and supremely frightening. And who am I to give an account of the incomprehensible being of the Lord, and of his face, so extremely strange and indescribable? And how many are his commands, and his multiple voice, and the Lord's throne, supremely great and not made by hands, and the choir stalls all around him, the cherubim and the seraphim armies, and their never-silent singing. Who can give an account of his beautiful appearance, never changing and indescribable, and his great glory? And I fell down flat and did obeisance to the Lord.

Andersen, "2 Enoch," 1.136.
223. Francis Andersen in his commentary on *2 Enoch* 22 notes the similarities between the fiery face in *2 Enoch* and the face of fire in the *Ladder of Jacob*. See Andersen, "2 Enoch," 1.137, n. 22d.
224. Both Slavonic pseudepigraphons in their description of the Face share the similar Slavonic terminology, words like face (*lice*); fiery (*ognena, iz ognja*); terrifying (*strashno*). See Franko, *Apokrifi i legendi*, 1.109; Pypin, *Lozhnye i otrechennye knigi russkoj stariny*, 27; Porfir'ev, *Apokrificheskie skazanija*, 138; Tihonravov, *Pamjatniki otrechennoj russkoj literatury*, 1.91; *Tolkovaja paleja 1477 goda*, 100b; and Macaskill, *The Slavonic Texts of 2 Enoch*, 100–101.

225. DeConick, *Seek to See Him*, 104–105.

226. The early traces of this tendency to identify *Kavod* with the Face within the Enochic tradition can be seen already in the *Book of the Watchers* 14 where the enthroned Glory is labeled as the Face. See *1 Enoch* 14:21: "And no angel could enter, and at the appearance of the face of him who is honored and praised no (creature of) flesh could look." Knibb, *Ethiopic Book of Enoch*, 2.99.

227. It is noteworthy that already in the classic description of God's Glory in Ezek 1:27, *Kavod* is described similarly to the portrayal of the Face in the *Ladder of Jacob*—namely, as the fiery *bust*: "Upward from what appeared like the loins I saw something like gleaming amber, something that looked like fire enclosed all around; and downward from what looked like the loins I saw something that looked like fire, and there was a splendor all around."

228. Exod 33:18–20: "Moses said, 'Show me your glory (כְּבֹדֶךָ), I pray.' And he said, 'I will make all my goodness pass before you, and will proclaim before you the name, 'The Lord'; and I will be gracious to whom I will be gracious, and will show mercy on whom I will show mercy. But,' he said, 'you cannot see my face (פָּנָי); for no one shall see me and live.'"

229. Lunt, "Ladder of Jacob," 2.408.

230. Andersen, "2 Enoch," 1.137.

231. "Before the face of your glory the six-winged seraphim are afraid, and they cover their feet and faces with their wings."

232. Alexander, "3 Enoch," 1.305. On the "danger motif" applied to the Face imagery, see Schäfer, *The Hidden and Manifest God*, 17; *Synopse* §§102, 159, 183, 189, 356.

233. MS S—*Chavod*; MS R—*Chavod*; MS F—*Chsavod*. See *Tolkovaja paleja 1477 goda*, 101b; Pypin, *Lozhnye i otrechennye knigi russkoj stariny*, 28; and Franko, *Apokrifi i legendi*, 1.110.

234. See Lunt, "Ladder of Jacob," 2.408, n. 2i.

235. Maher, *Targum Pseudo-Jonathan: Genesis*, 99–100; Díez Macho, *Targum Palaestinense in Pentateuchum*, 195–197.

236. "And here, The Glory of the Lord (יְקָרָא דּיי) was standing over him, and He said, 'I am the Lord, the God of your Father Abraham and the God of Isaac: the land on which you sleep I will give to you and to your offspring . . .' The Jacob awoke from his sleep and said, 'Truly the Glory of the Lord (יְקָרָא דּיי) dwells in this place, and I did not know it.'" *The Targum Onqelos to Genesis* (trans. B. Grossfeld; ArBib, 6; Wilmington: Michael Glazier, 1988), 104; *Targum Onkelos to Genesis: A Critical Analysis Together with an English Translation of the Text* (ed. M. Aberbach and B. Grossfeld; Denver: Ktav, 1982), 171.

237. Fossum, *Image of the Invisible God*, 135–151, esp. 143.

238. Böttrich notes that the complexity of the heavenly counterpart's imagery in the *Ladder of Jacob* posed some challenges for the transmitters of the text. He rightly notes that "the whole idea is very complex and puzzling here. Perhaps it was already unintelligible for the Slavonic translators or redactors." C. Böttrich, "Apocalyptic Tradition and Mystical Prayer in the *Ladder of Jacob*," *JSP* 23 (2014): 290–306 at 296–297.

239. Kugel, *In Potiphar's House*, 112–124; C. H. von Heijne, *The Messenger of the Lord in Early Jewish Interpretations of Genesis* (Berlin: Walter de Gruyter, 2010), 171ff; 356ff.
240. Lunt, "Ladder of Jacob," 2.403.
241. Kugel, *In Potiphar's House*, 119.
242. Rachel Neis observes that "it is conceivable that the 'face of Jacob' is used in a more generic sense for Jacob's image or likeness and could include a representation of his entire figure or bust. The bust, or portrait medallion, was ubiquitous in civic, funerary and religious art in Late Antiquity and Byzantine periods, and while emphasizing the face of the person portrayed could portray the upper torso and arms." Neis, "Embracing Icons," 42.
243. Kugel, *In Potiphar's House*, 119.
244. Kugel, *In Potiphar's House*, 119.
245. See also Rowland, "Jewish Apocalyptic and Targumic Tradition," 500–507; von Heijne, *Messenger of the Lord*, 177–178.
246. Fossum, *Image of the Invisible God*, 143, n. 30. I also previously argued for the existence of the heavenly counterpart traditions in the *Ladder of Jacob*. For my arguments, see Orlov, "The Face as the Heavenly Counterpart," 2.59–76.
247. Böttrich, "Apocalyptic Tradition and Mystical Prayer," 297.
248. Böttrich, "Apocalyptic Tradition and Mystical Prayer," 297.
249. Lunt, "Ladder of Jacob," 2.409.
250. In relation to these connections, Kugel observes that

> the same motif [of four empires] apparently underlies the *Ladder of Jacob*. Here too, it is Jacob's vision of the ladder that serves as the vehicle for a revelation of the "kings of the lawless nations" who will rule over Israel, and if this text does not specifically mention how many such nations there will be, it does go on to speak (as we have seen) of four "ascents" or "descents" that will bring Jacob's progeny to grief. Indeed, the continuation of our text alludes specifically to the last of the four empires, Rome: "The Most High will raise up kings from the grandsons of your brother Esau, and they will receive the nobles of the tribes of the earth who will have maltreated your seed." As is well known, Esau frequently represents Rome in Second Temple writings.

J. Kugel, "The Ladder of Jacob," *HTR* 88 (1995): 214.
251. Kugel, "The Ladder of Jacob," 214.
252. Freedman and Simon, *Midrash Rabbah*, 4.370. See also *Exodus Rabbah* 32:7: "God showed Jacob the guardian angels of every empire, for it says, And he dreamed, and behold a ladder set up on the earth (Gen 28:12). He showed him how many peoples, governors, and rulers would arise from each kingdom, and just as He displayed their rise, so he showed their fall, as it says, And behold, the angels of God ascending and descending on it." Freedman and Simon, *Midrash Rabbah*, 3.411.
253. Braude, *Midrash on Psalms*, 2.26–27. *Pesiqta de-Rab Kahana* 23 contains an almost identical tradition:

R. Nahman applied it to the episode in Jacob's life when He dreamed, and beheld a ladder . . . and angels of God (Gen 28:12). These angels, according to R. Samuel bar R. Nahman, were the princes of the nations of the earth. Further, according to R. Samuel bar Nahman, this verse proves that the Holy One showed to our father Jacob the prince of Babylon climbing up seventy rungs the ladder, then climbing down; the prince of Media climbing up fifty-two rungs and no more; the prince of Greece, one hundred and eighty rungs and no more; and the prince of Edom climbing and climbing, no one knows how many rungs. At the sight of Edom's climbing our father Jacob grew afraid and said: Is one to suppose that this prince will have no come-down? The Holy One replied: Be not dismayed, O Israel (Jer 30:10): Even if—as though such a thing were possible!—thou were to see him seated next to Me, I would have him brought down thence.

W. G. Braude and I. J. Kapstein, *Pesikta de-Rab Kahana: R. Kahana's Compilation of Discourses for Sabbaths and Festal Days* (Philadelphia: Jewish Publication Society of America, 1975), 353. See also *Zohar* I.149b:

And behold, the angels of God ascending and descending on it; this alludes to the Chieftains who have charge of all the nations, and who ascend and descend on that ladder. When Israel is sinful, the ladder is lowered and the Chieftains ascend by it; but when Israel are righteous, the ladder is removed and all the Chieftains are left below and are deprived of their dominion. Jacob thus saw in this dream the domination of Esau and the domination of the other nations. According to another explanation, the angels ascended and descended on the top of the ladder; for when the top was detached, the ladder was lowered and the Chieftains ascended, but when it was attached again, the ladder was lifted and they remained below.

Sperling and Simon, *The Zohar*, 2.79–80.
254. On this, see J. Kugel, *Traditions of the Bible: A Guide to the Bible as It Was at the Start of the Common Era* (Cambridge: Harvard University Press, 1998), 363.
255. Kugel, "Ladder of Jacob," 215.
256. Jonathan Smith observes that in five instances in *1 Enoch* (40:9; 54:6; 71:8, 9, 13), confined to the *Similitudes*, Phanuel replaces Uriel in a catalog of the four archangels. He also points out that while Sariel is a relatively unknown angelic figure, his name seems to be quite frequently conflated with Uriel, as in *1 Enoch* 9:1. Smith, "Prayer of Joseph," 2.708–709. For the discussion about Uriel-Sariel-Phanuel, see J. Greenfield, "Prolegomenon," in *3 Enoch or the Hebrew Book of Enoch*, xxxiv–xxxv; Lunt, "Ladder of Jacob," 2.405, n. 10; Milik, *Books of Enoch*, 170–174; Olyan, *A Thousand Thousands Served Him*, 105–109; Smith, "Prayer of Joseph," 270 and 227; G. Vermes, "The Archangel Sariel: A Targumic Parallel to the Dead Sea Scrolls," in *Christianity, Judaism and Other Greco-Roman Cults* (ed. J. Neusner; SJLA, 12.3; Leiden: Brill, 1975), 159–166; idem, "The Impact of the Dead Sea Scrolls on Jewish Studies," 13.
257. Smith, "Prayer of Joseph," 2.713.

258. McNamara, *Targum Neofiti 1: Genesis*, 158.
259. Vermes, "Impact of the Dead Sea Scrolls," 13; Smith, "Prayer of Joseph," 2.709.
260. Klein, *The Fragment-Targums of the Pentateuch*, 1.59 and 2.22.
261. MSS S, R, F. See *Tolkovaja paleja 1477 goda*, 101b; Pypin, *Lozhnye i otrechennye knigi russkoj stariny*, 28; Franko, *Apokrifi i legend*, 1.110.
262. Slav. "*uslazhdaemych*" can be literally translated as "sweetened." See *Staroslovjanskij slovar' po rukopisjam X–XI vekov* (ed. R. M. Cejtlin; Moscow: Russkij jazyk, 1994), 477; I. I. Sresnevskij, *Slovar' drevnerusskogo jazyka* (3 vols.; Moscow: Kniga, 1989), 3.1266.
263. Andersen, "2 Enoch," 1.139.
264. A visionary, therefore, becomes a reflection or even a representation of the Face/*Kavod*, a sort of vice-regent. Christopher Morray-Jones observes that "there is evidence, then, of the early existence of a tradition concerning the ascent to heaven of an exceptionally righteous man who beholds the vision of the divine *Kabod* upon Merkavah, is transformed into an angelic being and enthroned as celestial vice-regent, thereby becoming identified with the Name-bearing angel who either is or is closely associated with the *Kabod* itself and functions as a second, intermediary power in heaven." Morray-Jones, "Transformational Mysticism in the Apocalyptic-Merkabah Tradition," 10–11.
265. Gen 32:30: "For I have seen God face to face (פָּנִים אֶל־פָּנִים)."
266. The tradition of Jacob as the *Prince* of the Presence seems to be also reflected in *Targ. Onq.* to Gen 32:29: "Whereupon, he said, 'No longer shall your name be called Jacob, but rather Israel; for you are a *prince* before the Lord and among men; therefore have you prevailed.'" Grossfeld, *The Targum Onqelos to Genesis*, 116.
267. Geza Vermes notices that *Targ. Neof.* explains the etymology of Israel from שׂרר—to rule, to act as a prince. Vermes, "Impact of the Dead Sea Scrolls," 13.
268. C. Gieschen, *Angelomorphic Christology: Antecedents and Early Evidence* (AGAJU, 42; Leiden: Brill, 1998), 141–142.
269. The fact that Sariel-Uriel-Phanuel is known under several names might indicate that this angel also serves as a heavenly counterpart in the manner similar to other servants of the Face such as Jacob/Israel, Enoch/Metatron, and possibly Melchizedek/Michael. On the identification of Michael with Melchizedek, see Davila, "Melchizedek, Michael, and War in Heaven," 259–272; Hannah, *Michael and Christ*, 70–74.
270. Saul Olyan refers to Rashi's passage that identifies "the 'angel of his presence' of Isa 63:9 with Michael, the Prince of Presence." Olyan, *A Thousand Thousands Served Him*, 108.
271. The beginning of the second half of *Jos. Asen.* gives a description of Aseneth and Joseph visiting Jacob. *Jos. Asen.* 22:7–8 says that when Aseneth saw Jacob, she "was amazed at his beauty . . . his eyes (were) flashing and darting (flashes of) lightning, and his sinews and his shoulders and his arms were like (those) of an angel, and his thighs and his calves and his feet like (those) of a giant. And Jacob was like a man who had wrestled with God. And Aseneth saw him and was amazed, and prostrated herself before him face down to the ground." Burchard, "Joseph and Aseneth," 2.238. Reflecting on this scene, George Brooke suggests that "for those slow to see it, the author identifies Jacob's torso as angelic." Brooke, "Men and Women as Angels in Joseph and Aseneth," 171.
272. See Freedman and Simon, *Midrash Rabbah*, 2.626.

273. James Kugel argues that the similar development in which Jacob embodies the ladder might be present already in the *Ladder of Jacob*. He suggests that in the *Ladder* the top or the "head" of the ladder becomes Jacob's *iqonin*. He notes that

> For Jacob's "head" somehow reaches, via the ladder, to the Heavens either, as in the pseudepigraphon, an image of his head stands at the top of the ladder, or perhaps such an image ascends via the ladder into Heaven and the angels can thus go up and down between Jacob's heavenly head and his earthly one, presumably to admire both. In any case, one can easily see how this transformation of the ladder's "head" to a human head (already witnessed in the pseudepigraphon) could lead directly to the notion that some sort of bust, an *iqonin*, of Jacob existed on high.

Kugel, *In Potiphar's House*, 118–119.

274. Burney, *Aramaic Origin of the Fourth Gospel*, 115ff; Odeberg, *The Fourth Gospel*, 33–42.

275. Odeberg, *3 Enoch*, 123.

276. J. Z. Smith, *Map Is Not Territory: Studies in the History of Religions* (Leiden: Brill, 1978), 59. Smith suggests that the allusions to such an idea can be possibly found in Philo's *Somn.* I, 146ff and *Corpus Hermeticum* IV, 4 and X, 25.

277. Some scholars argue about the secondary nature of the Son of Man tradition found in this chapter of the Gospel of John. Thus, Raymond Brown writes the following: "At the very end of this part on the call of the disciples in the Jordan valley, there comes a verse that has caused as much trouble for commentators as any single verse in the Fourth Gospel. Our first question must be whether 1:51 has always been associated with the context in which it is now found. There are certain indications to the contrary." R. E. Brown, *The Gospel According to John* (2 vols.; AB, 29–29A; Garden City, NY: Doubleday, 1966), 1.88. Christopher Rowland also recognizes the secondary nature of John 1:51, by noting that "John 1.51 comes at the end of the first chapter of the gospel and is the climax of many Christological themes running throughout these verses, though it is probably an isolated logion of some antiquity which has been added by the evangelist at this point." Rowland, "Jewish Apocalyptic and Targumic Tradition," 500. On John 1:51 as an addition, see also R. Bultmann, *The Gospel of John* (Philadelphia: Westminster, 1971), 105–106; J. H. Neyrey, "The Jacob Allusions in John 1:51," *CBQ* 44 (1982): 586–605.

278. Commenting on John 1:51, Jarl Fossum argues that "Jesus, like Jacob-Israel, is both in heaven and on earth at the same time." Fossum, *Image of the Invisible God*, 149. See also Allison, *Constructing Jesus*, 300; Koch, "Questions Regarding the So-Called Son of Man in the Parables of Enoch," 237, n. 24.

279. On possible reasons why Jesus might use of the Son of Man title in third person, see E. M. Boring, *Sayings of the Risen Jesus: Christian Prophecy in the Synoptic Tradition* (Cambridge: Cambridge University Press, 1982), 239–250; W. Bousset, *Kyrios Christos: A History of the Belief in Christ from the Beginnings of Christianity to Irenaeus* (New York: Abingdon, 1970), 36; J. P. Brown, "The Son of Man: 'This Fellow,'" *Biblica* 58 (1977): 361–387 at 370–375; D. Burkett, *The Son of Man Debate: A History and*

Evaluation (SNTSMS, 107; Cambridge: Cambridge University Press, 2000), 32–42; A. Díez Macho, "L'usage de la troisième personne au lieu de la première dans le Targum," in *Mélanges Dominique Barthélemy* (ed. P. Casetti et al.; Göttingen: Vandenhoeck & Ruprecht, 1981), 61–89; idem, "La Cristologia del Hijo del Hombre y el uso de la tercera persona en vez de la primera," *ScrTh* 14 (1982): 189–201; E. Käsemann, *New Testament Questions of Today* (Philadelphia: Fortress, 1969), 82–137; T. W. Manson, *The Teaching of Jesus: Studies of Its Form and Content* (2nd ed.; Cambridge: Cambridge University Press, 1935), 228; S. Mowinckel, *He That Cometh* (New York: Abingdon, 1951), 447–450; R. Otto, *The Kingdom of God and the Son of Man* (2nd ed.; London: Lutterworth, 1943), 213–219; R. Schnackenburg, "Das kommende Reich Gottes und der Menschensohn," in R. Schnackenburg, *Gottes Herrschaft und Reich* (Freiburg: Herder, 1959), 110–122 at 116; P. Vielhauer, "Gottesreich und Menschensohn in der Verkündigung Jesu," in *Festschrift für Günther Dehn* (ed. W. Schneemelcher; Neukirchen: Erziehungsverein, 1957), 51–79; idem, "Jesus und der Menschensohn: Zur Discussion mit Heinz Eduard Tödt und Eduard Schweizer," *ZTK* 60 (1963): 133–177; J. Weiss, *Jesus' Proclamation of the Kingdom of God* (Philadelphia: Fortress, 1971); W. Wrede, "Zum Thema 'Menschensohn,'" *ZNW* 5 (1904): 359–360.

280. In this respect, it is symptomatic that Delbert Burkett, while analyzing various hypotheses about why Jesus speaks about the Son of Man in the third person, does not consider an option that he might refer to his heavenly counterpart. Burkett offers the following list of options:

> If Jesus used the expression "Son of Man," to whom did he refer? The question arises from the fact that in all the Son of Man sayings, Jesus speaks of the Son of Man in the third person, as if referring to someone else, though in most cases the context makes clear that he is speaking of himself. This oddity has given rise to five main interpretations that seek to account for it. (1) Jesus habitually referred to himself in the third person with a title. (2) Jesus referred to himself not with a title, but with an Aramaic idiom by which one could refer to oneself in the third person. Later the church misinterpreted the idiom as a messianic title. (3) Jesus referred not solely to himself, but to a collective or corporate entity which included himself. Later the church misinterpreted the collective reference as a reference to Jesus alone. (4) Jesus referred not to himself, but to another messianic figure distinct from himself. Later the church applied the messianic title to Jesus. (5) Jesus did not speak about himself in the third person, but the early church did.

Burkett, *The Son of Man Debate*, 32.

281. The polemical appropriation of Jacob's doppelganger traditions might be also present in the heterodox Christian traditions about James the Just. In this respect, it is intriguing that in the so-called *First Apocalypse of James*, where James is envisioned as Jesus' double, his upper identity in the form of Christ appears as the divine image. Thus, *NHC* V, 3, 25, 1–4 reads: "Since I am an image of Him-who-is. But I have brought forth

the image of [him] so that the sons of Him-who-is might know that things are theirs." Parrott, *Nag Hammadi Codices V, 2-5 and VI with Papyrus Berolinensis 8502, 1 and 4*, 69–71. Further, in the course of the adept's initiation, his doppelganger announces that James' name will be changed and he will no longer be James, but he will be the One-who-is. (HNC V, 3, 27,8–10). Parrott, *Nag Hammadi Codices V, 2-5 and VI with Papyrus Berolinensis 8502, 1 and 4*, 75. Here, like in Jacob's traditions, the adept's name is changed during the upper identity's acquisition. On James the Just as Jesus' double, see R. Uro, "'Who Will Be Our Leader?' Authority and Autonomy in the Gospel of Thomas," in *Fair Play: Diversity and Conflict in Early Christianity; Essays in Honour of Heikki Räisänen* (ed. I. Dunderberg et al; VTSup, 103; Leiden; Brill, 2002), 457–485 at 473–476.

282. Neyrey notes that "the question asked in John 4:12, 'Are you greater than our father Jacob?' . . . belongs to a theme in the Gospel which asserts Jesus' superiority to the founding fathers of traditional Israelite faith (see 1:17–18; 5:38; 6:32). The thrust of this question suggests not only that Jesus replaces Jacob, Abraham, and Moses vis-à-vis God's revelation, but that an absolute claim is made on his behalf: he is greater than all of these in that he supplants them with new revelation." J. Neyrey, *The Gospel of John in Cultural and Rhetorical Perspective* (Grand Rapids: Eerdmans, 2009), 107.

283. On the polemical tensions between the Book of Daniel and the Enochic literature, see Boccaccini, *Roots of Rabbinic Judaism*, 169ff.

284. Raymond Brown argues that exegetes at least since Augustine have entertained this connection between John 1:51 and Gen 28:12. Brown, *The Gospel According to John*, 1.89.

285. On the presence of Jacob traditions in the first chapter of the fourth gospel, see C. K. Barrett, *The Gospel According to St. John* (2nd ed.; London: SPCK, 1978), 186; Brown, *The Gospel According to John*, 1.89–90; E. G. Clarke, "Jacob's Dream at Bethel as Interpreted in the Targums and the New Testament," *SR* 4.4 (1974–1975): 367–377 at 371–372; S. Friedman, "Graven Images," *Graven Images* 1 (1994): 233–238; Kugel, *In Potiphar's House*, 115; L. Morris, *The Gospel According to John* (Grand Rapids, MI: Eerdmans, 1995), 149; J. Neeb, "Jacob/Jesus Typology in John 1:51," *Proceedings of Eastern Great Lakes and Midwest Biblical Societies* 12 (1992): 83–89; idem, "Origen's Interpretation of Genesis 28:12 and the Rabbis," in *Origeniana Sexta* (ed. G. Dorival and A. Le Boulluec; Louvain: Leuven University Press, 1995), 71–80; Neyrey, "Jacob Allusions in John 1:51," 586–605; Odeberg, *Fourth Gospel*, 33–42; W. Rordorf, "Gen 28,10ff und Joh 1,51 in der patristischen Exegese," in *Johannes-Studien* (Zürich: Theologischer Verlag, 1991), 39–46; Rowland, "Jewish Apocalyptic and Targumic Tradition," 495–507; J. M. Spiegelman, "Struggling with the Image of God," *JPsJ* 10 (1986): 100–111; P. Trudinger, "An Israelite in Whom There Is no Guile: An Interpretative Note on John 1:45:51," *EvQ* 54 (1982): 117–120; von Heijne, *Messenger of the Lord*, 351ff.

286. Neyrey, "Jacob Allusions in John 1:51," 589.

287. Neyrey, "Jacob Allusions in John 1:51," 589.

288. Neyrey, "Jacob Allusions in John 1:51," 591.

289. Thus, for example, in *Genesis Rabbah* 68:13–14, Jacob's ladder receives an anthropomorphic reinterpretation being identified with Nebuchadnezzar's statue from Daniel 2

"And he dreamed"—this hints at Nebuchadnezzar's dream. "And behold a ladder (*sulam*)" suggests Nebuchadnezzar's image, for *semel* (image) is identical with *sulam* (ladder). Another interpretation: "And he dreamed" foreshadowed Nebuchadnezzar's dream. "And behold a ladder"—And behold a great image, etc. (Dan 2:31). "Set upon the earth" And whose brightness was surpassing, stood before thee. "And the top of it reached to heaven"—This image which was mighty. "And behold the angels of God ascending"—this intimates two; "And ascending" another two: that alludes to the princes of the four empires whose power is complete through them. "Ascending and descending": it is not written, descending and ascending, but 'ascending and descending': they [the empires] do ascend [to power] and it is indeed an ascent for them, but each is nevertheless lower than the preceding. It is written, As for that image, its head was of fine gold, its breast and its arms of silver, etc. Babylon was the highest of all, as it is written, Thou art the head of gold; and it is written, And after thee shall arise another kingdom inferior to thee. Again, And another third kingdom of brass; while of the last is written, And as the toes of the feet were part of iron, and part of clay, so part of the kingdom shall be strong, and part thereof broken. "And, behold, the Lord stood beside him": Thus it is written, And in the days of those kings shall the God of heaven set up a kingdom, which shall never be destroyed.

Freedman and Simon, *Midrash Rabbah*, 2.628–629. In *Zohar* I.149b, Jacob appears to be envisioned as the anthropomorphic pillar: "And behold a ladder set up on the earth. This ladder signifies the grade on which the other grades rest, to wit, the 'Foundation of the world.' And the top of it reached to heaven, so as to be attached to it. For this grade is the conclusion of the Body standing between the upper and the lower world in the same way as the sign of the covenant is situated at the end of the trunk of the body, between the thighs." Sperling and Simon, *The Zohar*, 2.79. It should be noted that the symbolism of the pillar and the ladder is closely intertwined in the Jewish mystical lore. Thus, Moshe Idel notes that "in some parts of the *Zohar* the pillar recurrently serves as a conduit for the ascent of the souls of the deceased righteous from a lower paradise to a higher one." M. Idel, *Ascensions on High in Jewish Mysticism: Pillars, Lines, Ladders* (Past Incorporated; CEUSH, 2; Budapest: Central European University Press, 2005), 101.

290. Neyrey, "Jacob Allusions in John 1:51," 601.

291. Kugel, *In Potiphar's House*, 115. In relation to this conceptual link, Christopher Rowland also notes that in *Gen. Rab.* 68:12 "Jacob takes the place of the ladder as the means whereby the angels ascend and descend between heaven and earth. The reason for this is that the Hebrew בו in Gen 28:12 could be taken to indicate that Jacob, and not the ladder, was the means of the angels' ascent and descent." Rowland, "Jewish Apocalyptic and Targumic Tradition," 501.

292. Kugel, *In Potiphar's House*, 115.

293. Such a concept is also present in a Christian interpolation found in the *Ladder of Jacob* 7:1–2: "And as for the angels you saw descending and ascending the ladder, in the last years there will be a man from the Most High, and he will desire to join the upper (things) with the lower." Lunt, "Ladder of Jacob," 2.410.

294. Hugo Odeberg notes that "the disciples of Jesus will see the angels of God ascending and descending upon the son of man i.e., they will see the connection being brought about between the celestial appearance, the Glory of Christ, and his appearance in the flesh." Odeberg, *Fourth Gospel*, 36. He also points to close parallels between the Son of Man in John 1:51 and another crucial figure, prominent in the heavenly counterpart traditions—namely, Metatron. He notes that "the only parallel in Jewish writings to this feature of John 1:51 is the mystical conception of Metatron as himself being the Jacob's ladder of communication between heaven and earth, in the sense of the salvation-mysticism." Odeberg, *Fourth Gospel*, 39.

295. Another distinguished scholar of the Johannine traditions, Charles Kingsley Barrett, argued that "for the ladder John substitutes the Son of Man." Barrett, *Gospel According to St. John*, 187.

296. Brown, *Gospel According to John*, 1.90. On the Son of Man as the ladder in John 1:51, see also Ashton, *Understanding the Fourth Gospel*, 342–348; B. Lindars, *The Gospel of John* (London: NCBC, 1972), 121–122.

297. Neyrey, "The Jacob Allusions in John 1:51," 589. On this, see also Bultmann, *The Gospel of John*, 105 n. 3; W. Michaelis, "Joh. 1,51, Gen. 28,12 und das Menschensohn-Problem," *TLZ* 85 (1960): 564–566; R. Schnackenburg, *The Gospel According to St. John* (trans. K. Smyth et al., 3 vols.; London: Burns and Oates, 1968–1982), 1.320–321.

298. Thus, for example, Raymond Brown ascertained that the search for details, symbols, or metaphors for the fig tree are "pure speculations." Brown, *Gospel According to John*, 1.83.

299. On the motif of Nathaniel under the fig tree, see J. Jeremias, "Die Berufung des Nathanael," *Angelos* 3 (1928): 2–5; C. F. D. Moule, "A Note on 'Under the Fig-Tree' in John 1:48, 50," *JTS* 5.2 (1954): 210–211; J. R. Michaels, "Nathanael under the Fig Tree," *ExpTim* 78 (1966-1967): 182–183; R. Kysar, *John: The Maverick Gospel* (Atlanta: John Knox Press, 1976), 41; D. Burkett, *The Son of Man in the Gospel of John* (JSNTSS, 56; Sheffield: Sheffield Academic, 1991), 113–114; C. R. Koester, "Messianic Exegesis and the Call of Nathanael," *JSNT* 39 (1990): 23–34; A. R. Kerr, *The Temple of Jesus' Body: The Temple Theme in the Gospel of John* (JSNTSS, 220; Sheffield: Sheffield Academic Press, 2002), 139–142; H. J. Ellens, "A Christian Pesher: John 1:51," *Proceedings of Eastern Great Lakes and Midwest Biblical Societies* 25 (2005): 143–155.

300. Jeremias, "Die Berufung des Nathanael," 2–5.

301. Ginzberg, *The Legends of the Jews*, 5.97.

302. Anderson and Stone, *A Synopsis of the Books of Adam and Eve*, 58E. The Armenian and the Slavonic versions of the *Primary Adam Books* attest to a similar tradition. The Armenian version of the *Primary Adam Books* 20:4–5 reads: "In my parts of the Garden I sought leaves of a tree to cover [my nakedness], and I could not find any on all the trees. For, at that hour all the trees of the Garden became leafless, except for the fig-tree alone. I took (its leaves) and covered my nakedness, and I stood by the tree of which I had eaten." Anderson and Stone, *A Synopsis of the Books of Adam and Eve*, 58E. The Slavonic version of the *Primary Adam Books* 21–22 reads: "I however, gathered fig leaves to cover my shame. Because of how Paradise was apportioned, the one half to Adam, and the other to me, all the trees in my half had let fall all their leaves. The fig tree, however, did not do this. And I took from its leaves and wrapped myself." *A*

Synopsis of the Books of Adam and Eve, 58E. Cf. also the Georgian version of the *Primary Adam Books* 20:5: "I took some and made a covering for myself and stood by the tree of which I had eaten, my children." Anderson and Stone, *A Synopsis of the Books of Adam and Eve*, 58E.

303. "Except that Adam never said to his fig-tree, why hast thou made me thus? He confessed that he was led astray; and he did not conceal the seducer." *The Ante-Nicene Fathers: Translations of the Writings of the Fathers down to A.D. 325* (ed. A. Roberts and J. Donaldson; 10 vols.; New York: Charles Scribner's Sons, 1899), 3.298.

304. Freedman and Simon, *Midrash Rabbah*, 1.152.

305. Sperling and Simon, *The Zohar*, 1.136.

306. *Zohar* I.53b reads: "And they sewed fig leaves together. This means, as explained elsewhere, that they learnt all kinds of enchantments and magic, and clung to worldly knowledge, as has been said. At that moment the stature of man was diminished by a hundred cubits. Thus a separation took place (of man from God), man was brought to judgment, and the earth was cursed, all as we have explained." Sperling and Simon, *The Zohar*, 1.169.

307. Another salient "arboreal" connection that was invoked in later Christian interpretation is an understanding of Jacob's ladder as Christ's cross, which also often became envisioned as the Tree of Life. Thus, Didymus the Blind in *De trinitate* 1.15.103 offers the following interpretation of Jacob's ladder: "The ladder foreshadows the cross by which the believers are going up to the heavenly tabernacles; on this ladder God himself was leaning, the one who for us was voluntarily nailed on the cross." *Didymus der Blinde: De trinitate* (ed. J. Honscheid; Buch 1; BKP, 44; Meisenheim am Glan: Hain, 1975), 14:238. Aphrahat in his *On Prayer* 5 unveils a very similar tradition:

> Our father Jacob too prayed at Bethel and saw the gate of heaven opened, with a ladder going up on high. This is a symbol of our Savior that Jacob saw; the gate of heaven is Christ, in accordance with what he said, "I am the gate of life; everyone who enters by me shall live forever" [John 10:7]. David too said, "This is the gate of the Lord, by which the righteous enter" [Ps 117:20 LXX]. Again, the ladder that Jacob saw is a symbol of our Savior, in that by means of him the just ascend from the lower to the upper realm. The ladder is also a symbol of our Savior's cross, which was raised up like a ladder, with the Lord standing above it.

M. Sheridan, *Genesis 12–50* (Ancient Christian Commentary on Scripture. Old Testament, 2; Downers Grove, IL: InterVarsity Press, 2002), 188. On these traditions, see Sheridan, *Genesis 12–50*, 186ff; E. J. Pentuic, *The Old Testament in Eastern Orthodox Tradition* (Oxford: Oxford University Press, 2014), 235–236.

308. Neyrey, "Jacob Allusions in John 1:51," 588.

309. Neyrey, "Jacob Allusions in John 1:51," 588.

310. Von Heijne, *Messenger of the Lord*, 351. On this connection, see also Gieschen, *Angelomorphic Christology*, 281; J. C. O'Neill, "Son of Man, Stone of Blood (John 1:51)," *NovT* 45 (2003): 374–381; Hayward, *Interpretations of the Name Israel*, 312–320.

311. Friedländer, *Pirke de Rabbi Eliezer*, 260.

312. Both passages about the reviving dew might have their earlier background in Psalm 133:2-3 where the precious oil running down the head (כשמן הטוב על הראש ירד) of Aaron is compared with the dew of eternal life sent by the deity.

313. Sperling and Simon, *The Zohar*, 2.21.

314. It is significant for our study that in Philo the Logos is portrayed as the cosmic tree.

315. On this imagery, see M. Glovino, *The Assyrian Sacred Tree* (Fribourg: Academic Press/Göttingen: Vandenhoeck & Ruprecht, 2007); L. F. Hartman, "The Great Tree and Nabuchodonosor's Madness," in *The Bible in Current Catholic Thought* (ed. J. L. McKenzie; New York: Herder & Herder, 1962), 75–82; M. Henze, *The Madness of King Nebuchadnezzar: The Ancient Near Eastern Origins and Early History of Interpretation of Daniel 4* (JSJSS, 61; Leiden: Brill, 1999); S. Parpola, "The Assyrian Tree of Life: Tracing the Origins of Jewish Monotheism and Greek Philosophy," *JNES* 52 (1993): 161–208; S. J. Reno, *The Sacred Tree as an Early Christian Literary Symbol: A Phenomenological Study* (Saarbrücken: Homo et Religio, 1978); G. Widengren, *The King and the Tree of Life in Ancient Near Eastern Religion* (UUA, 4; Wiesbaden: Otto Harrassowitz/Uppsala: A.-B. Lundequistska Bohkhandeln, 1951).

316. Ezek 31:3-9 reads:

> Consider Assyria, a cedar of Lebanon, with fair branches and forest shade, and of great height, its top among the clouds. The waters nourished it, the deep made it grow tall, making its rivers flow around the place it was planted, sending forth its streams to all the trees of the field. So it towered high above all the trees of the field; its boughs grew large and its branches long, from abundant water in its shoots. All the birds of the air made their nests in its boughs; under its branches all the animals of the field gave birth to their young; and in its shade all great nations lived. It was beautiful in its greatness, in the length of its branches; for its roots went down to abundant water. The cedars in the garden of God could not rival it, nor the fir trees equal its boughs; the plane trees were as nothing compared with its branches; no tree in the garden of God was like it in beauty. I made it beautiful with its mass of branches, the envy of all the trees of Eden that were in the garden of God.

317. Dan 4:10-12 reads: "Upon my bed this is what I saw; there was a tree at the center of the earth, and its height was great. The tree grew great and strong, its top reached to heaven, and it was visible to the ends of the whole earth. Its foliage was beautiful, its fruit abundant, and it provided food for all. The animals of the field found shade under it, the birds of the air nested in its branches, and from it all living beings were fed."

318. Henze, *The Madness of King Nebuchadnezzar*, 78.

319. The traditions about the mythological tree are documented in several sources, including the Book of Erra, a Mesopotamian work dated between the eleventh and the eighth century BCE. The Book of Erra 1:150-156 reads: "Where is the mēsu tree, the

flesh of the gods, the ornament of the king of the uni[verse]? That pure tree, that august youngster suited to supremacy, whose roots reached as deep down as the bottom of the underwor[ld]: a hundred double hours through the vast sea waters; whose top reached as high as the sky of [Anum]?" L. Cagni, *The Poem of Erra* (SANE, 1/3; Malibu: Undena, 1977), 32.

320. Furthermore, in view of Christ's identification with the Logos in the beginning of the first chapter, it is noteworthy that some of Philo's texts attempt to apply arboreal imagery to the Logos. Thus, Philo in *De plantatione* 8–9 unveils the following tradition: "And that the everlasting Word of the eternal God is the very sure and staunch prop of the Whole. He it is, who extending Himself from the midst to its utmost bounds and from its extremities to the midst again, keeps up through all its length Nature's unvanquished course, combining and compacting all its parts. For the Father Who begat Him constituted His Word such a Bond of the Universe as nothing can break." Colson and Whitaker, *Philo*, 3.217. Some scholars previously argued that this passage appears to reflect the tradition about the Logos as the cosmic tree. On this, see M. C. Horowitz, *Seeds of Virtue and Knowledge* (Princeton: Princeton University Press, 1998), 60–62. Another instance of application of such arboreal symbolism to the Logos can be found in Philo's *De plantatione* 36–38 where the divine word is associated with the Tree of Life:

> So we must turn to allegory, the method dear to men with their eyes opened. Indeed the sacred oracles most evidently afford us the clues for the use of this method. For they say that in the garden there are trees in no way resembling those with which we are familiar, but trees of Life, of Immortality, of Knowledge, of Apprehension, of Understanding, of the conception of good and evil. And these can be no growths of earthly soil, but must be those of the reasonable soul, namely its path according to virtue with life and immortality as its end, and its path according to evil ending in the shunning of these and in death. We must conceive therefore that the bountiful God plants in the soul as it were a garden of virtues and of the modes of conduct corresponding to each of them, a garden that brings the soul to perfect happiness. Because of this He assigned to the garden a site most suitable, bearing the name of "Eden," which means "luxuriance," symbol of a soul whose eyesight is perfect, disporting itself in virtues, leaping and skipping by reason of abundance of great joy, having set before it, as an enjoyment outweighing thousands.

Colson and Whitaker, *Philo*, 3.231.

321. Ezek 31:6: "All the birds of the air made their nests in its boughs."

322. Dan 4:12: "The birds of the air nested in its branches."

323. Scholars note that the motif of the birds of the air in the Parable of Mustard Seed (Matt 13:31–32 = Mark 4:30–32 = Luke 13:18–19) "seems to be a deliberate allusion to Nebuchadnezzar's dream of the tree." C. Evans, "Daniel in the New Testament," in *The Book of Daniel: Composition and Reception* (ed. J. J. Collins and P. W. Flint; 2 vols.; VTSup, 83; Leiden: Brill, 2001), 2.522.

324. See Mk 4:30–32: "He also said, 'With what can we compare the kingdom of God, or what parable will we use for it? It is like a mustard seed, which, when sown upon the ground, is the smallest of all the seeds on earth; yet when it is sown it grows up and becomes the greatest of all shrubs, and puts forth large branches, so that the birds of the air can make nests in its shade'"; Luke 13:18–19: "He said therefore, 'What is the kingdom of God like? And to what should I compare it? It is like a mustard seed that someone took and sowed in the garden; it grew and became a tree, and the birds of the air made nests in its branches'"; Matt 13:31–32: "He put before them another parable: 'The kingdom of heaven is like a mustard seed that someone took and sowed in his field; it is the smallest of all the seeds, but when it has grown it is the greatest of shrubs and becomes a tree, so that the birds of the air come and make nests in its branches.'"

325. In later Jewish materials, Jacob's ladder is often understood as the path of the souls. Thus, the *Commentary on Sefer Ha-Temunah* fol. 9b reads:

> And the supernal angels ascend to that Image, and this Image symbolizes the order of emanation which contains the supernal Sanctuary. Our Father Jacob, who saw the ladder in his dream, knew that even as there is a Sanctuary in the [world of] emanation above, so there is a Sanctuary below, for it is written: "and this is the gate of heaven." And from the Upper Sanctuary to the one below there is a kind of ladder, that is to say, a well-known path, which leads from Sanctuary to Sanctuary, and on this path the angels ascend and descend, and so likewise do the souls.

Idel, *Ascensions on High*, 178. Moshe Idel notes that in this passage "not only the path and the ladder but also the souls are mentioned explicitly." Idel, *Ascensions on High*, 178. For Jewish and Muslim traditions in which Jacob's ladder is envisioned as the Tree of Life, see A. Altmann, "The Ladder of Ascension," in *Studies in Mysticism and Religion Presented to Gershom G. Scholem on his Seventieth Birthday* (ed. E. Urbach; Jerusalem: Magnes, 1967), 1–32 at 20.

326. G. Scholem, *Origins of Kabbalah* (ed. R. J. Zwi Werblowsky; Princeton: Princeton University Press, 1973), 71.

327. Scholem, *Origins of Kabbalah*, 153.

328. Scholem, *Origins of Kabbalah*, 72. Scholem notes that

> the totality of the powers of God thus constitutes a cosmic tree that is not only the tree of souls from which the souls of the righteous fly out and to which, apparently, they return, but a tree that also depends upon the deeds of Israel. . . . This symbolism of the tree stresses an element that was to become essential in the Kabbalistic doctrine of the mystical vocation of the Jew. The tree is not only kept alive and watered by the source; its flowering, growth, and prosperity, its vigor or, alternatively, its languor depend upon the deeds of Israel.

Scholem, *Origins of Kabbalah*, 75–79.

329. Burchard, "Joseph and Aseneth," 2.226–227.

330. The attention should be drawn also to an enigmatic depiction of Aseneth's honeycomb found in *Jos. Asen.* 16—a puzzling image that might be related to the seer's role as a metropolis of the heavenly counterparts. In *Jos. Asen.* 16, Aseneth's heavenly visitor, the Anthropos, performs the following actions with the mysterious honeycomb:

> And the man said to the comb, "Come." And bees rose from the cells of that comb and the cells were innumerable, ten thousand (times) ten thousand and thousands upon thousands. And the bees were white as snow, and their wings like purple and like violet and like scarlet (stuff) and like gold-woven linen cloaks, and golden diadems (were) on their heads, and they had sharp stings, and they would not injure anyone. And all those bees encircled Aseneth from feet to head. And other bees were great and chosen like their queens, and they rose from the damaged part of the comb and encircled Aseneth's mouth, and made upon her mouth and her lips a comb similar to the comb which was lying before the man. And all those bees ate of (is) the comb which was on Aseneth's mouth. And the man said to the bees, "Go off to your place." And all the bees rose and flew and went away into heaven. And those who wanted to injure Aseneth fell to the ground and died. And the man stretched out his staff over the dead bees and said to them, "Rise you, too, and go away to your place." And the bees who had died rose and went into the court adjoining Aseneth's house and sought shelter on the fruit-bearing trees.

Burchard, "Joseph and Aseneth," 229–230. It is possible that Aseneth's honeycomb full of innumerable bees serves here as a metaphor for an eschatological congregation of the doppelgangers of the elect. This enigmatic depiction of bees gathering has puzzled scholars of the pseudepigraphon for a long time. One researcher, Anathea Portier-Young, previously suggested that Aseneth's honeycomb might be related to her heavenly identity as City of Refuge. Drawing her attention to the second group of bees, great and chosen ones who encircle the seer's face and construct upon her mouth and her lips a honeycomb, Portier-Young suggests that "this group of bees likely represents the 'chosen ones of God' who eat of the honeycomb of life, described by the angel in 16:14." In the conclusion of her article, Portier-Young argues that after Aseneth has partaken of the honeycomb's substance, "and the bees have constructed a second honeycomb upon her lips, she is at last made pure and transformed into an agent of divine mercy for others. This is what it means to be 'City of Refuge.'" A. E. Portier-Young, "Sweet Mercy Metropolis: Interpreting Aseneth's Honeycomb," *JSP* 14 (2005): 133–157 at 140 and 155.

331. The longer recension of *2 Enoch* 65:1–11 details the following description of the last aeon:

> Listen my children! Before ever anything existed, and before ever any created thing was created, the Lord created the whole of his creation, visible and invisible. . . . And when the whole creation, visible and invisible, which

the Lord has created, shall come to an end, then each person will go to the Lord's great judgment. And then all time will perish, and afterwards there will be neither years nor months nor days nor hours. They will be dissipated, and after that they will not be reckoned. But they will constitute a single age. And all the righteous, who escape from the Lord's great judgment, will be collected together into the great age. And the great age will come about for the righteous, and it will be eternal. And after that there will be among them neither weariness nor sickness nor affliction nor worry nor want nor debilitation nor night nor darkness. But they will have a great light, a great indestructible light, and paradise, great and incorruptible. For everything corruptible will pass away, and the incorruptible will come into being, and will be the shelter of the eternal residences.

Andersen, "2 Enoch," 1.190–192.

332. It is possible that these entities are understood as divine beings. A suggestion of the divine nature of Adoil comes from the shorter recension of *2 Enoch* 24, which places God in the midst of the invisible preexistent things; it reads: "Before any visible things had come into existence, and the light had not yet opened up, I, in the midst of the light, moved around in the invisible things, like one of them, as the sun moves around from east to west and from west to east." This depiction of the deity "moving around" like the sun in the "invisible things" is reminiscent of a solar system in which God is envisioned as a chief luminary and the "invisible things," possibly, as planets. Such a depiction might envision the "invisible things" as "lesser deities" or as part of the divine Pleroma.

333. The longer recension of *2 Enoch* 25 portrays the following disintegration of Adoil:

> And I commanded the lowest things: "Let one of the invisible things descend visibly!" And Adoil descended, extremely large. And I looked at him, and, behold, in his belly he had a great light. And I said to him, "Disintegrate yourself, Adoil, and let what is born from you become visible." And he disintegrated himself, and there came out a very great light. And I was in the midst of the [great] light. And light out of light is carried thus. And the great age came out, and it revealed all the creation which I had thought up to create. And I saw how good it was. And I placed for myself a throne, and I sat down on it. And then to the light I spoke: "You go up higher (than the throne), and be solidified [much higher than the throne], and become the foundation of the higher things." And there is nothing higher than the light, except nothing itself.

Andersen, "2 Enoch," 1.144.

334. This concept is very similar to the notion of the Manichaean "Last Statue," the image that will be explored later in our study. In relation to this concept, Samuel Lieu notes that "the 'Last Statue' will gather up all the unredeemed Light Elements after

the final destruction of the World, i.e. the ultimate '*apokatastasis*' and return them to the Kingdom of Light." S. N. C. Lieu, *Manichaeism in the Later Roman Empire and Medieval China* (Tübingen: Mohr/Siebeck, 1992), 17.

335. Van den Broek, "The Cathars: Medieval Gnostics?," 101–102.

336. Gardner and Lieu underline the personified nature of this mediatorial entity by defining the Last Statue as the "eschatological divinity, that at the time of the great fire and dissolution of the universe will ascend; the final gathering in of the living soul by the counsel of life, so that the entire history of conflict and mixture is from the going down of the First Man to the rising up of the Last Statue." Gardner and Lieu, *Manichaean Texts from the Roman Empire*, 294. On the Last Statue, see also G. Widengren, *Mani and Manichaeism* (New York: Holt, Rinehart and Winston, 1965), 68; M. Heuser, "Manichaean Myth According to the Coptic Sources," in *Studies in Manichaean Literature and Art* (ed. M. Heuser and H.-J. Klimkeit; NHMS, 46; Leiden: Brill, 1998), 3–108 at 86–87.

337. Gardner, *The Kephalaia of the Teacher*, 32. Cf. also *Keph.* 54:

> Then the summons and the obedience, the great counsel that came to the elements, which are set in conjunction. It mixed with them, it was established in silence. It bears up until the end time when it can arise and stand firm in the great fire. It will gather to it its own soul, and sculpt it in the Last Statue. You will also find it sweeps out and casts from it the pollution that is foreign to it. However, the life and the light that are in all things it gathers in to it, and builds upon its body. Then when this Last Statue will be perfect in all its limbs, then it can become free and ascend from that great struggle through the Living Spirit its father, the one who comes and brings a limb. He brings it up from within this gathering, the melting down and destruction of all things.

Keph. 75: "The Last Statue will be sculpted from the remnant of all things." *Keph.* 81: "At the end also it can gather itself together and sculpt its own self in the Last Statue. And it separates light from darkness." *Keph.* 86: "Also another great and glorious work he will enact at the end is the Last Statue, which he will bring up to the aeons of light." Gardner, *The Kephalaia of the Teacher*, 58, 76, 83, and 89.

338. In relation to this process, Heuser observes that "the elements of Light which have gathered themselves to a totality, the Last Statue, on the basis of the Thought of Light which is effective within them, are brought back into the kingdom of Light by the Living Spirit, the creator of the world (*PsB* 11,13f.; *Keph.* 54,21f.)." Heuser, "Manichaean Myth According to the Coptic Sources," 87.

339. Gardner, *The Kephalaia of the Teacher*, 174. Cf. also *Keph.* 104: "The first death is from the time when the light fell to the darkness, and was mixed in with the rulers of darkness; until the time when the light will become pure, and be separated from the darkness in that great fire. The remainder left behind there can build and add to the Last Statue." Gardner, *The Kephalaia of the Teacher*, 107–108.

340. Gardner, *The Kephalaia of the Teacher*, 157–158.

341. One can see that the "gathering" mediators, coming at the end of time, in many ways mirror the protological figures. In this respect, it is significant that in later Jewish lore the concept of the "gathering" mediator was often associated with the Protoplast's figure. In these traditions, the original form of the Protoplast, the "image," was understood as a "vessel" that was incorporating all human souls. Alon Goshen Gottstein points to an existence of such a concept in rabbinic literature where the original creation of humanity "in the image" implied that all human souls became part of this "image." Goshen Gottstein draws attention to the following passage from *Gen. Rab.* 24:2:

> R. Tanhuma in R. Banayah's name, and R. Berekiah in R. Eleazar's name said: He created him a shapeless mass, and he lay stretching from one end of the world to the other; as it is written, "Thine eyes did see my shapeless mass." R. Judah b. R. Simon said: While Adam lay a shapeless mass before Him at whose decree the world came into existence, He showed him every generation and its Sages, every generation and its judges, scribes, interpreters, and leaders. Said He to him: "Thine eyes did see unformed substance: the unformed substance [viz. thy potential descendants] which thine eyes did see has already been written in the book of Adam."

Freedman and Simon, *Midrash Rabbah*, 1.199–200. Goshen Gottstein suggests that in view of this confluence between Adam's cosmic form and the future generations shown to him, these future generations might be envisioned as part of Adam's body. In his opinion, a similar idea can be found in *b. Yeb.* 63b where all souls are incorporated in the body (*guf*): "R. Assi stated: The son of David will not come before all the souls in *Guf* are disposed of; since it is said, For the spirit that enwrappeth itself is from Me, and the souls which I have made." Epstein, *The Babylonian Talmud. Yebamot*, 63b. Goshen Gottstein argues that "This *guf* (literally, 'body') may well be the great body of humanity, seen either as the body of the manifestation of God or as the incarnating body of the primordial Adam." Goshen Gottstein, "The Body as Image of God," 192.

342. Gardner, *The Kephalaia of the Teacher*, 73.
343. Freedman and Simon, *Midrash Rabbah*, 2.634.
344. M. Idel, *Ascensions on High*, 102. On the eschatological pillar of the souls in the Zoharic tradition, see idem, *Ascensions on High*, 101–133.
345. A. Jellinek, *Bet ha-Midrash* (6 vols.; Jerusalem: Bamberger and Wahrmann, 1938), 2.28.
346. Odeberg, *3 Enoch*, 123.
347. Nathaniel Deutsch observes that

> both Metatron and Abathur are associated with the care of human souls in other ways. Metatron is characterized as the teacher of "all the souls of the dead that have died in their mothers' wombs, and of the babies that have died at their mothers' breasts, and of the schoolchildren that have died while studying the five books of the Torah." Abathur's watch house is depicted as

the storage place for the pre-existent souls that have not yet descended to earth. Once again we observe the logic of the angelic vice regent: he is a guardian of the gate; a lord of mediation. Therefore, Metatron and Abathur are in charge of souls that are betwixt and between different modes of existence. In one case, the souls belong to those individuals who were never born or who died too young to receive a proper education; in the other case, the souls are waiting for their corresponding bodies to be born.

Deutsch, *Guardians of the Gate*, 99.
348. Deutsch, *Guardians of the Gate*, 99.
349. *b. Avodah Zarah* 3b depicts Metatron as a teacher of the souls of those who died in their childhood; it reads:

What then does God do in the fourth quarter?—He sits and instructs the school children, as it is said, Whom shall one teach knowledge, and whom shall one make to understand the message? Them that are weaned from the milk. Who instructed them theretofore?—If you like, you may say Metatron, or it may be said that God did this as well as other things. And what does He do by night?—If you like you may say, the kind of thing He does by day; or it may be said that He rides a light cherub, and floats in eighteen thousand worlds; for it is said, The chariots of God are myriads, even thousands shinan.

Epstein, *The Babylonian Talmud. Avodah Zarah*, 3b.
350. *Synopse* §75 (*3 Enoch* 48C:12) attests to a similar tradition; it reads:

Metatron sits for three hours every day in the heaven above, and assembles all the souls of the dead that have died in their mother's wombs, and of the babes that have died at their mothers' breasts, and of the schoolchildren beneath the throne of glory, and sits them down around him in classes, in companies, and in groups, and teaches them Torah, and wisdom, and haggadah, and tradition, and he completes for them their study of the scroll of the Law, as it is written, "To whom shall one teach knowledge, whom shall one instruct in the tradition? Them that are weaned from the milk, them that are taken from the breasts."

Alexander, "3 Enoch," 1.313. A similar tradition is also found in the *Alphabet of R. Akiba*. See S. A. Wertheimer, *Batei Midrashot* (2 vols.; Jerusalem: Mossad Harav Kook, 1950–1953), 2.333–477.
351. It is intriguing that *Numbers Rabbah* 12:12 depicts Metatron as being in charge of the souls of the righteous whom he offers as the atonement for the sins of Israel; it reads: "R. Simeon expounded: When the Holy One, blessed be He, told Israel to set up the Tabernacle He intimated to the ministering angels that they also should make a Tabernacle, and when the one below was erected the other was erected on high. The

latter was the tabernacle of the youth whose name was Metatron, and therein he offers up the souls of the righteous to atone for Israel in the days of their exile." Freedman and Simon, *Midrash Rabbah*, 5.482–483.

352. Metatron's role as the leader of the souls might also be reflected in an obscure passage from *Zohar* II.161b in which one can find a description of the mysterious angelic "officer" put in charge of the souls; it reads:

> And even today, all inhabitants of the world, before they come to this world, all stand in their images as they exist in this world, in a single treasure-house, where all souls of the world are clothed in their images. As they are about to descend to this world, the blessed Holy One calls upon one official whom He has appointed over all souls destined to descend to this world, and says to him, "Go, bring Me the spirit of so-and-so." At that moment the soul comes, clothed in the image of this world, and the official presents her before the Holy King. The blessed Holy One speaks to her and adjures her that when she descends to this world she will engage in Torah in order to know Him and to know the mystery of faith.

Matt, *The Zohar: Pritzker Edition*, 5.431. Here, similar to the Metatron passages found in *b. Avodah Zarah* and *Sefer Hekhalot*, one sees, again, the motif of the importance of the study of the Torah that coincides with the tradition about the angelic captain of the souls. The description found in the *Zohar* also refers to the imagery of the store-house of the souls, which in its turn brings to memory the motifs found in the Slavonic apocalypse, with its imagery of the protological and eschatological reservoirs, in the form of the womb of the primordial aeon Adoil and the final aeon during which all the righteous souls will be gathered.

353. Reflecting on the portrayal of the Theotokos as the ladder in eastern Orthodox liturgical materials, Paul Ladouceur notes that

> the liturgical texts of the Orthodox Church refer in numerous places to the Mother of God as "ladder." For example: "ladder and gate" (Matins of Annunciation, Exaposteilarion; *FM* 459); "Gate of heaven and spiritual Ladder" (Matins of the Nativity, ode 7; *FM* 120); "living ladder" (Matins of the Entrance, ode 8; *FM* 189); her tomb "becomes a ladder to heaven" (Vespers of the Dormition; *FM* 506). Matins of the Annunciation gives us the precise reference: "Jacob saw in days of old the ladder that prefigured you, and said: 'This is the stair on which God shall tread'" (Matins of the Annunciation, ode 9; *FM* 458). The source of the image is thus Jacob's dream or vision recounted in Genesis 28.

P. Ladouceur, "Old Testament Prefigurations of the Mother of God," *SVTQ* 50 (2006): 5–57 at 15.

354. "Curious to know knowledge what is knowable to no one, the Virgin cried out to the attendant: How is it possible for a son to be born of inviolate loins? Tell me

please. To whom the angel minister replied with fear, and cried out thusly: . . . Rejoice, heavenly ladder (κλίμαξ ἐπουράνιε) by which did God Himself descend; Rejoice, bridge that is conveying unto heaven earth-born men. Rejoice, immortal wonder most renowned of the Angels." *The Akathist Hymn and Small Compline* (ed. S. Dedes and N. M. Vaporis; Brookline: Holy Cross Orthodox Press, 1990), 9.

355. The similar connection with Jacob's ladder is present in Andrew of Crete's Homily III *On the Dormition of Our Most Holy Lady, the Mother of God*: "Behold the ladder that Jacob saw in a moment of divine revelation, on which he saw God's angels moving up and down—whatever that ascent and descent signified. This is the gate of heaven, of which Jacob said, 'How awe-inspiring is this place! It is nothing other than God's dwelling—it is itself the gate of heaven!'" *On the Dormition of Mary: Early Patristic Homilies* (ed. B. E. Daley; PPS, 18; Crestwood: St. Vladimir's Seminary Press, 1997), 147–148. See also Theodore the Studite's *Encomium on the Dormition of Our Holy Lady, the Mother of God*: "But this is what the blessed Apostles answered to her, either speaking on their own or quoting the words of the prophets: 'Hail,' one said, 'ladder set up from earth to heaven, on which the Lord came down to us and returned to heaven again, as in the vision of the great patriarch Jacob!'" Daley, *On the Dormition of Mary*, 253.

356. In his first homily, he offers the following interpretation:

> And I almost forgot Jacob's ladder! What, then? Is it not obvious to everyone that it too is an anticipation and a type of you? Just as [Jacob] saw that ladder joining heaven and earth by its [two] ends, so that angels could go up and down on it, and just as he saw the strong and unconquerable one symbolically struggling with him, so you, too, are an intermediary; you have joined distant extremes together, and have become the ladder for God's descent to us-the God who has taken up our weak material and has woven it into a unity with himself, making the human person a mind that sees God. Therefore angels came down to [Christ], worshipping their God and master; and human beings have taken on the angelic way of life, in order to lay hold of heaven.

Daley, *On the Dormition of Mary*, 193. John of Damascus' Homily III reveals a similar tradition: "Today the spiritual, living ladder, by which the Most High has appeared on earth to 'walk among human beings,' has herself climbed the ladder of death, and gone up from earth to heaven." Daley, *On the Dormition of Mary*, 232.

357. Eugene Pentiuc draws attention to a similar interpretation of the Holy Virgin as the ladder found in a Greek prayer to the Theotokos attributed to Ephrem the Syrian, where Mary is called the "heavenly ladder, through whom we, the earthlings, are running up to heaven . . . ladder through which the heavenly angels came down to us." Pentiuc, *The Old Testament in Eastern Orthodox Tradition*, 234.

358. K. Linardou, "Depicting the Salvation," in *The Cult of the Mother of God in Byzantium: Texts and Images* (ed. L. Brubaker and M. B. Cunningham; Burlington, VT: Ashgate, 2011), 136.

Chapter Four: The Heavenly Counterpart Traditions
in *Joseph and Aseneth*

1. *Jos. Asen.* has been dated from the second century BCE to the fourth century CE. The majority of scholars believe that the text was composed between the first century BCE and the second century CE in a Jewish community in Egypt. On the date of the text, see G. Bohak, *Joseph and Aseneth and the Jewish Temple in Heliopolis* (Atlanta: Scholars, 1996), 81–100; C. Burchard, "Zum Text von 'Joseph und Aseneth,'" *JSJ* 1 (1970): 3–34; R. D. Chesnutt, *From Death to Life: Conversion in Joseph and Aseneth* (JSPSS, 16; Sheffield: Sheffield Academic Press, 1995), 80–85; Kraemer, *When Aseneth Met Joseph*, 225–239; M. Philonenko, *Joseph et Aséneth: Introduction, texte critique, traduction et notes* (SPB, 13; Leiden: Brill, 1968), 108–109; A. Standhartinger, *Das Frauenbild im Judentum der hellenistischen Zeit: Ein Beitrag anhand von "Joseph und Aseneth"* (AGAJU, 26; Leiden: Brill, 1995), 14–20.

2. For published texts of *Jos. Asen.*, see C. Burchard, "Joseph und Aseneth serbisch-kirchenslawisch: Text und Varianten," in *Gesammelte Studien zu Joseph & Aseneth* (SVTP, 39; Leiden, Brill, 1996), 53–102; idem, *Joseph und Aseneth kritisch herausgegeben von Christoph Burchard mit Unterstützung von Carsten Burfeind & Uta Barbara Fink*; idem, *A Minor Edition of the Armenian Version of Joseph und Aseneth* (HUAS, 10; Leuven: Peeters, 2010); U. B. Fink, *Joseph und Aseneth Revision des griechischen Textes und Edition der zweiten lateinischen Übersetzung* (FSBP, 5; Berlin: Walter de Gruyter, 2008); idem, "Joseph und Aseneth: Text, Übersetzung und Anmerkungen," in *Joseph und Aseneth* (ed. E. Reinmuth; Sapere, 15; Tübingen: Mohr/Siebeck, 2009), 56–137; V. M. Istrin, "Apokrif ob Iosife I Asenefe," in *Drevnosti: Trudy Slavjanskoj Kommissii Imperatorskogo Moskovskogo Arheologicheskogo Obschestva* 2 (1898): 146–199; Philonenko, *Joseph et Aséneth*; P.-R. Tragan, *Josep i Àsenet: Introducció, text grec revisat i notes* (LIS, 4; Barcelona: Alpha, 2005). In this study, I will be mainly using the longer version of the text that in certain instances will be supplemented with readings of the shorter version.

3. The pseudepigraphon is an expansion of the story of Joseph and Aseneth's marriage, an event that is only briefly mentioned in Gen 41:45: "Pharaoh gave Joseph the name Zaphenath-paneah; and he gave him Aseneth, daughter of Potiphera, priest of On, as his wife."

4. Burchard, "Joseph and Aseneth," 2.224–225.

5. Later rabbinic materials appear to be also knowledgeable about the motif of Joseph's heavenly counterpart. Thus, *Gen. Rab.* 60:15 details the following tradition: "And she said unto the servants: what man is this (*ha-lazeh*) that walketh in the field to meet us? R. Berekiah said in the name of R. Hiyya his father: She saw that he was comely, [*halaseh* having the same meaning] as in the verse, Behold, this (*ha-lazeh*) dreamer cometh (Gen 37:19). The Rabbis said: It refers to his guardian (angel), *halazeh* meaning, this one [the angel] is for his service." Freedman and Simon, *Midrash Rabbah*, 2.536.

6. In relation to this terminology, Kraemer observes that the form of the celestial visitor "is that of an *anthropos*, which several English translations render by the technically accurate but insufficient term man." Kraemer, *When Aseneth Met Joseph*, 120.

7. Burchard, *Joseph und Aseneth kritisch herausgegeben von Christoph Burchard mit Unterstützung von Carsten Burfeind & Uta Barbara Fink*, 176.

8. On a heavenly double as "light" in some heterodox Christian developments, see Stang, *Our Divine Double*, 122.

9. On the φως traditions, see G. Quispel, "Ezekiel 1:26 in Jewish Mysticism and Gnosis," *VC* 34 (1980): 1–13 at 6–7; Fossum, *Name of God*, 280; idem, *Image of the Invisible God*, 16–17; Bunta, *Moses, Adam and the Glory*, 92ff.

10. C. Deutsch, "Aseneth: Ascetical Practice, Vision, and Transformation," in *With Letters of Light: Studies in the Dead Sea Scrolls, Early Jewish Apocalypticism, Magic and Mysticism* (ed. D. Arbel and A. Orlov; Ekstasis, 2; Berlin: Walter de Gruyter, 2010), 333.

11. Thus, *Jos. Asen.* 5:5 tells the following about "earthly" Joseph's appearance: "And Joseph was dressed in an exquisite white tunic, and the robe which he had thrown around him was purple, made of linen interwoven with gold, and a golden crown (was) on his head, and around the crown were twelve chosen stones, and on top of the twelve stones were twelve golden rays. And a royal staff was in his left hand." Burchard, "Joseph and Aseneth," 2.208.

12. Thus, in the course of her transformation, Aseneth emulates both earthly Joseph and his heavenly counterpart. Randall Chesnutt further reflects on the similarities between Joseph and Aseneth by noting that

> The author is even careful to portray Aseneth in terms which correspond in many specific ways to the portrayal of Joseph. . . . The description of Joseph in 6.2–6 borders on an ascription of angelic status, but the same can be said of the descriptions of Aseneth in 18.9–11 and 20.6–7: she is likened to the sun just as Joseph is; heavenly beauty is ascribed to both; and both are said to radiate great light. . . . When Joseph first arrives at the house of Pentephres, he is clad in an exquisite white tunic and a golden crown with precious stones and has a royal staff in his hand (5.5); later Aseneth too dresses in a radiant white garment and wears a golden crown with costly stones and has a scepter in her hand (14.12–15; 18.5–6) . . . Aseneth and Joseph are almost mirror images of each other.

Chesnutt, *From Death to Life*, 110–111. On this, see also R. C. Douglas, "Liminality and Conversion in Joseph and Aseneth," *JSP* 3 (1988): 31–42 at 35.

13. Thus, *Jos. Asen.* 18:3–6 reads:

> And Aseneth remembered the man (from heaven) and his commandment, and she hurried and entered her second chamber where the chests (containing) her ornaments were, and opened her big coffer and brought out her first robe, (the one) of wedding, like lightning in appearance, and dressed in it. And she girded a golden and royal girdle around (herself) which was (made) of precious stones. And she put golden bracelets on her fingers and on her feet golden buskins, and precious ornaments she put around her neck in which innumerable costly (and) precious stones were fastened and

a golden crown she put on her head, and on that crown, in front on her brow, was a big sapphire stone, and around the big stone were six costly stones. And with a veil she covered her head like a bride, and she took a scepter in her hand.

Burchard, "Joseph and Aseneth," 2.232.

14. Allison, *Constructing Jesus*, 299. Kraemer also notices some of these parallels. She observes that "Joseph becomes the commander of Pharaoh's house, as his angelic double in *Aseneth* is the commander of the house of the Lord (14.7). The human Joseph in *Aseneth* indeed rides in the chariot of Pharaoh's 'second-in-command,' while his angelic double ascends back to heaven in a fiery celestial chariot. Both the earthly and the heavenly Joseph wear 'garments of fine linen,' although those of the angel are distinguished by their fiery light." Kraemer, *When Aseneth Met Joseph*, 126. Reflecting on Joseph's garments and the attires of his heavenly twin, Kraemer further observes that "clearly, the source(s) or perhaps the explanation for the details of the description of Joseph must be found elsewhere, as also for the description of Joseph's angelic double, who appears in 14.8–9. . . . Joseph's clothing bears a broad resemblance to both priestly and royal garments in numerous ancient traditions." Kraemer, *When Aseneth Met Joseph*, 164.

15. Kraemer, *When Aseneth Met Joseph*, 123.

16. On the use of Enochic traditions in *Jos. Asen.*, see Kraemer, *When Aseneth Met Joseph*, 111–114.

17. Kraemer, *When Aseneth Met Joseph*, 121.

18. *2 Enoch* 1:4–5: "Then two huge men appeared to me, the like of which I had never seen on earth. Their faces were like the shining sun; their eyes were like burning lamps; from their mouths fire was coming forth; their clothing was various singing; their wings were more glistering than gold; their hands were whiter than snow." Andersen, "2 Enoch," 1.106.

19. Alexander, "3 Enoch," 1.256.

20. Celia Deutsch observes that "even the title 'chief of the Lord and commander of the whole host of the Most High' evokes the angelic beings of early Jewish materials and later hekhalot texts." Deutsch, "Aseneth: Ascetical Practice, Vision, and Transformation," 332.

21. Kraemer, *When Aseneth Met Joseph*, 125.

22. On Aseneth's heavenly visitor as the archangel Michael, see Philonenko, *Joseph et Aséneth*, 178; Burchard, "Joseph and Aseneth," 2.225, n. k. Ross Kraemer cautions against such precise identifications by arguing that through such parallels "Philonenko and Burchard impute to the angelic figure a fixed identity that obscures the fluidity of traditions about angels in the ancient sources." Kraemer, *When Aseneth Met Joseph*, 125. I agree with Kraemer on this.

23. Boccaccini, *Beyond the Essene Hypothesis*, 71.

24. Yet, some early Enochic booklets, like the *Animal Apocalypse*, appear to be exhibiting different tendencies concerning the heavenly counterparts acquisition. As one remembers, in *Animal Apocalypse*, the transition to the angelomorphic identities of Noah and Moses are established on earth, during the adept's entrance into the Ark and the

ascent to Mount Sinai. The Watchers also change their identities upon entrance into the lower earthly realm.

25. Jung Hoon Kim sees the anthropological significance of the garments' change. He observes that "Aseneth's abandoning her original, idolatrous garments and instead adorning herself with a new linen robe and a wedding garment seems to have particular relevance to the Pauline concept of putting off the old man and putting on the new man (Col 3.9–10; Eph 4.22–24; cf. Gal 3.27; Rom 13.14)." J. H. Kim, *The Significance of Clothing Imagery in the Pauline Corpus* (JSNTSS, 268; London: T&T Clark, 2004), 60. He further observes that "every step of her [Aseneth's] conversion is represented by her changing garments, which point to the transformation of her very being." Kim, *The Significance of Clothing Imagery*, 69.

26. Tyson Putthoff notes that "the Anthropos's promise serves as a paradigm for Aseneth's experience as it will unfold hereafter (cf. 8.9). She will experience a continued transformation from this day forward." T. L. Putthoff, "Aseneth's Gastronomical Vision: Mystical Theophagy and the New Creation in Joseph and Aseneth," *JSP* 24 (2014): 96–117 at 101.

27. Kraemer notices the similarities between Aseneth's reclothing and the developments found in *2* and *3 Enoch*. On this, see Kraemer, *When Aseneth Met Joseph*, 127–128.

28. Burchard, "Joseph and Aseneth," 2.225.

29. Burchard, "Joseph and Aseneth," 2.227.

30. Kraemer, *When Aseneth Met Joseph*, 266.

31. Kraemer points out that although "the angel does not himself dress Aseneth in new clothing . . . there is no question that both versions of the story have Aseneth dress in glorious new clothing, not once, but twice. Immediately after the angel appears in her bedroom, he instructs Aseneth to remove her garments of mourning, to wash her face with living water, and to put on a brand-new robe, together with the 'double girdle of her virginity,' all of which she does." Kraemer, *When Aseneth Met Joseph*, 128.

32. Kraemer, *When Aseneth Met Joseph*, 128.

33. Kraemer, *When Aseneth Met Joseph*, 128.

34. Burchard, "Joseph and Aseneth," 2.228. Burchard, *Joseph und Aseneth kritisch herausgegeben von Christoph Burchard mit Unterstützung von Carsten Burfeind & Uta Barbara Fink*, 208.

35. Burchard, "Joseph and Aseneth," 2.228–229.

36. The angel also uses his right hand when he restores the honeycomb at the end of the initiatory meal in *Jos. Asen.* 16:16: "And the man stretched out his right hand and touched the comb where he had broken off (a portion), and it was restored and filled up, and at once it became whole as it was in the beginning." Burchard, "Joseph and Aseneth," 2.229. See also *Jos. Asen.* 17:3–4: "And the man for the third time stretched out his right hand, and touched the damaged part of the comb, and at once fire went up from the table and consumed the comb, but the table it did not injure. And much fragrance came forth from the burning of the comb, and filled the chamber." Burchard, "Joseph and Aseneth," 2.230.

37. Burchard, "Joseph and Aseneth," 2.229.

38. Burchard, *Joseph und Aseneth kritisch herausgegeben von Christoph Burchard mit Unterstützung von Carsten Burfeind & Uta Barbara Fink*, 186.

39. Burchard, "Joseph and Aseneth," 2.225–226.

40. H. Stenström, "Masculine or Feminine? Male Virgins in Joseph and Aseneth and the Book of Revelation," in *Identity Formation in the New Testament* (ed. B. Holmberg and M. Winninge; WUNT, 227; Tübingen: Mohr/Siebeck, 2008), 199–222.

41. P. Brown, *The Body and Society: Men, Women, and Sexual Renunciation in Early Christianity* (London: Faber & Faber, 1989), 115.

42. Casey, *The Excerpta ex Theodoto of Clement of Alexandria*, 57. Einar Thomassen argues that in this passage "the distinction male/female is equivalent to that of angel/cosmic human." E. Thomassen, "Valentinian Ideas about Salvation as Transformation," in *Metamorphoses: Resurrection, Body and Transformative Practices in Early Christianity* (ed. T. K. Seim and J. Økland; Ekstasis, 1; Berlin: Walter de Gruyter, 2009), 169–186 at 179. A similar idea might be also reflected in *Zostrianos* 131:6–7 (NHC VIII, 1, 131, 6–7): "Flee from the madness and the bondage of femaleness, and choose for yourself the salvation of maleness." *Nag Hammadi Codex VIII* (ed. J. H. Sieber; NHS, 31; Leiden: Brill, 1991), 223.

43. The motif of Aseneth's becoming "male" might be also hinted at in another important motif in the text—namely, her eight-day transformation that some scholars believe corresponds to the eight-day period culminating in the circumcision of a newborn Israelite male. On this, see M. Thiessen, "Aseneth's Eight-Day Transformation as Scriptural Justification for Conversion," *JSJ* 45 (2014): 229–249.

44. DeConick notes that "many Christian and Greek thinkers associated sexual differentiation with the fall and embodiment of the soul." DeConick, *Seek to See Him*, 17. DeConick sees such developments in Logion 11 of the *Gospel of Thomas*, which "alludes to the pre-condition of Adam's Fall when the human separated into two sexes: 'On the day when you were one, you became two.' The division of the sexes was closely associated with Adam's sin. In order to return to the pristine state, this division must be rectified." DeConick, *Seek to See Him*, 17. On this, see also J. H. Waszink, *Quinti Septimi Florentis Tertulliani: De Anima* (SVC, 100; Leiden: Brill, 2010), 419–420.

45. Cf. *Zohar* II.167b: "The Archetypal Adam took shape and form without the co-operation of the Female, but a second Man was engraved and formed from the seed and energy of the first within a female. Archetypal Adam took shape and bodily image out of the substance of the Future World without the conjunction of male and female." Sperling and Simon, *The Zohar*, 4.78.

46. In this anthropological perspective, even human males in their current fallen condition also require restoration. In this respect, Antti Marjanen rightly observes that when these texts "speak about the transformation of 'female' into 'male' they mean everybody, both men and women. Men too are 'female,' if their life is controlled by cosmic powers." A. Marjanen, "Women Disciples in the Gospel of Thomas," in *Thomas at the Crossroads: Essays on the Gospel of Thomas* (ed. R. Uro; Edinburgh: T&T Clark, 1998), 102–103.

47. April DeConick notes that in this anthropological perspective "salvation is based on returning to Adam's Pre-Fall state before the division of the sexes, and subsequently before the tasting of the forbidden fruit, sexual intercourse. This notion . . . is best paralleled by the saying from the encratite *Gospel of the Egyptians*: 'When Salome asked when what she had inquired about would be known, the Lord said, When you have trampled on the garment of shame and when the two become one and the male

with the female (is) neither male nor female' (Clement of Alexandria, *Strom.* 3.13.92)." DeConick, *Seek to See Him*, 18.

48. Layton, *Nag Hammadi Codex II, 2–7*, 1.93.
49. DeConick, *Seek to See Him*, 18.
50. For a similar motif, see also *Gos. Thom.* 22:

> Jesus saw infants being suckled. He said to his disciples, "These infants being suckled are like those who enter the kingdom." They said to him, "Shall we then, as children, enter the kingdom?" Jesus said to them, "When you make the two one, and when you make the inside like the outside and the outside like the inside, and the above like the below, and when you make the male and the female one and the same, so that the male not be male nor the female; and you fashion eyes in place of an eye, and a hand in place of a hand, and a foot in place of a foot, and a likeness in place of a likeness; then will you enter [the kingdom]."

Layton, *Nag Hammadi Codex II, 2–7*, 1.63.

51. Kraemer, *When Aseneth Met Joseph*, 209.
52. Orlov, *Divine Scapegoats*, 80–96.
53. Kraemer, *When Aseneth Met Joseph*, 209.
54. Layton, *Nag Hammadi Codex II, 2–7*, 1.91.
55. Concerning this motif, Anathea Portier-Young notes, "[O]bserving that its breath is also like the breath of the mouth of her visitor, she infers that the honeycomb has emanated from his mouth, having come into being by his speech (16.9). The angel confirms her suspicion, smiling at her understanding; she now demonstrates knowledge of heavenly mysteries (16.12)." Portier-Young, "Sweet Mercy Metropolis," 139.
56. Burchard, "Joseph and Aseneth," 2.228.
57. Burchard, "Joseph and Aseneth," 2.228.
58. A. Lieber, "I Set a Table before You: The Jewish Eschatological Character of Aseneth's Conversion Meal," *JSP* 14 (2004): 63–77 at 68.
59. See also Matt 3:4: "And the tempter came and said to him, 'If you are the Son of God, command these stones to become loaves of bread.' But he answered, 'It is written, Man shall not live by bread alone, but by every word that proceeds from the mouth of God.'"
60. Kraemer, *When Aseneth Met Joseph*, 127.
61. M. Schneider, "Joseph and Aseneth and Early Jewish Mysticism," *Kabbalah* 3 (1998): 303–344 [Hebrew]. Concerning Aseneth's conversion and the tradition of opening the statue's mouth with the divine Name, see also M. Philonenko, "Initiation et mystère dans Joseph et Aséneth," in *Initiation* (ed. C. J. Bleeker; SHR, 10; Leiden: Brill, 1965), 147–153; C. Burchard, "The Present State of Research on Joseph and Aseneth," in *Religion, Literature, and Society in Ancient Israel, Formative Christianity and Judaism* (ed. J. Neusner et al.; NPAJ, 2; Lanham: University Press of America, 1987), 31–52; G. Bohak, "Asenath's Honeycomb and Onias' Temple: The Key to Joseph and Asenath," in *Proceedings of the Eleventh World Congress of Jewish Studies, Division A* (ed. D. Assaf; Jerusalem: Magness,

1994), 163–170; G. Y. Glazov, *The Bridling of the Tongue and the Opening of the Mouth in Biblical Prophecy* (JSOTSS, 311; Sheffield: Sheffield Academic Press, 2001), 379.

62. Scholars previously noted that one of the crucial aspects of the Egyptian ritual of the "opening of the mouth" was an establishment of a connection between the statue and its doppelganger, also known as the "Ka." Thus, Andrey Bolshakov observes that "without changing anything in the outer appearance of the statue, the 'opening' transformed its very nature: initially an animated substance, it became linked to the Double." A. J. Bolshakov, *Man and his Double in Egyptian Ideology of the Old Kingdom* (ÄAT, 37; Wiesbaden: Harrassowitz, 1997), 173.

63. Regarding ancient rituals of washing of the mouth and the opening of the mouth of cultic statues, see P. J. Boden, *The Mesopotamian Washing of the Mouth (Mīs Pî) Ritual* (PhD diss.; Johns Hopkins University, 1998); A. Berlejung, *Die Theologie der Bilder: Herstellung und Einweihung von Kultbildern in Mesopotamien und die alttestamentliche Bilderpolemik* (OBO, 162; Freiburg: Universitätsverlag, 1998); *Born in Heaven, Made on Earth: The Making of the Cult Image in the Ancient Near East* (ed. M. B. Dick; Winona Lake, IN: Eisenbrauns, 1999); *The Induction of the Cult Image in Ancient Mesopotamia: The Mesopotamian Mīs Pî Ritual; Transliteration, Translation, and Commentary* (ed. C. Walker and M. B. Dick; SAALT, 1; Helsinki: University of Helsinki, 2001); V. A. Hurowitz, "The Mesopotamian God Image, from Womb to Tomb," *JAOS* 123 (2003): 147–157; *Cult Image and Divine Representation in the Ancient Near East* (ed. N. H. Walls; ASOR, 10; Boston: American Schools of Oriental Research, 2005); V. A. Hurowitz, "What Goes in Is What Comes out: Materials for Creating Cult Statues," in *Text, Artifact, and Image: Revealing Ancient Israelite Religion* (ed. G. M. Beckman and T. J. Lewis; BJS, 346; Providence, RI: Brown Judaic Studies, 2006), 3–23; G. K. Beale, *We Become What We Worship: A Biblical Theology of Idolatry* (Downers Grove, IL: InterVarsity Press, 2008); M. S. Smith, *God in Translation: Deities in Cross-Cultural Discourse in the Biblical World* (Grand Rapids, MI: Eerdmans, 2010); M. J. Lundberg, "The *Mis-Pi* Rituals and Incantations and Jeremiah 10:1–16," in *Uprooting and Planting: Essays on Jeremiah for Leslie Allen* (ed. J. Goldingay; London: T&T Clark, 2007), 210–227.

64. M. Idel, "Hermeticism and Judaism," in *Hermeticism and the Renaissance: Intellectual History and the Occult in Early Modern Europe* (ed. I. Merkel and A. G. Debus; Washington, DC: Folger Library, 1988), 59–76; idem, *Golem: Jewish Magical and Mystical Traditions on the Artificial Anthropoid* (Albany, NY: SUNY Press, 1990).

65. G. Scholem, "The Idea of the Golem," in *On the Kabbalah and Its Symbolism* (trans. R. Manheim; New York: Schocken, 1965), 159–165; E. L. Greenstein, "God's Golem: The Creation of the Human in Genesis 2," in *Creation in Jewish and Christian Tradition* (ed. H. Reventlow and Y. Hoffman; JSOTSS, 319; Sheffield: Sheffield Academic Press, 2002), 219–239. In later rabbinic testimonies, not only Golem but also some infamous biblical idols are brought to life through the placement of the divine Name in their mouths. One such story occurs in *Zohar* II.175a, in which the idol of King Nebuchadnezzar is vivified when a vessel of the Temple with the divine Name is put in its mouth:

> King Nebuchadnezzar made an image of gold whose height was sixty cubits high and whose width was six cubits. Nebuchadnezzar said, "The image

that I saw had a head of gold and belly of silver. . . . I will make one all of gold, so that a lower coronet of gold will be upon its head." It has been taught: On that day he gathered all peoples, nations, and tongues to worship that image, and he took one of the vessels of the Temple upon which was engraved the Holy Name and put it in the mouth of that image, and it began speaking grandly until Daniel came and approached the image, and said, "I am the messenger of the supreme Lord. I decree upon you to leave here!" He invoked the Holy Name, and that vessel came out, and the image fell and broke.

Matt, *The Zohar: Pritzker Edition*, 5.520; PRE 55 suggests that another infamous biblical idol—the golden calf—was created with the help of the divine Name; it reads:

They broke off their earrings which were in their own ears, and they gave (them) to Aaron, as it is said, "And all the people brake off the golden rings which were in their ears" (Exod 32:3). "Which were in the ears of their wives" is not written here, but "which were in their ears." Aaron found among the earrings one plate of gold upon which the Holy Name was written, and engraved thereon was the figure of a calf, and that (plate) alone did he cast into the fiery furnace, as it is said, "So they gave it me: and I cast it into the fire, and there came out this calf." It is not written here, "And I cast them in," but "And I cast it in the fire, and there came out this calf." The calf came out lowing, and the Israelites saw it, and they went astray after it.

Friedländer, *Pirke de Rabbi Eliezer*, 354–355. For in-depth discussion of this tradition, see Scholem, *On the Kabbalah and Its Symbolism*, 182; Glazov, *The Bridling of the Tongue*, 382.

66. With respect to these traditions, see C. L. Beckerleg, *The "Image of God" in Eden* (PhD diss.; Harvard University, 2009).

67. In both texts, the spiritual feeding has salvific and eschatological significance. It returns a human seer to the protological condition when the protoplast was fed by the light of God's presence. As Ira Chernus rightly noted, this tradition of the protoplast's spiritual nourishment also appears to be reflected in *3 Enoch*. I. Chernus, *Mysticism in Rabbinic Judaism* (Studies in the History of Midrash; Berlin: Walter de Gruyter, 1982), 75–76. Thus, *3 Enoch* 5:3 says that "the first man and his generation dwelt at the gate of the garden of Eden so that they might gaze at the bright image of the Shekhinah." Alexander, "3 Enoch," 1.259. An early witness to such a tradition of the protoplast's feeding on the divine glory might also be reflected in *2 Enoch*, in which the deity orders the angel to open the heavens so Adam will gain access to the vision of Glory.

68. Concerning these traditions, see Idel, *Golem*, 31, 91–92, 103, 139.

69. Gieschen, *Angelomorphic Christology*, 71.

70. Smith, "Prayer of Joseph," 2.713; Denis, *Fragmenta pseudepigraphorum quae supersunt graeca*, 61.

71. Thus, *Sefer Haqqomah*, 155–164, reads:

> And (the) angels who are with him come and encircle the Throne of Glory. They are on one side and the (celestial) creatures are on the other side, and the Shekhinah is on the Throne of Glory in the center. And one creature goes up over the seraphim and descends on the tabernacle of the lad whose name is Metatron and says in a great voice, a thin voice of silence, "The Throne of Glory is glistening!" Immediately, the angels fall silent and the ʿirin and the qadushin are still. They hurry and hasten into the river of fire. And the celestial creatures turn their faces towards the earth, and this lad whose name is Metatron, brings the fire of deafness and puts (it) in the ears of the celestial creatures so that they do not hear the sound of the speech of the Holy One, blessed be He, and the explicit Name that the lad, whose name is Metatron, utters at that time in seven voices, in seventy voices, in living, pure, honored, holy, awesome, worthy, brave, strong, and holy Name.

M. Cohen, *The Shiʿur Qomah: Texts and Recensions* (TSAJ, 9; Tübingen: Mohr/Siebeck, 1985), 162–164. A similar motif can be found in the Hekhalot materials. Thus, *Synopse* §390 reads:

> One *hayyah* rises above the seraphim and descends upon the tabernacle of the youth whose name is Metatron, and says in a great voice, a voice of sheer silence: "The Throne of Glory is shining." Suddenly the angels fall silent. The watchers and the holy ones become quiet. They are silent, and are pushed into the river of fire. The *hayyot* put their faces on the ground, and this youth whose name is Metatron brings the fire of deafness and puts it into their ears so that they can not hear the sound of God's speech or the ineffable Name. The youth whose name is Metatron then invokes, in seven voices, his living, pure, honored, awesome, holy, noble, strong, beloved, mighty, powerful Name.

Schäfer et al., *Synopse*, 164.

72. Philo's *Conf.* 146 reads: "But if there be any as yet unfit to be called a Son of God, let him press to take his place under God's First-born, the Word, who holds the eldership among the angels, their ruler as it were. And many names are his, for he is called, 'the Beginning,' and the Name of God, and His Word, and the Man after His image, and 'he that sees,' that is Israel." Colson and Whitaker, *Philo*, 4.89–91. Richard Hayward also notes that "Philo's words in *De Abrahamo* 50–7 strongly suggest that, just as the three names Abraham, Isaac, and Jacob are inseparably bound up with the Divine Name given to human beings, so also the single name Israel is to be associated with the Divine Name. He does not state this explicitly; but it is a natural inference from what he has said here and in other places in his writings." Hayward, *Interpretations of the Name*, 184.

73. Fossum, *Name of God*, 314.
74. Fossum, *Name of God*, 314.
75. *Dialogue with Trypho* 75:2 reads: "Consider well who it was that led your fathers into the promised land, namely he who was first named Auses [Hosea], but later

renamed Jesus [Joshua]. If you keep this in mind, you will also realize that the name of him who said to Moses, My name is in him, was Jesus. Indeed, he was also called Israel. And he similarly bestowed this name upon Jacob." *St. Justin Martyr: Dialogue with Trypho* (trans. T. F. Falls and T. P. Halton; ed. M. Slusser; Washington, DC: Catholic University of America Press, 2003), 117.

76. Fossum, *Name of God*, 314.
77. Segal, *Two Powers in Heaven*, 200.
78. Gieschen, *Angelomorphic Christology*, 140.
79. *3 Enoch* 48C:7 reads: "I called him by my name, 'The lesser YHWH, Prince of the Divine Presence, knower of secrets.' Every secret I have revealed to him in love, every mystery I have made known to him in uprightness." Alexander, "3 Enoch," 1.312.
80. Alexander, "3 Enoch," 1.265–266.
81. *3 Enoch* 48:1 reads: "Metatron has seventy names, and these are they . . . lesser YHWH, after the name of his Master, as it is written, 'My name is in him.'" Alexander, "3 Enoch," 1.313–314.
82. Fossum, *Name of God*, 298.
83. Fossum, *Name of God*, 298.
84. See *b. Avodah Zarah* 3b; *3 Enoch* 48C:12. The connection between the possession of the divine Name and the guardianship of souls is also made in *Zohar* II.129a where the mysterious heavenly figure, named Jehudiam, responsible for the "celestial figures" of the righteous humans, is also associated with the divine Name. Thus, from *Zohar* II.129a, we learn the following: "An angel appears who is the storekeeper of the celestial figures of the righteous, and this angel's name is Jehudiam because of his office ('over the people of the Jews') and he is crowned with a crown on which is engraved the Holy Name . . . for there is no righteous person in the world whose image is not engraved in heaven under the authority of that angel." Sperling and Simon, *The Zohar*, 3.367.
85. For Michael's association with the divine Name, see J. Daniélou, *The Theology of Jewish Christianity* (London: Darton, Longman & Todd, 1964), 123–131.
86. Knibb, *Ethiopic Book of Enoch*, 2.162–163.
87. Knibb, *Ethiopic Book of Enoch*, 2.163–164.
88. C. Kaplan, "The Hidden Name," *JSOR* 13 (1929): 181–184. With respect to the oath imagery in *1 Enoch* 69, Daniel Olson notes that "it is common place in mystical Judaism that the Name of God is the force which binds and orders all things in creation, and a word that binds is by definition an oath. The idea is certainly old enough to appear in the 'Parables.'" Olson, *Enoch: A New Translation*, 271.
89. Regarding the association of the demiurgic name with the oath, see S. M. McDonough, *YHWH at Patmos: Rev. 1:4 in Its Hellenistic and Early Jewish Setting* (WUNT, 2.107; Tübingen: Mohr/Siebeck, 1999), 128–130; Fossum, *Name of God*, 257ff.
90. In this respect, it is intriguing that some rabbinic texts describe the process of cursing using the divine Name. One such tradition, for example, can be found in *Mekhilta de-Rabbi Ishmael*, which speaks about cursing using the Tetragrammaton: "[C]urse it means by using the divine name, so also when it says do not curse it means not to curse by using the divine name." *Mekhilta de-Rabbi Ishmael: A Critical Edition on the Basis of the Manuscripts and Early Editions with an English Translation, Introduction*

and Notes (ed. J. Z. Lauterbach; 2 vols.; Philadelphia: Jewish Publication Society, 2004), 2.388. Jonathan Ben-Dov notes that "oaths and the great name as elements of creation appear again in later Jewish literature such as Hekhalot and late midrash." J. Ben-Dov, "Exegetical Notes on Cosmology in the Parables of Enoch," in *Enoch and the Messiah Son of Man*, 143–150 at 149.

91. The demiurgic powers of the divine Name are also unfolded in the aforementioned passage from *3 Enoch* 12:1–2. The demiurgic list found in that passage is reminiscent of the list given in *1 Enoch* 69. Cf. also *3 Enoch* 41:1–3:

> R. Ishmael said: Metatron said to me: Come and I will show you the letters by which heaven and earth were created; the letters by which seas and rivers were created; the letters by which mountains and hills were created; the letters by which trees and grasses were created; the letters by which stars and constellations were created; the letters by which the orb of the moon and the disk of the sun, Orion and the Pleiades, and all the various luminaries of Raqia were created; the letters by which the ministering angels were created; the letters by which the seraphim and the creatures were created; the letters by which the throne of glory and the wheels of the chariot were created; the letters by which the necessities of the world were created; the letters by which wisdom and understanding, knowledge and intelligence, humility and rectitude were created, by which the whole world is sustained. I went with him and he took me by his hand, bore me up on his wings, and showed me those letters, engraved with a pen of flame upon the throne of glory, and sparks and lightnings shoot from them and cover all the chambers of Arabot.

Alexander, "3 Enoch," 1.292.

92. Cf. *Gen. Rab.* 12:10: "R. Berekiah said in the name of R. Judah b. R. Simeon: Not with labour or wearying toil did the Holy One, blessed be He, create the world, but: 'By the Word of the Lord, and the heavens were already made.' By means of *heh*, He created them." Freedman and Simon, *Midrash Rabbah*, 1.95; *Gen. Rab.* 12:10: "R. Abbahu said in R. Johanan's name: He created them with the letter *heh*. All letters demand an effort to pronounce them, whereas the *heh* demands no effort; similarly, not with labour or wearying toil did the Holy One, blessed be He, create His world." Freedman and Simon, *Midrash Rabbah*, 1.95; *Gen. Rab.* 12:10:

> With a *heh* created He them, it follows that this world was created by means of a *heh*. Now the *heh* is closed on all sides and open underneath: that is an indication that all the dead descend into *she'ol*; its upper hook is an indication that they are destined to ascend thence; the opening at the side is a hint to penitents. The next world was created with a *yod*: as the *yod* has a bent [curved] back, so are the wicked: their erectness shall be bent and their faces blackened [with shame] in the Messianic future, as it is written, And the loftiness of man shall be bowed down.

Freedman and Simon, *Midrash Rabbah*, 1.95; *b. Men.* 29b: "It refers to the two worlds which the Holy One, blessed be He, created, one with the letter *he* and the other with the letter *yod*. Yet I do not know whether the future world was created with the *yod* and this world with the *he* or this world with the *yod* and the future world with the *he*; but since it is written, These are the generations of the heaven and of the earth when they were created." Epstein, *The Babylonian Talmud. Menahoth*, 29b. Cf. also *3 Enoch* 15B:5, where Metatron reveals to Moses the letters of the divine Name that are understood there as an oath: "But Moses said to him, 'Not so! Lest I incur guilt.' Metatron said to him, 'Receive the letters of an oath which cannot be broken!'" Alexander, "3 Enoch," 1.304.

93. Concerning these traditions, see Fossum, *Name of God*, 253–256.

94. In the Palestinian targumic tradition (*Targ. Neof.*, *Frag. Targ.*), the divine command יהי uttered by God during the creation of the world is identified with the Tetragrammaton. For a detailed discussion of this tradition, see Fossum, *Name of God*, 80. Thus, *Targ. Neof.* reads: "He who spoke, and the world was there from the beginning, and is to say to it: יהי and it will be there,—He it is who has sent me to you." *Fragmentary Targum* attests to a similar tradition: "'He who said to the world from the beginning: יהי and it was there, and is to say to it: יהי and it will be there.' And He said: Thus you shall say to the Israelites: 'He has sent me to you.'" The connection between the divine command and the divine Name has very ancient roots and is found already in the *Prayer of Manasseh* (2 century BCE–1 century CE) in which the divine "Word of Command" and God's Name are put in parallel. *Prayer of Manasseh* 1–3 reads: "O Lord, God of our fathers, God of Abraham, Isaac, Jacob, and their righteous offspring; He who made the heaven and the earth with all their beauty; He who bound the sea and established it by the command of his word, He who closed the bottomless pit and sealed it by his powerful and glorious name." J. H. Charlesworth, "Prayer of Manasseh," in *The Old Testament Pseudepigrapha*, 2.625–637 at 634. Regarding the same tradition, see also *Samaritan Liturgy* 445.2: "It was created by a word, [namely, by] יהי and, in a flash, it was made new."

95. Hannah, *Michael and Christ*, 52.

96. It is significant for our study that the exemplars' endowment with both the divine Name and the heavenly identity occur in the same pivotal moment of the biblical hero's story. Thus, in Jacob's traditions, both the acquisition of the Name and the heavenly identity occur during the Jabbok encounter, and in Moses' traditions, the dual acquisition happens during the prophet's encounter with God on Horeb/Sinai.

97. On this tradition, see Fossum, *Name of God*, 87–94; Gieschen, *Angelomorphic Christology*, 77–78. It appears that in the Samaritan tradition Moses himself might become the divine Name. Thus, *Memar Marqa* IV.1 unveils this mysterious identification: "Where is there a prophet like Moses and who can compare with Moses, whose name was made the name of his Lord?" Reflecting on this passage, Macdonald observes that "the name משה is held to be the same in essence as שמה." J. Macdonald, *Memar Marqah: The Teaching of Marqah* (2 vols.; BZAW, 84; Berlin: Walter de Gruyter, 1963), 2.137. On this, see also Fossum, *Name of God*, 88. See also the *Samaritan Targum* to Exod 23:20–21.

98. The motif of the investiture with the divine Name can be found also in the *Samaritan Liturgy* (*Defter*), liturgical materials in which praise is given to the great

prophet who clad himself in the Name of the deity. For these materials, see A. E. Cowley, *The Samaritan Liturgy* (2 vols.; Oxford: Clarendon, 1908).

99. *Memar Marqah* I.1 reads: "He said Moses, Moses, revealing to him that he would be vested with prophethood and the divine Name." Macdonald, *Memar Marqah*, 2.4.

100. *Memar Marqah* I.9 iterates a similar tradition: "I have vested you with my Name." Macdonald, *Memar Marqah*, 2.32.; *Memar Marqah* II.12 reads: "Exalted is the great prophet Moses whom his Lord vested with His Name.... The Four Names led him to waters of life, in order that he might be exalted and honoured in every place: the name with which God vested him, the name which God revealed to him, the name by which God glorified him, the name by which God magnified him.... The first name, with which Genesis opens, was that which he was vested with and by which he was made strong." Macdonald, *Memar Marqah*, 2.80–81; *Memar Marqah* IV.7: "O Thou who hast crowned me with Thy light and magnified me with wonders and honoured me with Thy glory and hid me in Thy palm and brought me into the Sanctuary of the Unseen and vested me with Thy name, by which Thou didst create the world, and revealed to me Thy great name and taught me Thy secrets." Macdonald, *Memar Marqah*, 2.158.

101. On crowning with the divine Name in later Jewish mysticism, see A. Green, *Keter: The Crown of God in Early Jewish Mysticism* (Princeton: Princeton University Press, 1997), 42ff.

102. Macdonald, *Memar Marqah*, 2.31.

103. Jacobson, *The Exagoge of Ezekiel*, 54.

104. Fossum argues that "Moses' investiture and coronation, which usually were connected with his ascension of Mt. Sinai, were seen not only as a heavenly enthronement, but also as a restoration of the glory lost by Adam. The possession of this Glory was conceived of as a sharing of God's own Name, i.e., the divine nature." Fossum, *Name of God*, 94.

105. *Memar Marqah* VI.3 reads: "He [Moses] drew near to the holy deep darkness where the Divine One was, and he saw the wonders of the unseen—a sight no one else could see. His image dwelt on him. How terrifying to anyone who beholds and no one is able to stand before it!" Macdonald, *Memar Marqah*, 2.223.

106. Such developments might have biblical roots since in the fourth gospel the Name or the Logos appears to be understood as the heavenly alter ego of Jesus.

107. Fossum, *Name of God*, 95.

108. Layton, *Nag Hammadi Codex II, 2–7*, 1.147.

109. G. Quispel, "Gnosticism and the New Testament," in *The Bible in Modern Scholarship* (ed. J. P. Hyatt; Nashville: Abingdon Press, 1965), 252–271 at 267.

110. On this passage, see Fossum, *Name of God*, 95–96.

111. Casey, *The Excerpta ex Theodoto of Clement of Alexandria*, 57–59.

112. Several words should be said about the spatial settings in which Aseneth meets her heavenly visitor. In *Jos. Asen.* 14:5, Aseneth wonders how her heavenly visitor can enter her chamber: "And she said, Who is he that calls me, because the door of my chamber is closed, and the tower is high, and how then did he come into my chamber?"

Burchard, "Joseph and Aseneth," 2.224. Scholars previously noticed that the structure of Aseneth's palace is reminiscent of the tripartite structure of the Jerusalem Temple. So she encounters her heavenly guest literally in the "holy of holies" of her palace. Thus, Andrea Lieber observes that Aseneth's "chamber is configured like a temple. Her bedroom is situated in the third, innermost chamber of the palace, and she is attended by seven virginal guardians. . . . That the anthropomorphic angel appears in such a space is no surprise, as the setting is actually rather appropriate. Aseneth's chamber is the central component of what is effectively both palace and temple." Lieber, "I Set a Table before You," 67. Similarly Tyson Putthoff argues that Aseneth's "quarters have become an incubation chamber, modelled on Ezekiel's temple (Ezek 40–46), where she has summoned the divine to a meeting." Putthoff, "Aseneth's Gastronomical Vision," 100. On the temple structure of Aseneth's house, see also Bohak, *Joseph and Aseneth and the Jewish Temple in Heliopolis*, 68. If the interaction between the seer and the angel takes place in the "holy of holies" of Aseneth's temple, it is noteworthy that in some Christian traditions of the bridal chamber, it was closely associated with the Holy of Holies. Thus, Risto Uro notes that "the bridal chamber is compared to the holiest room in the temple of Jerusalem, 'the Holy of the Holies' (*Gos. Phil.* 69 [§76]; cf. 84 [§125]), and is generally used as expressing the highest revelation." R. Uro, "Gnostic Rituals from a Cognitive Perspective," in *Explaining Christian Origins and Early Judaism* (ed. P. Luomanen, I. Pyysiäinen, and R. Uro; BIS, 89; Leiden: Brill, 2007), 120. On the imagery of bridal chamber, see also R. Uro, "The Bridal Chamber and Other Mysteries: Ritual System and Ritual Transmission in the Valentinian Movement," in *Sacred Marriages: The Divine-Human Sexual Metaphor from Sumer to Early Christianity* (ed. M. Nissinen and R. Uro; Winona Lake, IN: Eisenbrauns, 2008), 457–486.

113. It is significant that throughout the narrative Aseneth is envisioned as a bride. Gilles Quispel notes that in the sacrament of the bridal chamber an adept becomes a bride. Quispel, "Genius and Spirit," 113.

114. It appears that some heterodox Christian materials operated with the notion of the celestial and terrestrial bridal chambers coexisting simultaneously and in some ways mirroring each other. Such traditions might be present in *Jos. Asen.* where two consummations are present: the celestial and the terrestrial that mirror each other. In relation to these conceptual currents, Risto Uro observes that "scholars' interpretations of the different uses of the bridal chamber vary greatly and it may be impossible to reach an agreement about the meaning and the content of the imagery in the *Gospel of Philip*. What seems to be relatively certain, however, is that the gospel envisions at least two bridal chambers: the 'great' celestial bridal chamber (*Gos. Phil.* 71 [§82]; see also 84–86 [§§125–127]) and a 'mirrored bridal chamber,' which could be understood as a kind of worldly counterpart of this celestial bridal chamber." Uro, "Gnostic Rituals from a Cognitive Perspective," 124.

115. In the view of the traditions of Aseneth's anointment with the "blessed ointment of incorruption," some scholars note that "the bridal chamber imagery is, on several occasions, associated with some ritual procedures, especially with chrism (*Gos. Phil.* 67 [§66]; 67 [§67]; 74 [§95]; cf. 84 [§125])." Uro, "Gnostic Rituals from a Cognitive Perspective," 124. On the oil imagery in *Jos. Asen.*, see R. D. Chesnutt, "Perceptions of Oil in Early Judaism and the Meal Formula in Joseph and Aseneth," *JSP* 14 (2005): 113–132.

116. DeConick argues that in Valentinian traditions the heavenly counterpart of the adept is represented sometimes by a gender counterpart. She notes that

> according to the *Gospel of Philip*, the angel with whom you are to be reunited is your sexual opposite. In 65:8–11, it is explained that no one can escape the sexual advances of the unclean spirits unless one has taken on the appropriate "male power" or "female power" which are respectively "the bridegroom and the bride." Thus "if the image and the angel are united with one another" the original androgyny is restored, and the unclean spirit can no longer violate the person (65:24–26). In the case of the *Excerpta ex Theodoto*, the angels are the "male" aspect of the original androgynous Man of Genesis 1:27, while the "superior seed" represents the female aspect. This seed was removed from Adam and became Eve. Those of the female "superior seed" must "become men" uniting with the male angel. In this way, the original androgyny of the primal Man is restored since Eve has reentered Adam. Thus: "we are raised up 'equal to angels,' and restored to unity with the males, member for member." Therefore, our angels are our "bridegrooms."

DeConick, *Seek to See Him*, 149–150.
117. Quispel, "Genius and Spirit," 104.
118. Quispel, "Genius and Spirit," 104.
119. See Burchard, "Joseph and Aseneth," 2.233–234; Kraemer, *When Aseneth Met Joseph*, 61.
120. In relation to the status of these apocryphal materials in early Christianity, Averil Cameron argues that "the apocryphal Acts cannot be marginalized; they too were integrally related to the general culture of the second and third centuries. But more specifically, they provided for Christians a set of texts in which the Christian self was expounded, first in narrative terms and then in terms of asceticism; the writing of Christian texts would shape Christian lives." A. Cameron, *Christianity and the Rhetoric of Empire: The Development of Christian Discourse* (SCL, 55; Berkeley: University of California Press, 1991), 116.
121. Kraemer, *When Aseneth Met Joseph*, 198.
122. Kraemer, *When Aseneth Met Joseph*, 261.
123. On the terminology of the bridal chamber in *Jos. Asen.*, see Burchard, "Joseph and Aseneth," 2.227, n. u; Philonenko, *Joseph et Aséneth*, 184.
124. Philonenko, *Joseph et Aséneth*, 184.
125. Kraemer, *When Aseneth Met Joseph*, 61; E. M. Humphrey, *Joseph and Aseneth* (Sheffield: Sheffield Academic Press, 2000), 70.
126. Burchard, "Joseph and Aseneth," 2.226–227.
127. See, for example, *Jos. Asen.* 7:8; 7:11.
128. Kraemer, *When Aseneth Met Joseph*, 130.
129. For the identification of Metanoia with Wisdom in the shorter and the longer versions of *Jos. Asen.*, see Standhartinger, *Das Frauenbild im Judentum der hellenistischen Zeit*, 189–204.

130. Kraemer, *When Aseneth Met Joseph*, 61. Kraemer also notes that "Metanoia closely resembles the portraits of Sophia and other feminine manifestations of the divine in gnostic texts." Kraemer, *When Aseneth Met Joseph*, 84.

131. On this juxtaposition of the symbolism of "mirror" and "image," see J. Jervell, *Imago Dei: Gen 1,26f. im Spätjudentum, in der Gnosis und in den paulinischen Briefen* (FRLANT, 76; Göttingen: Vandenhoeck & Ruprecht, 1960), 185; S. Kim, *The Origin of Paul's Gospel* (2nd ed.; WUNT, 2/4; Tübingen: Mohr/Siebeck, 1984), 232; H. Windisch, *Der zweite Korintherbrief* (KEK, 6; Göttingen: Vandenhoeck & Ruprecht, 1924), 128.

132. She notices that the "description of Metanoia, and indeed the entire personification of Metanoia, is unique to the texts of *Aseneth*." Kraemer, *When Aseneth Met Joseph*, 26.

133. Kraemer notes that "Aseneth receives a new name, City of Refuge, indicating her future role as the refuge and protection of all those who devote themselves to God in repentance, a role already played by Aseneth's heavenly double, the divine Metanoia (Repentance), the daughter of God." Kraemer, *When Aseneth Met Joseph*, 5.

134. Kraemer, *When Aseneth Met Joseph*, 131.

135. "I adjure you [Metatron], more beloved and dear than all heavenly beings, [faithful servant] of the God of Israel, the High Priest, chief of [the priest]s, you who poss[ess seven]ty names; and whose name [is like your Master's] . . . Great Prince, who is appointed over the great princes, who is the head of all the camps." L. H. Schiffman and M. D. Swartz, *Hebrew and Aramaic Incantation Texts from the Cairo Genizah* (Sheffield: Sheffield Academic Press, 1992), 145.

136. "Enmeduranki [king of Sippar], the beloved of Anu, Enlil [and Ea]." W. G. Lambert, "Enmeduranki and Related Matters," *JCS* 21 (1967): 126–138 at 132.

137. Kraemer, *When Aseneth Met Joseph*, 131.

138. Kraemer, *When Aseneth Met Joseph*, 130.

139. Deutsch, "Aseneth: Ascetical Practice, Vision, and Transformation," 335.

140. Deutsch, "Aseneth: Ascetical Practice, Vision, and Transformation," 335–336.

141. Kraemer, *When Aseneth Met Joseph*, 27.

142. Burchard, "Joseph and Aseneth," 2.231–233. In relation to this episode, Burchard asks and concludes, "Does this scene reflect magical practice involving the mirror effect of water in a basin (Philonenko, *Joseph et Aséneth*, p. 193)? Probably not, because the text neither says that Aseneth had anything but washing in mind, nor that she was transformed because she looked into the water. Aseneth's sudden beauty is in partial fulfillment of 16:16. She comes close to being an angelic creature (see 20:6; cf. Acts 6:15; 2 Cor 3:18)." Burchard, "Joseph and Aseneth," 2.232.

143. Andrew Chester observes that "the transformation that Aseneth thus undergoes appears very striking, even in context of the story as romance." A. Chester, *Messiah and Exaltation: Jewish Messianic and Visionary Traditions and New Testament Christology* (WUNT, 207; Tübingen: Mohr/Siebeck, 2007), 78.

144. It is important that earlier in *Jos. Asen.* 14 the Heavenly Man orders Aseneth to wash her face with living water: "Wash your face and your hands with living water." Deutsch notes the correspondences between the two events. She remarks that "in both

visions world and life-world of the narrative, Aseneth washes herself in 'living water' (14:15; 18:8–9)." Deutsch, "Aseneth: Ascetical Practice, Vision, and Transformation," 346.

145. Deutsch observes that "final ablution brings Aseneth the realization that her face is now 'like the sun,' and that her beauty has intensified in the course of her inner transformation (18:8–9). She, like Joseph, is 'like the sun.' The transformation is confirmed by her foster-father, who is alarmed at her beauty, and then 'was filled with great fear and fell at her feet,' responding as to a vision in the pattern of biblical and apocalyptical narratives (18:10–11)." Deutsch, "Aseneth: Ascetical Practice, Vision, and Transformation," 346.

146. Bringing attention to the *tropheus*' reaction, Ross Kraemer observes that "the response of the *tropheus* to Aseneth's new appearance is itself quite interesting. His reaction to her spectacular beauty follows precisely the pattern of Aseneth's own response to the angelic figure: he is alarmed, speechless, and frightened, and he ultimately falls at her feet." Kraemer, *When Aseneth Met Joseph*, 71. In relation to this episode, George Brooke also observes that "her [Aseneth's] angelic status is confirmed by the reaction of the first person to see her: and when he saw her he was alarmed and stood speechless for a long (time), and was filled with great fear and fell at her feet and said, 'What is this, my mistress, and what is this great and wonderful beauty?'(18.11). This is the common response of those who experience an angelophany." Brooke, "Men and Women as Angels in Joseph and Aseneth," 168.

147. Celia Deutsch observes that "through various ascetical performances Aseneth refashions herself. She does not make the ascent; rather, the heavenly Man descends to speak with her. Nonetheless, his appearance makes it clear that in the vision, Aseneth crosses the boundaries between earthly and heavenly. This is confirmed in 18:9 by her altered appearance." Deutsch, "Aseneth: Ascetical Practice, Vision, and Transformation," 336.

148. Burchard, "Joseph and Aseneth," 2.232. See also *Jos. Asen.* 20:6: "And they saw Aseneth like (the) appearance of light, and her beauty was like heavenly beauty." Burchard, "Joseph and Aseneth," 2.234.

149. See Philonenko, *Joseph et Aséneth*, 193, n. 18, 7. On Mesopotamian and Greco-Roman lecanomancy, see G. Pettinato, *Die Ölwahrsagung bei den Babyloniern* (StSem, 21–22; Roma: Istituto di studi del Vicino Oriente, 1966); D. Ogden, *Magic, Witchcraft and Ghosts in the Greek and Roman Worlds: A Sourcebook* (New York: Oxford University Press, 2002), 39–40; 205–6; N. Anor, *Reading the Oil Omens: A Study of Practice and Record of Mesopotamian Lecanomancy* (Jerusalem: Hebrew University, 2010). Reflecting on this praxis, Gilles Quispel notes that

> the most instructive example for our purpose is a lekanomanteia, a revelation of the deity through dish-divination. . . . The divinity has manifested itself to the magician in the water of the dish after he has invoked the god and impelled him to come down. The magician looks upon the water and sees there the reflection of the Lord: this vision grants participation in the divine nature (*isotheou physeōs kurieusas*). . . . In chapter 14 of the *Poimandres* this theme has been applied to the Anthropos, that is the *kabod* of

Ezekiel 1:26: he looks through the harmony of the seven spheres and shows his form. Nature becomes enamoured of him when she sees his reflection in the water and his shadow on the earth. Thereupon Man falls into the irrational body and becomes man. He becomes enamoured of his reflection in the water and wants to dwell there.

Quispel, "Judaism and Gnosis," in *Gnostica, Judaica, Catholica*, 553–555.

150. G. W. Dennis, "The Use of Water as a Medium for Altered States of Consciousness in Early Jewish Mysticism: A Cross-Disciplinary Analysis," *AC* 19 (2008): 84–106. Rebecca Lesses draws attention to this peculiar mystical ritual: "You will observe through the bowl—divination on whatever day or night you want, in whatever place you want, beholding the god in the water and hearing a voice from the god which speaks in verses in answer to whatever you want." R. M. Lesses, *Ritual Practices to Gain Power: Angels, Incantations, and Revelation in Early Jewish Mysticism* (Harrisburg, PA: Trinity Press International, 1998), 329.

151. M. Nissinen, "Sacred Springs and Liminal Rivers: Water and Prophecy in the Ancient Eastern Mediterranean," in *Thinking of Water in the Early Second Temple Period* (ed. E. Ben Zvi and C. Levin; Berlin: Walter de Gruyter, 2014), 35.

152. On this motif, see C. R. A. Morray-Jones, *A Transparent Illusion: The Dangerous Vision of Water in Hekhalot Mysticism; A Source-Critical and Tradition-Critical Inquiry* (JSJSS, 59; Leiden: Brill, 2002).

153. In relation to the tradition of Ezekiel's vision as in a mirror, Seyoon Kim observes, "Now, in light of the descriptions of epiphanic visions that we have examined, especially Ezek 1, we know that its primary sense is to 'behold as in a mirror.' . . . To see God in such a surrounding is like seeing him reflected in a mirror, that is seeing his mirror image. In Ezek 1.5 we are given a picture of a mirror in the midst of fire, in which God's throne and דמות כמראה אדם appear. So Ezekiel saw God 'as in a mirror.'" Kim, *The Origin of Paul's Gospel*, 232.

154. Halperin, *The Faces of the Chariot*, 265. Later midrashic accounts also underline the water provenance of revelations received by another great Jewish seer—Daniel. Thus, from *Mekhilta de-Rabbi Ishmael*, one learns the following: "Some say: Even though He did speak with them outside of the land, and because of the merit of the fathers, He did so only at a pure spot, near water, as it is said: 'And I was by the stream Ulai' (Dan 8:2). Again it says: 'As I was by the side of the great river, which is Tigris' (Dan 10:4); 'The word of the Lord came expressly unto Ezekiel the priest the son of Buzi, in the land of the Chaldeans by the river Chebar' (Ezek 1:3)." Lauterbach, *Mekhilta de-Rabbi Ishmael*, 1.4–5.

155. Halperin, *The Faces of the Chariot*, 230. Halperin also points to a haggadah in *Exodus Rabbah* 23:14, in which the celestial heights appear to the Egyptian horses in the Red Sea. *Exodus Rabbah* 23:14 reads: "*Ramah bayam* (he hath thrown into the sea) should be read *re'eh mah bayam*, 'Behold what is in the sea!' I behold in the sea the height (*rumo*) of the world." Freedman and Simon, *Midrash Rabbah*, 3.292.

156. Halperin, *The Faces of the Chariot*, 231.

157. Halperin, *The Faces of the Chariot*, 237.

158. *Lev. Rab.* 1:14 reads: "What difference is there between Moses and all other prophets? R. Judah b. Il'ai and the Rabbis [gave different explanations]. R. Judah said: Through nine mirrors did the prophets behold [prophetic visions]. This is indicated by what is said, And the appearance of the vision which I saw, was like the vision that I saw when I came to destroy the city; and the visions were like the vision that I saw by the River Chebar." Freedman and Simon, *Midrash Rabbah*, 4.17.

159. *Zohar* II.82b reads:

> R. Hiya also expounded, in accordance with the esoteric teaching, Ezekiel's vision: "Out of the midst thereof came the likeness of four living creatures, and this was their appearance, they had the likeness of a man," saying that there is a sacred Hall in which dwell four living Creatures, which are the most ancient celestial beings ministering to the Holy Ancient, and which constitute the essence of the Supernal Name; and that Ezekiel saw only the likeness of the supernal Chariots, because his beholding was from a region which was not very bright. He furthermore said that there are lower beings corresponding to these upper ones, and so throughout, and they are all linked one with another. Our teachers have laid down that Moses derived his prophetic vision from a bright mirror, whereas the other prophets derived their vision from a dull mirror. So it is written concerning Ezekiel: "I saw visions of God," whereas in connection with the difference between Moses and all other prophets it says: "If there is a prophet among you, I the Lord will make Myself known to him in a vision. . . . My servant Moses is not so, who is faithful in all my house: and with him I will speak mouth to mouth" (Num 12:7–8). R. Jose remarked that all the prophets are in comparison with Moses like females in comparison with males.

Sperling and Simon, *The Zohar*, 3.248.

160. "'What have you, my child, because your face has fallen so (much)?' And Aseneth said to him, 'My head is stricken with heavy pain, and the sleep kept away from my eyes and therefore my face has fallen.'"

161. "And Aseneth leaned (over) to wash her face and saw her face in the water. And it was like the sun."

162. "And her neck like an all-variegated cypress, and her breasts (were) like the mountains of the Most High God."

163. In rabbinic materials, the symbolism of Adam's image is often juxtaposed with the symbolism of his luminous face. Cf. *Lev. Rab.* 20.2: "Resh Lakish, in the name of R. Simeon the son of Menasya, said: The apple of Adam's heel outshone the globe of the sun; how much more so the brightness of his face! Nor need you wonder. In the ordinary way if a person makes salvers, one for himself and one for his household, whose will he make more beautiful? Not his own? Similarly, Adam was created for the service of the Holy One, blessed be He, and the globe of the sun for the service of mankind." Freedman and Simon, *Midrash Rabbah*, 4.252.

164. *Corp. Herm.* 1:12 reads: "The man was most fair: he had the father's image; and god, who was really in love with his own form, bestowed on him all his craftworks." B. P. Copenhaver, *Hermetica: The Greek Corpus Hermeticum and the Latin Asclepius in a New English Translation, with Notes and Introduction* (Cambridge: Cambridge University Press, 1995), 3.

165. *Corp. Herm.* 1:12. A. D. Nock and A.-J. Festugière, *Corpus Hermeticum* (Paris: Société d'Edition "Les belles lettres," 1945), 1.10.

166. Copenhaver, *Hermetica*, 3.

167. Copenhaver, *Hermetica*, 3.

168. G. G. Stroumsa, "Form(s) of God: Some Notes on Metatron and Christ," HTR 76 (1983): 269–288 at 275.

169. Koenen and Römer, *Der Kölner Mani-Kodex*, 8; Gardner and Lieu, *Manichaean Texts from the Roman Empire*, 49.

170. Stang, *Our Divine Double*, 168–169. Later in his study, Stang argues that "perhaps that 'mirror image' was introduced in a section now lost or illegible. Or perhaps that 'mirror image' is meant to refer back to the face of the man in the water (12,1–2), a figure whom I am inclined to identify as the twin-companion." Stang, *Our Divine Double*, 170.

171. Koenen and Römer, *Der Kölner Mani-Kodex*, 66; E. B. Aitken, "The Cologne Mani Codex," in *Religions of Late Antiquity in Practice* (ed. R. Valantasis; Princeton Readings in Religions; Princeton: Princeton University Press, 2000), 168.

172. Stang, *Our Divine Double*, 284. Stang draws his attention to another early tradition in which the heavenly counterpart imagery is juxtaposed with the motif of gazing into the water—namely, the story of Narcissus. Stang's research demonstrates that this mythological motif became an important narrative vehicle for conveying the doppelganger traditions both in Plato and Plotinus. On this, see Stang, *Our Heavenly Double*, 213ff.

173. *Jos. Asen.* 20:6 reads: "And her father and mother and his whole family came from the field which was their inheritance. And they saw Aseneth like (the) appearance of light, and her beauty was like heavenly beauty." Burchard, "Joseph and Aseneth," 2.234.

174. Kraemer, *When Aseneth Met Joseph*, 72–73.

175. See *Jos. Asen.* 19:4: "And Aseneth went out of the entrance to meet Joseph, and Joseph saw her and was amazed at her beauty, and said to her, 'Who are you? Quickly tell me.'" Burchard, "Joseph and Aseneth," 2.233.

Bibliography

I. Texts and Translations

Aberbach, Moses, and Grossfeld, Bernard. *Targum Onkelos to Genesis: A Critical Analysis Together with an English Translation of the Text.* Denver: Ktav, 1982.

Alexander, Philip. "3 (Hebrew Apocalypse of) Enoch." In *The Old Testament Pseudepigrapha.* Edited by J. H. Charlesworth, 1.223–315. 2 vols. New York: Doubleday, 1983–1985.

Andersen, Francis. "2 (Slavonic Apocalypse of) Enoch." In *The Old Testament Pseudepigrapha.* Edited by J. H. Charlesworth, 1.91–221. 2 vols. New York: Doubleday, 1983–1985.

Anderson, Gary, and Stone, Michael. *A Synopsis of the Books of Adam and Eve.* 2nd rev. ed. EJL 17. Atlanta: Scholars, 1999.

Armstrong, Arthur Hilary. *Plotinus: Enneads.* 7 vols. LCL. Cambridge, MA: Harvard University Press, 1966–1988.

Aune, David. *Revelation 1–5.* WBC 52A. Nashville: Thomas Nelson, 1997.

Barrett, Charles Kingsley. *The Gospel According to St. John.* London: SPCK, 1978.

Berger, Klaus. *Das Buch der Jubiläen.* JSHRZ 2.3. Gütersloh: Gütersloher Verlaghaus, 1981.

Black, Matthew. *The Book of Enoch or 1 Enoch.* SVTP 7. Leiden: Brill, 1985.

Blanc, Cécile. *Origène, Commentaire sur Saint Jean. Tome I (Livres I–V).* SC 120. Paris: Cerf, 1966.

Böttrich, Christfried. *Das slavische Henochbuch.* JSHRZ 5. Gütersloh: Gütersloher Verlaghaus, 1995.

Bowman, John. *Samaritan Documents Relating to Their History, Religion and Life.* Pittsburgh: Pickwick, 1977.

Braude, William. *The Midrash on Psalms.* 2 vols. YJS 13. New Haven: Yale University Press, 1959.

Braude, William, and Kapstein, Israel. *Pesikta de-Rab Kahana: R. Kahana's Compilation of Discourses for Sabbaths and Festal Days.* Philadelphia: Jewish Publication Society of America, 1975.

Brown, Raymond. *The Gospel According to John.* AB 29–29A. 2 vols. Garden City, NY: Doubleday, 1966.

Bultmann, Rudolph. *The Gospel of John: A Commentary*. Philadelphia: Westminster, 1971.
Burchard, Christoph. "Joseph and Aseneth." In *The Old Testament Pseudepigrapha*. Edited by J. H. Charlesworth, 2.177–247. 2 vols. New York: Doubleday, 1983–1985.
———. "Joseph und Aseneth serbisch-kirchenslawisch: Text und Varianten." In *Gesammelte Studien zu Joseph & Aseneth*. Edited by C. Burchard and C. Burfeind, 53–102. SVTP 39. Leiden: Brill, 1996.
———. *Joseph und Aseneth kritisch herausgegeben von Christoph Burchard mit Unterstützung von Carsten Burfeind & Uta Barbara Fink*. PVTG 5. Leiden: Brill, 2003.
———. *A Minor Edition of the Armenian Version of Joseph und Aseneth*. HUAS 10. Leuven: Peeters, 2010.
Cagni, Luigi. *The Poem of Erra*. SANE 1/3. Malibu: Undena, 1977.
Cameron, Ron, and Dewey, Arthur. *The Cologne Mani Codex: "Concerning the Origin of His Body."* SBLTT 15. ECLS 3. Missoula, MT: Scholars, 1979.
Casey, Robert Pierce. *The Excerpta ex Theodoto of Clement of Alexandria*. London: Christophers, 1934.
Charles, Robert Henry. *The Book of Jubilees or the Little Genesis*. London: Black, 1902.
Charles, Robert Henry, and Forbes, Nevill. "The Book of the Secrets of Enoch." In *The Apocrypha and Pseudepigrapha of the Old Testament*. Edited by R. H. Charles, 2.425–269. 2 vols. Oxford: Clarendon, 1913.
Charles, Robert Henry, and Morfill, William. *The Book of the Secrets of Enoch*. Oxford: Clarendon, 1896.
Charlesworth, James. "Prayer of Manasseh." In *The Old Testament Pseudepigrapha*. Edited by J. H. Charlesworth, 2.625–637. 2 vols. New York: Doubleday, 1983–1985.
———. "Odes of Solomon." In *The Old Testament Pseudepigrapha*. Edited by J. H. Charlesworth, 2.726–771. 2 vols. New York: Doubleday, 1983–1985.
Cohen, Martin. *The Shi'ur Qomah: Texts and Recensions*. TSAJ 9. Tübingen: Mohr/Siebeck, 1985.
Collins, John. *Daniel: A Commentary on the Book of Daniel*. Hermeneia. Minneapolis: Fortress, 1993.
Colson, Francis Henry, and Whitaker, George Herbert. *Philo*. 10 vols. LCL. Cambridge, MA: Harvard University Press, 1929–1964.
Conzelmann, Hans. *Acts of the Apostles*. Hermeneia. Philadelphia: Fortress, 1987.
Cooper, James, and Maclean, Arthur. *Testament of Our Lord*. Edinburgh: T&T Clark, 1902.
Copenhaver, Brian. *Hermetica: The Greek Corpus Hermeticum and the Latin Asclepius in a New English Translation, with Notes and Introduction*. Cambridge: Cambridge University Press, 1995.
Cowley, Arthur Ernest. *The Samaritan Liturgy*. 2 vols. Oxford: Clarendon, 1908.
Daley, Brian. *On the Dormition of Mary: Early Patristic Homilies*. PPS 18. Crestwood: St. Vladimir's Seminary Press, 1997.
Davila, James. *Hekhalot Literature in Translation: Major Texts of Merkavah Mysticism*. SJJTP 20. Leiden: Brill, 2013.
Dedes, Seraphim, and Vaporis, Michael. *The Akathist Hymn and Small Compline*. Brookline: Holy Cross Orthodox Press, 1990.

De Lacy, Phillip, and Einarson, Benedict. *Plutarch's Moralia*. 15 vols. LCL. Cambridge, MA: Harvard University Press, 1959.
Denis, Albert-Marie. *Fragmenta pseudepigraphorum quae supersunt graeca*. PVTG 3. Leiden: Brill, 1970.
Dibelius, Martin. *Der Hirt des Hermas*. HNT. Die Apostolischen Väter 4. Tübingen: Mohr/Siebeck, 1923.
Díez Macho, Alejandro. *Neophiti 1: Targum Palestinense MS de la Biblioteca Vaticana*. Madrid: Consejo Superior de Investigaciones Científicas, 1968.
Dodge, Bayard. *The Fihrist of al-Nadīm: A Tenth-Century Survey of Muslim Culture*. New York: Columbia University Press, 1970.
Dörries, Hermann et al. *Die 50 Geistlichen Homilien des Makarios*. PTS 4. Berlin: Walter de Gruyter, 1964.
Drijvers, Han. "The Acts of Thomas." In *New Testament Apocrypha*. Edited by E. Hennecke and W. Schneemelcher, 2.322–411. 2 vols. Louisville, KY: Westminster John Knox, 2003.
Epstein, Isidore. *The Babylonian Talmud*. London: Soncino, 1935–1952.
Ferreira, Johan. *The Hymn of the Pearl: The Syriac and Greek Texts with Introduction, Translations, and Notes*. Sydney: St. Pauls Publications, 2002.
Fink, Uta. *Joseph und Aseneth Revision des griechischen Textes und Edition der zweiten lateinischen Übersetzung*. FSBP 5. Berlin: Walter de Gruyter, 2008.
———. "Joseph und Aseneth. Text, Übersetzung und Anmerkungen." In *Joseph und Aseneth*. Edited by E. Reinmuth, 56–137. Sapere 15. Tübingen: Mohr/Siebeck, 2009.
Foerster, Werner. *Gnosis: A Selection of Gnostic Texts*. 2 vols. Oxford: Clarendon, 1972.
Franko, Ivan. *Apokrifi i legendi z ukrains'kih rukopisiv*. Monumenta Linguae Necon Litterarum Ukraino-Russicarum (Ruthenicarum). 5 vols. L'vov: Shevchenka, 1896–1910.
Freedman, Harry, and Simon, Maurice. *Midrash Rabbah*. 10 vols. London: Soncino, 1961.
Friedländer, Gerald. *Pirke de Rabbi Eliezer*. 2nd ed. New York: Hermon Press, 1965.
García Martínez, Florentino, and Tigchelaar, Eibert. *The Dead Sea Scrolls Study Edition*. 2 vols. Leiden: Brill, 1997.
Gardner, Iain. *The Kephalaia of the Teacher: The Edited Coptic Manichaean Texts in Translation with Commentary*. NHMS 37. Leiden: Brill, 1995.
Gardner, Iain, and Lieu, Samuel. *Manichaean Texts from the Roman Empire*. Cambridge: Cambridge University Press, 2004.
Grossfeld, Bernard. *The Targum Onqelos to Genesis*. ArBib 6. Wilmington, DE: Michael Glazier, 1988.
Hennecke, Edgar, and Schneemelcher, Wilhem. *New Testament Apocrypha*. 2 vols. Louisville, KY: Westminster John Knox, 2003.
Holladay, Carl. *Fragments from Hellenistic Jewish Authors*. 3 vols. SBLTT 30. Pseudepigrapha Series 12. Atlanta: Scholars, 1989.
Honscheid, Jürgen. *Didymus der Blinde. De trinitate*. BKP 44. Meisenheim am Glan: Hain, 1975.
Jacobson, Howard. *The Exagoge of Ezekiel*. Cambridge: Cambridge University Press, 1983.

———. *A Commentary on Pseudo-Philo's Liber Antiquitatum Biblicarum, with Latin Text and English Translation.* 2 vols. AGAJU 31. Leiden: Brill, 1996.
James, Montague Rhodes. *The Lost Apocrypha of the Old Testament: Their Titles and Fragments.* Eugene, OR: Wipf and Stock, 2007.
Jellinek, Adolph. *Beth ha-Midrash.* 6 vols. Jerusalem: Wahrmann, 1967.
Jenott, Lance. *The Gospel of Judas.* STAC 64. Tübingen: Mohr/Siebeck, 2011.
Junod, Eric, and Kaestli, Jean-Daniel. *Acta Iohannis.* 2 vols. Corpus Christianorum. Series Apocryphorum 1–2. Turnhout: Brepols, 1983.
Kaler, Michael, and Rosenstiehl, Jean-Marc. *L'Apocalypse de Paul.* Québec: Presses de l'Université Laval, 2005.
Kasser, Rodolphe. *The Gospel of Judas from Codex Tchacos.* Washington, DC: National Geographic Society, 2006.
Klein, Michael. *The Fragment-Targums of the Pentateuch According to Their Extant Sources.* 2 vols. AnBib 76. Rome: Biblical Institute Press, 1980.
Klijn, Albertus Frederik Johannes. *The Acts of Thomas: Introduction, Text, and Commentary.* 2nd ed. Leiden: Brill, 2003.
Knibb, Michael. *The Ethiopic Book of Enoch: A New Edition in the Light of the Aramaic Dead Sea Fragments.* 2 vols. Oxford: Clarendon, 1978.
———. "Martyrdom and Ascension of Isaiah." In *The Old Testament Pseudepigrapha.* Edited by J. H. Charlesworth, 2.143–176. 2 vols. New York: Doubleday, 1983–1985.
Koenen, Ludwig, and Römer, Cornelia. *Der Kölner Mani-Kodex: Über das Werden seines Leibes. Kritische Edition.* Papyrologica Coloniensia 14. Opladen: Westdeutscher Verlag, 1988.
Lanfranchi, Pierluigi. *L'Exagoge d'Ezéchiel le Tragique: Introduction, texte, traduction et commentaire.* SVTP 21. Leiden: Brill, 2006.
Lauterbach, Jacob Zallel. *Mekhilta de-Rabbi Ishmael: A Critical Edition on the Basis of the Manuscripts and Early Editions with an English Translation, Introduction and Notes.* 2 vols. Philadelphia: Jewish Publication Society, 2004.
Layton, Bentley. *Nag Hammadi Codex II, 2–7.* 2 vols. NHS 20. Leiden: Brill, 1989.
Lidzbarski, Mark. *Ginza, der Schatz oder das große Buch der Mandäer.* Göttingen: Vandenhoeck & Ruprecht, 1925.
Lindars, Barnabas. *The Gospel of John.* London: NCBC, 1972.
Lunt, Horace. "Ladder of Jacob." In *The Old Testament Pseudepigrapha.* Edited by J. H. Charlesworth, 2.401–411. 2 vols. New York: Doubleday, 1983–1985.
Macaskill, Grant. *The Slavonic Texts of 2 Enoch.* SJS 6. Leiden: Brill, 2013.
MacDonald, Dennis. *The Acts of Andrew and the Acts of Andrew and Matthias in the City of the Cannibals.* Texts and Translations 33. Christian Apocrypha 1. Atlanta: Scholars, 1990.
Macdonald, John. *Memar Marqah: The Teaching of Marqah.* 2 vols. BZAW 84. Berlin: Walter de Gruyter, 1963.
MacRae, George, and Murdock, William. "The Apocalypse of Paul." In *Nag Hammadi Codices V, 2–5 and VI with Papyrus Berolinensis 8502, 1 and 4.* Edited by D. M. Parrott, 47–63. NHS 11. Leiden: Brill, 1979.

Maher, Michael. *Targum Pseudo-Jonathan: Genesis*. ArBib 1B. Collegeville, MN: Liturgical Press, 1992.
Maloney, George. *Pseudo-Macarius: The Fifty Spiritual Homilies and the Great Letter*. New York: Paulist Press, 1992.
Mandelbaum, Bernard. *Pesikta de Rav Kahana According to an Oxford Manuscript, with Variants from All Known Manuscripts and Genizoth Fragments and Parallel Passages*. 2 vols. New York: Jewish Theological Seminary of America, 1962.
Matt, Daniel. *The Zohar: Pritzker Edition*. 12 vols. Palo Alto, CA: Stanford University Press, 2003.
McNamara, Martin. *Targum Neofiti 1: Genesis*. ArBib 1A. Collegeville, MN: Liturgical Press, 1992.
McNamara, Martin et al. *Targum Neofiti 1 and Pseudo-Jonathan: Exodus*. ArBib 2. Collegeville, MN: Liturgical Press, 1994.
Milik, Józef Tadeusz. *The Books of Enoch: Aramaic Fragments of Qumrân Cave 4*. Oxford: Clarendon, 1976.
Mopsik, Charles. *Le Livre hébreu d'Hénoch ou Livre des palais*. Paris: Verdier, 1989.
Morris, Leon. *The Gospel According to John*. Grand Rapids, MI: Eerdmans, 1995.
Mras, Karl. *Eusebius, Praeparatio Evangelica*. GCS 43.1-2. Leipzig: J. C. Hinrichs, 1954-1956.
Murray, Augustus Taber. *Homer: The Iliad*. 2 vols. LCL. Cambridge, MA: Harvard University Press, 1924.
———. *Homer: The Odyssey*. 2 vols. LCL. Cambridge, MA: Harvard University Press, 1945.
Nickelsburg, George. *1 Enoch 1: A Commentary on the Book of 1 Enoch: Chapters 1-36; 81-108*. Hermeneia. Minneapolis: Fortress, 2001.
Nickelsburg, George, and VanderKam, James. *1 Enoch 2: A Commentary on the Book of 1 Enoch: Chapters 37-82*. Hermeneia. Minneapolis: Fortress, 2012.
Nock, Arthur, and Festugière, Andre-Jean. *Corpus Hermeticum*. 4 vols. Paris: Les Belles Lettres, 1954-1960.
Novickij, P. *Tolkovaja paleja 1477 goda. Vosproizvedenie Sinodal'noj Rukopisi No 210*. St. Petersburg: Tipografia Imperatorskoj Akademii Nauk, 1892.
Odeberg, Hugo, *The Fourth Gospel: Interpreted in Its Relation to Contemporary Religious Currents in Palestine and the Hellenistic-Oriental World*. Uppsala: Almqvist & Wiksell, 1929. repr. Chicago: Argonaut, 1968.
———. *3 Enoch or the Hebrew Book of Enoch*. New York: Ktav, 1973.
Olson, Daniel. *Enoch: A New Translation: The Ethiopic Book of Enoch, or 1 Enoch*. North Richland Hills, TX: Bibal Press, 2004.
Osiek, Carolyn. *Shepherd of Hermas*. Hermeneia. Minneapolis: Fortress, 1999.
Paleja tolkovaja po spisku sdelannomu v gorode Kolomne v 1406 g. Trud uchenikov N.S. Tihonravova. Moscow: Gerbek, 1892.
Parrott, Douglas. *Nag Hammadi Codices V, 2-5 and VI with Papyrus Berolinensis 8502, 1 and 4*. NHS 11. Leiden: Brill, 1979.
Pervo, Richard. *The Acts of John*. Edited by J. V. Hills. Salem, OR: Polebridge Press, 2015.

Philonenko, Marc. *Joseph et Aséneth: Introduction, texte critique, traduction et notes*. SPB 13. Leiden: Brill, 1968.

Porfir'ev, Ivan. *Apokrificheskie skazanija o vethozavetnyh licah i sobytijah po rukopisjam soloveckoj biblioteki*. SORJS 17.1. St. Petersburg: Tipografia Imperatorskoj Academii Nauk, 1877.

Pypin, Aleksandr. *Lozhnye i otrechennye knigi russkoj stariny*. Pamjatniki starinnoj russkoj literatury, izdavaemye Grafom Grigoriem Kushelevym-Bezborodko 3. St. Petersburg: Kulish, 1862.

Rahmani, Ignatius Ephraem. *Testamentum Domini Nostri Jesu Christi*. Moguntiae: F. Kirchheim, 1899.

Resch, Alfred. *Agrapha: Aussercanonische Schriftfragmente*. Leipzig: J. C. Hinrichs, 1906.

Roberts, Alexander, and Donaldson, James. *The Ante-Nicene Fathers: Translations of the Writings of the Fathers down to A.D. 325*. 10 vols. New York: Charles Scribner's Sons, 1899.

Robertson, R. G. "Ezekiel the Tragedian." In *The Old Testament Pseudepigrapha*. Edited by J. H. Charlesworth. 2.803-819. 2 vols. New York: Doubleday, 1983-1985.

Robinson, Joseph Armitage. *Origen, Philocalia*. Cambridge: Cambridge University Press, 1893.

Santos Otero, de Aurelio. "Libro de los secretos de Henoc (Henoc eslavo)." In *Apócrifos del Antiguo Testamento*. Edited by A. Díez Macho, 4.147-202. 5 vols. Madrid: Ediciones Christiandad, 1984.

Schäfer, Peter, Schlüter, Margaret, and von Mutius, Hans George. *Synopse zur Hekhalot-Literatur*. TSAJ 2. Tübingen: Mohr/Siebeck, 1981.

Schäfer, Peter, and Shaked, Saul. *Magische Texte aus der Kairoer Geniza*. TSAJ 64. Tübingen: Mohr/Siebeck, 1997.

Schiffman, Lawrence, and Swartz, Michael. *Hebrew and Aramaic Incantation Texts from the Cairo Genizah*. Sheffield: Sheffield Academic Press, 1992.

Schmidt, Carl, and MacDermot, Violet. *Pistis Sophia*. NHS 9. Leiden: Brill, 1978.

Schnackenburg, Rudolf. *The Gospel According to St. John*. 3 vols. London: Burns and Oates, 1968-1982.

Sieber, John. *Nag Hammadi Codex VIII*. NHS 31. Leiden: Brill, 1991.

Slusser, Michael, ed. *Dialogue with Trypho. By St. Justin Martyr*. Washington, DC: Catholic University of America Press, 2003.

Smith, Jonathan. "Prayer of Joseph." In *The Old Testament Pseudepigrapha*. Edited by J. H. Charlesworth. 2.699-714. 2 vols. New York: Doubleday, 1983-1985.

Snell, Bruno. *Tragicorum graecorum fragmenta I*. Göttingen: Vandenhoeck & Ruprecht, 1971.

Snell, Bruno, and Maehler, Herwig. *Pindari carmina cum fragmentis. Pars I Epinicia*. Leipzig: B. G. Teubner, 1980.

Snyder, Graydon. "The Shepherd of Hermas." In *Apostolic Fathers*. Edited by R. M. Grant. 6 vols. Camden, NJ: Nelson, 1969.

Sokolov, Matvej. "Materialy i zametki po starinnoj slavjanskoj literature. Vypusk tretij. VII. Slavjanskaja Kniga Enoha Pravednogo. Teksty, latinskij perevod i izsledovanie. Posmertnyj trud avtora prigotovil k izdaniju M. Speranskij." *COIDR* 4 (1910): 1-167.

Sperber, Alexander. *The Bible in Aramaic Based on Old Manuscripts and Printed Texts.* 5 vols. Leiden: Brill, 1959.
Sperling, Harry, and Simon, Maurice. *The Zohar.* 5 vols. London: Soncino, 1933.
Stinespring, William. "Testament of Isaac." In *The Old Testament Pseudepigrapha.* Edited by J. H. Charlesworth. 1.903–911. 2 vols. New York: Doubleday, 1983–1985.
Stone, Michael. *The Penitence of Adam.* CSCO 429–430. Louvain: Peeters, 1981.
———. *Texts and Concordances of the Armenian Adam Literature.* EJL 12. Atlanta: Scholars, 1996.
Stoops, Robert. *The Acts of Peter.* Edited by J. V. Hills. Salem, OR: Polebridge Press, 2012.
Tihonravov, Nikolaj. *Pamjatniki otrechennoj russkoj literatury.* 2 vols. St. Petersburg: Obshestvennaja Pol'za, 1863.
Tishby, Isaiah. *The Wisdom of the Zohar.* 3 vols. London: Littman Library of Jewish Civilization, 1994.
Tragan, Pius-Ramon. *Josep i Àsenet: Introducció, text grec revisat i notes.* LIS 4. Barcelona: Alpha, 2005.
Valavanolickal, Kuriakose. *Aphrahat, Demonstrations I.* Kerala: St. Ephrem Ecumenical Research Institute, 2005.
Van der Horst, Peter, and Newman, Judith. *Early Jewish Prayers in Greek.* CEJL. Berlin: Walter de Gruyter, 2008.
VanderKam, James. *The Book of Jubilees.* 2 vols. CSCO 510–511. Scriptores Aethiopici 87–88. Leuven: Peeters, 1989.
Vogt, Ernst. *Tragiker Ezechiel.* JSHRZ 4.3. Gütersloh: Mohn, 1983.
Waldstein, Michael, and Wisse, Frederik. *The Apocryphon of John: Synopsis of Nag Hammadi Codices II, 1; III, 1; and IV, 1 with BG 8502, 2.* NHMS 33. Leiden: Brill, 1995.
Waszink, Jan Hendrik. *Quinti Septimi Florentis Tertulliani. De Anima.* SVC 100. Leiden: Brill, 2010.
Wertheimer, Solomon. *Batei Midrashot.* 2 vols. Jerusalem: Mossad Harav Kook, 1950–1953.
Whittaker, Molly. *Tatian, Oratio ad Graecos and Fragments.* Oxford: Clarendon, 1982.
Wieneke, Joseph. *Ezechielis Judaei poetae Alexandrini fabulae quae inscribitur Exagoge fragmenta.* Münster: Monasterii Westfalorum, 1931.
Windisch, Hans. *Der zweite Korintherbrief.* KEK 6. Göttingen: Vandenhoeck & Ruprecht, 1924.

II. Secondary Literature

Aaron, David. "Shedding Light on God's Body in Rabbinic Midrashim: Reflections on the Theory of a Luminous Adam." *HTR* 90 (1997): 299–314.
Adrianova, Varvara. *K literaturnoj istorii Tolkovoj Palei.* Kiev: Petr Barskij, 1910.
Albrile, Ezio. "Shining like a Star Man: Iranian Elements in the Gospel of Judas." In *The Gospel of Judas in Context: Proceedings of the First International Conference on the Gospel of Judas.* Edited by M. Scopello, 277–292. NHMS 62. Leiden: Brill, 2008.
Alexander, Philip. "The Historical Setting of the Hebrew Book of Enoch." *JJS* 28 (1977): 156–180.

Allison, Dale. *Constructing Jesus: Memory, Imagination, and History*. Grand Rapids, MI: Baker Academic, 2010.

Altmann, Alexander. "The Gnostic Background of the Rabbinic Adam Legends." *JQR* 35 (1945): 371–391.

———. "The Ladder of Ascension." In *Studies in Mysticism and Religion Presented to Gershom G. Scholem on His Seventieth Birthday*. Edited by E. Urbach, 1–32. Jerusalem: Magnes, 1967.

Anderson, Gary. "The Exaltation of Adam and the Fall of Satan." In *Literature on Adam and Eve: Collected Essays*. Edited by G. Anderson, M. E. Stone, and J. Tromp, 83–110. SVTP 15. Leiden: Brill, 2000.

Angel, Joseph. *Otherworldly and Eschatological Priesthood in the Dead Sea Scrolls*. STDJ 86. Leiden: Brill, 2010.

Anor, Netanel. *Reading the Oil Omens: A Study of Practice and Record of Mesopotamian Lecanomancy*. Jerusalem: Hebrew University, 2010.

Aptowitzer, Victor. "The Celestial Temple as Viewed in the Aggadah." In *Binah: Studies in Jewish Thought*. Edited by J. Dan, 1–29. Binah: Studies in Jewish History, Thought, and Culture 2. New York: Praeger, 1989.

Ashton, John. *Understanding the Fourth Gospel*. Oxford: Oxford University Press, 1991.

Assefa, Daniel. *L'Apocalypse des animaux (1Hen 85–90): Une propagande militaire? Approches narrative, historico-critique, perspectives théologiques*. JSJSS 120. Leiden: Brill, 2007.

Barker, Margaret. *The Gate of Heaven: The History and Symbolism of the Temple in Jerusalem*. London: SPCK, 1991.

Bauckham, Richard. "The Throne of God and the Worship of Jesus." In *Jewish Roots of Christological Monotheism: Papers from the St Andrews Conference on the Historical Origins of the Worship of Jesus*. Edited by C. C. Newman, J. Davila, and G. Lewis, 43–69. Leiden: Brill, 1999.

Beale, Gregory. *The Temple and the Church's Mission*. NSBT 17. Downers Grove, IL: InterVarsity Press, 2004.

———. *We Become What We Worship: A Biblical Theology of Idolatry*. Downers Grove, IL: InterVarsity Press, 2008.

Beckerleg, Catherine Leigh. *The "Image of God" in Eden*. PhD diss. Harvard University, 2009.

Ben-Dov, Jonathan. "Exegetical Notes on Cosmology in the Parables of Enoch." In *Enoch and the Messiah Son of Man: Revisiting the Book of Parables*. Edited by G. Boccaccini, 143–150. Grand Rapids, MI: Eerdmans, 2007.

Berlejung, Angelika. *Die Theologie der Bilder: Herstellung und Einweihung von Kultbildern in Mesopotamien und die alttestamentliche Bilderpolemik*. OBO 162. Freiburg: Universitätsverlag, 1998.

Bernstein, Moshe. "Noah and the Flood at Qumran." In *The Provo International Conference on the Dead Sea Scrolls: Technological Innovations, New Texts, and Reformulated Issues*. Edited by D. W. Parry and E. Ulrich, 199–231. STDJ 30. Leiden: Brill, 1999.

Blenkinsopp, Joseph. *Sage, Priest, Prophet; Religious and Intellectual Leadership in Ancient Israel*. Louisville, KY: Westminster John Knox, 1995.

Boccaccini, Gabriele. *Beyond the Essene Hypothesis: The Parting of the Ways between Qumran and Enochic Judaism*. Grand Rapids, MI: Eerdmans, 1998.

———. *Roots of Rabbinic Judaism: An Intellectual History from Ezekiel to Daniel*. Grand Rapids, MI: Eerdmans, 2002.

Boden, Peggy. *The Mesopotamian Washing of the Mouth (Mīs Pî) Ritual*. PhD diss. Johns Hopkins University, 1998.

Bohak, Gideon. "Asenath's Honeycomb and Onias' Temple: The Key to Joseph and Asenath." In *Proceedings of the Eleventh World Congress of Jewish Studies, Division A*. Edited by D. Assaf, 163–170. Jerusalem: Magnes, 1994.

———. *Joseph and Aseneth and the Jewish Temple in Heliopolis*. Atlanta: Scholars, 1996.

Bolshakov, Andrey. *Man and His Double in Egyptian Ideology of the Old Kingdom*. ÄAT 37. Wiesbaden: Harrassowitz, 1997.

Boring, Eugene. *Sayings of the Risen Jesus: Christian Prophecy in the Synoptic Tradition*. Cambridge: Cambridge University Press, 1982.

Böttrich, Christfried. "Palaea/Paleja. Ein byzantinisch-slavischer Beitrag zu den europäischen Historienbibeln." In *Fragmentarisches Wörterbuch: Beiträge zur biblischen Exegese und christlichen Theologie. Horst Balz zum 70. Geburtstag*. Edited by K. Schiffner, K. Wengst, and W. Zager, 304–313. Stuttgart: W. Kohlhammer, 2007.

———. "Apocalyptic Tradition and Mystical Prayer in the Ladder of Jacob." *JSP* 23 (2014): 290–306.

Bousset, Wilhelm. "Manichäisches in den Thomasakten: Ein Beitrag zur Frage nach den christlichen Elementen im Manichäismus." *ZNW* 18 (1917/18): 1–39.

———. *Die Religion des Judentums in späthellenistischen Zeitalter*. 3rd ed. HNT 21. Tübingen: Mohr/Siebeck, 1926.

———. *Kyrios Christos: A History of the Belief in Christ from the Beginnings of Christianity to Irenaeus*. New York: Abingdon, 1970.

Boustan, Raʿanan. *From Martyr to Mystic: Rabbinic Martyrology and the Making of Merkavah Mysticism*. TSAJ 112. Tübingen: Mohr/Siebeck, 2005.

Boyce, Mary. "The Absorption of the Fravašis into Zoroastrianism." *AOASH* 48.1–2 (1995): 26.

———. "Fravaši." *Encyclopedia Iranica*. Edited by E. Yarshater, 10.195–199. Vol. 1–16. Costa Mesa: Mazda, 2001.

Bremmer, Jan. *The Early Greek Concept of the Soul*. Princeton: Princeton University Press, 1983.

Britt, Brian. *Rewriting Moses: The Narrative Eclipse of the Text*. JSOTSS 402. London: T&T Clark, 2004.

Brock, Sebastian. "Clothing Metaphors as a Means of Theological Expression in Syriac Tradition." In *Typus, Symbol, Allegorie bei den östlichen Vätern und ihren Parallelen im Mittelalter*. Edited by M. Schmidt, 11–40. EB 4. Regensburg: Friedrich Pustet, 1982.

Brooke, George. "Men and Women as Angels in Joseph and Aseneth." *JSP* 14 (2005): 159–177.

Brown, John. "The Son of Man: 'This Fellow.'" *Biblica* 58 (1977): 361–387.

Brown, Peter. *The Body and Society: Men, Women, and Sexual Renunciation in Early Christianity*. London: Faber & Faber, 1989.

Brown, Raymond. *The Death of the Messiah: From Gethsemane to the Grave: A Commentary on the Passion Narratives in the Four Gospels.* 2 vols. New Haven: Yale University Press, 1998.
Buckley, Jorunn. "The Mandaean Sitil as an Example of 'The Image Above and Below.'" *Numen* 26 (1979): 185–191.
———. "Two Female Gnostic Revealers." *HR* 19 (1980): 259–269.
———. "A Rehabilitation of Spirit Ruha in Mandaean Religion." *HR* 21 (1982): 60–84.
———. *The Mandaeans: Ancient Texts and Modern People.* Oxford: Oxford University Press, 2002.
Bucur, Bogdan. *Angelomorphic Pneumatology: Clement of Alexandria and Other Early Christian Witnesses.* SVC 95. Leiden: Brill, 2009.
Bunta, Silviu. *Moses, Adam and the Glory of the Lord in Ezekiel the Tragedian: On the Roots of a Merkabah Text.* PhD diss. Marquette University, 2005.
Burchard, Christoph. "Zum Text von 'Joseph und Aseneth.'" *JSJ* 1 (1970): 3–34.
———. "The Present State of Research on Joseph and Aseneth." In *Religion, Literature, and Society in Ancient Israel, Formative Christianity and Judaism.* Edited by J. Neusner, 31–52. NPAJ 2. Lanham: University Press of America, 1987.
Burkett, Delbert. *The Son of Man in the Gospel of John.* JSNTSS 56. Sheffield: Sheffield Academic Press, 1991.
———. *The Son of Man Debate: A History and Evaluation.* SNTSMS 107. Cambridge: Cambridge University Press, 2000.
Burney, Charles Fox. *The Aramaic Origin of the Fourth Gospel.* Oxford: Clarendon, 1922.
Cameron, Averil. *Christianity and the Rhetoric of Empire: The Development of Christian Discourse.* SCL 55. Berkeley: University of California Press, 1991.
Cartlidge, David. "Transfigurations of Metamorphosis Traditions in the Acts of John, Thomas, and Peter." In *The Apocryphal Acts of the Apostles.* Edited by D. MacDonald, 53–66. Semeia 38. Decatur, GA: Scholars, 1986.
Catchpole, David. "The Angelic Son of Man in Luke 12:8." *NovT* 24 (1982): 255–265.
Cejtlin, Raisa. *Staroslovjanskij slovar' po rukopisjam X–XI vekov.* Moscow: Russkij jazyk, 1994.
Charlesworth, James. "A Rare Consensus among Enoch Specialists: The Date of the Earliest Enoch Books." *Henoch* 24 (2002): 255–234.
———. "The Date and Provenience of the Parables of Enoch." In *Parables of Enoch: A Paradigm Shift.* Edited by D. Bock and J. Charlesworth, 37–57. London: T&T Clark, 2013.
Chernus, Ira. *Mysticism in Rabbinic Judaism: Studies in the History of Midrash.* SJ 11. Berlin: Walter de Gruyter, 1982.
Chesnutt, Randall. *From Death to Life: Conversion in Joseph and Aseneth.* JSPSS 16. Sheffield: Sheffield Academic Press, 1995.
———. "Perceptions of Oil in Early Judaism and the Meal Formula in Joseph and Aseneth." *JSP* 14 (2005): 113–132.
Chester, Andrew. *Messiah and Exaltation: Jewish Messianic and Visionary Traditions and New Testament Christology.* WUNT 207. Tübingen: Mohr/Siebeck, 2007.
Chilton, Bruce. "(The) Son of (the) Man, and Jesus." In *Authenticating the Words of Jesus.* Edited by B. Chilton and C. A. Evans, 259–288. Leiden: Brill, 1999.

Clarke, Ernest. "Jacob's Dream at Bethel as Interpreted in the Targums and the New Testament." *SR* 4.4 (1974–1975): 367–377.
Collins, John. *The Apocalyptic Vision of the Book of Daniel.* HSM 16. Missoula, MT: Scholars, 1977.
———. "The Heavenly Representative: The 'Son of Man' in the Similitudes of Enoch." In *Ideal Figures in Ancient Judaism: Profiles and Paradigms.* Edited by J. Collins and G. Nickelsburg, 111–133. SBLSCS 12. Missoula, MT: Scholars, 1980.
———. "A Throne in the Heavens: Apotheosis in Pre-Christian Judaism." In *Death, Ecstasy, and Other Worldly Journeys.* Edited by J. J. Collins and M. Fishbane, 43–57. Albany: SUNY Press, 1995.
———. *The Apocalyptic Imagination: An Introduction to Jewish Apocalyptic Literature.* 2nd ed. Grand Rapids, MI: Eerdmans, 1998.
———. *Between Athens and Jerusalem. Jewish Identity in the Hellenistic Diaspora.* 2nd ed. Grand Rapids, MI: Eerdmans, 2000.
———. "Enoch and the Son of Man: A Response to Sabino Chialà and Helge Kvanvig." In *Enoch and the Messiah Son of Man: Revisiting of the Book of Parables.* Edited by G. Boccaccini, 216–227. Grand Rapids, MI: Eerdmans, 2007.
Colpe, Carsten. "Daēnā, Lichtjungfrau, Zweite Gestalt: Verbindungen und Unterschiede zwischen zarathustrischer und manichäischer Selbst-Anschauung." In *Studies in Gnosticism and Hellenistic Religions, Presented to Gilles Quispel on the Occasion of His 65th Birthday.* Edited by R. van den Broek and M. J. Vermaseren, 58–77. EPRO 91. Leiden: Brill, 1981.
Corbin, Henry. "The Time of Eranos." In *Man and Time: Papers from the Eranos Yearbooks.* Edited by J. Campbell, xiii–xx. Princeton: Princeton University Press, 1957.
———. *The Man of Light in Iranian Sufism.* Translated by N. Pearson. New Lebanon, NY: Omega, 1971.
———. *Avicenna and the Visionary Recital.* Translated by W. R. Trask. Bollingen Series 66. Princeton: Princeton University Press, 1986.
———. *Spiritual Body and Celestial Earth: From Mazdean Iran to Shīʿite Iran.* Translated by N. Pearson. Princeton: Princeton University Press, 1989.
Czachesz, Istvan. *The Grotesque Body in Early Christian Discourse: Hell, Scatology, and Metamorphosis.* New York: Equinox, 2012.
Dahl, Nils Alstrup, and Hellholm, David. "Garment-Metaphors: The Old and the New Human Being." In *Antiquity and Humanity: Essays on Ancient Religion and Philosophy. Presented to Hans Dieter Betz on His Seventieth Birthday.* Edited by A. Yarbro Collins and M. M. Mitchell, 139–158. Tübingen: Mohr/Siebeck, 2001.
Daniélou, Jean. *The Theology of Jewish Christianity.* London: Darton, Longman & Todd, 1964.
Davila, James. "Melchizedek, Michael, and War in Heaven." *SBLSP* 35 (1996): 259–272.
———. "Heavenly Ascents in the Dead Sea Scrolls." In *The Dead Sea Scrolls after Fifty Years: A Comprehensive Assessment.* Edited by P. W. Flint and J. C. VanderKam, 2.461–485. 2 vols. Leiden: Brill, 1998–1999.
———. "Melchizedek, the 'Youth,' and Jesus." In *The Dead Sea Scrolls as Background to Postbiblical Judaism and Early Christianity: Papers from an International Conference at St. Andrews in 2001.* Edited by J. R. Davila, 248–274. STDJ 46. Leiden: Brill, 2003.

De Blois, François. "Manes' 'Twin' in Iranian and Non-Iranian Texts." In *Religious Themes and Texts of Pre-Islamic Iran and Central Asia: Studies in Honour of Professor Gherardo Gnoli on the Occasion of His 65th Birthday on 6th December 2002.* Edited by C. G. Cereti, M. Maggi and E. Provasi, 7–16. BI 24. Wiesbaden: Ludwig Reichert, 2003.

DeConick, April. *Seek to See Him: Ascent and Vision Mysticism in the Gospel of Thomas.* SVC 33. Leiden: Brill, 1996.

———. "Heavenly Temple Traditions and Valentinian Worship: A Case for First-Century Christology in the Second Century." In *The Jewish Roots of Christological Monotheism.* Edited by C. C. Newman, J. R. Davila, and G. S. Lewis, 308–341. JSJSS 63. Leiden: Brill, 1999.

———. *Voices of the Mystics: Early Christian Discourse in the Gospels of John and Thomas and Other Ancient Christian Literature.* London: T&T Clark, 2001.

———. *Recovering the Original Gospel of Thomas: A History of the Gospel and Its Growth.* London: T&T Clark, 2005.

DeConick, April, and Fossum, Jarl. "Stripped before God: A New Interpretation of Logion 37 in the *Gospel of Thomas*." *VC* 45 (1991): 123–150.

De Jonge, Marinus, and Tromp, Johannes. *The Life of Adam and Eve and Related Literature.* GAP. Sheffield: Sheffield Academic Press, 1997.

De Jonge, Marinus, and van der Woude, Adam. "11QMelchizedek and the New Testament." *NTS* 12 (1966): 301–326.

Delcor, Mathias. "Melchizedek from Genesis to the Qumran Texts and the Epistle to the Hebrews." *JSJ* 2 (1971): 115–135.

———. "La naissance merveilleuse de Melchisédeq d'après l'Hénoch slave." In *Kecharitomene. Mélanges René Laurentin.* Edited by C. Augustin et al., 217–229. Paris: Desclée, 1990.

Dennis, Geoffrey. "The Use of Water as a Medium for Altered States of Consciousness in Early Jewish Mysticism: A Cross-Disciplinary Analysis." *AC* 19 (2008): 84–106.

Deutsch, Celia. "Aseneth: Ascetical Practice, Vision, and Transformation." In *With Letters of Light: Studies in the Dead Sea Scrolls, Early Jewish Apocalypticism, Magic and Mysticism.* Edited by D. Arbel and A. Orlov, 325–348. Ekstasis 2. Berlin: Walter de Gruyter, 2010.

Deutsch, Nathaniel. *The Gnostic Imagination: Gnosticism, Mandaeism, and Merkabah Mysticism.* Leiden: Brill, 1995.

———. *Guardians of the Gate: Angelic Vice Regency in Late Antiquity.* BSJS 22. Leiden: Brill, 1999.

Dick, Michael. *Born in Heaven, Made on Earth: The Making of the Cult Image in the Ancient Near East.* Winona Lake: Eisenbrauns, 1999.

Díez Macho, Alejandro. "L'usage de la troisième personne au lieu de la première dans le Targum." In *Mélanges Dominique Barthélemy.* Edited by P. Casetti et al., 61–89. Göttingen: Vandenhoeck & Ruprecht, 1981.

———. "La Cristologia del Hijo del Hombre y el uso de la tercera persona en vez de la primera." *ScrTh* 14 (1982): 189–201.

Dimant, Devorah. "The Sons of Heaven: The Theory of the Angels in the Book of Jubilees in Light of the Writings of the Qumran Community." In *A Tribute to Sarah: Studies in Jewish Philosophy and Cabala Presented to Professor Sara A. Heller-Wilensky*. Edited by M. Idel, D. Dimant, and S. Rosenberg, 97–118. Jerusalem: Magnes, 1994. [Hebrew]

———. "Men as Angels: The Self-Image of the Qumran Community." In *Religion and Politics in the Ancient Near East*. Edited by A. Berlin, 93–103. STJHC 1. Bethesda, MD: University Press of Maryland, 1996.

———. "Noah in Early Jewish Literature." In *Biblical Figures Outside the Bible*. Edited by M. E. Stone and T. A. Bergren, 123–150. Harrisburg: Trinity Press International, 1998.

Dodd, Charles. *The Interpretation of the Fourth Gospel*. Cambridge: Cambridge University Press, 1953.

Douglas, Conrad. "Liminality and Conversion in Joseph and Aseneth." *JSP* 3 (1988): 31–42.

Dozeman, Thomas. *God on the Mountain*. Atlanta: Scholars, 1989.

Drower, Ethel. *The Secret Adam*. Oxford: Oxford University Press, 1960.

Drower, Ethel, and Macuch, Rudolph. *A Mandaic Dictionary*. Oxford: Clarendon, 1963.

Dunn, James. *Christology in the Making: A New Testament Inquiry into the Origins of the Doctrine of the Incarnation*. Grand Rapids, MI: Eerdmans, 1996.

Ego, Beate. "'Im Himmel wie auf Erden.'" WUNT 2.34. Tübingen: Mohr/Siebeck, 1989.

———. "Heilige Zeit—heiliger Raum—heiliger Mensch: Beobachtungen zur Struktur der Gesetzesbegründung in der Schöpfungs- und Paradiesgeschichte des Jubiläenbuches." In *Studies in the Book of Jubilees*. Edited by M. Albani, J. Frey, and A. Lange, 207–219. TSAJ 65. Tübingen: Mohr/Siebeck, 1997.

Elior, Rachel. "From Earthly Temple to Heavenly Shrines: Prayer and Sacred Song in the Hekhalot Literature and Its Relation to Temple Traditions." *JSQ* 4 (1997): 217–267.

———. *The Three Temples: On the Emergence of Jewish Mysticism*. Oxford: Littman Library of Jewish Civilization, 2005.

Ellens, Harold. "A Christian Pesher: John 1:51." *Proceedings of Eastern Great Lakes and Midwest Biblical Societies* 25 (2005): 143–155.

Erho, Ted, and Stuckenbruck, Loren. "A Manuscript History of Ethiopic Enoch." *JSP* 23 (2013): 87–133.

Evans, Craig. "Daniel in the New Testament." In *The Book of Daniel: Composition and Reception*. Edited by J. J. Collins and P. W. Flint, 2.489–527. 2 vols. VTSup 83. Leiden: Brill, 2001.

Fauth, Wolfgang. "Manis anderes Ich: Gestalthafte Metaphysik in Kölner Mani-Kodex." In *Gnosis und Philosophie: Miscellanea*. Edited by R. Berlinger and W. Schrader, 75–114. Elementa 59. Amsterdam: Rodopi, 1994.

———. "Syzygos und Eikon." In *Gnosis und Philosophie: Miscellanea*. Edited by R. Berlinger and W. Schrader, 115–139. Elementa 59. Amsterdam: Rodopi, 1994.

Fishbane, Michael. "Through the Looking-Glass: Reflections on Ezek. 43.4, Num. 12.8 and 1 Cor. 13.8." *HAR* 10 (1986): 63–75.

Fleddermann, Harry. "The Flight of a Naked Young Man (Mark 14:51–52)." *CBQ* 41 (1979): 412–418.

Fletcher-Louis, Crispin. *Luke–Acts: Angels, Christology and Soteriology.* WUNT 2.94. Tübingen: Mohr/Siebeck, 1997.

———. "The Worship of Divine Humanity as God's Image and the Worship of Jesus." In *The Jewish Roots of Christological Monotheism: Papers from the St. Andrews Conference on the Historical Origins of the Worship of Jesus.* Edited by C. Newman et al., 112–128. JSJSS 63. Leiden: Brill, 1999.

———. *All the Glory of Adam: Liturgical Anthropology in the Dead Sea Scrolls.* STDJ 42. Leiden: Brill, 2002.

———. *Jesus Monotheism: Volume 1; Christological Origins: The Emerging Consensus and Beyond.* Eugene, OR: Cascade Books, 2015.

Foltz, Richard. *Religions of Iran: From Prehistory to the Present.* London: Oneworld, 2013.

Fossum, Jarl. *The Name of God and the Angel of the Lord: Samaritan and Jewish Mediation Concepts and the Origin of Gnosticism.* WUNT 36. Tübingen: Mohr/Siebeck, 1985.

———. *The Image of the Invisible God: Essays on the Influence of Jewish Mysticism on Early Christology.* NTOA 30. Fribourg: Universitätsverlag Freiburg Schweiz. Göttingen: Vandenhoeck & Ruprecht, 1995.

Foster, Paul. "Polymorphic Christology: Its Origins and Development in Early Christianity." *JTS* 58 (2007): 66–99.

Frankfurter, David. "The Legacy of Jewish Apocalypses in Early Christianity: Regional Trajectories." In *The Jewish Apocalyptic Heritage in Early Christianity.* Edited by J. C. VanderKam and W. Adler, 129–200. CRINT 3.4. Assen: Van Gorcum, 1996.

Franzmann, Majella. *Jesus in the Manichaean Writings.* London: T&T Clark, 2003.

Freedman, David Noel. "Temple without Hands." In *Temples and High Places in Biblical Times: Proceedings of the Colloquium in Honor of the Centennial of Hebrew Union College–Jewish Institute of Religion, Jerusalem, 14–16 March 1977.* Edited by A. Biran, 21–30. Jerusalem: Hebrew Union College–Jewish Institute of Religion, 1981.

Friedman, Shamma. "Graven Images." *Graven Images* 1 (1994): 233–238.

Gallusz, Laszlo. *The Throne Motif in the Book of Revelation.* London: Bloomsbury, 2014.

Garcia, Hughes. "La polymorphie du Christ dans le christianisme ancien: Remarques sur quelques définitions et quelques enjeux." *Apocrypha* 10 (1999): 16–55.

García Martínez, Florentino. *Qumran and Apocalyptic.* STDJ 9. Leiden: Brill, 1992.

———. "Interpretation of the Flood in the Dead Sea Scrolls." In *Interpretations of the Flood.* Edited by F. García Martínez and G. P. Luttikhuizen, 86–108. TBN 1. Leiden: Brill, 1998.

———. *Qumranica Minora II: Thematic Studies on the Dead Sea Scrolls.* Edited by E. Tigchelaar. Leiden: Brill, 2007.

Gathercole, Simon. *The Preexistent Son: Recovering the Christologies of Matthew, Mark, and Luke.* Grand Rapids, MI: Eerdmans, 2006.

Gieschen, Charles. *Angelomorphic Christology: Antecedents and Early Evidence.* AGAJU 42. Leiden: Brill, 1998.

Ginzberg, Louis. *Legends of the Jews.* 7 vols. Baltimore: Johns Hopkins University Press, 1998.

Glazov, Gregory. *The Bridling of the Tongue and the Opening of the Mouth in Biblical Prophecy*. JSOTSS 311. Sheffield: Sheffield Academic Press, 2001.

Glovino, Mariana. *The Assyrian Sacred Tree*. Fribourg: Academic Press. Göttingen: Vandenhoeck & Ruprecht, 2007.

Goshen-Gottstein, Alon. "The Body as Image of God in Rabbinic Literature." HTR 87 (1994): 171–195.

Green, Arthur. *Keter: The Crown of God in Early Jewish Mysticism*. Princeton: Princeton University Press, 1997.

Greenstein, Edward. "God's Golem: The Creation of the Human in Genesis 2." In *Creation in Jewish and Christian Tradition*. Edited by H. Reventlow and Y. Hoffman, 219–239. JSOTSS 319. Sheffield: Sheffield Academic Press, 2002.

Griffith, Terry. "Eidolon as 'Idol' in Non-Jewish and Non-Christian Greek." JTS 53 (2002): 95–101.

Gruenwald, Ithamar. *From Apocalypticism to Gnosticism: Studies in Apocalypticism, Merkavah Mysticism and Gnosticism*. BEATAJ 14. Frankfurt am Main: Peter Lang, 1988.

———. *Apocalyptic and Merkavah Mysticism*. 2nd ed. Leiden: Brill, 2014.

Gutman, Yehoshua. *The Beginnings of Jewish-Hellenistic Literature*. 2 vols. Jerusalem: Mosad Bialik, 1958–1963. [Hebrew]

Hadas, Moses. *Hellenistic Culture: Fusion and Diffusion*. Morningside Heights, NY: Columbia University Press, 1959.

Hakl, Hans Thomas. *Eranos: An Alternative Intellectual History of the Twentieth Century*. Translated by C. McIntosh. London: Routledge, 2014.

Halperin, David. "Heavenly Ascension in Ancient Judaism: The Nature of the Experience." SBLSP 26 (1987): 218–231.

———. *The Faces of the Chariot: Early Jewish Responses to Ezekiel's Vision*. TSAJ 16. Tübingen: Mohr/Siebeck, 1988.

Hamerton-Kelly, Robert. "The Temple and the Origins of Jewish Apocalyptic." VT 20 (1970): 1–15.

Hannah, Darrell. *Michael and Christ: Michael Traditions and Angel Christology in Early Christianity*. WUNT 2.109. Tübingen: Mohr/Siebeck, 1999.

———. "Guardian Angels and Angelic National Patrons in Second Temple Judaism and Early Christianity." In *Angels, the Concept of Celestial Beings: Origins, Development and Reception*. Edited by F. V. Reiterer, T. Nicklas, and K. Schöpflin, 413–435. Deuterocanonical and Cognate Literature Yearbook. Berlin: Walter de Gruyter, 2007.

Hartman, Louis. "The Great Tree and Nabuchodonosor's Madness." In *The Bible in Current Catholic Thought*. Edited by J. L. McKenzie, 75–82. New York: Herder & Herder, 1962.

Hayward, Richard. *Interpretations of the Name Israel in Ancient Judaism and Some Early Christian Writings*. Oxford: Oxford University Press, 2005.

Heath, Jane. "Homer or Moses? A Hellenistic Perspective on Moses' Throne Vision in Ezekiel Tragicus." JJS 58 (2007): 1–18.

Henrichs, Albert, and Koenen, Ludwig. "Ein griechischer Mani-Codex (P. Colon. inv. nr. 4780)." ZPE 5 (1970): 97–216.

Henrichs, Albert et al. "Der Kölner Mani-Kodex (P. Colon. inv. nr. 4780)." *ZPE* 19 (1975): 1–85.

Henze, Matthias. *The Madness of King Nebuchadnezzar: The Ancient Near Eastern Origins and Early History of Interpretation of Daniel 4*. JSJSS 61. Leiden: Brill, 1999.

Heuser, Manfred. "Manichaean Myth According to the Coptic Sources." In *Studies in Manichaean Literature and Art*. Edited by M. Heuser and H. Klimkeit, 3–108. NHMS 46. Leiden: Brill, 1998.

Himmelfarb, Martha. "The Experience of the Visionary and Genre in the Ascension of Isaiah 6–11 and the Apocalypse of Paul." In *Early Christian Apocalypticism: Genre and Social Setting*. Edited by A. Y. Collins, 97–111. Semeia 36. Decatur, GA: Scholars, 1986.

———. "From Prophecy to Apocalypse: The Book of the Watchers and Tours of Heaven." In *Jewish Spirituality: From the Bible through the Middle Ages*. Edited by A. Green, 145–165. New York: Crossroad, 1986.

———. "Apocalyptic Ascent and the Heavenly Temple." *SBLSP* 26 (1987): 210–217.

———. *Ascent to Heaven in Jewish and Christian Apocalypses*. New York: Oxford University Press, 1993.

———. "The Practice of Ascent in the Ancient Mediterranean World." In *Death, Ecstasy, and Other Worldly Journeys*. Edited by J. J. Collins and M. Fishbane, 123–137. Albany: SUNY Press, 1995.

Holladay, Carl. "The Portrait of Moses in Ezekiel the Tragedian." *SBLSP* 10 (1976): 447–452.

Horton, Fred. *The Melchizedek Tradition: A Critical Examination of the Sources to the Fifth Century A.D. and in the Epistle to the Hebrews*. SNTSMS 30. Cambridge: Cambridge University Press, 1976.

Humphrey, Edith McEwan. *Joseph and Aseneth*. GAP 8. Sheffield: Sheffield Academic Press, 2000.

Hurowitz, Victor. "The Mesopotamian God Image, from Womb to Tomb." *JAOS* 123 (2003): 147–157.

———. "What Goes in Is What Comes out: Materials for Creating Cult Statues." In *Text, Artifact, and Image: Revealing Ancient Israelite Religion*. Edited by G. M. Beckman and T. J. Lewis, 3–23. BJS 346. Providence, RI: Brown Judaic Studies, 2006.

Hurtado, Larry. *One God, One Lord: Early Christian Devotion and Ancient Jewish Monotheism*. Philadelphia: Fortress, 1988.

Idel, Moshe. "Hermeticism and Judaism." In *Hermeticism and the Renaissance: Intellectual History and the Occult in Early Modern Europe*. Edited by I. Merkel and A. G. Debus, 59–76. Washington, DC: Folger Shakespeare Library, 1988.

———. "Enoch Is Metatron." *Imm* 24/25 (1990): 220–240.

———. *Golem: Jewish Magical and Mystical Traditions on the Artificial Anthropoid*. Albany: SUNY Press, 1990.

———. "Panim: On Facial Re-Presentations in Jewish Thought: Some Correlational Instances." In *On Interpretation in the Arts, Interdisciplinary Studies in the Honor of Moshe Lazar*. Edited by N. Yaari, 21–56. Tel Aviv: Tel Aviv University, 2000.

———. *Ascensions on High in Jewish Mysticism: Pillars, Lines, Ladders*. Past Incorporated. CEUSH 2. Budapest: Central European University Press, 2005.

———. *Old Worlds, New Mirrors: On Jewish Mysticism and Twentieth-Century Thought.* Philadelphia: University of Pennsylvania Press, 2010.

———. "The Changing Faces of God and Human Dignity in Judaism." In *Moshe Idel: Representing God.* Edited by H. Tirosh-Samuelson and A. W. Hughes, 103–122. LCJP 8. Leiden: Brill, 2014.

Istrin, Vasilij. "Zamechanie o sostave Tolkovoj Palei." *IORJS* 2.1 (1897): 175–209.

———. "Apokrif ob Iosife i Asenefe." *Drevnosti. Trudy Slavjanskoj Kommissii Imperatorskogo Moskovskogo Arheologicheskogo Obschestva* 2 (1898): 146–199.

———. "Redakcii Tolkovoj Palei." *IORJS* 10.4 (1905): 150–151.

Jacobson, Howard. "Mysticism and Apocalyptic in Ezekiel's Exagoge." *ICS* 6 (1981): 273–293.

Jaeger, Werner. *The Theology of the Early Greek Philosophers.* Oxford: Clarendon, 1947.

Jeremias, Joachim. "Die Berufung des Nathanael." *Angelos* 3 (1928): 2–5.

Jervell, Jacob. *Imago Dei. Gen 1,26f. im Spätjudentum, in der Gnosis und in den paulinischen Briefen.* FRLANT 76. Göttingen: Vandenhoeck & Ruprecht, 1960.

Junod, Eric. "Polymorphie du Dieu sauver." In *Gnosticisme et monde hellénistique.* Edited by J. Ries et al., 38–46. Publications de l'Institut orientaliste de Louvain 27. Louvain-la-Neuve: Université Catholique de Louvain, Institut orientaliste, 1982.

Kamchatnov, Aleksandr. "Paleja Tolkovaja." In *Idejnye techenija russkoj mysli.* Edited by M. N. Gromov and V. V. Mil'kov, 571–677. St. Petersburg: RHGI, 1999.

———. "Paleja Tolkovaja." In *Filosofskie i bogoslovskie idei v pamjatnikah drevnerusskoj mysli.* Edited by M. N. Gromov and V. V. Mil'kov, 114–169. Moscow: Nauka, 2000.

Kaplan, Chaim. "The Hidden Name." *JSOR* 13 (1929): 181–184.

Käsemann, Ernst. *New Testament Questions of Today.* Philadelphia: Fortress, 1969.

Kerr, Alan. *The Temple of Jesus' Body: The Temple Theme in the Gospel of John.* JSNTSS 220. Sheffield: Sheffield Academic Press, 2002.

Kim, Jung Hoon. *The Significance of Clothing Imagery in the Pauline Corpus.* JSNTSS 268. London: T&T Clark, 2004.

Kim, Seyoon. *The Origin of Paul's Gospel.* 2nd ed. WUNT 2/4. Tübingen: Mohr/Siebeck, 1984.

Kim Harkins, Angela. *Reading with an "I" to the Heavens: Looking at the Qumran Hodayot through the Lens of Visionary Traditions.* Ekstasis: Religious Experience from Antiquity to the Middle Ages 3. Berlin: Walter de Gruyter, 2012.

Knibb, Michael. "Messianism in the Pseudepigrapha in the Light of the Scrolls." *DSD* 2 (1995): 177–180.

Knox, John. "A Note on Mark 14:51–52." In *The Joy of Study: Papers on New Testament and Related Subjects Presented to Honor Frederick Clifton Grant.* Edited by S. Johnson, 27–30. New York: Macmillan, 1951.

Kobelski, Paul. *Melchizedek and Melchireša^c.* CBQMS 10. Washington, DC: Catholic Biblical Association of America, 1981.

Koch, Klaus. "Questions Regarding the So-Called Son of Man in the Parables of Enoch: A Response to Sabino Chialà and Helge Kvanvig." In *Enoch and the Messiah Son of Man: Revisiting of the Book of Parables.* Edited by G. Boccaccini, 228–237. Grand Rapids, MI: Eerdmans, 2007.

Koenen, Ludwig. "Augustine and Manichaeism in Light of the Cologne Mani Codex." *ICS* 3 (1978): 154–195.
Koester, Craig. *The Dwelling of God: The Tabernacle in the Old Testament, Intertestamental Jewish Literature and the New Testament.* CBQMS 22. Washington, DC: Catholic Biblical Association of America, 1989.
———. "Messianic Exegesis and the Call of Nathanael." *JSNT* 39 (1990): 23–34.
Kraemer, Ross. *When Aseneth Met Joseph: A Late Antique Tale of the Biblical Patriarch and His Egyptian Wife, Reconsidered.* New York: Oxford University Press, 1998.
Kugel, James. *In Potiphar's House: The Interpretive Life of Biblical Texts.* San Francisco: Harper Collins, 1990.
———. "The Ladder of Jacob." *HTR* 88 (1995): 209–227.
———. *Traditions of the Bible: A Guide to the Bible as It Was at the Start of the Common Era.* Cambridge, MA: Harvard University Press, 1998.
———. *A Walk through Jubilees: Studies in the Book of Jubilees and the World of Its Creation.* JSJSS 156. Leiden: Brill, 2012.
Kuiper, Koenraad. "De Ezekiele Poeta Iudaeo." *Mnemosyne* 28 (1900): 237–280.
———. "Le poète juif Ezéchiel." *REJ* 46 (1903): 48–73, 161–177.
Kvanvig, Helge. *Roots of Apocalyptic: The Mesopotamian Background of the Enoch Figure and of the Son of Man.* WMANT 61. Neukirchen-Vluyn: Neukirchener Verlag, 1988.
———. "The Son of Man in the Parables of Enoch." In *Enoch and the Messiah Son of Man: Revisiting of the Book of Parables.* Edited by G. Boccaccini, 197–210. Grand Rapids, MI: Eerdmans, 2007.
Kysar, Robert. *John: The Maverick Gospel.* Atlanta: John Knox Press, 1976.
Ladouceur, Paul. "Old Testament Prefigurations of the Mother of God." *SVTQ* 50 (2006): 5–57.
Lambert, Wilfred. "Enmeduranki and Related Matters." *JCS* 21 (1967): 126–138.
Lambrecht, Jan. "Transformation in 2 Cor 3,18." *Biblica* 64 (1983): 243–254.
Lankarny, Firouz-Thomas. *Daēnā in Avesta: Eine Semantische Untersuchung.* SII 10. Reinbek: Verlag für Orientalistische Fachpublikationen, 1985.
Leicht, Reimund. "Qedushah and Prayer to Helios: A New Hebrew Version of an Apocryphal Prayer of Jacob." *JSQ* 6 (1999): 140–176.
Lesses, Rebecca. *Ritual Practices to Gain Power: Angels, Incantations, and Revelation in Early Jewish Mysticism.* Harrisburg, PA: Trinity Press International, 1998.
Levenson, Jon. "The Temple and the World." *JR* 64 (1984): 275–298.
———. "The Jerusalem Temple in Devotional and Visionary Experience." In *Jewish Spirituality: From the Bible through the Middle Ages.* Edited by A. Green, 32–59. New York: Crossroad, 1986.
Lewis, Jack. *A Study of the Interpretation of Noah and the Flood in Jewish and Christian Literature.* Leiden: Brill, 1968.
Liddell, Henry George et al. *A Greek-English Lexicon with a Revised Supplement.* Oxford: Clarendon, 1996.
Lieber, Andrea. "I Set a Table before You: The Jewish Eschatological Character of Aseneth's Conversion Meal." *JSP* 14 (2004): 63–77.

Lieu, Samuel. *Manichaeism in the Later Roman Empire and Medieval China*. Tübingen: Mohr/Siebeck, 1992.

Linardou, Kallirroe. "Depicting the Salvation." In *The Cult of the Mother of God in Byzantium: Texts and Images*. Edited by L. Brubaker and M. B. Cunningham, 133–149. Burlington, VT: Ashgate, 2011.

Litwa, David. "Transformation through a Mirror: Moses in 2 Cor. 3.18." *JSNT* 34 (2012): 286–297.

Lundberg, Marilyn. "The *Mis-Pi* Rituals and Incantations and Jeremiah 10:1–16." In *Uprooting and Planting: Essays on Jeremiah for Leslie Allen*. Edited by J. Goldingay, 210–227. London: T&T Clark, 2007.

Luttikhuizen, Gerard. "The Hymn of Jude Thomas, the Apostle, in the Country of the Indians." In *Apocryphal Acts of Thomas*. Edited by J. N. Bremmer, 101–114. Leiden: Brill, 2001.

Manson, Thomas. *The Teaching of Jesus: Studies of Its Form and Content*. 2nd ed. Cambridge: Cambridge University Press, 1935.

Marjanen, Antti. "Women Disciples in the *Gospel of Thomas*." In *Thomas at the Crossroads: Essays on the Gospel of Thomas*. Edited by R. Uro, 89–106. Edinburgh: T&T Clark, 1998.

McDonough, Sean. *YHWH at Patmos: Rev. 1:4 in Its Hellenistic and Early Jewish Setting*. WUNT 2.107. Tübingen: Mohr/Siebeck, 1999.

McNicol, Allan. "The Heavenly Sanctuary in Judaism: A Model for Tracing the Origin of the Apocalypse." *JRelS* 13 (1987): 66–94.

Meeks, Wayne, *The Prophet-King: Moses Traditions and the Johannine Christology*. NovTSup 14. Leiden: Brill, 1967.

———. "Moses as God and King." In *Religions in Antiquity: Essays in Memory of Erwin Ramsdell Goodenough*. Edited by J. Neusner, 354–371. SHR 14. Leiden: Brill, 1968.

Michaelis, Wilhelm. "Joh. 1,51, Gen. 28,12 und das Menschensohn-Problem." *TLZ* 85 (1960): 564–566.

Michaels, Ramsey. "Nathanael under the Fig Tree." *ExpTim* 78 (1966–1967): 182–183.

Mihajlov, Aleksandr. "Obshij obzor sostava, redakcij i literaturnyh istochnikov Tolkovoj Palei." *VUI* 7 (1895): 1–21.

Molé, Marijan. "Daēnā, Le Pont Činvat et l'initiation dans le Mazdéisme." *RHR* 157 (1960): 155–185.

Montgomery, James. *The Samaritans*. New York: Ktav, 1968.

Morray-Jones, Christopher. "Transformational Mysticism in the Apocalyptic-Merkabah Tradition." *JJS* 43 (1992): 1–31.

———. "The Temple Within: The Embodied Divine Image and Its Worship in the Dead Sea Scrolls and Other Jewish and Christian Sources." *SBLSP* 37 (1998): 400–431.

———. *A Transparent Illusion: The Dangerous Vision of Water in Hekhalot Mysticism: A Source-Critical and Tradition-Historical Inquiry*. JSJSS 59. Leiden: Brill, 2002.

Moule, Charles Francis Digby. "A Note on 'Under the Fig-Tree' in John 1:48, 50." *JTS* 5.2 (1954): 210–211.

Moulton, James Hope. "'It Is His Angel.'" *JTS* 3 (1902): 514–527.

———. "Fravashi." In *Encyclopaedia of Religion and Ethics*. Edited by J. Hastings, 5.116–118. 12 vols. Edinburgh: Charles Scribner's Sons, 1913.

———. *Early Zoroastrianism: Lectures Delivered at Oxford and in London February to May 1912*. London: Constable & Company, 1926.

Mowinckel, Sigmund. *He That Cometh*. New York: Abingdon, 1951.

Murmelstein, Benjamin. "Adam, ein Beitrag zur Messiaslehre." *WZKM* 35 (1928): 242–275.

Nagel, Peter. "Die apokryphen Apostelakten des 2. und 3. Jahrhunderts in der manichäischen Literatur: Ein Beitrag zur Frage nach den christlichen Elementen im Manichäismus." In *Gnosis und Neues Testament: Studien aus Religionswissenschaft und Theologie*. Edited by K.-W. Tröger, 149–182. Gütersloh: Mohn, 1973.

———. "Der Parakletenspruch des Mani (Keph. 14,7–11) und die altsyrische Evangelienübersetzung." In *Festschrift zum 150-jährigen Bestehen des Berliner Ägyptischen Museums*, 303–313. MAS 8. Berlin: Akademie-Verlag, 1974.

Najman, Hindy. "Angels at Sinai: Exegesis, Theology and Interpretive Authority." *DSD* 7 (2000): 313–333.

Neeb, John. "Jacob/Jesus Typology in John 1:51." *Proceedings of Eastern Great Lakes and Midwest Biblical Societies* 12 (1992): 83–89.

———. "Origen's Interpretation of Genesis 28:12 and the Rabbis." In *Origeniana Sexta: Origène et la Bible*. Edited by G. Dorival and A. Le Boulluec, 71–80. Louvain: Leuven University Press, 1995.

Neis, Rachel. "Embracing Icons: The Face of Jacob on the Throne of God." *Images: A Journal of Jewish Art and Visual Culture* 1 (2007): 36–54.

Newsom, Carol. "'He Has Established for Himself Priests': Human and Angelic Priesthood in the Qumran Sabbath Shirot." In *Archaeology and History in the Dead Sea Scrolls: The New York University Conference in Memory of Yigael Yadin*. Edited by L. H. Schiffman, 101–120. JSPSS 8. Sheffield: JSOT Press, 1990.

Neyrey, Jerome. "The Jacob Allusions in John 1:51." *CBQ* 44 (1982): 586–605.

———. *The Gospel of John in Cultural and Rhetorical Perspective*. Grand Rapids: Eerdmans, 2009.

Nickelsburg, George. "Enoch, Levi, and Peter: Recipients of Revelation in Upper Galilee." *JBL* 100 (1981): 575–600.

———. "The Apocalyptic Construction of Reality in 1 Enoch." In *Mysteries and Revelations: Apocalyptic Studies since the Uppsala Colloquium*. Edited by J. J. Collins, 51–64. JSPSS 9. Sheffield: JSOT Press, 1991.

Nissinen, Martti. "Sacred Springs and Liminal Rivers: Water and Prophecy in the Ancient Eastern Mediterranean." In *Thinking of Water in the Early Second Temple Period*. Edited by E. Ben Zvi and C. Levin, 29–48. Berlin: Walter de Gruyter, 2014.

Ogden, Daniel. *Magic, Witchcraft and Ghosts in the Greek and Roman Worlds: A Sourcebook*. New York: Oxford University Press, 2002.

Olson, Daniel. *A New Reading of the Animal Apocalypse of 1 Enoch: "All Nations Shall be Blessed."* SVTP 24. Leiden: Brill, 2013.

Olyan, Saul. *A Thousand Thousands Served Him: Exegesis and the Naming of Angels in Ancient Judaism*. TSAJ 36. Tübingen: Mohr/Siebeck, 1993.

O'Neill, John Cochrane. "Son of Man, Stone of Blood (John 1:51)." *NovT* 45 (2003): 374–381.

Orlov, Andrei. "'Noah's Younger Brother': Anti-Noachic Polemics in 2 Enoch." *Henoch* 22 (2000): 259–273.
———. "Noah's Younger Brother Revisited: Anti-Noachic Polemics and the Date of 2 (Slavonic) Enoch." *Henoch* 26 (2004): 172–187.
———. "The Face as the Heavenly Counterpart of the Visionary in the Slavonic Ladder of Jacob." In *Of Scribes and Sages: Early Jewish Interpretation and Transmission of Scripture*. Edited by C. A. Evans, 2.59–76. SSEJC 9. 2 vols. London: T&T Clark, 2004.
———. *The Enoch-Metatron Tradition*. TSAJ 107. Tübingen: Mohr/Siebeck, 2005.
———. "Moses' Heavenly Counterpart in the Book of Jubilees and the Exagoge of Ezekiel the Tragedian." *Biblica* 88 (2007): 153–173.
———. "In the Mirror of the Divine Face: The Enochic Features of the Exagoge of Ezekiel the Tragedian." In *The Significance of Sinai: Traditions about Sinai and Divine Revelation in Judaism and Christianity*. Edited by G. Brooks, H. Najman, and L. Stuckenbruck, 183–199. TBN 12. Leiden: Brill, 2008.
———. *Selected Studies in the Slavonic Pseudepigrapha*. SVTP 23. Leiden: Brill, 2009.
———. *Dark Mirrors: Azazel and Satanael in Early Jewish Demonology*. Albany: SUNY Press, 2011.
———. "The Sacerdotal Traditions of 2 Enoch and the Date of the Text." In *New Perspectives on 2 Enoch: No Longer Slavonic Only*. Edited by A. Orlov, G. Boccaccini, and J. Zurawski, 103–116. SJS 4. Leiden: Brill, 2012.
———. *Divine Scapegoats: Demonic Mimesis in Early Jewish Mysticism*. Albany: SUNY Press, 2015.
Ort, Lodewijk Josephus Rudolf. *Mani: A Religio-Historical Description of His Personality*. Leiden: Brill, 1957.
Otto, Rudolph. *The Kingdom of God and the Son of Man*. 2nd ed. London: Lutterworth, 1943.
Parpola, Simo. "The Assyrian Tree of Life: Tracing the Origins of Jewish Monotheism and Greek Philosophy." *JNES* 52 (1993): 161–208.
Patai, Raphael. *Man and Temple in Ancient Jewish Myth and Ritual*. New York: Ktav, 1967.
Penn, Michael. "Identity Transformation and Authorial Identification in Joseph and Aseneth." *JSP* 13 (2002): 171–183.
Pentuic, Eugen. *The Old Testament in Eastern Orthodox Tradition*. Oxford: Oxford University Press, 2014.
Peters, Dorothy. *Noah Traditions in the Dead Sea Scrolls: Conversations and Controversies of Antiquity*. Atlanta: Scholars, 2008.
Pettinato, Giovanni. *Die Ölwahrsagung bei den Babyloniern*. StSem 21–22. Roma: Istituto di studi del Vicino Oriente, 1966.
Philonenko, Marc. "Initiation et mystère dans Joseph et Aséneth." In *Initiation*. Edited by C. J. Bleeker, 147–153. SHR 10. Leiden: Brill, 1965.
Pinnick, Avital. *The Birth of Moses in Jewish Literature of the Second Temple Period*. PhD diss. Harvard University, 1996.
Poirier, Paul-Hubert. "L'Hymne de la Perle et le manichéisme à la lumière du Codex manichéen de Cologne." In *Codex Manichaicus Coloniensis: Atti del Simposio Internazionale (Rende-Amantea 3–7 settembre 1984). Università degli studi della Cal-

abria, Centro interdipartimentale di science religiose. Edited by L. Cirillo, 235–248. Studi e ricerche 4. Cosenza: Marra, 1986.

Portier-Young, Anathea. "Sweet Mercy Metropolis: Interpreting Aseneth's Honeycomb." *JSP* 14 (2005): 133–157.

Principe, Concetta. *Secular Messiahs and the Return of Paul's "Real": A Lacanian Approach*. New York: Palgrave Macmillan, 2015.

Puech, Henry-Charles. "Doctrines ésotériques et thèmes gnostiques dans L'Évangile selon Thomas." *ACF* 63 (1963): 199–213.

Putthoff, Tyson. "Aseneth's Gastronomical Vision: Mystical Theophagy and the New Creation in Joseph and Aseneth." *JSP* 24 (2014): 96–117.

Quispel, Gilles. "Gnosticism and the New Testament." In *The Bible in Modern Scholarship*. Edited by J. P. Hyatt, 252–271. Nashville: Abingdon, 1965.

———. "Das ewige Ebenbild des Menschen: Zur Begegnung mit dem Selbst in der Gnosis." *Eranos-Jahrbuch* 36 (1967): 9–30.

———. "Jewish Gnosis and Mandaean Gnosticism." In *Les textes de Nag Hammadi*. Edited by J.-É. Ménard, 82–122. NHS 7. Leiden: Brill, 1975.

———. "Ezekiel 1:26 in Jewish Mysticism and Gnosis." *VC* 34 (1980): 1–13.

———. "Gnosis and Psychology." In *The Rediscovery of Gnosticism*. Edited by B. Layton, 1.17–31. 2 vols. SHR 41. Leiden: Brill, 1981.

———. *Gnostica, Judaica, Catholica: Collected Essays of Gilles Quispel*. Edited by J. van Oort. NHMS 55. Leiden: Brill, 2008.

Reeves, John. "Utnapishtim in the Book of Giants?" *JBL* 12 (1993): 110–115.

———. *Heralds of that Good Realm: Syro-Mesopotamian Gnosis and Jewish Traditions*. NHMS 41. Leiden: Brill, 1996.

———. *Prolegomena to a History of Islamicate Manichaeism*. Comparative Islamic Studies. Sheffield: Equinox, 2011.

Reno, Stephen Jerome. *The Sacred Tree as an Early Christian Literary Symbol: A Phenomenological Study*. Saarbrücken: Homo et Religio, 1978.

Rordorf, Willy. "Gen 28,10ff und Joh 1,51 in der patristischen Exegese." In *Johannes-Studien*, 39–46. Zürich: Theologischer Verlag, 1991.

Rose, Eugen. *Die Manichäische Christologie*. SOR 5. Wiesbaden: Harrassowitz, 1979.

Rowland, Christopher. "The Visions of God in Apocalyptic Literature." *JSJ* 10 (1979): 137–154.

———. *The Open Heaven: A Study of Apocalyptic in Judaism and Early Christianity*. London: SPCK, 1982.

———. "John 1.51, Jewish Apocalyptic and Targumic Tradition." *NTS* 30 (1984): 498–507.

Rowland, Christopher, and Morray-Jones, Christopher. *The Mystery of God: Early Jewish Mysticism and the New Testament*. CRINT 12. Leiden: Brill, 2009.

Rubin, Nissan, and Kosman, Adniel. "The Clothing of the Primordial Adam as a Symbol of Apocalyptic Time in the Midrashic Sources." *HTR* 90 (1997): 155–174.

Ruffatto, Kristine. "Polemics with Enochic Traditions in the Exagoge of Ezekiel the Tragedian." *JSP* 15 (2006): 195–210.

———. "Raguel as Interpreter of Moses' Throne Vision: The Transcendent Identity of Raguel in the Exagoge of Ezekiel the Tragedian." *JSP* 17 (2008): 121–139.

Sacchi, Paolo. "The 2005 Camaldoli Seminar on the Parables of Enoch: Summary and Prospects for Future Research." In *Enoch and the Messiah Son of Man: Revisiting of the Book of Parables*. Edited by G. Boccaccini, 499–512. Grand Rapids, MI: Eerdmans, 2007.

Santos Otero, de Aurelio. "Alttestamentliche Pseudepigrapha und die sogenannte 'Tolkovaja Paleja' [TP]." In *Oecumenica et Patristica. FS für W. Schneemelcher zum 75. Geburtstag*. Edited by D. Papandreou, W. A. Bienert, and K. Schäferdieck, 107–122. Stuttgart: W. Kohlhammer, 1989.

Schäfer, Peter. *The Hidden and Manifest God: Some Major Themes in Early Jewish Mysticism*. Albany: SUNY Press, 1992.

———. *The Origins of Jewish Mysticism*. Tübingen: Mohr/Siebeck, 2009.

Schnackenburg, Rudolf. "Das kommende Reich Gottes und der Menschensohn." In *Gottes Herrschaft und Reich*. Edited by R. Schnackenburg, 110–122. Freiburg: Herder, 1959.

Schneider, Michael. "Joseph and Aseneth and Early Jewish Mysticism." *Kabbalah* 3 (1998): 303–344. [Hebrew]

Scholem, Gershom. *Jewish Gnosticism, Merkabah Mysticism, and Talmudic Tradition*. New York: Jewish Theological Seminary of America, [1960] 1965.

———. *On the Kabbalah and Its Symbolism*. Translated by R. Manheim. New York: Schocken, 1965.

———. *Origins of Kabbalah*. Edited by R. J. Zwi Werblowsky. Princeton: Princeton University Press, 1973.

———. *On the Mystical Shape of the Godhead: Basic Concepts in Kabbalah*. New York: Schocken, 1976.

Schwartz, Howard. *Tree of Souls: The Mythology of Judaism*. Oxford: Oxford University Press, 2004.

Scott, James. "Geographic Aspects of Noachic Materials in the Scrolls of Qumran." In *The Scrolls and the Scriptures: Qumran Fifty Years After*. Edited by S. E. Porter and C. E. Evans, 368–381. JSPSS 26. Sheffield: Sheffield Academic Press, 1997.

———. *Geography in Early Judaism and Christianity: The Book of Jubilees*. SNTSMS 113. Cambridge: Cambridge University Press, 2002.

———. *On Earth as in Heaven: The Restoration of Sacred Time and Sacred Space in the Book of Jubilees*. JSJSS 91. Leiden: Brill, 2005.

Segal, Alan. *Two Powers in Heaven: Early Rabbinic Reports about Christianity and Gnosticism*. Leiden: Brill, 1977.

———. "Heavenly Ascent in Hellenistic Judaism, Early Christianity and Their Environment." *ANRW* 2.23.2 (1980): 1333–1394.

———. *Paul the Convert: The Apostolate and Apostasy of Saul the Pharisee*. New Haven: Yale University Press, 1990.

———. "The Afterlife as Mirror of the Self." In *Experientia: Volume 1: Inquiry into Religious Experience in Early Judaism and Christianity*. Edited by F. Flannery, C. Shantz, and R. A. Werline, 19–40. SBLSS 40. Atlanta: SBL, 2008.

Segal, Michael. *The Book of Jubilees: Rewritten Bible, Redaction, Ideology and Theology*. JSJSS 117. Leiden: Brill, 2007.

Shaked, Shaul. *Dualism in Transformation: Varieties of Religion in Sasanian Iran.* Jordan Lectures. London: School of Oriental and African Studies, 1994.
Sheridan, Mark. *Genesis 12-50.* Ancient Christian Commentary on Scripture. Old Testament 2. Downers Grove, IL: InterVarsity Press, 2002.
Smagina, Evgenia. *Maniheistvo po rannim istochnikam.* Moscow: Vostochnaja Literatura, 2011.
Smelik, Willem. "On Mystical Transformation of the Righteous into Light in Judaism." *JSJ* 26 (1995): 131-141.
Smith, Jonathan. "The Garments of Shame." *HR* 5 (1965/1966): 217-238.
———. "The Prayer of Joseph." In *Religions in Antiquity: Essays in Memory of Erwin Ramsdell Goodenough.* Edited by J. Neusner, 253-294. SHR 14. Leiden: Brill, 1968.
———. *Map Is Not Territory: Studies in the History of Religions.* Leiden: Brill, 1978.
Smith, Mark. "Biblical and Canaanite Notes to the Songs of the Sabbath Sacrifice from Qumran." *RevQ* 12 (1987): 585-588.
———. *God in Translation: Deities in Cross-Cultural Discourse in the Biblical World.* Grand Rapids, MI: Eerdmans, 2010.
Spiegelman, Marvin. "Struggling with the Image of God." *JPsJ* 10 (1986): 100-111.
Sreznevskij, Izmail. *Slovar' drevnerusskogo jazyka.* 3 vols. Moscow: Kniga, 1989.
Standhartinger, Angela. *Das Frauenbild im Judentum der hellenistischen Zeit: Ein Beitrag anhand von "Joseph und Aseneth."* AGAJU 26. Leiden: Brill, 1995.
Stang, Charles. *Our Divine Double.* Cambridge, MA: Harvard University Press, 2016.
Starobinski-Safran, Esther. "Un poète judéo-hellénistique: Ezéchiel le Tragique." *MH* 3 (1974): 216-224.
Steiner, Richard. "The Heading of the Book of the Words of Noah on a Fragment of the Genesis Apocryphon: New Light on a 'Lost' Work." *DSD* 2 (1995): 66-71.
Stenström, Hanna. "Masculine or Feminine? Male Virgins in Joseph and Aseneth and the Book of Revelation." In *Identity Formation in the New Testament.* Edited by B. Holmberg and M. Winninge, 199-222. WUNT 227. Tübingen: Mohr/Siebeck, 2008.
Stichel, Rainer. *Die Namen Noes, seines Bruders und seiner Frau. Ein Beitrag zum Nachleben jüdischer Überlieferungen in der außerkanonischen und gnostischen Literatur und in Denkmälern der Kunst.* AAWG 3.112. Göttingen: Vandenhoeck & Ruprecht, 1979.
Stone, Michael. "Noah, Books of." *Encyclopaedia Judaica,* 12.1198. Jerusalem: Keter, 1971.
———. "The Book of Enoch and Judaism in the Third Century B.C.E." *CBQ* 40 (1978): 479-492.
———. "The Axis of History at Qumran." In *Pseudepigraphic Perspectives: The Apocrypha and the Pseudepigrapha in Light of the Dead Sea Scrolls.* Edited by E. Chazon and M. E. Stone, 133-149. STDJ 31. Leiden: Brill, 1999.
———. "The Fall of Satan and Adam's Penance: Three Notes on the Books of Adam and Eve." In *Literature on Adam and Eve: Collected Essays.* Edited by G. Anderson, M. Stone, and J. Tromp, 43-56. SVTP 15. Leiden: Brill, 2000.
Stone, Michael et al. *Noah and His Book(s).* Atlanta: Scholars, 2010.
Stroumsa, Gedaliahu. "Form(s) of God: Some Notes on Metatron and Christ." *HTR* 76 (1983): 269-288.

———. *Another Seed: Studies in Gnostic Mythology*. Leiden: Brill, 1984.
Stroumsa, Gedaliahu, and Fredriksen, Paula. "The Two Souls and the Divided Will." In *Self, Soul, and Body in Religious Experience*. Edited by A. I. Baumgarten et al., 198–208. Leiden: Brill, 1998.
Stuckenbruck, Loren. "The Lamech Narrative in the Genesis Apocryphon (1QapGen) and Birth of Noah (4QEnoch^c ar): A Tradition-Historical Study." In *Aramaica Qumranica*. Edited by K. Berthelot and D. Stökl Ben Ezra, 253–271. STDJ 94. Leiden: Brill, 2010.
Sullivan, Kevin. *Wrestling with Angels: A Study of the Relationship between Angels and Humans in Ancient Jewish Literature and the New Testament*. AGAJU 55. Leiden: Brill, 2004.
Sundermann, Werner. "Der Paraklet in der ostmanichäischen Überlieferung." In *Manichaean Studies: Proceedings of the First International Conference on Manichaeism, August 5–9, 1987*. Edited by P. Bryder, 201–212. LSAAR 1. Lund: Plus Ultra, 1988.
Suter, David. "Enoch in Sheol: Updating the Dating of the Book of Parables." In *Enoch and the Messiah Son of Man: Revisiting the Book of Parables*. Edited by G. Boccaccini. 415–443. Grand Rapids, MI: Eerdmans, 2007.
Sweeney, Leo. "Mani's Twin and Plotinus: Questions on 'Self.'" In *Neoplatonism and Gnosticism*. Edited by R. T. Wallis and J. Bregman, 381–424. Albany: SUNY Press, 1992.
Testuz, Michel. *Les idées religieuses du livre des Jubilés*. Geneva: Droz, 1960.
Thiessen, Matthew. "Aseneth's Eight-Day Transformation as Scriptural Justification for Conversion." *JSJ* 45 (2014): 229–249.
Thomassen, Einar. "Valentinian Ideas about Salvation as Transformation." In *Metamorphoses: Resurrection, Body and Transformative Practices in Early Christianity*. Edited by T. K. Seim and J. Økland, 169–186. Ekstasis 1. Berlin: Walter de Gruyter, 2009.
Trudinger, Paul. "An Israelite in Whom There Is no Guile: An Interpretative Note on John 1:45:51." *EvQ* 54 (1982): 117–120.
Tvorogov, Oleg. "Paleja Tolkovaja." In *Slovar' knizhnikov i knizhnosti Drevnei Rusi (XI–pervaja polovina XIV v.)*. Edited by D. S. Lihachev, 285–288. Leningrad: Nauka, 1987.
Uro, Risto. "'Who Will Be Our Leader?' Authority and Autonomy in the Gospel of Thomas." In *Fair Play: Diversity and Conflict in Early Christianity: Essays in Honour of Heikki Räisänen*. Edited by I. Dunderberg et al., 457–485. VTSup 103. Leiden: Brill, 2002.
———. "Gnostic Rituals from a Cognitive Perspective." In *Explaining Christian Origins and Early Judaism*. Edited by P. Luomanen, I. Pyysiäinen, and R. Uro, 115–137. BIS 89. Leiden: Brill, 2007.
———. "The Bridal Chamber and Other Mysteries: Ritual System and Ritual Transmission in the Valentinian Movement." In *Sacred Marriages: The Divine-Human Sexual Metaphor from Sumer to Early Christianity*. Edited by M. Nissinen and R. Uro, 457–486. Winona Lake, IN: Eisenbrauns, 2008.
Uspenskij, Vladimir. *Tolkovaja Paleja*. Kazan', 1876.
Van den Broek, Roelof. "The Cathars: Medieval Gnostics?" In *Gnosis and Hermeticism from Antiquity to Modern Times*. Edited by R. van den Broek and W. J. Hanegraaff,

87-108. SUNY Series in Western Esoteric Traditions. Albany, NY: SUNY Press, 1997.

Van der Horst, Peter. "De Joodse toneelschrijver Ezechiël." *NedTT* 36 (1982): 97-112.

———. "Moses' Throne Vision in Ezekiel the Dramatist." *JJS* 34 (1983): 21-29.

———. "Some Notes on the Exagoge of Ezekiel." *Mnemosyne* 37 (1984): 364-365.

VanderKam, James. *Textual and Historical Studies in the Book of Jubilees*. HSM 14. Missoula, MT: Scholars, 1977.

———. "The Righteousness of Noah." In *Ideal Figures in Ancient Judaism: Profiles and Paradigms*. Edited by J. J. Collins and G. W. E. Nickelsburg, 13-32. SBLSCS 12. Chico, CA: Scholars, 1980.

———. *Enoch and the Growth of an Apocalyptic Tradition*. CBQMS 16. Washington, DC: Catholic Biblical Association of America, 1984.

———. "The Birth of Noah." In *Intertestamental Essays in Honor of Jósef Tadeusz Milik*. Edited by Z. J. Kapera, 213-231. QM 6. Krakow: Enigma Press, 1992.

———. "Righteous One, Messiah, Chosen One, and Son of Man in 1 Enoch 37-71." In *The Messiah: Developments in Earliest Judaism and Christianity: The First Princeton Symposium on Judaism and Christian Origins*. Edited by J. H. Charlesworth et al., 169-191. Minneapolis: Fortress, 1992.

———. "The Origins and Purposes of the Book of Jubilees." In *Studies in the Book of Jubilees*. Edited by M. Albani, J. Frey, and A. Lange, 3-24. TSAJ 65. Tübingen: Mohr/Siebeck, 1997.

———. "The Angel of the Presence in the Book of Jubilees." *DSD* 7 (2000): 378-393.

VanderKam, James and Boesenberg, Dulcinea. "Moses and Enoch in Second Temple Jewish Texts." In *Parables of Enoch: A Paradigm Shift*. Edited by D. Bock and J. Charlesworth, 124-158. London: T&T Clark, 2013.

Van De Water, Rick. "Moses' Exaltation: Pre-Christian?" *JSP* 21 (2000): 59-69.

Vanhoye, Albert. "La fuite du jeune homme nu (Mc 14,51-52)." *Biblica* 52 (1971): 401-406.

Van Oort, Johannes. "Mani and the Origins of a New Church." In *The Apostolic Age in Patristic Thought*. Edited by A. Hilhorst, 139-157. SVC 70. Leiden: Brill, 2004.

Van Peursen, Wido. "Who Was Standing on the Mountain? The Portrait of Moses in 4Q377." In *Moses in Biblical and Extra-Biblical Traditions*. Edited by A. Graupner and M. Wolter, 99-114. BZAW 372. Berlin: Walter de Gruyter, 2007.

Van Ruiten, Jacques. *Abraham in the Book of Jubilees: The Rewriting of Genesis 11:26-25:10 in the Book of Jubilees 11:14-23:8*. JSJSS 161. Leiden: Brill, 2012.

Vermes, Geza. "The Archangel Sariel: A Targumic Parallel to the Dead Sea Scrolls." In *Christianity, Judaism and Other Greco-Roman Cults*. Edited by J. Neusner, 159-166. SJLA 12.3. Leiden: Brill, 1975.

———. "The Impact of the Dead Sea Scrolls on Jewish Studies." *JJS* 26 (1975): 1-14.

Vernant, Jean-Pierre. "Psuche: Simulacrum of the Body or Image of the Divine?" In *Mortals and Immortals*. Edited by F. I. Zeitlin, 186-187. Princeton: Princeton University Press, 1991.

———. "The Figuration of the Invisible and the Psychological Category of the Double: The Kolossos." In *Myth and Thought among the Greeks*. Edited by J.-P. Vernant, 321-332. New York: Zone Books, 2005.

Vielhauer, Philipp. "Gottesreich und Menschensohn in der Verkündigung Jesu." In *Festschrift für Günther Dehn*. Edited by W. Schneemelcher, 51–79. Neukirchen: Erziehungsverein, 1957.

———. "Jesus und der Menschensohn: Zur Discussion mit Heinz Eduard Tödt und Eduard Schweizer." *ZTK* 60 (1963): 133–177.

Vodolazkin, Evgenij. "O Tolkovoj Palee, Zlatoj Matice i 'estestvenno nauchnyh' compiljacijah." *TODRL* 51 (1999): 80–90.

———. *Vsemirnaja istorija v literature Drevnej Rusi (na materiale hronograficheskogo i palejnogo povestvovanija XI–XV vekov)*. SSS 26. München: Sagner, 2000.

Von Gall, August Freiherr. *Basileia tou theou: Eine religionsgeschichtliche Studie zur vorkirchlichen Eschatologie*. Heidelberg: Carl Winter, 1926.

Von Heijne, Camilla. *The Messenger of the Lord in Early Jewish Interpretations of Genesis*. Berlin: Walter de Gruyter, 2010.

Waetjen, Herman. "The Ending of Mark and the Gospel's Shift in Eschatology." *ASTI* 4 (1968): 114–131.

Walker, Christopher et al. *The Induction of the Cult Image in Ancient Mesopotamia: The Mesopotamian Mīs Pî Ritual: Transliteration, Translation, and Commentary*. SAALT 1. Helsinki: University of Helsinki, 2001.

Walls, Neal. *Cult Image and Divine Representation in the Ancient Near East*. ASOR 10. Boston: American Schools of Oriental Research, 2005.

Weiss, Johannes. *Jesus' Proclamation of the Kingdom of God*. Philadelphia: Fortress, 1971.

Werman, Cana. "Qumran and the Book of Noah." In *Pseudepigraphic Perspectives: The Apocrypha and the Pseudepigrapha in Light of the Dead Sea Scrolls*. Edited by E. Chazon and M. E. Stone, 171–181. STDJ 31. Leiden: Brill, 1999.

Widengren, Geo. *The King and the Tree of Life in Ancient Near Eastern Religion*. UUA 4. Wiesbaden: Otto Harrassowitz, 1951.

———. *Mani and Manichaeism*. New York: Holt, Rinehart and Winston, 1965.

Windisch, Hans. "Die göttliche Weisheit der Juden und die paulinische Christologie." In *Neutestamentliche Studien für Georg Heinrici zu seinem 70*. Edited by A. Deissmann and H. Windisch, 220–234. UNT 6. Leipzig: J. C. Hinrichs, 1914.

Wolfson, Elliot. "The Image of Jacob Engraved upon the Throne." In *Along the Path: Studies in Kabbalistic Myth, Symbolism, and Hermeneutics*. Edited by E. Wolfson, 1–62. Albany, NY: SUNY Press, 1995.

———. "The Face of Jacob in the Moon: Mystical Transformations of an Aggadic Myth." In *The Seductiveness of Jewish Myth*. Edited by S. D. Breslaur, 235–270. Albany, NY: SUNY Press, 1997.

Wrede, William. "Zum Thema 'Menschensohn.'" *ZNW* 5 (1904): 359–360.

Index

Aaron, 29, 57, 68, 175, 179–180, 237, 254
Abatur, 117, 195, 243–244
Abraham, 17, 18, 91, 95–96, 160, 188–189, 199, 201, 221, 227, 233, 255, 258
  heavenly counterpart of, 17–18
Acherusian Lake, 181
Achilles, 73, 206
Adoil, 114, 241, 245
Aeneas, 72, 206
Akae, 134
Alchasai, 77, 146, 210
Angel of the Lord, 130–133, 171, 186
Angels of Holiness, 52
Anthropos, 49, 113, 120–121, 125, 127–128, 130, 137, 139–140, 145, 148, 240, 250, 263
Anu, 262
Apollo, 72, 206
Apostle of Light, 146, 210, 217, 220
ᶜArabot, 96, 132, 357
archon, 121
Arpad, 14
Artemis, 206
Aruchas, 114
Asael, 158
Aseneth, 4, 31, 35–36, 49, 113–114, 119, 120–131, 137–148, 170, 174, 179, 182, 186, 189, 195, 230, 240, 247–252, 259–266
  as City of Refuge, 113–114, 139, 240, 262

  as "youth," 31
  heavenly counterpart of, 139–141
  her reclothing, 35–36
Assyria, 237
astral body, 70, 71, 202, 204
Athene, 72
ᶜAzaʾel, 29, 83, 164
Azazel, 153, 158
ᶜAzzah, 29, 83, 164

Babylon, 99, 100, 229, 234
Barbelo, 195
Belial, 33–34
Beqa, 133
Bethel, 61, 123, 150, 233, 236
Bezalel, 56, 57
Bridal Chamber, 4, 137–139, 260, 261
Buddha, 146
Buzi, 41, 264

Cathars, 114–115, 211, 220, 242
Chebar, 8, 41, 55, 143–144, 191, 264–265
Cherubim, 9, 12, 160
circumcision, 52, 251
City of Refuge, 113–114, 139, 240, 262

daēnā, 2, 154
daimon, 2, 59, 80, 154
Day of Atonement, 158
Demiurge, 209
Dinah, 51
Diomedes, 72, 206

Divine Face, 153
dmuta, 39, 75, 209
   as garment, 39, 75
Drusiana, 167

Ea, 262
Eden, 3, 32, 37, 69, 112, 128, 144, 150, 176, 178, 180, 191, 237–238, 254
Edessa, 210
Edom, 99, 100, 229
Egypt, 27, 182, 202, 247
eidōlon, 72–74, 205–209
Elijah, 7, 203
Elpenor, 205
Endzeit, 50, 51, 187
Enlil, 262
Enmeduranki, 41, 262
Enoch, 3, 4, 7–59, 66, 81–106, 109, 114–116, 121–125, 132–135, 147, 149–150, 153, 156–166, 172–179, 183–186, 189–190, 198–203, 213–216, 224, 226–227, 229–231, 240–244, 249–250, 254, 256–258
   as mirror, 59
   as scribe, 53
   as "youth," 25–31
   heavenly counterpart of, 7–41
Esau, 52, 98–99, 110, 215, 228–229
Eumelus, 72
Eve, 37, 83, 108–109, 126–128, 173, 180–183, 213–214, 222, 235–236, 261

Festival of Weeks, 51
Flood, 22, 29, 32–33, 165, 174, 176
fravaši, 2, 154–155
frozen angel, 40–41, 185

Gabriel, 12, 25, 30, 38, 81, 165–166, 181, 195
garment, 16, 26–28, 34–36, 38–39, 41, 69–70, 75, 78–79, 92, 109, 123–124, 134, 172, 182, 195, 202–203, 209–210, 248, 250–251
   as heavenly counterpart, 34–41

   as mirror, 38
   removal of, 39–41
garments of light, 37–39, 69, 179
garments of skin, 35, 37–38
genius, 2, 80
Giants, 174
Golem, 130, 253–254
Greece, 14, 99–100, 220, 229

Hades, 72, 74, 205–206, 208
Hamath, 14
Hayyot, 144
Head of Days, 12
heavenly counterpart, 7, 31, 34, 43, 48, 52, 54, 61, 87, 97, 104, 113, 119, 128, 130, 139, 153, 155, 183, 190, 199, 228, 247
   as angel of the Presence, 24–25
   as *dmuta*, 39, 75, 209
   as *eidōlon*, 72–74, 205–209
   as garment, 34–41
   as guardian of the scribal tradition, 52–54
   as image, 61–84
   as *iqonin*, 50, 67–68, 79–80, 92, 97–98, 138, 144, 200, 209, 231
   as mirror, 58–59
   as Paraclete, 87–89
   as shadow, 71–72
   as spirit, 87–91
   as "youth," 25–34
Heavenly Man, 140, 262
Heavenly Tablets, 187
Heavenly Temple, 8–10, 156, 185
Hebe, 72
Hera, 72
Heracles, 72
Herod, 159
Holy of Holies, 9–10, 67, 158, 260
Holy Spirit, 1, 18, 78–79, 87–90, 92, 114, 115, 161, 210–211, 220, 222–223
honeycomb, 125, 128–130, 150, 240, 250, 252

Icarius, 72

icon, 63, 80–81, 197, 201
idolatry, 253
Image, Divine, 61–83
    as garment, 39
    as heavenly counterpart, 61–84
Iphthime, 72
iqonin, 50, 67, 68, 79–80, 92, 97, 98, 138, 144, 200, 209, 231
Isaac, 17–18, 63, 85, 91, 95–96, 109–110, 133, 160, 163, 188, 199, 201–202, 204, 221, 227, 255, 258
Israel, 15, 25, 29, 45, 52, 63–68, 70, 85–87, 91, 93, 99–103, 108, 110, 131, 157, 160, 162, 166, 178, 184, 187–191, 197, 200–202, 215–217, 221–222, 228–231, 236, 239, 244–245, 252, 255–256, 262
    as heavenly counterpart of Jacob, 84–86

Jabbok, 91, 93, 123, 150, 258
Jacob, 4, 7, 10, 13, 15, 18, 22–25, 31, 39, 44, 49–68, 75, 80–123, 130–131, 136, 144, 150, 153, 159–166, 174, 178, 186, 190–217, 221–239, 245–246, 255–256, 258
    as mirror, 59, 67
    as "youth," 31
    face of, 65
    heavenly counterpart of, 61–117
    image of, 61–93
Jared, 22, 83
Jehudiam, 202, 256
Jesus, 14–16, 25–28, 49–50, 76–77, 87, 89, 92, 104–108, 110, 113, 127–128, 131, 136–138, 146, 161–163, 166–171, 173, 179, 184, 213, 215–217, 219, 223, 231–235, 249, 252, 256, 259
    as ladder, 104–106
    as mirror, 58
    as "youth," 25–28
    heavenly counterpart of, 14–16
    his clothing with the divine Name, 136
    his polymorphism, 166–167

Jordan, 136–137, 155, 231
Joseph, 4, 7, 13, 15, 22, 25, 27, 31, 36, 49–50, 84–86, 90–93, 101–103, 108, 119–124, 127–131, 137–142, 148, 150, 160, 164, 166, 170–171, 174, 178–179, 182, 185–186, 189, 201, 215–217, 221–223, 229–230, 240, 247, 248–252, 254, 260–263, 266
    heavenly counterpart of, 119

Ka, 253
Kavod, 13, 16, 23–25, 44–45, 48, 56–58, 62, 64, 94–96, 103, 143, 144, 146, 148–149, 164, 189–191, 193, 227, 230
Kesbeel, 133

ladder, 61–64, 66, 81, 93–94, 96–100, 104, 106–107, 110, 112–113, 116–117, 160, 201, 226, 228–229, 231, 233–236, 239, 245–246
Last Statue, 115–116, 241–242
Lebanon, 237
lecanomancy, 143, 263
Left Side, 71, 194
Lesser YHWH, 21, 131–132
Leto, 206
Levi, 29, 63, 66, 100, 141, 157, 179, 181, 188, 197–198, 202
Light Form, 76–77
Logos, 58, 126, 169, 196, 215, 222, 237–238, 259
    as mirror, 58
Lord of Spirits, 12–13, 93, 224

Maccabean Revolt, 155
Manashar, 171
Mani, 1, 76–77, 87–89, 122, 146, 154, 165, 169, 186, 189, 195–196, 208–209, 217–220, 242, 266
    his heavenly counterpart, 1, 76–77, 87–89
manna, 129–130
Media, 99–100, 229

Melchirešaᶜ, 34
Melchizedek, 7, 21, 28, 32–34, 122, 133, 173, 175–178, 230
 as heavenly counterpart, 33–34, 177
 as "youth," 32–34
Messalians, 114, 115
Mēsu-Tree, 111, 237–238
Metanoia, 114, 125, 127, 137, 139–141, 261–262
Metatron, 4, 19–22, 25, 28–30, 34–35, 44, 46, 48–49, 53–54, 58–59, 83, 102–104, 117, 121–122, 131–135, 141, 149–150, 153, 159, 163–166, 173, 178–179, 184–185, 189–190, 196, 198, 230, 235, 243–245, 255–258, 262, 266
 as "Beloved," 141
 as heavenly counterpart of Enoch, 19–22
 as "Lesser YHWH," 21, 131–132
 as mirror, 58–59
 as Prince of the World, 21, 173
Methuselah, 177
Michael, 12–14, 17, 20–21, 23, 31–35, 38, 49, 81–82, 103, 122, 124, 133–134, 159, 165–166, 176–179, 181, 187, 213–214, 227, 230, 249, 256, 258
Miriam, 57
mirror, 2, 5, 38, 41, 46, 50–59, 67, 76–77, 88, 121, 127, 138, 140–150, 172, 187–198, 208, 243, 248, 260, 262, 264–266
Moses, 4, 7, 8, 11, 19–21, 24, 28, 33, 36, 41–59, 67–68, 83, 95, 108, 120, 122, 125, 134–136, 144, 147–150, 153, 157, 159, 175–179, 183–196, 199–201, 204, 227, 233, 248–249, 256, 258–259, 265
 as mirror, 59
 as scribe, 53
 heavenly counterpart of, 43–59
 his crowning with the divine Name, 135
 his *iqonin*, 67–68
 his reclothing, 36
 his standing, 46–48
Mšunia Kušta, 75

Narcissus, 74, 153, 266
Nathanael, 105, 108, 110, 235
Nebuchadnezzar, 233–234, 237–238, 253
Nir, 175–176, 178
Noah, 3, 7, 21, 32–33, 174–177, 249
 miraculous birth of, 32
 as "youth," 32
Nous, 88, 219

oath, 133–134, 194, 256, 258
Odysseus, 72, 205
oil of resurrection, 109
opening of the mouth, 130, 253
opposition, angelic, 64, 91–92, 99
Orion, 257
Orphics, 73
Ozel, 38

Panim, 15, 17, 24, 47–48, 54–57, 66, 82, 84, 90, 94–95, 102–103, 131, 146, 149, 189, 194, 196–198, 201, 204, 212
 as mirror, 54–59
Paraclete, 1, 76, 87–89, 219, 220
 as heavenly counterpart of Mani, 76, 87–89
Paradise, 38–39, 109, 116, 202–203, 235
Parthia, 76, 87
Parvain, 177
Patroclus, 73, 206
Penelope, 72
Peniel, 166
Persia, 14, 76, 88, 218
phantom, 49, 72–74, 205–206, 223
Phanuel, 12, 24–25, 100–103, 166, 229–230
 as custodian of heavenly identities, 24–25
Pharaoh, 121, 247, 249
Pherae, 72

Pleiades, 257
Pleroma, 126, 137, 241
Potiphera, 247
Prince of the Presence, 166, 230
Promised Land, 93, 95
Protoktistoi, 90, 221
Protoplast, 130, 144, 220, 243
psychē, 70, 73, 205, 208
Ptahil, 195
Pythagoreans, 73, 206–207

Raguel, 36, 43, 45, 184
Raphael, 12, 165–166
Red Sea, 264
Repentance, 113, 139–141, 262
Rome, 79, 99, 181, 228

Salome, 251
Sariel, 24–25, 93–94, 100–103, 166, 229–230
    as custodian of heavenly identities, 24–25
Satan, 39, 81–82, 92, 173, 180, 213–214
Seraphim, 12, 160
Seth, 28, 80, 109, 172
    as "youth," 28
shadow, 5, 56, 57, 70–73, 145, 194, 204–207, 264
    as heavenly counterpart, 71–72
Shechemites, 51
Shekinah, 21, 56, 67, 97, 121, 177, 191, 194, 254–255
Shiʿur Qomah, 132
Sinai, 8, 29, 41–46, 50, 55, 57, 67, 123, 147, 149, 153, 159, 185–188, 194, 250, 258–259
Son of Man, 4, 11–16, 20, 24, 34, 45, 53, 93, 100, 104–117, 145, 149, 158–165, 174, 178, 207, 224, 231–236, 257
    as heavenly counterpart of Enoch, 11–15
    as heavenly counterpart of Jesus, 14–16, 104–107
    as path of the heavenly counterparts, 108–117

    as vessel of the heavenly counterparts, 108–117
Sophia, 1, 49, 92, 140, 169, 186, 209, 223, 262
    as mirror, 140
Sothonim, 175–176
Spirit, 49, 50, 78–79, 87–92, 114–115, 154, 161, 169, 187, 198, 209–212, 218–223, 242, 260–261
    as heavenly counterpart, 87–91
syzygia, 138, 210, 220
syzygos, 146, 210

Tabernacle, 56, 156, 179, 244
Tetragrammaton, 130–131, 134–135, 256
Theoclymenos, 205
Theon, 168
Theotokos, 28, 117, 245–246
    as ladder, 117
Tigris, 264
Torah, 8, 21, 38, 117, 200, 202–204, 222, 243–245
Tree of Knowledge, 108–109, 150
Tree of Life, 109, 111–112, 116, 173, 236–239
Trisagion, 96

Uriel, 24–25, 52–53, 85–86, 91, 100–103, 131, 165–166, 216, 229–230
    as custodian of heavenly identities, 24–25
Urzeit, 50–51, 187
ʿUzzah, 29, 83, 164

veneration, angelic, 30, 81–84, 212–213
Vereveil, 24, 52–53, 100, 102, 165, 189
vice-regent, 35, 44, 171, 230
Vizan, 171, 187

washing of the mouth, 130, 253
Watchers, 4, 8–11, 13, 106, 122, 149, 156–158, 160, 173, 227, 250

Yahoel, 20, 21
Yom Kippur, 10

yored merkavah, 55
"Youth," 21–22, 25–31, 49, 83, 126, 164–165, 170, 173, 213
    as heavenly counterpart, 25–34

Zadok, 155
Zadokites, 7–8, 122, 155
Zeus, 72
Zoroaster, 146, 209

www.ingramcontent.com/pod-product-compliance
Ingram Content Group UK Ltd.
Pitfield, Milton Keynes, MK11 3LW, UK
UKHW041925140426
5217IPUK00014B/312